DEMYSTIFYING THERAPY

Also by Ernesto Spinelli

The Interpreted World: An Introduction to
Phenomenological Psychology

DEMYSTIFYING
THERAPY

Ernesto Spinelli

Constable · London

First published in Great Britain 1994
by Constable and Company Ltd
3 The Lanchesters, 162 Fulham Palace Road
London W6 9ER
Copyright © Ernesto Spinelli 1994
The right of Ernesto Spinelli to be identified as the author
of this work has been asserted by him in accordance
with the Copyright, Designs and Patents Act 1988
ISBN 0 09 472940 9
Set in Linotron Sabon 10½ pt by
Rowland Phototypesetting Ltd
Bury St Edmunds, Suffolk
Printed in Great Britain by
St Edmundsbury Press Ltd
Bury St Edmunds, Suffolk

A CIP catalogue record for this book
is available from the British Library

For my father
Who thinks that therapy is a load of nonsense,

For my mother
Who takes the opposite point of view,

And for my students and clients
Who have had to put up with the divided loyalties
Of yet one more dutiful son.

CONTENTS

INTRODUCTION

We're playing those mind games together.
— John Lennon

Try to imagine a world where psychotherapy or counselling do not exist. Imagine that not only are there no more private practices for those who can afford to pay specialists to listen to and assist them in dealing with their problems, nor are there any similar services provided by local authorities, community groups and educational or religious establishments, but also that there are no longer any telephone help-lines such as the Samaritans, Childline, and so forth, nor are there any problem pages in your newspaper or magazine, nor any radio station 'agony aunts' and 'uncles', nor any self-help books, or 'pop' psychology manuals, to help you cope with stress or sexual problem or to teach you to live more suitable or hedonistic or caring or fulfilling lifestyles. And consider, as well, how much less 'psychobabble' there would be for morning television hosts to endlessly chat on about or to find ways of having you reveal, live, on the air, the various concerns and dilemmas you face each day or can no longer live with. Consider as well the nature of the everyday conversations you might engage in with your colleagues, friends, children, spouse or partner, and how much of their content would now be bereft of notions and ideas that would be derived from popular usage of therapeutic terminology. How great would be the gaps in people's thinking and communicating about themselves and others? How would people cope with the myriad variety of problems that psychotherapists and counsellors (both trained and self-made) are experts in dealing with? How would they even recognize them or discern their existence?

11

A colleague of mine once pointed out to me that the basic premise of Woody Allen's film *A Midsummer Night's Sex Comedy* lay in its attempt to present a world of social and intimate relations which existed prior to the advent of Freud's psychology and the dramatic, lasting cultural changes it would bring forth. Perhaps it was the very 'strangeness' of this world, and the irksome naïveté of its characters, which invoked in me, and in a great many others who saw the film, a sense of disgruntlement that made the cinematic experience seem so disappointing. Like Adam and Eve, it would seem, once we have eaten of the tree of knowledge, we can never return to that prior state of innocence. Nor, perhaps, can we fully re-experience it.

Whatever the case, it would appear that, at the close of this century, Western culture and society (and, increasingly, a great many other cultures and societies that have been influenced for good or ill by the West) have succumbed to the 'triumph of the therapeutic' to the extent that vast amounts of our understanding about our desires and motives, our explanations of our behaviour and perceived needs, our aspirations and desires, even our very sense of ourselves as human beings, are largely derived from notions and hypotheses gleaned from theories that have either originated from psychotherapeutic assumptions or have been extrapolated from more general theories of psychology, philosophy, the social, biological and physical sciences and so forth, in order to amplify, clarify or substantiate therapeutic claims.

However much the majority of lay individuals who employ such ideas may have overextended, trivialized or even misunderstood a great many of the terms employed in order to explain or make sense of their own, or others', beliefs and behaviours, it remains the case that these ideas have entered common parlance, and, in so doing, have shaped, and continue to shape, fundamental views we hold about ourselves. It would be surprising, for instance, for most of us not to assume such things as the existence of an 'unconscious mind', or to disavow the notion that experiences and 'traumas' from an individual's infancy and childhood provide the key to the understanding of his or her adult personality. We speak authoritatively, if not glibly, about

12

archetypal individuals such as 'the archetypal' hero, sex goddess, or football player; we recognize the hidden (often erotic or aggressive) meanings of all manner of *symbolic* images and verbal allusions employed by novelists, film directors and advertising agencies; we would find it surprising if one were to suggest that each of us does not harbour seemingly forgotten (or *repressed*) memories which, nevertheless, continue to exert their psychic hold upon us.

As we approach the end of the twentieth century and begin to assess and stamp it with an instantly identifiable label which seeks to capture its fundamental 'essence', we are immediately presented with the wide selection of candidates available to our consideration: the 'Communication Revolution', the 'Nuclear Age', the 'Electronics Explosion', to mention just three. During this century we have seen the creation of technological marvels and monstrosities, we have witnessed the sudden rise, spread, and even more sudden fall of political ideologies, we have toyed with genetics, our reproductive systems, subatomic quanta, and we have invented a form of music whose popularity and adaptability appears to be worldwide. But, most 'essential' of all, I would suggest, in that it has fundamentally shifted the very means by which we think of and try to understand ourselves, and, therefore, has set the parameters of our objectives, aspirations and achievements, has been the birth, steady rise and ever-increasing reliance upon, and use of, therapeutic thought and practice. Like it or not, we (particularly we in the West) are the 'children' of Freud and all his many and diverse followers, re-interpreters, rivals and detractors. Even if we, ourselves, have not been in, nor practised, psychotherapy or counselling, it would be surprising if we did not know or were unable to name someone in our circle of family, friends and acquaintances who has.

I have been a practising psychotherapist and counsellor for some fourteen years. My name appears on the register of psychotherapists of the United Kingdom Council for Psychotherapy (UKCP) and on the list of accredited counsellors of the British Association of Counselling (BAC). Over the last decade, I have devised, directed and taught various academic and professional

13

training programmes in psychotherapy and counselling. I have been employed as a counsellor for the NHS and for an international college and continue to maintain a private practice working with adult individuals and couples. I state all this not in order to elevate myself, or to prove my credentials, but, rather, in order to present a paradox. While I have clearly dedicated a large part of my life to therapeutic practice and to the dissemination of therapeutic thought, and while I can truthfully state that my enjoyment – even love – of my work has not diminished over time (if anything, I have grown even more entranced and engaged with the nature of my chosen profession), nevertheless I hold a high degree of scepticism for many of the claims made for psychotherapy and counselling – particularly with regard to the specialist (some might say 'quasi-magical') 'skills' or 'powers' of psychotherapists and counsellors, the specific and unique outcome characteristics of therapeutic encounters, and, perhaps most importantly, the unnecessarily mystificatory assumptions and near-tenets underlying the theoretical underpinnings and practices held by most practitioners.

Increasingly, a number of authors have pointed out the potentials for, as well as actual incidents of, physical and sexual abuse of clients by their therapists (Masson, 1989; Rutter, 1990; Russell, 1993). While I share these authors' concerns, I am convinced that there exists a much more subtle and prevalent problematic area that has not been sufficiently analysed. Generally speaking, it has to do with the distinct form of subtle (and sometimes not so subtle) potentially debilitating influences engendered by a variety of *assumptions* held by psychotherapists and counsellors regarding their role and function, their employment of specialist skills and their (sometimes unquestioning) reliance upon, and belief in, the 'truths' of their theories. Over time, I have increasingly questioned the significance of these assumptions and have tended towards a conclusion that their principal function is not to provide the means of alleviating the various forms of human misery with which clients present their therapists, but rather to invest therapists, and the therapeutic process, with a sense of *special and unique authority and wisdom* which serves as a distinguishing hallmark of both the profession and its practitioners. I have felt this tendency to be increasingly disturbing and problematic not only because of the potentially abusive expressions of *power* that it offers to therapists, but, just as significantly, because of its inclination towards the unnecessary *mystification* of therapy.

I readily admit that I am not the first to voice such concerns, but it is my intent, in writing this text, to present them from a point of focus that I hope will be seen to be both novel and instructive. As I have written elsewhere (Spinelli, 1989), I subscribe to an *existential-phenomenological* orientation. This approach, I believe, readily lends itself to a sceptical stance – by which I don't mean to suggest a stance of closed-mindedness, but rather its opposite – which seeks to counter-balance those tendencies mentioned above by its attempts to avoid reliance upon seemingly fixed or unshakeable 'truths' or universal 'facts' in order to imbue its arguments with the stamp of authority, and which takes its fundamental project to be that of clarification and, hence, demystification.

I feel that I should be clear from the outset that this will be an opinionated and critical text. But, just as I hope that the opinions expressed will be viewed by readers as being balanced and worthy of their consideration, so, too, is it my hope that the criticisms expressed will be seen to have constructive, rather than destructive, intent.

Readers will have noticed by now that I have employed the terms 'psychotherapy' and 'counselling' synonymously. While each exists as a separate professional body, it is fair to say that a great deal of overlap exists in the theoretical foundations of the various approaches associated with each, and, also, in their applications at the consultative, or therapeutic, level. I have taken this stance in order to clarify that my concerns and interests lie in the analysis and examination of *all* approaches that take as their main area of concentration a structured therapeutic focus. While I am aware that many colleagues would prefer (if not insist upon) a clear line of demarcation, I am not entirely in agreement with them for reasons that will be made clear in Part 1 of this text. But this issue raises a far more fundamental problem – that of *defining* the terms 'psychotherapy' and

15

'counselling' themselves. This issue, too, will be considered in Part 1. Nevertheless, for the time being at least, rather than continue to employ both these terms throughout the text (which seems to be rather an unwieldy and irksome exercise for both writer and reader!), I will, instead, employ the lexicons 'therapy' or 'therapeutic process' as overall, inclusive terms for both psychotherapy and counselling and the theories, practices, skills and assumptions underlying both, and will employ the separate terms only when considering their avowed distinction or in deference to other authors whose texts and/or personal preferences refer explicitly to one or other label.

In a similar fashion, I will employ the term 'client' rather than 'patient' throughout the text. Although I remain dissatisfied with the former, the medical implications of the latter make it, to me at least, an even more disingenuous term. There is, I think, much to be said for the term 'analysand' which is employed by a number of psycho-analytically influenced therapists. However, as these seem to be the only therapists to employ this label, my use of it would run the risk of imposing an unnecessary theoretical or practice-based restriction upon it. Having racked my brain in vain for years in search of a better term than those currently available, I have settled for 'client' until a more appropriate term is suggested by someone far more capable and linguistically creative than me.

Finally, for reasons of space and added complexity of argument, I will limit the discussion in this text to issues of therapy as practised with individuals whose degree of felt disturbance, anxiety, inability to cope or fragmentation falls within those boundaries that were once largely distinguished as 'neurotic' rather than 'psychotic'. Although I believe that much of what I have to say applies equally to more serious or pervasive instances of mental disturbance, I have elected to focus upon those therapeutic interventions that are most prominently observable in private practices, counselling agencies and NHS surgeries that offer consultations with registered or accredited therapists.

As I have already indicated, Part 1 of this text will focus on questions related to the ostensible similarities and differences between psychotherapy and counselling, and the various attempts that have been made to define the nature, boundaries and concerns of each in order that the unnecessarily mystificatory tendencies that such definitions impose can be clearly demonstrated. Part 1 will also consider a number of important critiques made of therapy and will examine the main findings arrived at concerning the general efficacy or 'success' of therapy in fulfilling its stated (or implied) aims to 'cure', 'help' or 'change' clients.

Part 2 will principally consider the question of *power* in the therapeutic relationship. In particular, it will focus on the existing evidence for the serious misuse and abuse of therapeutic power as expressed in the sexual, physical and financial abuse of clients by therapists, and via forms of therapeutic indoctrination. It will also consider the conclusions arrived at by critics of therapy, in particular those set forth by Jeffrey Masson, with regard to the significance of power and its abusive potentials and argue that such critiques, while valuable and requiring attention by therapists, themselves add to the unnecessary mystification of the therapeutic process.

Parts 3 and 4 will focus on a variety of important elements found in the principal theoretical models upon which most therapists rely in order to 'do' therapy. Part 3 will examine a number of the major 'theory-led' assumptions of the psychoanalytic model such as the role of the past, unconscious processes, and the issue of transference, and will provide a critique of these, as well as the notion of analytic interpretation. In a similar fashion, Part 4 will consider certain fundamental assumptions found within the cognitive-behavioural and humanistic models of therapy focusing in particular on issues dealing with the 'objectivity' of the therapist and assumptions concerning the nature of 'the self'. Once again, the principal aim in criticizing these views will be to expose those implicit mystificatory tendencies contained within them which serve to imbue therapists with unnecessary and potentially abusive power.

Having addressed the major mystificatory concerns raised about therapeutic theory and practice, Part 5, 'Demystifying the Therapeutic Relationship', will present an alternative orientation towards therapy, derived from existential-phenomenological investigation, which concentrates on the potentials for a more open encounter between therapist and client by concentrating its attention on issues surrounding the relational qualities of 'being' within the therapeutic relationship. Further, it will examine both the potentials and limitations of therapy so that more adequate expectations, process possibilities and outcomes can be identified.

Throughout the text, my overall contention will be that, however unwittingly, therapists have tended to mystify both the therapeutic process and themselves as its expert practitioners. As a result, these mystificatory tendencies have helped to promote the increasingly prominent public view that therapy is both a special and necessary 'cure' for human misery and that therapists, correspondingly, are the qualified agents of that 'cure'. These views demand serious questioning not least because the failure to fulfil the expectations that clients have tended to set upon therapy and their therapists – and which therapists, as well, have been inclined to set upon their profession and themselves – is all too likely to create increasing frustration and criticism. Already, the initial signs of a 'backlash' against therapy are evident – paradoxically just at the moment when therapists are stepping up their attempts to regulate their profession. Along with such safeguards, however, therapists must be prepared to practise what they preach in that they must be willing to look honestly at the enterprise they engage in and confront that which they have allowed, or encouraged, to be mystified.

It is the intent of this text to assist therapists, and their clients, in the task of demystification. In taking these initial steps, perhaps it will become evident to all concerned that the task has long been overdue.

PART ONE

DEMYSTIFYING SOME FUNDAMENTAL IDEAS ABOUT THERAPY

Whatever you say it is, it isn't.
– Alfred Korzybski

Human beings ask questions. Our success as a species is due, in no small part, to our quest for knowledge. Underlying a great deal of both what we ask and how we formulate our queries has been our attempt to arrive at an increasingly adequate understanding of ourselves. Over time – and especially during this century – we have gained significant skills for clarifying and (at least partially) alleviating many forms of distress, dissonance and disorganization that any one of us is likely to experience either within ourselves or between ourselves and others. In this sense, Sigmund Freud's own evaluation of his theories as being equal in revolutionary import and significance to those of Copernicus and Darwin is almost certainly valid. For while there may be sufficient cause to doubt the specific conclusions that Freud derived from his theories, it seems to me undeniable that, in general terms at least, his ideas have provided the impetus with which to address our questions in a manner that is fundamentally characteristic of this century.

Freud's 'talking-cure', which served as genesis to his developing theory and technique of psycho-analysis, for good or ill, has shaped our age to the extent that ever-increasing numbers of us turn to such forms of dialogue the moment we are confronted with the mysteries, conflicts, dilemmas and disruptions that intrude and impinge upon our lives no matter how mundane or cataclysmic they may appear to be.

Therapy has never been as popular, or as available, as it is today. More people than ever before are 'in' therapy or are training to be therapists. For instance, when I first joined the School of Psychotherapy and Counselling, in October 1989, the only programme on offer to trainees was its MA in Psychotherapy and Counselling. Less than five years later, the school has expanded its programmes to such an extent that it currently offers not only the MA programme (with three annual intakes), but also a substantial number of short courses in psychotherapy and counselling, a one-year certificate in the Foundations of Psychotherapy and Counselling (six intakes), a diploma in Counselling (two annual intakes), an advanced diploma in Existential Psychotherapy (one annual intake) and, most recently, a PhD in Psychotherapy and Counselling which is the first of its kind in the UK. This dramatic growth in the numbers of programmes is by no means unique; various colleges and training establishments can as easily provide similar wide-ranging lists of their own.

In parallel to this development, public demand for therapy has increased substantially. Dr Raj Persaud, in a recent *Sunday Times* article entitled 'Talking your way out of trouble', has stated that there are:

> currently 30,000 people earning their living from counselling and a further 270,000 in the voluntary sector. Research conducted on behalf of the Department of Employment suggests that over 2.5 million use counselling as a major component of their jobs ... The BAC [British Association for Counselling] has over 10,000 members and receives over 60,000 calls per year ... (Persaud, 1993:8).

Similarly, there exists a large number of applications for therapy through the NHS or via private-practice contacts. In the light of such, and a great many more examples that would amplify this contention, Dr Persaud has suggested that '[p]sychotherapy is the growth industry of the 1990s – being chic now means being in treatment' (Persaud, 1993:8).

But the great interest in, and demand for, therapy has also created significant worries. Most recently, serious concerns about various aspects of therapy have been raised by a number of journalists and writers critical of the increasing public use of, and dependence on, therapy. A notable example of this has been the furore raised by Fay Weldon's novel *Affliction* (1994) and her subsequent highly disparaging remarks concerning the potentially abusive and manipulative interventions of therapists (Freely, 1994). Ms Weldon's critiques seem to have struck a responsive chord in the British media to the extent that even the free weekly London careers magazine *Ms London* recently ran an article on this topic which was cover-headlined as 'Psycho-babble: decoding the jargon of therapy' (Bartlett, 1994). In effect, the result of this current wave of articles and exposés has been to inform the public of something that many 'insiders' have known all along: the values and foundations of therapeutic practice are riddled with insufficiently questioned assumptions.

Currently, anyone in Britain can call himself or herself a thera-pist and offer such services since it remains the case that no therapeutic body or organization has as yet been granted a Royal Charter or legal status (as is the case for psychology). In their concern and desire to remedy this situation, if only to protect the public, most of the major psychotherapy organizations in the UK have joined together to form the United Kingdom Coun-cil for Psychotherapy (UKCP) which, in May 1993, published its first (voluntary) list of registered psychotherapists. In a similar fashion, the British Association for Counselling (BAC) has, for several years now, maintained a publicly available list of its members (both accredited and non-accredited) and of BAC-registered training programmes. In addition, consultations with comparable therapeutic organizations throughout Europe have been initiated with the aim of establishing common regulations governing the practice of therapy within the European Com-munity.

Such developments – as time-consuming, exasperating and imperfect as some insiders and outsiders have judged them to be – are generally praiseworthy and, in the final analysis, necessary. However, it remains the case that, in emphasizing such issues as what constitutes adequate training in therapy and which rules and requirements will govern the registration of therapists, a fundamental question is not being properly addressed. For such has been the belief and dependence on the alleviating or curative properties of therapy that all concerned rarely stop to ask themselves just what it is that therapy provides, or *can* provide.

1. SEVERAL (FAILED) ATTEMPTS AT DEFINING THERAPY AND ONE NOVEL ALTERNATIVE

As I will endeavour to show throughout this first part of the text, what responses have been provided, or assumed, tend to be *mystificatory* in that they impose on therapy (and therapists) an aura of 'specialness', uniqueness and expertise derived from its theories, practices and training components which, however desirable to some, clearly lack sufficient supportive evidence from research studies.

However, just in case readers are beginning to suspect that they are in for another round of 'therapy-bashing', allow me to inject a note of reassurance: I *do* think that therapy offers something that is both unique and worthwhile and I will seek to clarify and examine that which I believe makes it so. But in doing this, I will also have to question and criticize numerous assumptions – some of which may seem fundamental – currently held by many therapists (and clients) which seem to me to be not only unnecessary but also detrimental to the understanding and practice of therapy and, more importantly, to the enhancement of its potentials. In order to engage in an attempt to demystify therapy, the most obvious and logical place to begin would be to describe and define what therapy is, or has been said to be – even if, as we shall see, as is often the case with issues dealing with human relations, obviousness and logic do not unfortunately seem to play a governing role in the matter.

A. *Some Initial Difficulties*

While anyone reading this text may well have a sense, or 'gut feeling', either from previous readings or from his or her own experience of 'being in therapy' – either as a therapist or as a client – of what therapy is or means to them, and, if pressed, might well be able to put such into a sufficiently suitable and representative statement, nevertheless it would appear to be the case that any such statement, while by no means incorrect, would almost certainly remain incomplete and open to some degree of dispute.

While a common resolution to a problem of this sort would be to turn to a suitable dictionary for definitional guidance, in this case dictionary definitions turn out to be misleading and problematic. My copy of the *Concise Oxford Dictionary*, for instance, defines *therapy* as a form of medical treatment, and associates the word *therapeutic* with terms such as curative, healing arts, and medical treatment of disease. Similarly, *psychotherapy* is defined as a psychological form of disease (or disorder) treatment, and while the term *counselling* does not appear, the word *counsel* is given the meaning of consultation and giving advice professionally on social problems, just as, similarly, a *counsellor* is said to be an advice-giver. All these definitions, while not entirely incorrect, are certainly confusing and would be rejected in whole or in part by many therapists. Further, in their employment of terms such as disease and medical treatment, and in the implicitly directive quality of words such as advising, they impose unnecessary definatory restrictions that, once again, a great many therapists (myself included) would dispute as being antithetical to both the understanding and practice of therapy.

As if such complexities were not enough to confound and demoralize us, Jeremy Holmes and Richard Lindley point out in their important text *The Values of Psychotherapy* (1989) that the activity we call therapy has failed to establish itself with a degree of unity of function and purpose since its basis lies in no agreed-on theoretical foundation, and, indeed, encompasses procedures and ideologies that range from the established and conventional to cult-like fringe systems. The full impact of this statement is made eminently clear when it is realized that somewhere in the region of 460 diverse forms of therapy are now claimed to be in existence (Omer and London, 1988). Each of these has its own particular perspective on what therapy is and what it claims to offer or promote, ranging from quasi-medical 'curative or symptom-removal' stances (as might be suggested in the literature of behavioural therapies (Corey, 1991)) to views of therapy as a form of 'applied philosophy' (as advocated by British existential therapists (van Deurzen-Smith, 1988)).

Therapies can be classified in a variety of ways – founder, orientation, directiveness, reflectiveness, expressiveness, length, and so forth (Holmes and Lindley, 1989), such that 'clusters' of therapies may be formed.

I have elected to distinguish four general models or 'thematic stances' of therapy. Three of these, the *psycho-analytic* (e.g. Freudian psycho-analysis, Kleinian psycho-analysis), the *humanistic* (e.g. person-centred therapy, gestalt therapy) and the *cognitive-behavioural* (e.g. Beck's cognitive therapy, Rational-Emotive Behaviour Therapy) are widely known and, together, cover the central emphases and divergences within the great majority of theories and approaches to therapy. The fourth model, the *existential-phenomenological model*, is far less well known and is derived from the writings of various existentially influenced therapists, including the present author (e.g. May, 1983; van Deurzen-Smith, 1988; Spinelli, 1989). The fundamental ideas, practices and attitudes to therapy of the first three models are summarized in the appropriate sections (i.e. Parts 3 and 4) of this text; the fourth model primarily informs the last section of the book.

To complicate matters even further, the general public (like the dictionary and, perhaps, like some therapists as well) also tends to confuse therapy with broadly related areas of guidance, advice, socio-legal and job-related assistance, and so forth. And, while all such enterprises may involve some elements of 'therapy-based skills', it is necessary to clarify how these differ from 'therapy proper'. As these distinctions are by far the most clear-cut, it would seem appropriate to begin with them and then move on to more contentious areas.

B. Distinguishing Therapy from Commonly Associated Terms

Recently, the BAC has provided a most interesting and relevant document entitled *A Report on Differentiation between Advice, Guidance, Befriending, Counselling Skills and Counselling* which was commissioned by the Department of Employment (Russell, Dexter and Bond, 1993). As the title of the report suggests, its principal task is to provide the basis for clarifying the different aims and realms of discourse contained in the above-stated terms, since their distinctiveness is by no means clear to a great many members of the public (and possibly to a good number of 'service providers' as well!)

Advice may be defined as a brief consultation the aim of which is to provide the client with appropriate and accurate information and to offer informed suggestions about how to act upon that information. Advice-giving focuses on the widening of clients' knowledge of their options and choices with regard to their socio-legal rights, potential action programmes, and so forth. The *Citizens Advice Bureau* is almost certainly the most well-known advice-giving organization in the UK. Though advising is such a commonly employed term, taking in a wide variety of styles and attitudes ranging from the facilitative to the authoritarian, in this more restricted sense it focuses particularly on areas and issues related to problem-solving via the dissemination of accurate and appropriate information and assistance with related practical tasks such as official letter-writing, professional telephone contacts, and so forth.

Guidance involves the use of an extended consultation or a series of consultations the aim of which is to assist the client to explore a particular concern via the provision of appropriate and accurate information and the giving of both suggestions and support as to how to act upon that information. A good example of a British guidance organization would be *Relate* or, as it was known until a few years ago, the *National Marriage Guidance Council*. Guidance services are often confidential and involve specific contractual criteria setting out such parameters as the designated time, focus and duration of the service. While the guidance-provider will certainly apprise the client of accurate and relevant information required to make appropriate decisions, it is equally (if not more significantly) the task of guidance to afford clients with the opportunity to explore possibilities and to develop various skills designed to enhance decision-making. Guidance clearly requires the development and maintenance of a close relationship between client and guidance-provider, but while in some cases it may aim for a more or less egalitarian basis (as in Relate), it may also be explicitly unequal (as in career guidance).

The term *befriending* involves a relationship between two individuals, one of whom agrees (either within clearly demarcated or flexible and negotiable boundaries) to take on the role of friend to someone who is socially isolated and who then, in his or her capacity as a 'befriender', offers practical and emotional support. Although it is the least frequently employed and possibly least familiar of all the terms under consideration, references to befriending appear as far back as 1879 'when lay missionaries were appointed to advise, befriend and help offenders and their families' (Russell, Dexter and Bond, 1993:3). Probably the best-known befriending organization in the UK is the *Samaritans*. The founder of the Samaritans, Chad Varah, distinguished befriending from counselling in terms of befriending's greater flexibility in being accessible and available to the individual seeking help. Befriending is most accurately associated with such services as telephone help-lines, hospice assistance, and juvenile offender schemes which may be complementary or alternative to the judicial system. Befriending differs from the other related approaches under consideration in that it emphasizes its informality, it remains deliberately non-professional in order to remain as flexible as possible with regard to its style of assistance (so that, for instance, the term 'client' is avoided in order to emphasize an egalitarian, humane form of contact), and it takes its principal task and service to be the 'sharing', rather than the management or solution, of problems.

Counselling skills focus on the employment of communication and social skills that may benefit or enhance the offering of advice, guidance, and befriending or which may be employed while in the process of nursing, educating, policing, medically diagnosing, and so forth. 'Counselling skills do not constitute a role in themselves . . . but need to be identified within a framework of values which facilitate someone's capacity for self-determination and a pattern of communication which flows mostly from that person to the facilitator' (Russell, Dexter and Bond, 1993:19). Counselling skills focus upon the facilitative element that underlies communication and social skills. As such, members of the *'caring' professions*, such as nursing, for example, will employ counselling skills as part of their task or goal-oriented work and such skills may well provide therapeutic benefit though, clearly, the person employing such skills would not lay claim to being a therapist.

Lastly, and most pertinently, the BAC-derived definition of *counselling* focuses on a specific relationship, established and maintained via clearly demarcated and mutually agreed guidelines or boundaries, the aim of which is to facilitate the means by which the client may initiate personal work designed to promote a more satisfying life-experience in a manner that respects 'the client's values, personal resources and capacity for self-determination' (Russell, Dexter and Bond, 1993:20). Since the 1920s, counselling has been defined as the application of psycho-social care. More pertinently, the term was initially employed by Carl Rogers in reaction to his not being permitted to label himself a psychotherapist and practise psychotherapy on the grounds that he was a psychologist rather than a medical doctor (thankfully – in my view, anyway – in most instances these restrictive criteria would no longer hold today). 'Imported' to the UK in the mid-1950s, counselling today tends to assume the requirement of extensive training for counsellors and differs from all the previous terms in its emphasis on the exploration of the unique meaning-world of the client and on the possibilities and limitations that such a view expresses and contains.

While the influence of Rogers' person-centred approach on counselling must be acknowledged, nevertheless counsellors today may be adherents of as wide a variety of theoretical perspectives (i.e. cognitive-behavioural counselling, psycho-analytic counselling, existential counselling) as would be encountered in a directory of psychotherapeutic approaches.

The very fact that most practitioners distinguish 'psychotherapy' from 'counselling' further aggravates the problem of defining therapy. Can psychotherapy be differentiated from counselling? And if so, how? Both are broadly agreed to be 'therapeutic enterprises', yet in the UK (and elsewhere) each is represented by separate 'host bodies' (i.e. the UKCP and the BAC). Whether there exist more subject- or enterprise-based distinctions is an additional area of complexity and controversy that will be discussed later in this section. Nevertheless, while acknowledging that I have not yet made the case for such, and begging the reader's temporary indulgence, I have opted to employ the term *therapy* as a 'generic' one that includes both psychotherapy and counselling. As such, the terms 'counselling skills' and 'counselling' discussed above may be equally designated – for the time being, at least – as 'therapeutic skills' and 'therapy'.

C. *Some Further Problems*

While the differentiation guidelines just discussed are useful in allowing a clearer understanding of what is not therapy, they still tell us very little about what it is. Acknowledging this same difficulty in a recent paper entitled 'Core skills for psychotherapy', Ian Owen has written:

> It is easy to define what therapy is not. It is not lecturing, not moralizing, patronizing nor befriending. It is not the use of counselling skills by non-mental health professionals in interviewing or management (Owen, 1993:15).

This point of view, while perhaps seeming initially unhelpful, nevertheless contains an implicit issue of substantive importance which is rarely made explicit: both practitioners and critics tend to speak of 'therapy' *in a singular or all-embracing sense*. While such a stance might be understandable for the purposes of simplicity and convenience, even so it is highly misleading. Therapy, as we have begun to see, is far more diffuse and complex a term than we might have originally assumed it to be. Indeed, when one considers the great variety of approaches and techniques that refer to themselves as therapies, one is struck as much by the substantial differences and contradictions between these as by any immediately apparent or obvious similarities.

Freud's now-famous description of psycho-analysis as an 'impossible profession' resulting from his certainty that it could never hope to provide entirely satisfactory results (Freud, 1937a) would seem to take on an added and more general significance in that the statement would also seem to fit all too accurately the current condition in which therapy in general finds itself with regard to attempts at its definition for the purposes of both clarity and criticism.

But if it seems impossible to define the term therapy (other than in terms of what it is not) then perhaps there may be some value in returning to the initial distinctions that were made – between psychotherapy and counselling – in order to consider how these terms have been defined. Possibly, in this way, we might gain some helpful entry-point leading to the definition of therapy.

D. Defining Psychotherapy

Eloquently taking on the challenge of attempting a definition of psychotherapy, Jeremy Holmes and Richard Lindley have argued that one way of approaching the possibility of extracting 'the basic elements to be found in all forms of therapy' (Holmes and Lindley, 1989:3) is to consider it from the standpoint of structure, space and relationship (Holmes and Lindley, 1989).

The notion of *structure*, that is to say the basic conditions such as the meeting-time, the location where psychotherapeutic sessions are to be conducted, the 'contractual' conditions that both psychotherapist and client agree to, and so forth, while clearly variable and distinct between one theoretical approach and another, and, indeed, between any one psychotherapist and another, nevertheless offers a broadly common purpose. For the structure offers, at least potentially, a secure environment which promotes the exploration of cognitions, affects and behaviours in a manner that seeks to allow greater honesty and the expression of thoughts and feelings that might not otherwise be allowed direct expression in another structure.

This 'safe' structure, while clearly unusual or, indeed, 'unreal', may sometimes prove to be cathartic or emotionally explosive and, in this way, the psychotherapeutic structure may be likened to that of theatre (particularly in the original Greek sense of the word), in that 'as in the theatre, there is a suspension of disbelief, which allows powerful emotions and actions to be explored safely without the consequences that might follow in everyday life' (Holmes and Lindley, 1989:5). Further, as in theatre, this very 'unreality' may expose and clarify the underlying features of the client's everyday, lived 'reality' in a more intense and direct fashion. As such, the psychotherapeutic structure seeks to promote and enhance the client's experience of being 'held' by and within the psychotherapeutic process.

In so doing, however, a novel and possibly unique *space* is created which seeks to enable or facilitate the clarification or discovery of previously unconsidered or superficially examined feelings, attitudes, assumptions, and viewpoints held by the client. In this exploratory space, then, the possibilities emerge for greater, more honest self-challenge and discovery. Again, however, as has been pointed out by various authors, an important paradox emerges. For while the psychotherapeutic space is likely to foster the client's experience of increased autonomy, this experience seems to require in the first instance an *abdication of autonomy* via the acceptance of the structure which, however much 'democratically negotiated' between psychotherapist and client, will nevertheless contain a number of rules, restrictions and conditions that are non-negotiable and which have been effectively imposed on the client by the psychotherapist, or by the psychotherapist's allegiance to a particular approach to psychotherapy – conditions that raise crucial questions concerning the *unequal power base* of the therapeutic process.

Finally, for most psychotherapists, regardless of the orientation they represent or advocate, the *relationship* between psychotherapist and client is considered to be the most fundamental element in the psychotherapeutic process. Indeed, many would go so far as to state that the very success of psychotherapy, however defined, is first and foremost dependent on the quality of the relationship that has been established and the possibilities contained within it for furthering the likelihood of productive or positively experienced change. It remains to be asked, however, just what there might be that is special or different about a psychotherapeutic relationship as opposed to any other, or indeed whether differing models of therapy promote the establishment of varying kinds of relationships.

E. *Defining Counselling*

Founded in 1977, the British Association for Counselling (BAC) has established itself in the UK as the principal organization promoting counselling and both accrediting individual counsellors and registering counselling training institutes. In its 'Code of Ethics and Practice for Counsellors', it is stated that:

> The term 'counselling' includes work with individuals, pairs or groups of people often, but not always, referred to as 'clients'. The objectives of particular counselling relationships will vary according to the client's needs. Counselling may be concerned with developmental issues, addressing and resolving specific problems, making decisions, coping with crisis, developing personal insight and knowledge, working through feelings of inner conflict or improving relationships with others. The counsellor's role is to facilitate the client's work in ways which respect the client's values, personal resources and capacity for self-determination.
> Only when both the user and the recipient explicitly agree to enter into a counselling relationship does it become 'counselling' rather than the use of 'counselling skills' (BAC, 1993: section 3).

While denoting a sense of offering a service, this definition avoids greater specificity on the grounds that

> While it is essential to have some consensus about counselling as a service, it is not useful to attempt to specify in detail how the counselling task is undertaken. This might lead to an exclusive set of assumptions about how human beings learn, develop, and cope with the changing needs and resources in themselves and their environment (BAC, 1991: section 1).

> People become engaged in counselling when a person, occupying regularly or temporarily the role of counsellor, offers or agrees explicitly to offer time, attention and respect to another person or persons temporarily in the role of client. (BAC, 1991: section 2).

In a BAC document written by Hetty Einzig aimed at the potential 'consumer', the counsellor is presented as being supportive but unwilling to provide direct advice, 'since the aim is to help you develop insight into your problems' (Einzig, 1991:3). Equally, the counsellor examines and clarifies the client's communications so that they can become both clearer and more direct in their meaning. Throughout, the counsellor employs such skills as 'knowing how and when to ask the right questions' (Einzig, 1991:4) which have been 'developed through training and experience' (Einzig, 1991:4). She goes on to state:

> Most of all, the counselling process can help you to feel more in control of your life and able to do something *yourself* about what isn't right for you, about the feelings distressing you or about a difficult relationship, rather than feeling helpless, angry or frustrated. You don't *have* to be a victim in your life (Einzig, 1991:4).

When the separate definitions of psychotherapy and counselling just outlined are analysed in conjunction with one another, there is little that emerges which offers a significant distinction between the two enterprises. Other than differences in terminology (i.e. psychotherapy vs. counselling), and a more clearly 'service-offering' slant in the statements concerning counselling, it is evident that the three principal elements of structure, space and relationship which informed the previous discussion on psychotherapy (Holmes and Lindley, 1989) are also emphasized in the BAC literature on counselling. Has something been left out which would clarify just what is different between the two processes?

F.   A Critique of the Suggested Differences Between Psychotherapy and Counselling

Sigmund Freud viewed psycho-analysis as a profession that was neither for physicians nor priests but, rather, as that of professionals who minister to the other's needs (Freud used the word *seelsorger*, which has tended to be translated into English in terms suggesting 'secular minister of the soul'). Similarly, Thomas Szasz has pointed out that 'Aeschylus actually had a name for what we now call psychotherapy. He called it the employment of *iatroi logoi*, or "healing words". In these ancient roots, then, lies our proper term for the modern, secular cure of souls . . .' (Szasz, 1978:208).

While the term 'cure' might initially suggest that psychotherapy – as opposed to counselling – is deeply embedded in a medical tradition, such a conclusion would be inaccurate. Although it is true that the great majority of the pioneers of psycho-analysis were indeed medical doctors, and that in some countries, such as the United States, medical training was (and, to a lesser extent, remains) a requirement for entering into psycho-analytic training, this was never the case in the UK (among other countries), and Freud himself (as the previous paragraph suggests) was in favour of 'lay', or non-medical, analysts (Freud, 1926).

'Cure', in the psychotherapeutic sense, extends the meaning of the word far beyond the boundaries set by medical diagnosis and treatment. V. M. Axline, in her well-known book *Dibs: in search of self*, for instance, speaks of psychotherapeutic cure as 'a chance to feel worthwhile. A chance to be a person wanted, respected, accepted as a human being worthy of dignity' (Axline, 1964:22). Similarly, Abraham Maslow's view that the deepest psychological miseries encountered in living result from 'the sin of failing to do with one's life all that one knows one could do' (Maslow, 1968:5) captures, for many psychotherapists, the essence of what psychotherapy deals with and seeks to 'cure'.

Such distinctions might best be understood from the standpoint of the difference between *problems and dilemmas*. Problems require solutions, while dilemmas can only be explored and lived with in a more or less satisfactory manner. While the medical doctor deals primarily with problems, psychotherapists' principal endeavours focus on their clients' dilemmas.

For all the above reasons, psychotherapy – like counselling – excludes from its definition the more medically based approaches to the cure or alleviation of symptoms as exemplified by drug-based or physicalist-based interventions (such as, for instance, electro-convulsive treatment (ECT)) and, instead, typically emphasizes interventions that rely in whole or in part on verbal and non-verbal communication.

As was stated before, the modern-day employment of the term 'counselling' came about when Carl Rogers found himself prevented from practising psychotherapy in the United States because he had not been medically trained. Rogers called what he did 'counselling' not because he wished to make a distinction with psychotherapy but because he quite simply was not allowed to label himself a psychotherapist. His agenda was the same as that of the psychotherapist and, as such, in this instance, we must conclude that no substantive distinction between psychotherapy and counselling is apparent.

Clare Townsend (1993) has argued that the distinction is principally one of *status* based on the questionable assumption that counselling is somehow inferior to psychotherapy. Once again, this view probably has its origins in psychotherapy's (tenuous) relationship with medicine and the possibility that the high regard in which the latter was held in some ways 'transferred' on to the former. It must be said, however, that today it is by no means certain as to whether medical training necessarily infers higher status upon a psychotherapeutic practitioner; indeed, for some, the opposite view may well be the case!

For the general public (and, perhaps, for some psycho- therapists and counsellors), counselling clearly has a 'populist' appeal, while psychotherapy, again possibly owing to its histori- cal development, retains an 'élitist' element. Particularly in a class-conscious society such as that to be found in Britain, these distinctions may say more about social divisions than about theory or practice-based differences, or, indeed, about differ- ences in the quality or effectiveness of the therapeutic process. Certainly, there is a currently held belief that counselling 'can be provided to many more people than psychotherapy can and in a wider variety of contexts' (Townsend, 1993:252).

For many, psychotherapy suggests the idea of lengthy treat- ment involving several weekly meetings, while counselling is perceived as being relatively brief and usually requiring, at most, once-weekly meetings. For some, the *number of weekly sessions* in which therapy occurs is sufficient distinction between psycho- therapy and counselling, so that whereas counselling is seen to occur typically on a once-weekly basis, psychotherapy sessions may take place anywhere between three and five times per week. This purely quantitative (as opposed to qualitative) distinction seems to me to be somewhat arbitrary and artificial in that there exist numerous instances where psychotherapists will see clients on a once-weekly basis and, equally, counsellors may meet with their clients for several sessions in the same week. It would not be surprising if this distinction (more commonly raised by psychotherapists trained within the psycho-analytic model) were not one based once again more on perceived status than on process or outcome effects. Though largely anecdotal, Towns- end's point that, while professionals might be impressed by someone who is in therapy three times per week, the general public would regard that individual with some degree of sus- picion and might go so far as to view him or her as being mentally unbalanced, suggests, if not the truth, then at least something approximating it. Certainly, given the requirements of personal on-going psychotherapy for trainees on the great majority of psychotherapy training programmes, it remains the case that a significant proportion of psychotherapy's clientele is made up of students of psychotherapy. Such requirements are less common within counselling training programmes, where, while at least some experience of counselling from the standpoint of a client is strongly encouraged by most training programmes as a means of clarifying the various dynamics of the counselling relationship, it may not be required.

Some have argued the distinction between psychotherapy and counselling on the basis that counselling tends to focus on a specific and currently experienced life-issue and, in this sense, is focused on problem-exploration, while psychotherapy deals with more deep-seated, less easily definable or compartmentalizable issues, exploration of which may bring about general, permanent and profound changes in a client's whole attitude to life. Translated into the language of advertising, what is being claimed is that the psychotherapeutic process 'reaches those parts that counselling cannot'.

Still others have taken as their focus point for distinction the argument that while counselling is largely 'present-focused', emphasizing the 'here and now' aspects of experience, psychotherapy is more concerned with the exploration of the past, focusing on infant and childhood relations with 'significant others' (such as one's parents) in order to expose and bring to the client's awareness how such relationships may have imposed negative or 'neurotic' patterns of thought and behaviour. In this way, it is further argued, while the nature of the counselling relationship is straightforward, direct and focused on the dynamics between counsellor and client, the psychotherapeutic relationship emphasizes and relies on the 'subtextual elements' (i.e. transferential elements) in the relationship.

Finally, some have suggested that the main distinction between psychotherapy and counselling is that while the former requires clients to recline on a couch, the latter only provides an armchair. I leave it to readers to decide whether this variation provides a sufficient point for demarcation.

Needless to say, all these distinctions are open to argument and are clearly not generalizable. In all cases, examples can be presented which not only raise significant doubt as to the general validity of a particular point of divergence, but also provide the means for arguing the very opposite – such that distinctive features or categories said to belong to psychotherapy can be seen to be, in certain circumstances, central to the counselling process under consideration, and vice versa.

It is possible that the difference between counselling and psychotherapy has more to do with 'image marketing' than with revealing any genuine process- or outcome-related differences. Equally, contextual factors may play a role in whether a practitioner defines himself or herself as a psychotherapist or a counsellor. In my own case, for instance, being both a UKCP-registered psychotherapist and a BAC-accredited counsellor, I cannot, in all honesty, say that I am aware of any differences when I say I am being one or the other! Usually, in fact, my title is determined by my clients' wants or assumptions, or which referral list they selected my name from. It is possible that, just as some might feel that the issues in their lives merited the attention of a psychotherapist, others might be intimidated by the perceived 'grandiosity' of such a title and would feel more at ease talking to a 'humble' counsellor.

My own conclusion is that it is not possible to make a generally accepted differentiation between counselling and psychotherapy and that it is clear that, regardless of the many and varied distinctions that some have sought to impose on them, the terms may be employed interchangeably. Indeed, it may well be the case that the desire to impose or avoid distinctions has more to say about the allegiance of the institution in which a practitioner has trained, the setting in which he or she might typically work, and the personalities involved, than about specific distinctive features of practice.

As such, it may be more helpful to acknowledge the similarities between the two terms:

1. Both involve methods for (primarily) verbal exploration of psychological difficulties.
2. Both terms 'house' a variety of differing (even competing) theories and methodologies the precise goals of which may vary significantly.

3. In general, both seek to assist individuals in clarifying and resolving their own emotional predicaments and thereby gain greater clarity and increase the possibility of bringing about change in their way of relating to themselves, to others, and to the world in general.
4. Both share common theoretical underpinnings in that both are based on the work of the same authors and on the same theoretical constructs.
5. Both emphasize the establishment and development of a particular and specific relationship which is itself viewed as essentially therapeutic or at least containing essential elements necessary for therapeutic benefit.

All in all, then, if there exist significant differences between psychotherapy and counselling, they are not easily forthcoming. As such, my case for employing the term 'therapy' as one that encompasses both psychotherapy and counselling can be seen to have sufficient validity to merit its continuation.

G.   The Definition of Therapy Revisited

Nevertheless, since both psychotherapy and counselling have each provided their own definition, albeit a definition that seems equally applicable to the other, can it be that our initial task of defining therapy has finally reached its fruition?

Unfortunately, the answer must remain 'no'. For while at first sight the given definitions would seem to be as accurate and inclusive as one might realistically hope for, on closer inspection they reveal assumptions and gaps in logic which require eluci-dation. Not wishing to burden the reader any more than is necessary with regard to this issue, I will endeavour to expose these by focusing on a critique of the BAC definition of coun-selling provided by Alex Howard (1992) which, hopefully, the reader will recognize as being equally applicable to a definition of psychotherapy, or, indeed, of therapy in general.

In considering the BAC's definition of counselling, Alex Howard has written:

40

It ought to be obvious that BAC's definition of counselling is just about as vague as it can be ... BAC refers to the 'task' of counselling; but prescribes nothing about the means and methods. It tells you *what* counsellors are trying to do, but nothing about *how* they do it. Such coyness is understandable, for three reasons:

a) There is very little consensus among counsellors and psychotherapists about methods that work and don't work.

b) Counsellors and psychotherapists, in their urge to show toleration, warmth and humanity, don't like to explore their differences very energetically.

c) Counsellors, in the process of marketing their wares to the wider world, are keen to show an underlying unity of purpose. Therefore they are most reluctant to face, or reveal, the fundamental divisions about methods which run, like deep fissures, through the very heart of their activities (Howard, 1992:90).

But how is counselling distinct from the myriad forms of 'care' that others may offer? Howard points out that the

BAC does, of course, stipulate that counselling is occuring only when people explicitly adopt the role of 'counsellor' and 'client' ... But we still end up with a circular definition. Ask: 'What is counselling?' and you get the answer: 'It is what counsellors and clients explicitly agree to do together.' But what *do* they do together? The answer: 'Counsellors do counselling and clients have it done to them'! ... This tells us nothing more about the nature of counselling but it reveals a great deal about the, human enough, search for power, status and a secure income (Howard, 1992:91).

While one might wish to take issue with the tone of Howard's critique, its basic argument, however unpalatable, nevertheless strikes home. It may well be the case that a definition of therapy involves *therapists' definitions and views of themselves as therapists* (for whatever reasons and purposes) as much as having something to say about the act and purpose of therapy.

H. A Final – and Novel – Attempt to Define Therapy

As we can see, then, the various attempts to define the broad field of therapy have not succeeded in providing an agreed-on statement. Does this mean that the field cannot be defined? Possibly. But before entirely subscribing to this conclusion, let us consider the possibility that there may be something in the nature of the question itself which provokes (if not forces) such a conclusion upon us. All the approaches and attempts to define therapy discussed so far reveal a *Socratic stance* in that they seek to ask the question 'what is therapy?' in the hope that an answer will emerge which will provide the necessary and sufficient properties of this term. This is clearly a laudable aim, and it is one that permeates most attempts to define a realm of discourse. Indeed, for many centuries, philosophers in the West subscribed to this approach as being the *sole* means of arriving at suitable definitions.

It was only towards the middle of this century that this approach was challenged in a substantial manner by the Cambridge philosopher Ludwig Wittgenstein (1953). Wittgenstein forcefully argued that:

> most concepts or categories do not possess a set of characteristics shared by all members of the category. Rather, category members are united by strands of similarity, or what are called 'family resemblances' ... [They] are open concepts, which possess no set of necessary and sufficient properties but are held together by a network of overlapping and crisscrossing similarities (Winner, 1982:5)

Wittgenstein's famous example of this argument was the concept of *games*. While it may seem, at first, to be the easiest thing in the world to define a game, nevertheless, as Wittgenstein so ably showed, this is far from the case. For the concept of games is an open one in that, on closer inspection, there exist no features that are common to *all* games. Monopoly, poker and football are all games, but what do they have in common? One might first say that they all involve some sort of competition between at least two game-players. But is competition a *necessary* condition to a game? Clearly not; in recent years there has been the development of a wide range of 'fantasy' board and computer games that emphasize co-operation or exploration rather than competition. Yet there is no doubt in participants' minds that they are engaged in game-playing. Nor does a game require a minimum of two players. Games such as solitaire, for instance, can only be played by one person. While all games share *some* properties with some other games, no games share *all* properties with all other games. And further, as Wittgenstein argues, when a new game is invented, it is understood to be a game because it is in some ways similar to *some* established game, not because it is similar to *all* games in any exact manner.

The philosopher Nelson Goodman (1977), clearly influenced by Wittgenstein's line of argument, approached this same issue with regard to our attempts to define art. While it may be justifiably argued that all art is in some way 'symbolic', being symbolic is not in itself a necessary and sufficient defining feature of art since much can be symbolic that is not 'art-laden', such as Ordnance Survey maps or numbers. At the same time, however, it is not inconceivable that an art gallery (which, one would expect, houses works of art) might purchase an Ordnance Survey map taped on to a piece of hardboard or a line of numbers painted on to a canvas and promote such as examples (perhaps even exemplary examples) of contemporary art. We can all easily think of real controversies generated by diverse views on the issue of what constitutes a work of art. Goodman provides an original (and, I believe, highly significant) alternative to such controversies by arguing that, rather than ask the question '*What* is art?', we should be asking instead '*When* is art?' Consider Goodman's own example of a stone lying in a driveway. In such circumstances, the stone is neither a symbol nor a work of art. But consider the same stone inside a geological museum. The stone may now, as a representative of stones of a given geological period, be symbolic, but it is still not a work of art. Now place the stone inside an art gallery. The stone here, under observation, may also be seen to be symbolic, but its symbolic nature will not be the same as that of the stone in the geological museum. Rather, it may be symbolic of all manner of aesthetic qualities by virtue of its shape, colour, smoothness or roughness of texture and so forth. It may also be symbolic in terms of the 'mood' that some observers might claim it to exemplify. Put more simplistically, although the stone itself might be unchanged, it is the *context* under which the stone is observed which provides it with its differing meanings and classifications.

Following both Wittgenstein and Goodman, I would propose that our concerns with the nature of therapy reveal similar issues. Therapy cannot be fully defined in that it, too, is an 'open concept' – the varying forms or categories of therapy do not possess sets of characteristics shared by *all* members of the category 'therapy'. Rather, category members are united by 'family resemblances' the varying similarities of which overlap and criss-cross one another. Similarly, it may well be far more useful and satisfactory for us to ask '*When* is therapy?' rather than '*What* is therapy?'. For in doing so we can then begin to focus on the *contextual* features of therapy rather than continue with our vain attempts to eke out their definitional properties.

Again, to return to the example of art, something is a representative of art when it is *located* in a specifically designated artistic environment (such as an art gallery), when it is *labelled* as art by an authoritative individual or body (such as an art critic or the gallery's body of governors), and/or when an individual's experience of, or *encounter* with, the said object is experienced in such a manner that the individual labels that object-in-context as 'a work of art'.

Let us consider what emerges when we apply the same criteria to therapy. Therapy is such when it occurs in a specifically designated environment (such as the therapist's office or the 'psychological frame' under which therapy occurs), and when a process of encounter occurs under conditions that have been labelled as 'a therapeutic encounter' by a designated authority (i.e. the therapist and/or the registering authority that attests to the therapist's credentials), and/or when the experiential features of the encounter are defined as 'therapeutic' by at least one participant in the process.

Therapy, in this sense, acknowledges the vast realm of possibilities inherent within the term, while containing such under the limits (or 'givens') specified above. Equally, it focuses the term within a *contextual frame of reference* within which the notion of 'encounter' is central. In doing so, it shifts our focus away from 'doing' or 'done to' characteristics to, broadly speaking, 'being' (or, more accurately, as I will discuss in Part 5, 'being-for' and 'being-with') variables that involve both the therapist and client. Most significantly, perhaps, this stance exposes the mystificatory possibilities and tendencies that are most likely to emerge when one attempts to impose defining characteristics on therapy which are fixed on its 'whatness'.

It is precisely this realm of definition which, I believe, has led numerous critics of therapy to express their concerns or to polemicize against its practice (or its practitioners). Unlike a number of my colleagues, I do not take the position that such views are entirely misguided, or are the expressions of the critic's personal neurosis, or that the best means of dealing with them is to pay them no attention whatsoever in the hope that they will disappear or be revealed to be absurd at some future point in time. Equally, however, I remain sceptical of the conclusions drawn by such critics because they, too, in their critiques, reveal their allegiance to the imbuing of therapy with quasi-magical, 'doing-specific' properties. For me, it is not a question of 'white magic' versus 'black magic'; it is the doing away with the 'magical beliefs' themselves which should concern us.

My attempt to refocus the definition of therapy in the manner suggested above may not be entirely satisfactory, but it would seem to be an improvement over previous attempts at defining the term in that:

1. It allows for all the various competing (and often conflicting) theories of, and approaches, styles and attitudes to, therapy to co-exist within the broad realm of 'family resemblances' by de-emphasizing specific skills, aims, goals

45

and outcomes claimed to be necessary, desirable, or specific to therapy (e.g. curing, helping and/or directly changing the client).

2. It circumvents notions of therapy that are reliant on the idea that therapy is 'done to' someone (the client) and is 'done by' someone else (the therapist).

3. It acknowledges the significance of the labels, or titles, of 'therapist' and 'client' as being, in and of themselves, essential defining components of the therapeutic process.

4. While recognizing the 'specialness' or uniqueness of therapeutic encounters, it nevertheless diminishes the tendency to view any events that might emerge in seeming consequence to such encounters (e.g. alleviation of symptoms, beneficial help, etc.) as being possible *only* under the specific set of theoretical conditions and assumptions believed in, espoused and imposed by the therapist (or the 'school' or approach that he or she has been trained in and represents), or, indeed, by the therapeutic process in general – that is to say, the 'specialness' of therapy lies within the *relationship or encounter* that is made possible rather than in the *consequences or outcomes* of such.

This last point may be seen by some as being somewhat problematic since its intent is to redirect the emphasis of therapeutic encounters *away from* such notions as might be associated with medically modelled ideas of diagnostic intervention, alleviation and cure and *towards* the idea that the object and focus of therapy is principally the formation of the relationship and the exploration of the possibilities contained therein. This is not to say that the experience of (and, indeed, evidence for) psychophysical benefit, alleviation of disturbing and disorientating symptoms, and even 'cures' are not possible through therapy. Such a statement would be clearly absurd! *But what is being suggested is that just as therapy cannot lay claim to be the sole, or even established, means of producing these consequences, in the same way it should not make the production of these outcomes its point of focus or its 'reason for being'.*

I realize that this view will not sit well with a great many people, not least a good number of my therapeutic colleagues. Equally, the stance I am taking begs the question: 'Then why go to, or engage in, therapy at all? What is the point?' I will endeavour to address this question and provide what I hope will be a sufficiently satisfactory answer. But some patience is required of the reader; we must first consider the various critiques raised against therapy.

2. CRITIQUES OF THERAPY

Even if the difficulties surrounding the very definition of therapy were to be agreed as having been partially surmounted, we have still to face an equally problematic question: Is there any evidence that therapy is effective in alleviating distress, or even curing it? Indeed, is there any evidence that therapy is at least *as effective* in these goals as any other activity that would not be defined as therapy? And, as well, is there any evidence that would suggest that therapy not only is not effective but might actually be harmful or likely to increase or prolong distress in individuals?

These are fair questions to ask and, once again, as I will seek to demonstrate, there are no straightforward answers to *any* of these concerns.

The harshest critics of therapy, though often focusing their attacks on psycho-analysis (Eysenck and Wilson, 1973; Masson, 1984, 1988; Gellner, 1985), have raised serious objections to the vagueness, lack of scientific evidence and rigour and possible inaccuracies in most (if not all) theories that underlie therapeutic practice. Some have suggested that therapy is a modern form of religion requiring unquestioning faith in both its 'priests' (i.e. therapists) and its 'congregation' (i.e. clients) and is thus closed to objective criticism, measurement and scientific falsifiability. Others, on the other hand, while acknowledging that at least some therapies are open to scientific investigation, claim that therapy has been found to be ineffective, or unable to substantiate its claims. Still others have attacked therapy not from a scientific perspective but from a socio-political one, arguing that therapy 'may be used essentially as a palliative, diverting attention away from the true cause of human unhappiness' (Holmes and Lindley, 1989:13), such that therapy degrades, mystifies and moulds individuals to accept, even embrace, as personally tolerable situations that should continue to be seen as socially intolerable. Equally, these latter critics argue as unacceptable the elevation of the individual and the 'psycho-political' competition that such an elevation creates or aggravates between individuals, social classes, cultures, races and genders. Clearly, all these separate criticisms require consideration and response if we are to remain broadly in favour of the therapeutic enterprise.

Generally speaking, however, it must be noted that all such critiques are, in significant ways, far from neutral. Each has as its basis an alternative view of social vicissitudes to promote and, indeed, elevate. This is not to say that the critiques are to be swept aside, but rather that they must be placed into their proper context in order that suitable discussion and analysis can proceed. I feel it necessary to make my own position clear in this matter. While I am in no doubt that there is much to criticize therapy for, as this text will hopefully make clear, nevertheless there is also much to be said in its favour. While there are certainly individuals who have suffered and been injured in numerous ways as a result of their involvement with therapy, it is important to acknowledge that many have also found therapy to be literally life-saving or life-enhancing. If therapy can be accused of doing wrong to people, it must also be praised for doing something right. If therapy, as it currently exists, is imperfect, then we are left with two broad options: either to give up on it and seek alternative enterprises that will fulfil therapy's promise and avoid its inadequacies and inconsistencies, or alternatively seek to clarify both what therapy *can* offer and what ill-considered, misleading and potentially disruptive and abusive assumptions therapy carries with it might be removed or at least minimized from its agenda. Both approaches seem to me to be valid and worth promoting. But just as the first alternative must acknowledge that, after much deliberation and proposal of alternatives, as yet no entirely suitable substitute for therapy has been found (Masson, 1993), so, too, does it remain a possibility that the clarification of the therapeutic process may reveal destructive assumptions that are so fundamental to its entire enterprise that they are embedded in its definition and application. I believe that the most honest answer we can provide with regard to this dilemma is to acknowledge that we simply do not know as yet. As such, it would seem sensible to me to maintain a view that promotes further exploration of *both* stances. This text takes as its main focus the investigation of those issues and concerns that arise when one adopts the second option, in that its principal aim is to consider critically the possibilities and concerns which emerge when one makes therapy itself the focus point of investigation. That is to say, if it were to be the case that therapy offers *unique* possibilities in understanding and alleviating at least some aspects of human misery and disturbance, then what are its potentials, limitations and points of danger?

A. Critiques Linking Therapy to Religion

One recurring theme that arises in many discussions on therapy, in particular the very idea of therapy, is that it is in some way linked to, or a contemporary form of, *religion*. Such views have been advocated by both defenders and critics (or, if you will, 'believers' and 'heretics') of either therapy in general or of specific models of therapy (particularly the psycho-analytic model). Freud himself was well aware of this tendency and, in a now-famous letter to his friend Oskar Pfister, railed against the possibility of psycho-analysis being in any way associated with religion. Indeed, it was his aim to find the means of protecting it from its influence (as well as that of physicians) (Freud and Meng, 1963).

On one level, it is easy to understand why, in spite of Freud's protests, such analogies continue to be made. Partly as a result of the first phase of the development of psycho-analytic theory and practice, the Freudian legacy of which included 'inner circles', testaments of faith, apostates, heroic myths, and so forth, some therapy institutes have retained (perhaps even fostered) an aura of secrecy and mystery that suggests more the initiation rites and ceremonies of secret societies than an academic or professional training. But it would be unfair to suggest that this is so for most modern-day training programmes. Nevertheless, something (at least vaguely) akin to Christian religious practices (such as the Catholic confessional) might be seen to have their parallels in the therapeutic process, and for these reasons there has been some interest in considering and promoting such potential similarities.

Halmos (1965), for instance, in considering the status of therapy, argues that therapy is more dependent on the 'faith' of therapists in maintaining their beliefs in the beneficial possibilities of therapy than on any significant scientific bases. In this way, he suggests, therapy is best understood as a secularized form of religion exchanging the notion of the struggle between good and evil for that of mental health versus mental disruption.

Rieff (1979), among others, sees the therapist's 'own value system as central to the therapeutic relationship' (Holmes and Lindley, 1989:119). As such, he argues, therapy can be understood

> as a form of 'moral pedagogy', and therapists as latter-day priests who wrap up their covert moral message in a pseudo-scientific garb . . .
> In his view it is only a short step from the confessional to the couch . . . He characterizes Freud's 'fundamental rule' of psychoanalysis – the 'candour' expected of the patient – as a sacrament . . . (Holmes and Lindley, 1989:119).

In this fashion, Rieff suggests, that which can be clearly seen as moral discourse takes on the guise of science.

In a similar fashion, Rustin and Rustin (1960) take the view that therapy is the religion of humanism which, in being so, emphasizes the value in the exploration of individual experience.

Taking a more controversial stance on the issue, Dr Kenneth Calestro observed somewhat caustically that psychotherapy is the bastard progeny of a long tradition of neo-religious and magical practices that have risen up in every unit of human culture (Calestro, 1972:83).

In order to provide substance to such claims, E. F. Torrey (1986) goes on to compare therapists with those whom Westerners have somewhat derogatorily labelled as 'witch doctors' and lists various points which he sees as being of convergence. These include: symptom removal, attitude and behaviour change, insight, improved interpersonal relationships, and improved social efficiency (Torrey, 1986).

While these views may be appealing to some, and indeed may contain some intriguing possibilities for exploration, they are likely to be as misleading as they are potentially useful. I agree entirely with Holmes and Lindley when, in addressing this issue, they write that the attempt to reinterpret psychotherapy in terms of its potential resonances with religion

> misses . . . the heart of what is special about analytic psycho-therapy. Interesting and illuminating parallels exist between, say, the findings of modern physics and Taoist philosophy . . . but to reduce one to the other or to conflate them would be absurd (Holmes and Lindley, 1989:122–3).

Equally, to stretch these similarities in order to suggest the lack of distinction between therapy and religion is, ultimately, abusive to both systems. Better then to acknowledge that, while potential points of contact and dialogue may exist and may be worthwhile pursuing, nevertheless each has its own unique foundational emphases and concerns which are as much its defining characteristics as any statements or conclusions it might share with alternate, or competing, systems.

Nevertheless, something of relevance is contained in such views. In her paper, 'The myth of therapist expertise' (1992), Katharine Mair compares the current position of therapists with that of physicians during the first decade of this century since, in each case, their patients' faith in their expertise, their understanding of the nature of the problems and their ability to remedy the complaints are far less than might be imagined or conveyed. Equally, just as physicians undertook a specialized training which claimed to provide a model with which to understand the illness and a methodology for treatment they believed in because it seemed to work, so, too, does the modern-day therapist function under similar, and equally questionable, guidelines. While Mair accepts that therapy can be of significant value to people, she argues that

> its efficacy is not due primarily to the models and methods that it uses (which may be as irrelevant to the patient's problems as the application of leeches was to the curing of a fever eighty years ago), and that too blind a faith in them may actually interfere with therapists' ability to help their patients (Mair, 1992:135).

Echoing Torrey, Mair makes the point that all societies seem to designate certain individuals as their 'healers' whose wisdom, authority and ability to carry out effective interventions are accepted with little, if any, doubt. All forms of therapy rely upon or make use of this mystique even in those instances where the task of therapy is defined in terms of providing ways of enabling individuals to heal themselves. 'Psychotherapy, like medicine, is said to be based on knowledge. Perhaps, like the medicine of eighty years ago, its true foundation is on the myth of knowledge' (Mair, 1992:136).

B. Socio-Political Critiques

Socio-political critiques of therapy present quite a different area of concern which the psychologist and counsellor, Phillida Salmon, has succinctly summarized:

> Historically, psychotherapy has been something of a special preserve, separated off from the social world. At worst, it has reduced social structures to inner feelings, psychologising – often pathologising – material, political or cultural realities.

Even at its best it has tended to ignore and bypass these realities, treating them merely as the context for its focus: individual, private worlds, intra-personal or inter-personal processes. Psychotherapy has, in general, affirmed the primacy of inner events, and paid little attention to the ways in which social and cultural structures actually *shape* personal experience. This situation is surely not the outcome of a lack of awareness . . . The problem, for psychotherapists, is rather the lack of a language in which to formulate the meaning of sociocultural realities in relation to the work they do. The need is not just for a new kind of understanding of how the outer world may have brought about the pain, bewilderment and suffering of therapeutic clients. A still greater problem is that, within our available conceptual repertoire, there is no adequate way of formulating the meaning of psychotherapy itself as socio-cultural practice (Salmon, 1991:50).

Following this line of argument, David Pilgrim has presented a critical perspective which posits that while it was the case that therapy from the mid-1960s to the mid-1970s stood in opposition to the orthodoxy of mental health and both sided with and informed progressive, even radical, social movements, this is no longer the case. The current 'reductionist, socially blinkered understandings of therapy can be traced back to the sectional interests of professionalism . . . What is on offer, in professional practice, is typically élitist and self-interested' (Salmon, 1991:50).

Pilgrim criticizes the tendency to employ forms of 'psychological reductionism' that re-interpret and reduce actions that are arguably valid within their social context to instances of (neurotic) individual motives. For example, Chasseguet-Smirgel and Grunberger (1986) take the stance that trade union activists may be considered to have 'authority problems' and revolutionaries may be deemed to be suffering from 'an omnipotent infantile fixation'. In a broader manner, such approaches assume the validity of considering parts of a system not only in isolation from their wider context, but also in a manner that excludes all variables other than those deemed to be 'psychological'. In this way, for instance, 'discourse . . . has been associated with reducing social policy decisions about mental health to psychological considerations of child care (particularly mothering) and reducing class-derived industrial conflict to tensions in and between small and large groups . . .' (Pilgrim, 1991:53).

Further, these questionable stances tend to be validated by means of naive invocations of individual responsibility and choice which both elevate the individual and disenfranchize social criticism.

In a similar vein, David Smail (1991) has presented the argument that:

> [p]sychotherapists . . . are trapped within a fundamental dilemma. Explanations of the origins of suffering usually make reference to the material world. But the claim to universal curative powers leads to a formulation of therapeutic work in terms that are purely psychological . . . This results in the psychological reductionism pointed out by Pilgrim: the conversion of real powerlessness into personal inadequacies supposedly remediable by social skills or stress management training – or conversely, the reading of socio-political advantage as inner strength (Salmon, 1991:51).

This suggests the kind of 'get on yer bike' philosophy advocated by the Thatcherite ideology that was so seemingly popular during the 1980s but which has since been largely discredited even by those who, at the time, were its staunchest defenders. For example, the Institute of Economic Affairs (the free-market 'think tank' so venerated by Mrs Thatcher which initiated many of her economic ideas) now acknowledges that Thatcherism failed to address 'the deeper questions facing any civilization', and that, contrary to the view attributed to the Prime Minister, there is such a thing as a society (*Guardian*, 27/09/1993:3).

More extreme stances have argued that therapy can be seen as a means of suppressing social dissent and advocating social conformity. They view therapy as a panacea for the privileged classes which allows these to view and deal with their problems in ways that elevate the individual and, by so doing, strengthen the inhuman relations between classes, cultures, races, genders, members of differing sexual orientations; in short, between the various group classifications to be found in contemporary Western society. Further, they argue that therapy offers false promises since the underlying causes of human misery and unhappiness are fundamentally socio-political, not psychological; as such, all therapy can truly offer is a conformist acceptance of life lived in 'quiet desperation'.

Russell Jacoby (1975), for instance, arguing the case that the humanistic psychology of Carl Rogers provides a subtle means of making the intolerable and unacceptable both tolerable and acceptable, writes:

> Rogers in *Encounter Groups* writes that 'the encounter group movement will be a growing counterforce to the dehumanization of our culture.' Proposed is not the dissolution of dehumanization, but its humanization. The brutal totality is accepted as given . . . The unholy alliance between monopoly capital and the Center for Studies of the Person is no sacrilege. The concern of the former for pacifying its employees, like the concern of the latter, is not malicious but is grounded in the lie of bourgeois society that they both share: the ills are subjective . . .
>
> The endless talk of human relations and responses is utopian; it assumes what is obsolete or yet to be realized: *human* relations. Today these relations are inhuman; they partake more of rats than of humans, more of things than of people. And not because of bad will but because of evil society. To forget this is to indulge in the ideology of sensitivity groups that work to desensitize by cutting off human relations from the social roots that have made them brutal. More sensitivity today means revolution or madness. The rest is chatter (Jacoby, 1975:88–9).

While Jacoby's argument may have become even more relevant to the 1990s given the rise of a substantial number of organizations that employ humanistic and encounter-oriented techniques in order to 'better empower' employees to work harder and feel happier within their company rather than question its principles or hierarchical structures, nevertheless there remains an under-lying logical error in his stance. If therapy increases an indi-vidual's chances of survival in an inhumane society, it does not follow that that individual has now come to believe that society is humane. If anything, the experience of many who have been in therapy is quite the opposite in that they begin to recognize much that they have gone along with or merely tolerated in the past as being no longer acceptable or tolerable. While it is poss-ible for an individual to emerge from therapy in a state that may be categorized as being far more complacent, it is equally possible that another may emerge far more socially responsible and active.

In the same fashion, it remains just as erroneous to assume that all forms of psychic disturbance are *solely* the result of social forces. That individuals from the same social group experience life at varying levels of disturbance or dissociation would suggest that other, psychological, forces are at work. Is it not more likely that *both* elements (and any number of others) play a role in the matter? And, in the same way, it seems sensible to consider that if therapy can at least minimize those elements of disempowerment experienced at the psychic level, then this in itself, however partial and imperfect it may be, is of some worth.

One of my clients, Donna, a woman deeply involved in social causes, experienced through her therapeutic work the realization that an underlying theme to what she sought to accomplish was an increasingly punitive and intolerable psychic command to push herself further and further into 'service for others'. Driven as she was, unable to consider or 'have a say' in her actions, Donna had begun to lose all sense of care and concern for both her work and for those who benefited from it. Although her actions were socially laudable and significant, she felt herself to be lost within them to the extent that she experienced as little choice in the living out of her life as those who see themselves as having no option in resisting the social injustices they perceive as prevalent in the world we inhabit. Through therapy, Donna began to regain a sense of choice in her work; she shifted from a position of 'must do' to that of 'can do' and, in so doing, regained not only a sense of value in her work but also in herself. Before, she had perceived herself as being machine-like, compelled to carry out her actions not because they were socially just but because they were her 'command programme'. Her life had become as full of embitterment and helplessness as that of many an employee working in a capitalist organization. By the end of her therapy, her commitment to her work had, if anything, increased – not dissolved, as Jacoby would suggest – because, as she put it: 'it's no longer something that I *have to* do, it's what I *want to* do.' Just as significantly, Donna had discovered that this shift restored to her a greater sense of responsibility than she had felt for a good many years. As liberating as this responsibility was to her, it also gave her the insight to recognize how much more difficult it was to work from this stance than from her previous one – and, equally, how much more *human* it was.

With regard to such criticisms, it seems to me fair to conclude that therapy clearly emphasizes the significance of 'the inner world' – the realm of meaning, reason and imagination – that each of us brings into our private and public relations with the world. Equally, one must acknowledge therapists' claims that, by means of the examination of such, therapy opens up the possibility for mental and behavioural change that promotes the development of increasing autonomy and self-awareness so that the experience of living is imbued with greater responsibility, tolerance (of self and others) and respect. In this regard, however, given the make-up of contemporary society, the possibility exists that therapy may well have become an essential means to examine and analyse, both within 'its private encounter with the patient and in its public face . . . a part of human experience that, in our society, only *it* takes seriously' (Holmes and Lindley, 1989:14).

I believe that we are in no position to ignore or 'wish away' the social impact and existence of therapy – whatever concerns we might have about it in its current guise and regardless of the questions it raises about itself and the society that has become increasingly dependent on, and defined by, its very presence. Nevertheless, there is an important note of caution to be acknowledged from the various socio-political critiques of therapy.

In their evangelical fervour to promote the cause of therapy, individual therapists have tended to present therapy as the principal – if not sole – means of resolving the problems of human relations and of transforming society. Such extremist viewpoints, while being directly opposite in their stance to that adopted by some socio-political critics, are based on similar errors of logic. To be fair, I have myself written from a standpoint that argued that if socio-political relations between individuals, groups, cultures and societies can possibly be improved or fundamentally changed, then what appears to me to be required is an adoption of a phenomenologically informed perspective on the issues that both unite and divide us (Spinelli, 1989). I still stand by that view, but I also want to stress that it is far from the stance being criticized above. It is one thing to say that a particular theoretically infused viewpoint may provide significant ways and means to approach or clarify issues of human relations; it is quite another to state that that particular perspective is *itself the solution* to the issues under consideration.

In the same way, it is one thing to argue that therapy, in its general sense, may provide us with significant – if not unique – means to understand, address and seek to ameliorate many problems of private and public social relations, but this is not the same as stating that therapy in and of itself can resolve many – if any – such concerns. Therapy can *inform* the task so that more adequate analyses and resolutions may be attempted, but to claim that therapy is itself the means to reducing or removing social problems is both simplistic and potentially dangerous.

I emphasize this point because I believe that it contains within itself a fundamental misunderstanding of therapy which both its critics and many of its advocates continue to promote. Therapy, it seems to me, can at best provide the means to explore, better understand and reassess various issues in one's life so that an individual gains a more adequate means of acting upon, accepting, or changing his or her perspectives and behaviours. It is, broadly speaking, *a means towards the acceptance and clarification of the possibilities for change rather than the instigator or cause of change.*

It is this very distinction which reveals a fundamental flaw in the arguments raised by both the critics of therapy (including the socio-political critics currently under consideration and, as we shall see below, the scientifically oriented critics), as well as those who present themselves as extreme advocates of therapy. All such groups have imposed a *causal* assumption between therapy and some aspect of change (whether change is seen as 'cure' or 'panacea') and in so doing have substantially misunderstood or misrepresented the possibilities that therapy may offer. As I will argue below, the main thrust of the great majority of 'outcome studies' has been based on this false assumption of a causal relationship between therapeutic intervention and (measurable) change, just as most critiques – and defences – of therapy have also based themselves on this same assumption. This is no moot point. In equating therapy with change, therapists themselves have fallen into the trap of emphasizing change for its own sake (presumably in order to give meaning to their enterprise). But this stance, as we shall see, is itself deeply problematic, not merely because of its implicit arrogance (*is* change always for the private and public good?) but because it imposes limits and constraints on the possibilities of relationship between therapist and client – limits that may themselves significantly aggravate the elements of power within the therapeutic process and which may, however inadvertently, promote various forms of both overt and subtle abuse.

C. *The Argument against State-Funded or Assisted Therapy*

Another, related, line of argument argues not so much against therapy itself as the assumption that therapy has become an essential constituent of modern society and that, as such, it should not be solely available to those who can afford it but should be *publicly* funded in a manner similar to the National

Health Service and state education. Like it or not, here in the UK, public opinion appears to be largely in favour of publicly funded therapy. Increasingly, GP surgeries are making such available to their patients and more and more patients are responding to this offer. Such developments have fuelled various movements to lobby both Parliament and medical agencies to make provisions for NHS-funded therapy.

Among critics of this viewpoint, Thomas Szasz, himself a therapist and member of the American Psychiatric Association, is perhaps the most well-known opponent of publicly funded therapy. While much of his critique is aimed specifically at the psychiatric and psycho-analytic professions, it is equally applicable to a state-based therapy. Szasz has argued that once therapy comes under the governance of the state, then, like psychiatry, it can become persecutory and a major mechanism for the imposition of moral standards that are more in the state's interest to promote than to the individual's benefit, in that such institutions then become (or, at the very least, risk becoming) coercive and inegalitarian (Szasz, 1974b). Szasz has presented throughout his writing a great number of historical examples to back up his views that, in the service of the state, psychiatry and psychiatrically related professions such as therapy become the means for the state to define (usually through pseudo-medical language and diagnostic terminology) and persecute 'deviants'. In the past, such 'deviants' included witches and religious heretics. In current times, they include schizophrenics, drug-takers, homosexuals, and single parents (Szasz, 1974b, 1992b).

For Szasz, the involvement of the state places psychiatrists and therapists in an insurmountable dilemma. For, in having become representatives and employees of the state, they must ally themselves either with the state – and thereby persecute the 'deviant' – or, alternatively, must ally themselves with the 'deviants' – and, in so doing, find themselves branded as irresponsible or 'rogue'. It is only by remaining independent of the state, Szasz argues, that both the therapist and the client can remain protected.

Szasz's argument is a serious one. There is abundant evidence to demonstrate that institutionalized psychiatry has oppressed some individuals (Laing, 1967; Masson, 1988; Breggin, 1993). Szasz's own encounters with the American Psychiatric Association provide testimony for this and it is arguable that, in the UK, R. D. Laing's critiques of medically based theories of psychiatry 'branded' him as an irresponsible, dangerous, and even 'mad' practitioner. As such, the question to be asked is not *can* state-funded therapy be persecutory (for surely it can), but rather is state-funded therapy *inevitably* persecutory?

While I have a great deal of sympathy for Szasz's arguments, and certainly share his concerns, and, as well, agree with him that state-funded therapy raises specific issues that require continual monitoring and protective measures to minimize, if not ensure against, persecution of both therapist and client, I am not fully convinced of the inevitability of his scenario for several reasons.

Firstly, it is surely the case that many of those who advocate state-funded therapy – and this includes both therapists and members of the medical profession – do so precisely because they are both aware of and concerned by instances of medically focused theoretical biases that might lead to the mistreatment, abuse or persecution (whether intentional or not) of individuals and who view the establishment of state-funded therapy both as a beneficial complement to medical diagnosis and treatment and as a protection against such biases and their consequences.

Secondly, there is a clear difference between making therapy available to a great many people who could not otherwise afford it and imposing or forcing it on them. I agree with Szasz that such instances can and do occur, but it is possible to set up protective measures to prevent such. In the UK, for instance, the British Medical Association's vociferous stance against forcing certain individuals to take blood tests in order to ascertain whether they are infected by the HIV virus – a stance that remains deeply unpopular with a substantial proportion of the British public and with a good many Members of Parliament – suggests that the institutionalized medical establishment is not *always* at the service of those who would seek to add new categories of 'deviancy'. Considering the argument more broadly, it is important to distinguish between recommendation and imposition and it is clear that such distinctions can be incorporated into those regulations which govern the establishment or extension of state-funded therapy.

Thirdly, Szasz himself reminds us that for psychotherapy to work the patient must actively *want* it rather than just passively accept it, and be prepared to give up something in order to achieve success (Szasz, 1992a). Presumably, that individual bases the decision on the judgement that the choice of being in therapy is potentially more worthwhile than another. But what if I, as an individual, choose to enter therapy but find that I cannot because I do not have the financial means to do so? Szasz's stance seems to suggest that the poor and the uneducated require jobs, money, knowledge and skills rather than therapy* (Szasz, 1974c). But does this statement differ markedly from that of those whom Szasz criticizes? Is not Szasz also imposing a view that restricts freedom of choice on questionable grounds? I agree with him that the poor and the uneducated may want or require all of the above, but are they to be dictated to as to what they require simply because they are poor and uneducated? Can it not be the case that such ethical discussions might also benefit the poor and uneducated not because, as Szasz argues, they might simply reveal previously unforeseen facets of personal freedom (Szasz, 1974c) – though that in itself might be of some value – but because the process may well expose additional factors that aggravate their physical and mental impoverishment? I agree with Szasz that no amount of therapy is going to reduce or remove social oppression or political disenfranchisement, but it may well reveal additional variables that make an individual's life experience even more miserable and debilitating. If therapy can at least offer this much to the poor and uneducated, if some of the poor and uneducated would choose it were it not for its financial cost, and if it seems reasonable to test the hypothesis that state-funded therapy may provide some possibly significant novel and unique personal and social benefits which

---

* Szasz's argument is actually specifically directed at psycho-analysis, but I extended the term to therapy on the assumption (based on a discussion I had with him) that this more general term would not affect his critique.

other services are unable to provide, then is not a just and humane society duty-bound to provide the means at least to explore such possibilities?

Nevertheless, I agree with Szasz that potentials for abuse and coercion exist within such developments and if they were to come into being suitable protective measures must be contemplated and established from the start. These would focus on issues of availability versus imposition as well as on controls designed to protect both practitioners and clients from unnecessary and abusive institutional interference. Szasz's critiques should not be dismissed as extremist or unduly pessimistic. We simply do not have the evidence as yet to conclude whether they are or not. On balance, I believe that the enterprise is worth attempting so long as we remain cognizant of its potential dangers and are entrusted with sufficient means to protect against them.

I also believe that Szasz is correct in his insistence that no one *needs* therapy in the sense that it is both a necessary and singular means to greater self-awareness, empowerment, authenticity, greater autonomy or any other of the jargon words that therapists and clients might employ. That it is certainly a *unique* means to deal with all such is not being disputed, but those who go so far as to stress that therapy is the *sole* means to such goals simply overstate the matter. Even so, the fact that it *is* a means, and is at least potentially a very good means, would suggest that it would be somewhat irresponsible to make it available only to those who can afford its financial costs. In this latter sense, I would disagree with Szasz's argument that public funding for therapy is a dangerous and unnecessary development. Insofar as it might allow the state to honour and advance its commitments to the provision of structured assistance to those experiencing mental disquiet and 'dis-ease', but who cannot afford the cost of private consultations, therapy may well be both a viable and cost-effective option worthy of serious consideration (Holmes and Lindley, 1989).

D. Gender-Based and Multi-Cultural Critiques

In relation to the last point raised above, numerous feminist critics of therapy continue to point out that many of its assumptions and practical applications are still infused with patriarchal and paternalistic tendencies – even when practised by female therapists. Is this another unavoidable or unresolvable dilemma for therapy? I think not. Modern feminism gained much of its impetus and clarification of its critiques of patriarchal society from the 'consciousness-raising' groups developed in the 1970s. Both the rationale and practices of such groups were based on therapeutic models and techniques and provided powerful means for self-challenge, critical awareness and increased autonomy which allowed many women to consider more honestly the roles they had adopted in their personal and public relations, to question and challenge such roles, and to strive to find the means to change them in whole or in part. If, as I believe, therapy is a dynamic process, open to the exposure and re-evaluation of its tenets and assumptions, then the challenges of feminism require critical and non-defensive consideration which might in numerous ways influence the development of both its theories and practices.

The same clearly holds for challenges from other cultures, both within and outside a therapeutically influenced society. The question of whether therapy can adapt to differing socio-cultural conditions or be seen to offer and fulfil its promise as a valid enterprise beyond the Western milieu remains unanswered in significant ways. For, although therapy obviously exists in various forms and emphases in many diverse cultures, it is unclear as to whether it has been adopted because it is a valid and capable response to those cultures' internally perceived concerns and dilemmas, or, alternatively, whether therapy has become an important means to promote and partially fulfil those cultures' tendencies to be seen to be increasingly 'Westernized' through their adoption of Western ideals and aspirations, fashion styles, popular arts such as music, cinema and television, and, as well, those 'Western neuroses' that might best be explored via a Western form of therapy.

As to sub-cultures within a dominant Western culture, as is the case in the UK, one can observe an acceptance of the value of therapy so long as it is in the hands of therapist-representatives from within that same culture. The argument here runs along the lines that only therapists from the same culture as their clients can understand and deal with the particular issues and concerns brought to them. In this way, non-Caucasian groups within the UK have argued the case for 'Black Therapy' or 'Afro-Caribbean Therapy' or 'Asian Therapy', and so forth. In turn, this has led to movements which advocate that therapeutic encounters be segregated on the basis of sexual orientation (e.g. gay and lesbian therapists for gay and lesbian clients), religious affiliation (e.g. Christian therapy), or gender (e.g. female therapists for female clients), or any combination of the above (e.g. Gay Asiatic Christian Therapy). While the stimulus for such movements is partially understandable given the increasing socio-cultural schisms that currently exist in a society such as that of the UK, where change towards a more culturally diversified community has not yet been substantially acknowledged or accepted by its dominant culture, nevertheless the underlying logic of these movements remains open to question. It seems necessary to point out, for instance, that while such stances may remove or restrict possible inter-cultural biases and assumptions that in a microcosmic fashion reflect the aspects of the broader cultural imperialism of the West towards other cultures, nevertheless it remains important to expose and challenge the great variety of possible inter-cultural biases that might enter the therapeutic relationship and thereby inhibit the exploration of individual differences or divergent views. Is there not the possibility that similar tendencies, unhelpful as they are to clients, might not occur in therapeutic encounters that are segregated on the basis of various similarities between therapists and clients? Worse than this, however, as socio-cultural critics themselves point out, therapy can easily become employed as a means of imposing normative standards of thought and behaviour and, just as one group or culture can seek to impose its views and standards on another through therapy, so, too, can it be the case that this act of imposition can be carried out within the same group or culture so that the therapeutic process becomes something more akin to 'thought reform' or the inculcation of various forms of 'correct' thought and practice. This is not to say that the very idea of segregated therapy is fundamentally erroneous, but merely to point out that it is by no means devoid of potential dangers. The problems encountered might be different to those that might be found when individuals from divergent representative groups engage in therapy, but problems are still likely to arise and must be seriously considered – just as the possible advantages of engaging in therapy with individuals from divergent cultures or sub-groups should also be studied.

There remain two major forms of critique against therapy to be considered. The first, most famously argued by Jeffrey Masson (1988), focuses its attention on the *unequal distribution of power in the therapeutic relationship*, which Masson takes as being unresolvable and which, as a consequence, turns therapy into an *unavoidably abusive* enterprise, and will be left to Part 2 of this text in order to provide the fuller discussion that it, and its implications, require. The second area, dealing with the *scientific critiques* of therapy, actually contains not one general issue but several, each of which has been of significant public and specialist interest. For these reasons, I have chosen to address these critiques separately in the following section.

3. SCIENTIFIC CRITIQUES OF THERAPY

With regard to a scientifically based case either for or against therapy, there continue to be two main issues that have interested critics and researchers. The first has focused on the question regarding the scientific status of therapy while the second, more common, concern, concentrating on 'outcome' studies, has studied the effects – positive, negative and negligible – of therapeutic interventions. I will summarize the major findings of each individually.

A. Critiques Questioning the Scientific Basis of Therapy

On considering the scientific basis or status of therapy, initial investigations have exposed several immediate difficulties hindering any simple or straightforward conclusions. Firstly, as ever, the very *variety* of currently existing therapies has confounded discussion. Many critiques of therapy tend to focus exclusively on the scientific status of psycho-analysis (e.g. Farrell, 1981). Yet even here to speak of psycho-analysis as a unified field of enquiry is somewhat misleading since there exist many diverse forms of psycho-analysis (e.g. Freudian, Jungian, Kleinian, American and British object-relations theories, Lacanian, etc.), all of which exemplify significant divergences between one another both at the theoretical and applied levels and many of which also contain within themselves differing emphases that reveal important implications for their development of hypotheses and practice. At the other end of the scale, cognitive-behavioural therapies have tended to attract the least scientific challenge owing to their claims to being direct applied off-shoots of dominant trends in academic, experimentally focused psychology (e.g. Beck, 1976). Between these two extremes lies a broad range of humanistic therapies which, while not immune from critique as to their scientific status, have themselves developed critiques of statistically oriented, quantitatively focused empirical approaches to scientific enquiry and have played a major role in promoting scientific investigation that is, at least initially, qualitatively oriented and focused on the exploration and clarification of subjective experience rather than objective measurement (Shaffer, 1978).

This latter enterprise reveals a subsidiary area of concern – namely, that scientific evaluation can take many forms. Not surprisingly, perhaps, the most vociferous critics of the scientific status of therapy tend to be exponents of a view of science that is grounded in, and dominated by, a stance on experimental findings based exclusively on quantifiable and repeatable controlled studies best exemplified by laboratory-based research that seeks to isolate specific variables and study their influence and effects under strictly manipulated conditions (e.g. Eysenck,

1952, 1983). While the value and advantages of such a stance are obvious, perhaps even desirable, it is quite another matter to suggest that these are the *only* acceptable or proper means of engaging in scientific enquiry. Further, it is debatable that such forms of enquiry can approach an area of such variable complexity as the therapeutic process without imposing serious limitations on both the nature, the quality or the significance of any of the available findings.

For many scientists, the essential criterion as to whether a theory can be said to be scientific is its *falsifiability*. So if, for instance, I were to argue that everything that human beings think and do is caused by invisible, supernatural rays originating from the dark side of the Moon, my theory might be believed to be correct by myself and any number of other individuals, but could not be said to be a scientific theory since it could not, at this point in time at least, be falsified. Any objection that anyone raised against my contention would have little, if any, impact on my stance and, indeed, I might even be able to interpret such an objection as further 'evidence' for the accuracy of my argument. As such, while my theory might seem to explain everything, it actually explains nothing. An apt, if disconcerting, example should clarify the issue. In *The Interpretation of Dreams* (Freud, 1900), Freud recounts that one of his patients refused to accept his contention that all dreams were disguised attempts at wish-fulfilment. She produced a dream for him that seemed to prove her point. On the contrary, Freud asserted, the dream *did* fulfil a wish – the wish to prove Freud wrong! Now perhaps Freud was right and his intervention provided beneficial therapeutic insight for his patient. But this is not the issue: was Freud's theoretical reasoning *scientific*? On the grounds of falsifiability, in this instance, it clearly wasn't.

Psycho-analysis has often been singled out as being an unfalsifiable theory and, therefore, as an unscientific one (Popper, 1960). But this conclusion has been contested not only by defenders of psycho-analysis (Edelson, 1984) but also by theorists who remain deeply critical of psycho-analysis for other reasons (Grünbaum, 1984). Unfortunately, as my earlier example suggests, a great deal of ammunition has been given to their critics by psycho-analysts themselves. For instance, Freud himself argued that many critiques of his theories were not based on logic but on the psychology of the critic (Freud, 1925). This view has persisted in many forms so that genuine criticisms have been dismissed and left unconsidered and, instead, have been 'explained away' as examples of the critic's pathology. Jeffrey Masson's critiques of certain aspects of Freudian psycho-analysis have tended to be dealt with in this way by the psycho-analytic establishment (Masson, 1992). In a similar fashion, when recently, in my capacity as Acting Chair of the Society for Existential Analysis, I invited Masson to speak at its annual conference, I was told by various psycho-analytic colleagues that 'the man was clearly mad and had nothing to say' and that the very act of my inviting him suggested 'disturbing destructive tendencies in my own psyche'! Needless to say, I find such attitudes deeply disturbing and of no benefit to the status of therapy. To dismiss what is being said solely on the basis of who says it, to equate criticism with personality, is nothing less than intellectual fascism of the most insidious kind. It was precisely on such grounds that individuals were arrested, placed into psychiatric clinics or executed in Stalin and Brezhnev's USSR. It may well be the case that Masson's 'pathology' or my own 'destructive tendencies' fuel or direct our interests and criticisms, but such explanations say nothing at all about the possible validity of the criticism in and of itself and only succeed in giving credence to those who would characterize therapy as something more akin to religion than to a philosophically or scientifically infused enterprise.

Is the *whole* of therapy based on unfalsifiable theoretical assumptions? The available evidence is clear that even if it were to be found that *some* approaches to therapy – in whole or in part – were based on unfalsifiable theories, there is no basis to any contention that the theoretical underpinnings of therapy are, *of necessity*, unfalsifiable.

As such, the question of the scientific status of therapy, while by no means satisfactorily answered in the eyes of its most extreme critics, seems to be sufficiently resolved for everyone else – critics and advocates alike. For them, the crucial question is not whether therapy is scientific or not but whether it achieves its claims of reducing or removing a great deal of psychic disturbance, misery and pain.

B. Critiques of the Efficacy of Therapy

How is efficacy to be measured?

Understandably, a substantial amount of literature exists on this topic with most of the research tending to concentrate on *treatment or outcome studies* – that is to say, the evidence for or against any discernible (i.e. 'objective') effects (whether positive or negative) of therapeutic interventions. But here, too, we are immediately faced with serious limitations and challenges to the evidence obtained from such studies. How, for instance, are outcomes to be measured? Is a client's subjective experience of the beneficial effects of therapy in and of itself a suitable 'measurement' of the efficacy of therapy? Or must there be some observable or measurable changes in the client which are open to quantitative analyses? And if no notable behavioural changes following therapy are to be found, does this necessarily imply a failure in the therapeutic process?

To aggravate the situation further, the very aims or goals that therapists may set for therapy might, in themselves, not only vary, but also prove not to be overly amenable to experimental research.

Freud, for instance, saw the possibilities of his technique as allowing individuals to enhance their ability to 'love and work', or, alternatively, 'to transform hysterical misery into common unhappiness' (Freud and Breuer, 1895).

In a similar vein, the psycho-analyst Roy Schafer takes the position that an analysis can be said to be successful when it produces

> a more united, subjective self, one which has more room in it for undisguised pleasure, but also for control, delay, renunciation, remorse, mourning, memories, anticipation,

ideals, moral standards, and more room too for a keen sense of real challenges, dangers and rewards in one's current existence. The childlike regression and nostalgia are reduced in influence (Schafer, 1976:147).

And Owen emphasizes that

> the purpose of meetings is to give clients the space in which to unfold their problems in a professional's presence. Therapists must put aside their cares and needs and be 'introverted', that is, let clients speak and use the time as they wish . . . (Owen, 1993a:15).

I am in broad agreement with all these aims and stances, but it is also clear to me that it would be an extremely difficult task to set about *measuring* any or all of these effects on the behaviour of an individual or, indeed, to demonstrate that they were the direct outcome or result of therapeutic intervention.

As such, the scientific evaluation of the efficacy of therapy is a notoriously difficult enterprise which has, so far at least, provided very few reliable and valid conclusions. Kline (1984), for example, having scrupulously examined the available research evidence concerning the effectiveness of psycho-analytic therapy, concludes that

> it is wrong to say that psychoanalysis is an effective therapy. It is equally wrong to say that it is ineffective. There is no evidence either way . . . The criteria of success of psychoanalytic therapy are difficult to define (Kline, 1984:19).

This assertion is echoed by Anthony Storr (1966):

> [T]he view that psychoanalysis cures anyone of anything is so shaky as to be practically non-existent (Storr, 1966:58).

Evidence for the beneficial and harmful effects of therapy

In general, however, the accumulated evidence of outcome studies at least suggests that therapy tends to be beneficial (Luborsky et al, 1975, 1985; Smith et al, 1980), and that some aspects of therapy seem to be more important than others in bringing about beneficial change.

For instance, the six-year-long, ten-million-dollar study funded by the National Institute of Mental Health concluded that therapy is as effective as drug treatment in alleviating clinical depression. Analysing the results obtained over a sixteen-week test period, it was found that while the drug treatment (employing the anti-depressant drug imipramine) was initially quicker in producing ameliorative results, therapy eventually caught up and was shown to be equally effective in eliminating the most serious symptoms of clinically diagnosed depression in over 50 per cent of the randomly assigned individuals. Similar percentages of success were obtained with individuals assigned to drug treatment. These results contrasted significantly with those obtained from a control group of individuals who had been prescribed placebos and were provided with regular statements of verbal support in that only some 29 per cent of control group individuals no longer displayed serious symptoms (Leo, 1986).

While these findings are clearly of importance in arguing the case for therapy as a suitable, possibly even preferable, alternative to drug treatments, nevertheless when one considers that nearly 50 per cent of the individuals in the two experimental study groups were not helped significantly by either therapeutic intervention or by drug treatment, and, alternatively, that some 29 per cent of the control study group improved somewhat 'spontaneously', the actual effectiveness of therapy is not as great as one might initially be led to believe (Leo, 1986).

If there exists at least some evidence to suggest that therapy can be beneficial, is there any that would suggest that therapy can also be harmful or damaging? McCord (1978) traced 250 treated clients thirty years after termination of treatment and 250 from a matched control group. Although 80 per cent of the treated group thought they had benefited from counselling (which was person-centred supplemented by educational help and training in social skills and lasted five years in most cases), the employment, criminal and health records of both groups showed the treated group to have done less well in all respects than the control group. A number of other studies, as summarized by Mays and Franks (1985), have also pointed out the existence of negative outcomes in therapy.

Research design problems in outcome studies

Overall, then, while a substantial number of studies dealing with the outcomes of therapy exist, their findings, whether positive or negative, have to be treated with considerable caution, owing to various and significant methodological problems and weaknesses in research design which, in some cases, render the studies essentially valueless.

Restricting himself to a review of quantitatively based outcome studies of psychotherapy on the grounds that it is from the evidence obtained from these that claims for the scientific basis of psychotherapy are usually made, Paul Kline points out a number of significant problematic areas present in all of them. These include: issues dealing with the meaning of recovery; problems of client diagnosis; variance among therapists; variance among clients; therapist–client interaction variables; difficulties arising out of the need for control groups; variables dealing with instances and regularity of 'spontaneous remission'; the validity and reliability of the psychological tests; length of follow-up studies; biases in the research design, and so forth (Kline, 1992). Each of these areas raises important difficulties for the researcher. Just to take one of them as an illustrative example, let us consider the issue of recovery. The fundamental problem here is that it is by no means an easy task to define the meaning of recovery. Is recovery to be understood as the remission of symptoms? Or can recovery simply mean that clients feel more able to deal with life, or are just generally more cheerful? Or does recovery entail some dramatic change in their behaviour? (Kline, 1992). These, and a great many more, possibilities can be argued to be examples of recovery. But not all therapists and researchers would agree that any, or even most, of such instances constitute recovery. The question of recovery, as Kline quite rightly points out, conceals a far more formidable conceptual difficulty in the investigation of psychotherapy. What is deemed to constitute recovery must depend upon how psychotherapy is conceived. This varies from the simple (behavioural therapy) to the complex (psychoanalytic therapies) and to its virtual denial ... Clearly what constitutes recovery is no simple matter to decide (Kline, 1992:65).

If such are the difficulties to be encountered with just one variable of a possible research design, then 'it can be seen that the ideal research, with proper sampling and valid measures, constitutes a massive practical problem demanding enormous resources' (Kline, 1992:83). And yet to compromise one's research opens it to the risk of being judged invalid. Perhaps unsurprisingly, given the massive problems involved, Kline concludes that 'the case for the effects of psychotherapy remains to be made. This is not to say that it is ineffectual, simply that it remains unproven, despite the weight of research findings (from experiments which have not overcome these problems) in its favour' (Kline, 1992:83–4). As to the possibility that such problems may be fully overcome at some future point, Kline remains cautious. His task, he tells his readers, was simply to sensitize us to the problems involved. Whether we respond to these optimistically or pessimistically 'is perhaps a matter of personality rather than logic' (Kline, 1992:98).

Other researchers (e.g. Stiles and Shapiro, 1988) have also criticized a number of important assumptions of outcome studies on the grounds that, being a usually lengthy interaction, 'it is by no means a clear and easy task in therapy to separate process from outcome'. Further, they point out that these approaches to the question of therapeutic efficacy tend to take medically focused outcome studies of the effectiveness of a particular drug as their model. But, while such models may be valid when it is possible to isolate and measure the effects of a specific variable (i.e. the drug in question), such that the researcher can obtain a linear dose-response curve which can then be analysed and measured for its effectiveness, in therapy, where no specific variable can be easily isolated, and where it is more likely that the variables are both far more complex, interactive and interdependent, then the accumulated data may be minimally significant, seriously flawed or misleading such that a zero, or even a negative correlation between therapeutic intervention and outcome, may still be masking the effectiveness of the encounter.

Placebo effects

It is precisely because such issues have not been properly addressed, and hence the distinction between specific and non-specific variable effects has not been properly acknowledged, that some critics have suggested that the effectiveness of therapy is best understood in terms of a *placebo effect*.

To consider this argument constructively, it becomes important to clarify firstly a distinction between an *intentional* and an *inadvertent* placebo. An intentional placebo refers to a treatment variable that has been designed to have no effect in itself on a particular disorder. An inadvertent placebo, on the other hand, refers to a treatment variable that is intended to have an effect on a particular disorder by a specified means, but which is subsequently found to produce its effect in some other manner which remains unknown or inexplicable to the investigator. Intentional placebos such as sugar pills are commonly employed in medical tests measuring the effectiveness of a new drug. On the other hand, it now seems likely that most medical and surgical procedures before this century were in fact inadvertent placebos and some of them may have been highly effective. Intriguingly, Frank (1989) has argued that placebos may best be understood as a form of therapy since a placebo is a 'symbolic communication that combats demoralisation by inspiring the patient's hopes for relief ... It is therefore not unsurprising that placebos can provide marked relief in patients who seek psychotherapy' (Frank, 1989:97).

The relationship between theoretical models and therapeutic effectiveness

Nevertheless, it remains a possibility that should not be entirely discounted that *therapy itself may be an inadvertent placebo*. This would suggest that while therapy can be shown to be effective, *the reasons for its effectiveness are not those that we have tended to assume*. Some initial evidence in favour of this view would be obtained if it were to be shown that in spite of the fact that each of the 400-plus approaches to therapy attributes its effectiveness to its specific theory and methodology, in fact no evidence exists which demonstrates that some theoretical approaches to therapy are more effective than others (Kazdin, 1986).

As it happens, there is actually a good deal of evidence in favour of this very contention. Smith and Glass (1977), for instance, having reviewed almost 400 controlled evaluations of counselling and psychotherapy, concluded, in line with other outcome studies, that, on balance, therapy was effective. However, their research went on to argue that there were, at best, only 'negligible differences' between the different schools of treatment. In the same way, Beutler (1979) could not find any evidence to show that any one form of therapeutic treatment was consistently better than any other. Differing theoretical orientations produced no significant differences in outcome.

Similarly, in the National Institute for Mental Health project discussed above, part of the research involved the comparison of the effectiveness of the two forms of brief therapy employed in the study (these were cognitive-behavioural therapy and inter-personal therapy). The researchers were unable to find any significant evidence for the greater effectiveness of one over the other (Leo, 1986).

In line with these conclusions, the following statement by Ian Howarth, a vociferous critic of therapy, deserves serious consideration:

It is now clear from meta-analyses of almost 500 evaluative studies (e.g. Smith, Glass and Miller, 1980) that most forms of psychotherapy and counselling are approximately 50 per cent more likely to produce an improvement than would occur without treatment, provided the outcome is assessed from the client's subjective reports. These same meta-analyses mostly fail to show any difference between different forms of treatment, no matter how different in philosophy . . . or how different the procedures . . . and no matter what the disorder being treated . . . The non-specificity of treatment is confirmed by the failure to demonstrate any effect of training on the effectiveness of therapy (e.g. the meta-analysis of Berman and Norton, 1985). One is driven to the simple conclusion that psychotherapists do not know what they are doing and cannot train others to do it, whatever it is (Howarth, 1989:150).

Clients' views on the effectiveness of therapy

There is the strong possibility, then, that therapeutic efficacy may have little to do with a particular theory being espoused and that therapists have emphasized the wrong reasons for the effectiveness of therapy. Perhaps it would be wise to turn to the *statements and views of clients* in order to consider their stance on the matter. Somewhat amazingly, given the large amount of studies dealing with therapy and therapists, there exist very few extensive studies that focus exclusively on the client's experience of therapy. Recently, a text entitled *On Being a Client* by David Howe (1993) has provided an important analysis of this subject area.

Howe argues that, from their perspectives, clients tend to see the therapeutic process as one composed of three 'movements' or sequences:

1. Accept me.
2. Understand me.
3. Talk with me.

With regard to the last point, Feifel and Eells (1963) studied sixty-three clients of psychotherapy and found that simply *the opportunity to talk* topped the list of what clients found to be most helpful from the therapeutic process.

A major factor which clients return to again and again in their assessment of therapeutic effectiveness, and which seems to be a fundamental underlying factor in all assessment ratings, is 'the warmth and friendliness' of the therapist (Strupp et al, 1969). Similarly, one study showed that clients tended to feel that therapists should be interested in them as people, not as potential or actual cases (Sainsbury et al, 1982).

Summarizing many of these findings, Howe points out that, generally, clients tend to prefer therapists who seem to them to have their own personality, sense of humour and particular characteristic 'quirks'. Clients also typically tend to prefer engagement and dialogue with the therapists and tend to experience the therapist's unwillingness to engage verbally with them, or to remain silent, as being artificial, threatening, or rejecting. Anne France (1988), taking up this issue from the client's standpoint, argues that while she doesn't want the therapist's views to swamp and overwhelm her own, nevertheless she does want to know them.

Similarly, clients tend to define the good therapist as one who attempts to enter their world-view empathically and non-judgmentally. This belief that another is able at least to partially understand them and have some sense of their suffering, confusion or distress is, in itself, perceived as being deeply therapeutic.

Clients also want their therapists to be interested in them. Kline et al (1974) found that accurate insight and the perceived interest shown in them by the therapist were variables defined as being of major importance by the client group that had been interviewed.

As to the therapeutic process itself, clients identify the *quality* of the relationship as being of central defining importance in that it fosters both acceptance and understanding which will enable the necessary sense of trust and security required for honest exploration, but which also seeks to avoid rejection, criticism, ridicule, inconsistency and judgement. This view is backed by Lomas (1981), Oldfield (1983) and France (1988) among others. Strupp and his associates aptly sum up these issues when they conclude:

It seems that the amount of improvement noted by a patient in psychotherapy is highly correlated with his attitudes to the therapist ... More important, the therapist's warmth, his respect and interest ... emerged as important ingredients in the amount of change reported ... the more uncertain the patient felt about the therapist's attitude toward him, the less change he tended to experience (Strupp et al, 1969:77).

As to clients' views on factors that may impede the therapeutic process, McLeod's (1990) review of clients' conclusions noted that:

First, clients felt that things went badly when they did not co-operate with the therapist by being silent, by talking super-ficially or by not daring to talk about some things. Secondly, problems in the relationship between therapist and client were seen as a hindrance (for example, the therapist not being warm enough, confronting too much or too little, not valuing or accepting the client enough). Thirdly, clients found it unhelpful when their therapists made interventions which took them off their own 'track', when the therapist said things that 'did not feel right' (McLeod, 1990:15).

Howe amplifies these findings by arguing that the therapeutic process itself is impaired when therapists fail to understand, or even attempt to understand, their clients. Worse, under such circumstances, clients' sense of isolation is likely to increase when therapists seek to impose their own explanations on the client's experience (Howe, 1993).

Noting important perceptual differences in the therapeutic process between therapists and clients, Maluccio (1979) has shown that when counsellors are asked to recall the first session, they typically focus on the problems and issues presented. Clients, on the other hand, tend to remember the feelings they had and their reactions to the therapist. In a similar fashion, Feifel and Eells (1963) found that whereas therapists emphasize changes in behaviour and relief of symptoms as the main indi-cators of success, clients placed the accent on insight and understanding as the most appropriate measures of satisfaction.

Oldfield (1983) presented four main aims that clients tend to want to achieve through their therapy:

1. To change their feelings, gain relief from distressing emotional states and increase their self-esteem and confidence.
2. To gain greater understanding, both of self and of problems to be dealt with.
3. To regain their ability to cope with life, and be able to work effectively again.
4. To improve their relationships with others.

Clients' perspectives on the therapeutic process are valuable not only for what they state but also for what is not said. Like the research findings discussed earlier, client views do not seem to hold the therapist's allegiance to any particular theory as being of great significance – indeed, this issue is rarely, if ever, mentioned by them! Once again, then, we are faced with the possibility that the effectiveness of therapy is based on previously unforeseen factors. But if this is so, then what other factors may be worth considering?

Personality factors and therapeutic effects

Some researchers have suggested that variances in therapeutic efficacy may be due to the *personality factors* associated with the therapist. McConnaughy, for instance, found that a significant positive correlation existed between the most consistent beneficial therapeutic results and minimal emotional disturbance in the therapist (McConnaughy, 1987).

In the *OPUS Report* which was drawn out of a series of discussions with forty-three therapists representing sixteen therapeutic 'schools' or approaches, it was argued that there exists the distinct possibility that the best therapists are 'born' rather than 'made' in that their ability to deal effectively with others is ultimately more a reflection of the therapists' personality and life experiences than of any specifically taught techniques. Further, it was suggested that most, if not all, therapists are drawn to the profession as much out of a personal curiosity and desire to understand and deal with aspects of their own lives which remain unresolved or problematic as they are by the desire to help others (Broadbent et al, 1983). More problematically, this same report also addressed the possibility that some may have been drawn to the profession at least partially by their wish for power (Broadbent et al, 1983).

Training and therapeutic efficacy

These viewpoints raise significant questions concerning the value and effectiveness of *training* individuals to become therapists. In recent years, partly owing to the desire to promote the professional status of therapy, and to enhance client protection against various forms of abuse perpetrated by 'rogue' therapists and to provide some suitable means of securing clients' ability to address their complaints to the proper authoritative bodies, therapeutic institutes and 'host' bodies such as the UKCP and BAC have increasingly emphasized the necessity of suitable training for therapists.

Now while it would seem to me that, for all the reasons given above, training is an important, not to say essential, safeguard for both therapists and clients the value of which should in no way be minimized, the assumption that training itself is directly related to effective therapy remains an open question.

In addressing this point, perhaps somewhat facetiously, Mair concludes that therapists 'do seem to be able to help people; perhaps because they often manage to outgrow the handicaps imposed by their training' (Mair, 1992:152). As a back-up to this somewhat disturbing statement, she reminds her readers of some intriguing research (Hattie et al, 1984) that reviewed forty-three studies in which the effectiveness of the interventions of 'professionals' (defined as those who had undergone formal clinical training in psychology, psychiatry, social work or nursing) were compared with those of 'para-professionals' (educated people with no clinical training). The findings obtained from this study concluded that, on average, the para-professionals' interventions were significantly *more* effective than those of the professionals. Not surprisingly, criticism of these findings was sought and, to be fair, was found in that there was sufficient evidence of an arbitrariness in designating the two groups such that, for instance, some of those labelled as professionals had had no training in psychology and some of the para-professionals had had academic training that was of at least tangential relevance to therapy. Nevertheless, when Berman and Norton (1985) eliminated eleven of the forty-three studies on such grounds, they found that although the analysis of the remaining thirty-two studies eliminated the statistically significant advantage of the para-professionals, even so, the accumulated data now showed that both groups were *equally* effective both at the end of treatment and in follow-up studies. When further differential treatment effects were considered separately, the only variables that distinguished the two groups were that the professionals' interventions were more effective with older clients while the para-professionals' interventions had a greater beneficial impact with younger clients, and that professionals' interventions proved to be better in longer treatments (Berman and Norton, 1985).

Such findings raise potentially significant, if embarrassing, questions about the nature of therapist expertise and the inherent value of training. In entering a training process which is likely to last a minimum of four years (often many more) and which requires a good deal of financial and emotional investment, the successful graduate will, in the end, gain sound knowledge of one or more relevant theories, the ability to employ various skills and techniques, and the status of recognition as a 'professional'. All these may well be of importance and value for a variety of reasons, including those pertaining to the provisions of 'safety mechanisms' and controls designed to protect both therapists and clients from various forms of abuse and to provide the means to ensure that suitable avenues of complaint procedures and allegiance to standards of ethical practice are both implemented and practised. But in terms of either gauging or ensuring the most effective therapeutic interventions, therapeutic training can make no indisputable claims as to its merits or even its necessity.

Some preliminary conclusions

It would seem that all the points discussed with regard to the evidence for the efficacy of therapy do not tell us very much that is either conclusive or overly explanatory as to either the efficacy of therapy or the reasons as to why it should be efficacious. On the basis of these studies, it would seem fair to conclude that therapy is *usually* beneficial to people, at least in so far as clients judge it to be so and as far as a term as vague as 'beneficial' can be measured by means of quantitative outcome studies. Nevertheless, when researchers have tried to identify those variables that can be identified with, or related to, therapeutic effectiveness, none of the obvious ones – such as theory or training – have been found to be of significance.

In the light of such failures, various sceptics such as Mair (1992) have suggested that therapy gains its authority simply because it reflects the attitudes of society in the guise of scientific 'truths'. In a similar fashion, Frank (1973) has written that differing therapies with similar levels of effectiveness share, in common with all healing arts (both scientific and magical), rationales or 'mythologies' that contain within them explanations of illness, deviancy and normality. For Frank, therapies rely on persuasion designed to allow or convince the client to accept and enter into the mythological system. The relative effectiveness of therapy, then, rests not on its scientific veracity but, rather, in its compatibility with 'the cultural world view shared by the patient and the therapist' (Frank, 1973:327), and in its ability to protect therapists' authority and hence maintain clients' confidence in their therapists' ability to 'heal' them.

An example provided by Mair should clarify this line of argument. About one hundred years ago, many psychiatrists claimed, on scientific grounds, that masturbation was a major cause of insanity. These claims were not challenged, nor, indeed, were they even properly tested. Nevertheless, they were accepted as scientifically sound because they 'made sense' to them and to their society in that they accurately reflected the attitudes, biases and fears of that society. It was only when society itself began to reconsider its attitudes and values that such claims became open to doubt and criticism and were subsequently rejected as false (Mair, 1992).

These views can be seen to underline the fact that all knowledge, even 'scientific' knowledge, cannot be isolated from its psycho-social context. Truth is neither pure nor permanent but a more or less adequate construct which is at the very least influenced by all manner of socially based variables. Several writers who have focused on the history and development of science and medicine (e.g. Koestler, 1959; Foucault, 1961; Boorstin, 1985) have arrived at similar conclusions. Nevertheless, there remains a deep resistance to such views, not only by those whose power and authority rest on the 'truth' of science, but also by those who bestow such authority upon them. Uncertainty does not appear to be highly valued in our society. Once again, Mair provides a further example which makes this point somewhat obvious.

Deciding to test 'whether an honest admission of uncertainty would have any effect on the progress of his patients' (Mair, 1992:137), a general practitioner truthfully told half his experimental sample of patients that he was uncertain as to what it was that was wrong with them; to the remaining half he provided an authoritative, but fraudulent, hypothesis and told them that they would be better in a few days. Two significant findings emerged. Firstly, as an immediate response to the GP's statement, the latter group of patients tended to express greater satisfaction with the consultation, felt that their doctor had understood them and voiced their sense of having been helped. Two weeks later, 64 per cent of the second group stated that they were now cured or at least felt better. On the other hand, only 39 per cent of the first group claimed to be over their illness or felt better. The GP's conclusion was 'that honest doubt had actually prolonged some of his patients' symptoms since they would normally be expected to clear up within the two weeks' (Mair, 1992:137).

What might this tell us about therapy? Therapists tend to both believe in and present themselves as 'learned experts' whose methods depend on an established theory (the basis of which is usually claimed to be 'scientifically sound') and on the training they have received. But, as we have seen, conclusive evidence for such views has hardly been forthcoming. Yet therapists' insistent beliefs in such is understandable. At a time when dubious 'new age psychobabble' is capitalizing on the demand for guidance and enlightenment, most professionally trained therapists vehemently distance themselves from anything that smacks of charlatanism and (I believe quite correctly) express heartfelt horror at having therapy equated with such on the basis that it is 'just another placebo' – however well it works. But, equally, therapists remain on dangerous ground if their insistence is based on assumptions and arguments, such as those discussed, the validity of which may be minimal or even non-existent.

Alternative possibilities and the 'Dumbo Effect'

Those of us who are prepared to accept inconclusive research findings but do not remain entirely convinced by the alternative explanations proposed by Mair and Frank may have yet another option to consider. It is possible that much of the problem lies principally with the research methods that researchers have tended to employ and their underlying assumptions.

> After decades of research the amount of well-established knowledge about what affects therapeutic outcomes is disappointingly meagre. Research of the sort done in the last decade, although approaching clinical relevance, still has not offered much to practising clinicians (Greenberg, 1981:34).

Echoing this view, John Rowan has criticized the conclusion that therapists of all persuasions, trained or untrained, obtain much the same results. He argues that the point is dubious because, once again, it relies on outcome research which is perhaps the weakest area in the whole field of psychological research. Considering the findings of Garfield and Bergin (1986) (which are generally viewed as the standard critical review of outcome research), he notes that:

> every single piece of research turns out to be minimally revealing. In each case, whatever variable one looks at, the

answer seems to be the same – either there is no effect, or the effect is very small, or the answers are confused in some way. No clear results emerge at all (Rowan, 1992:162).

Considering what might be done about this state of affairs, Rowan has emphasized the distinction between outcome research and *process research* (i.e. research that focuses on what takes place in therapy as it is in the process of occurring) and advocates that more of the latter seems required. Further, he has argued that both forms of research are mutually necessary in that each offers different, if equally significant, emphases which *only when taken together* may provide researchers with a more realistic basis for their conclusions (Rowan, 1992). The current tendency in therapeutic research, however, is to focus on one or the other (and usually just on outcome studies), but rarely, if ever, on both together, and thus the derived results are, at best, limited and more often inadequate and one-sided. The relationship of variables in therapist intervention is both difficult and complex. In the words of Greenberg and Pinsof, it 'appears to be beyond the capabilities of current research procedures' (Greenberg and Pinsof, 1986:726). Perhaps, as Rowan suggests, there exists the 'need for new paradigm research that does not even attempt to talk about variables, but which talks instead about people, and to people, and with people' (Rowan, 1992:163).

Like Rowan, it seems to me that in the current state of affairs, while it might be rash to claim, on the basis of currently existing, if still inadequate, evidence, that all therapists and therapeutic processes are equal, nevertheless the fairest conclusion we can arrive at is that 'we simply do not have the evidence to conclude whether they are or not' (Rowan, 1992:163).

In the light of this, a recent, highly interesting study by Aebi (1993) considered the question of how therapeutic change is achieved. Aebi noted that one way of approaching this question would be initially to differentiate between *specific* and *nonspecific* factors that might influence therapeutic outcomes. Specific factors are those that are claimed to be essential ingredients and characteristics of a particular therapeutic approach. These are perceived to be active agents of change and are centrally related to that therapy's theoretical underpinnings. Examples of specific factors include 'transference', 'systematic desensitization' and so forth. Non-specific factors, on the other hand, refers to those factors that seem common to different approaches, or which have not been specified as active ingredients, or which are not considered to be sufficient, or even necessary, in bringing about change, or which are employed incidentally rather than deliberately to achieve or promote change. In some instances, non-specific factors may even be likened to inadvertent placebos.

Now while it is obvious that all therapeutic approaches agree that clients are capable of beneficial change, there exists little, if any, agreement as to how this change can best be brought about. Clients are, in most instances, motivated to change and, arguably, prime themselves for such simply by beginning therapy (Garfield, 1989). In a similar fashion, therapists in general tend to expect clients to change in therapy not only because they might be caring individuals who want the best for their clients, but also because therapeutic change is one means of confirming that one is a good therapist and, as well, justifies one's advocacy of a particular theoretical approach and its specific applications. I feel certain that all therapists more or less adopt this stance and, in most instances, it seems a perfectly reasonable thing to do. It only begins to become questionable when therapists find themselves (as, I confess, I have at times found myself) reacting angrily to their clients' announcements of major insights or breakthroughs brought about by dialogues or events occurring *outside* of the therapeutic sessions. Having found, through discussions with my students and colleagues, that this is not an uncommon event, it seems well worth asking why we should react in this way. Aebi's study points to obvious, if unpalatable, possibilities: if clients are able to achieve such significant therapeutic changes with others who are neither trained therapists nor possess the deep theoretical understanding (or, indeed, *any* relevant theoretical understanding) that therapists do, then both the 'specialness' of therapists and the 'specialness' of the theory they subscribe to and believe in are called into question.

If, rather than dismiss this anxiety-provoking challenge, therapists were seriously to examine their assumptions, then one possibility that emerges, as Aebi suggests, is that perhaps their emphasis on and belief in the specific factors in therapeutic models are somewhat misguided and bereft of significant evidence since, as we have seen, although the research evidence for outcome studies is at best partial and certainly imperfect in its experimental procedure, nevertheless its conclusions remain consistent: there exists no evidence to show that any one approach is any more effective than any other. Added to that, research on named specific factors such as systematic desensitization (a technique employed by some cognitive-behavioural approaches which pairs anxiety-provoking stimuli with relaxation training until the anxiety response is eliminated), while generally agreeing that it is an effective form of treatment, also concludes that there is currently little understanding as to how or why this procedure should work (Aebi, 1993). Indeed, there is a singular failure of evidence correlating specific therapeutic impact with specific factors (Aebi, 1993). Could it be the case that *non-specific factors may play a more important, if not central, role in the therapeutic process* while those factors that have been labelled (and valued) as being specific are not, in themselves, significant but rather, as Aebi suggests, are specified as important only because they provide therapists with a *rationale* for their interventions?

In working with students, I have referred to what I have facetiously named the *Dumbo Effect*. In the Disney cartoon, Dumbo the elephant is able to fly because he has convinced himself that he possesses a magic feather that grants him this ability. So long as Dumbo continues to believe this, the feather takes on fundamental significance and is seen as essential to both Dumbo's powers and self-esteem. It is only when the feather is lost and Dumbo discovers, much to his initial astonishment, that he can still fly without it, that the feather is seen as an initially necessary 'trick' or focal point which is, in and of itself, possessed of nothing special or magical. This simple little allegory seems to me to encapsulate the issue under discussion.

Consider, for example, the power of the therapeutic 'frame'

or structure. For example, therapists tend to believe that the physical environment in which therapy is conducted plays a significant role in the relationship that is generated. As such, they go about fashioning an environment that is in keeping with the theoretical views they hold concerning a proper frame. Is the room to be 'neutral' or filled with objects that belong, or have some personal meaning, to the therapist? How should the furniture be arranged? Indeed, *what* furniture should there be in the room? What clothes should be worn by the therapist during therapeutic sessions? Should paper tissues be provided for clients or would their availability relay the implicit message that the client is expected to cry? (Some readers may find this difficult to believe but this last point has generated a good deal of debate within and between certain models of therapy!) If asked why they are concerned with such questions, therapists are likely to respond that these (and many other) frame issues have been shown to be of major significance to the success, or possibility of success, of therapy. But this assertion is highly debatable as there exists no substantive evidence which demonstrates a correspondence between any of these frame issues and successful outcome. But to suggest that therefore all frame-related concerns should be dismissed would be missing a significant point. The frame issues may not be important in themselves, but may rather have the same effect as Dumbo's magic feather. In other words, their importance lies in the fact that *the therapist believes them to be necessary in order for the 'magic' of therapy to work.* Behaviourist psychologists refer to such beliefs as 'superstitious learning' in that it points to unnecessary behaviour that has been incorrectly associated with necessary behaviour leading to a desired goal. In simple language, what is being referred to are those 'superstitious' beliefs which all of us hold to some extent that allow us to 'explain' various successes or failures in our lives. Where behaviourists go wrong, I believe, is when they denigrate such beliefs and seek to find ways of expunging them from our 'repertoire of responses'. What they forget is that one person's superstitious belief may well be another's reason for living. Worse, they fail to consider how much of what they, or anyone else, might take as being 'non-superstitious' might well be so. The history of science and medicine provides numerous examples of this very phenomenon.

In any case, the point being made here is that it is far more likely (though far less palatable to therapists) that their concerns and beliefs with regard to various frame-related issues reveal their dependence on the Dumbo Effect.

But this effect extends to clients as well in that they, too, might believe that the presence or lack of a couch, therapists' personal objects, boxes of tissues or whatever are necessary for the 'magic' of therapy to be effective on them. For instance, some prospective clients have told me on their first meeting that they could not consider me as their therapist because my clothes were too casual. Alternatively, others decide to work with me precisely because the clothes I wear reveal (to them) that I am an easy-going and caring person who will be more interested in them than in himself.

The problem is that, as much of the discussion has shown, there seems to be very little in therapy that is not *a Dumbo Effect.*

Just like Dumbo, therapists may have found their 'magic feather' through their theories and, as well, have rationalized that the 'magic' they are able to achieve comes from their theories and their applications. Perhaps, as is being suggested, their powers are not derived from the 'truths' they hold, but from therapists' beliefs in them, and, through them, in themselves. If so, an examination of those non-specific factors that have been thus far identified might initiate the process whereby therapists, like Dumbo, might discover what is still possible without the feather.

The main non-specific factors that have been identified by Aebi include:

1. The therapeutic relationship itself.
2. The therapeutic frame (which is the term initially coined in 1952 by the psycho-analyst Marion Milner, who took the metaphor from painting; it refers to the 'ground rules', or structure, of therapy, including practical issues such as procedure, logistics, time and duration factors, etc.); therapist/

client protection issues such as confidentiality, taping of sessions, etc; and process issues such as the clarification and agreement between therapist and client as to the possibilities and purpose of their therapeutic sessions and what is expected of each of them.

3. Therapist reinforcement (which refers to therapists' encouragements to their client that they are willing to listen and to attend to them (e.g. head-nodding, summarizing, etc.))

4. Arousal (that is the expression of emotions through which there emerges the increased likelihood of client receptivity to change).

5. Interpretation (which refers to the inclination on the part of all therapists to present their clients with theoretically derived interpretative hypotheses focusing on the clients' meaning-world, self–other relations, behaviours, and so forth).

In a similar fashion, Orlinsky and Howard (1986) reviewed 1,100 outcome studies, spanning thirty-five years, and were able to single out what they considered to be *the crucial factor* in all cases of effective therapy. As might be expected, it was *not* the theory behind the therapy or on which its practices and interventions were based, nor was it any explicit factor related to training, nor was it the nature or quality of the therapists' interpretations and interventions. Rather, it was the *bond that therapists form with their clients*.

For many reasons, this conclusion should not come as any major surprise. It will be recalled that the *BAC Report on Differentiation* discussed earlier emphasized *the relationship* itself as a central defining characteristic of therapy, just as Aebi's findings summarized above placed the therapeutic relationship as a focus point of virtually unanimous agreement among therapeutic approaches.

Nevertheless, beyond acknowledgement of its being of major significance to the therapeutic enterprise, both the structure and meaning of this relationship is by no means agreed on by therapists. While some approaches (such as the cognitive-behavioural approach) emphasize the importance of the development of a therapeutic relationship largely as a means to a specified, goal-directed end, other approaches (such as the person-centred approach or psycho-analytic models) view the properties or the possibilities of this relationship as themselves being the 'essence' or catalyst to beneficial change, conflict resolution, growth, 'making the unconscious conscious', and so forth. But, even in this latter grouping, the meaning, function, essential defining characteristics, and the therapist's role or task within the relationship differ widely. So, for instance, while the person-centred therapist emphasizes such features as the therapist's aim of providing or expressing congruence, empathy and unconditional positive regard within the relationship, psycho-analytic therapists emphasize the transferential possibilities contained within the therapeutic alliance.

It would seem essential, then, to examine the therapeutic relationship in order to expose its possibilities and limitations and to discover what there may be about it which allows or encourages the beneficial processes and outcomes of therapy. For instance, it would seem to be the case that, in its widest or most accepted sense, the bond or relationship between therapist and client focuses on the cognitive, affective and behavioural elements in the client's experience and that its primary function would be the investigation of some or all of these elements (depending, at least partly, on the therapist's theoretical allegiance) in order to facilitate the possibility of ameliorative change.

What might there be in, or about, this bond that is so significant? Some clues from the research discussed so far – clues concerning therapists' ability and willingness to listen to and be with and for their clients – have emerged. Similarly, such investigations also point out two distinct emphases within therapists' understanding of the relationship – that is therapists' tendencies to stress either the 'doing' or the 'being' elements or qualities that they bring to the relationship and how the emphasis on one or the other has a major impact on the therapeutic relationship and, indeed, significantly alters not only its structure but also its direction and possibilities. However, the reader's patience is required. These issues will form the basis of discussion in Part 5 of this text. Before we can begin to consider them with some degree of adequacy, a number of related and relevant concerns must first be addressed.

In my analysis of various critiques of therapy, I set aside the currently dominant issue of the *distribution of power* within the therapeutic relationship. This issue, perhaps above all others, demands our initial attention since, as I will seek to demonstrate in Part 2, it is only by means of its clarification, and the subsidiary examination of the various potentialities of the therapist's *misuse and abuse of power in the therapeutic relationship*, that the beneficial possibilities of therapeutic encounters can begin to be suitably analysed and assessed.

PART TWO

DEMYSTIFYING THE ISSUE
OF POWER IN THE
THERAPEUTIC RELATIONSHIP

Mystery evokes the illusion of power;
transparency dissolves it.

– David Mearns and Brian Thorne

The great majority of therapeutic institutions see their principal *raison d'être* as that of training suitable candidates to become therapists rather than as being centres for intellectual discourse focused on the critical analysis and development of a particular theoretical approach or of therapy in general. Indeed, my own experience, and that of many colleagues and students with whom I have discussed such issues, would suggest that in a number of established institutes critically focused discussion of theoretical assumptions and their practical applications is not only *not* viewed with favour but, rather, is either 'nipped in the bud', or may be employed as evidence for the unsuitability of the critical trainee. In its most pernicious form, this 'protection of the faith' may extend to such lengths that criticisms will be 'explained' or 'interpreted' by the institute as unconscious expressions of the critic's 'unresolved psychic conflicts'. As an example of this, the following encounter, which I had some years ago as a trainee in one such institute, should substantiate my contention.

As part of the foundational year of training at this institute, I was a participant in weekly two-hour group therapy led by two trainers – one male, one female. About four weeks into the group process, the male trainer strongly urged the group to begin to address him and his colleague as 'Daddy' or 'Mum' in order to expose long-term conflicts which, he declared, each of us held in our unconscious. This request struck me, as well as several other trainees, as being somewhat ludicrous and I voiced my

97

disdain of what I saw as the heavy-handed attempt to impose a 'transferential relationship' on us and questioned its basis. Cutting my argument short, the male trainer intoned: 'Mr Spinelli, it is understandable that you have such a reaction to my suggestion since you are, of course, an orphan.'

When I responded to this by reminding the trainer that both my parents happened to be alive and in good health, his reply to me was: 'This is beside the point! It doesn't matter whether your parents are actually alive or not, the issue is that you are a *psychic* orphan!'

I remained with that training institute until the completion of the year, but I chose not to continue this training any further. In any case, I suspect that I would not have been invited to continue – unless I resolved my conflicts concerning my 'psychic orphanhood' (among others, I suppose) with the help of a suitable therapist.

My point here is not to deny *any* validity in the trainer's comment. There may well have been some element of truth in his interpretation which would have clarified some possible issues concerning my then current relations with my parents. I don't know. Whatever the case, the issue here seems to me to be one of *how* the interpretation was presented to me. The trainer quite obviously and honestly was convinced of the truth of his statement and wished me to confirm it. That I rejected it was to him by no means any indication that he may have been in error. Rather, my 'resistance' convinced him all the more of the accuracy of his conclusion since he returned to it several times subsequently and, although on each occasion I continued to 'deny' him, he appeared to remain confident that he had hit upon an important element in a chain of defences that expressed both my conflict and the stance I had adopted with regard to authority figures such as himself. Even the fact that I made it clear to him that what authority he believed me to have invested him with was minimal, if not non-existent, did not shake him from his stance. He was my 'father substitute' and that was that.

Now, again, as much as I am willing to concede a potential value in his point, the arrogance with which it was presented to me clearly added further conscious resistances to any unconscious ones that may have been there. These conscious resistances had less to do for me with the wide issue of 'authority figures' than they had with the specific issue of what I considered then, and still consider now, to be a flagrant and specific misuse of authority. More to the point, I felt *unheard* and, what is more, concluded, rightly or wrongly, that this person would never really hear me as long as he remained stuck in his interpretation.

Today, thinking back to that incident, recognizing the hurt and confusion it left me with – no less because, up until that point, I had been committed to the pursuit of therapeutic training specializing in the particular theoretical model offered at that institute – I am grateful for that interaction since it clearly – perhaps too clearly – pointed out to me both the danger and abusive possibilities inherent in *therapeutic dialogue.*

For it seems to me that this example points to a number of important issues that therapy must address if it is ever to hope to begin sufficiently to defend itself from the attacks of its critics and detractors. The concerns presented seem to me to be so fundamental that I will spend the entirety of this part of the text considering the effects of this stance and how, to me at least, it addresses forms of abuse, both subtle and flagrant, which, however inadvertently, may be carried out on clients in the name of successful therapy.

1. PHYSICAL AND SEXUAL ABUSE IN THE THERAPEUTIC RELATIONSHIP

I believe that it would be accurate to state that *all* therapeutic models contain within them the possibility of therapeutic interventions being experienced as abusive by clients. Equally, I believe that there is a case to be made for the argument that all models of therapy contain the means both to recognize and, equally importantly, minimize such instances for the sake of both the client and the therapist. Broadly speaking, all forms of abuse within therapy – as practised or experienced – originate from the related issue of *power in the therapeutic relationship*, particularly when the relationship is structured in such a way as to imbalance the experience of power so that it is heavily weighted in favour of the therapist. Instances of physical and sexual abuse of clients by their therapists provide the most obvious examples of this power imbalance, but, perhaps far more significantly, there also exist far more subtle expressions of this imbalance. Needless to say, each form has its consequences – for both clients and therapists – as the following discussion will, hopefully, make clear.

A. Abuse versus Misuse: a suggested distinction

I must first inject a cautionary note. In recent years, concern about abuse in various settings and relationships appears to have gained a great degree of attention. It has become an almost everyday phenomenon to hear or read of instances of abuse in the family, the workplace, social relations, and so forth. While I do not wish to deny either the value or significance of questioning and analysing what abusive elements may exist in our various encounters with others, and how they may be expressed, the widespread and indiscriminatory employment of the term has tended to promote various stances of 'correctness' in thought and behaviour which have fostered increasing degrees of fear and isolation in many peoples' relations with one another.

Equally, if paradoxically, these concerns may have not only added to (rather than diminished) the already large number of 'neuroses' individuals may feel they have or express in their relations with both themselves and with others, but also, more pertinently, may have increased, rather than reduced, the incidence of aggressive thoughts and behaviours directed towards oneself or others. In addition, in focusing on the potentially abusive elements contained in any relation, the very term 'abuse' has become so distilled and weakened in its impact and meaning that its current indiscriminatory usage may, however inadvertently, be adding further injury to those who have suffered the consequences of serious, even life-threatening, physical and sexual violence.

While I am ready and willing to admit that an act such as unilaterally opting to invade the personal space of another either physically or verbally may be experienced as improper, uncalled-for, embarrassing, problematic or even abusive by the 'invaded' person, nevertheless it does seem to me to be important to distinguish this in some way from instances of physical violence and rape. I am well aware that this is no simple issue to resolve since we are dealing with questions of *lived reality* such that, for instance, having a part of one's body touched unwillingly or prior to some signal of permission may be experienced as powerfully *as if* one had been raped (in the socio-legal sense of the term).

Nevertheless, it seems sensible to uphold some kind of distinction between the acts. I have never myself (thankfully!) been raped, but I have, for example, suffered the pain, anger, guilt and shame of having been unwillingly 'touched up' by a stranger sitting next to me in a cinema. I can recall the overwhelming sense of personal psychic powerlessness, the inability to carry out any form of defensive or retaliatory action, and the deep contempt for both the stranger and myself which I felt then. And while I may have been able to make use of this experience, among others, in seeking to imagine and enter into various clients' accounts of their experience of having been raped or physically abused, it seems wrong (and somehow degrading of my clients' experiences) for me to assert that I, too, like them, have been raped.

Again, the issue is far too complex and problematic to be pursued any further in this text. But I raise it here because of its relevance to the concerns being addressed since I too, like those I am to some degree criticizing in introducing this topic, have employed the term 'abuse' (or 'abusive') in an indiscriminatory fashion. As such, in order at least to suggest some sort of distinction at the non-experiential level, I will employ the term *abuse of therapeutic power* only when the behaviour of the therapist is premeditative, principally physical and enters the realms of legally defined criminality. All those instances involving subtle, unpremeditated and principally verbal, theoretical or practice-led exploitative violence towards the client I have opted to label as illustrations of *misuse of therapeutic power*.

An example of abuse of therapeutic power would be the appalling list of physical and psychological violations of clients carried out by Dr John Rosen and his associates in the name of *Direct Analytic Therapy* (Masson, 1988). The example of my training experience that was discussed earlier, on the other hand, would be an instance of misuse of therapeutic power.

Nevertheless, such demarcations cannot be seen as all-encompassing. Issues surrounding financial improprieties, for instance, may in many instances 'straddle' the dividing line between these two terms. Similarly, changes in cultural attitudes and mores remind us that such terms are at least influenced by, if they are not reflections of, alterations in cultural perceptions. Fritz Perls, the co-founder of *Gestalt Psychotherapy*, for example, made it no secret that he had had sexual relations with several of his clients. At the time when these events took place, Perls's behaviour was viewed by many therapists, political activists and feminist theorists as acceptable, 'freeing' for the client, and therapeutically laudable. Today, it would be judged by virtually all contemporary representatives of these groups as being blatantly abusive and open to criminal indictment. As such, the definition of terms like abuse must acknowledge both its context and its flexibility.

The two main forms of *abuse of therapeutic power* that have been addressed with increasing forthrightness by both critics of therapy and by therapists themselves over the last few years have been those concerned with instances of *physical and psychological violence* carried out on clients by their therapists and the effects of therapists and clients *engaging in sexual relations* either during, or shortly following the termination of, therapy.

B. *Physical and Psychological Violence*

While concerns about physical and psychological abuse of clients in the name of therapeutic benefit have been raised by a variety of therapists over the last thirty years or more (Laing, 1967; Cooper, 1967; Szasz, 1974a; Breggin, 1993), I think it would be fair to say that it was the publication of Alice Miller's *Thou Shalt Not Be Aware* (1985) and Jeffrey Masson's *The Assault on Truth: Freud's suppression of the seduction theory* (1984) and *Against Therapy* (1988) which both re-awakened and intensified public and professional concern about the use of physical and psychological techniques the curative aims of which employed blatant forms of coercion, indoctrination, and the employment of physical violence of such extremes that it was virtually indistinguishable from torture.

The chronicles of inflicted pain detailed by these authors, Masson in particular, make valuable, if deeply disturbing, reading.

It should come as no surprise, then, that the vast majority of therapists clearly do not condone and, indeed, are repelled by these abuses of power and have taken several important steps to make this stance explicit through the development of clearly stated ethical codes and standards of behaviour. Both the BAC and the UKCP, for example, have published explicit codes of ethics and practice which their members and registered practitioners are obliged to adhere to. In addition, various means have been created for individuals who believe that they have been abused in various ways by their therapists to present their cases to the appropriate complaints and ethical standards committees of these institutions either directly or through their member organizations. The BAC has even begun to publish in its main journal *Counselling* both the notice of current cases under its Ethical Standards Committee's consideration, as well as the name of the counsellor under investigation, and the conclusions arrived at by this committee once it has reached its decision. In some instances, where serious abuse has been ascertained, the practitioner in question has been struck off the BAC membership list either permanently or until such a time as he or she has demonstrated sufficient change in his or her professional and personal stance to ensure as far as is possible that such practices have been abandoned.

While these measures are by no means perfect, in that they cannot guarantee the prevention of further instances of physical abuse of clients by therapists, nevertheless it is evident that they are likely to be sufficient in most instances. In the UK, the issue is exacerbated somewhat by the current non-existence of a mandatory register of therapists which would oblige all those who practise therapy to agree to specified ethical codes and standards. Even so, the general public, in my experience at least, has become increasingly aware of the existence of the main professional bodies and, over the years, prospective clients have tended to enquire as to the registered or accredited status of the therapist they have contacted.

In any case, thankfully, in the UK recorded instances of physical and extreme psychological abuse of clients by therapists (as opposed to other professions) remain a rarity.

C. Sexual Relations between Therapists and Clients

The issue of therapists and clients engaging in sexual relations with one another has also been a matter of increasing concern. Peter Rutter's *Sex in the Forbidden Zone* (1990) and Janice Russell's *Out of Bounds: sexual exploitation in counselling and therapy* (1993) are two recent examples of texts detailing and analysing the incidence and effects of sexual involvement between therapist and client. As this form of abuse would seem to be the more prevalent and morally problematic of the two, it is worthwhile considering it in greater detail.

As with the issue of physical and extreme psychological abuse, there is, currently, almost universal agreement among therapists that sexual relations between therapists and their clients are wrong. Why should such a hard line be adopted? Could there be any circumstances in which sexual relations between therapist and client might provoke beneficial effects for the client? And, equally, might it not be possible that, in the course of the evolving close, intimate relationship that therapy can engender, a sexual expression of this bond might be acceptable and realistic, particularly when both parties are adults who have expressed their *consent*?

These questions, at first glance, seem proper ones to ask. Nevertheless, even under these instances the possibility of there being an *exploitative* element – however remote – seems to be sufficient reason for nearly all individual therapists, as well as professional and training institutions, to proscribe it on the grounds that it is inappropriate, and usually harmful, to the client.

Even so, it remains to be asked whether therapists tend to do what they say. Is there evidence that a significant number of therapists continue to have sexual relations with their clients? And, further, is there any suitable proof that these relations are harmful to clients? The answers to both these questions, as we shall see below, while by no means final and complete, are clearly affirmative.

Although violations involving sexual intimacy between therapists and clients tend to make up over 50 per cent of the disciplinary actions taken up by the main American psychotherapy and counselling licensing agencies (Vinson, 1987), and damages awarded to clients who successfully take abusive therapists to court can reach multi-million-dollar levels (Pope, 1990), surprisingly, there exists as yet virtually no empirically based evidence delineating the extent of sexual relations between therapists and their clients in the UK. (One recent exception to this is Janice Russell's *Out of Bounds : sexual exploitation in counselling and therapy* (1993).) The current Chair of the Registration Board of the UKCP, Michael Pokorny, has been quoted as stating that '[n]obody really knows how common sexual activity is between therapist and patient' (Troupp, 1991). Nevertheless, it remains the case that well-known therapists such as Carl Gustav Jung, Fritz Perls and Masud Khan did have sexual relations with a number of their clients and there exists substantial American research evidence on this issue which suggests that it is more widespread than might have initially been supposed (Llewelyn, 1992).

Research data on the incidence and effects of therapist–client sexual relations

In their recently published survey of existing literature on therapist–client sexual contact, Kasia Szymanska and Stephen Palmer (1993) note that until the late 1960s the topic was avoided and was rarely referred to in practitioner codes of ethics. Similarly, several researchers have pointed out that data on this issue tended not to be published on the grounds that the topic was simply too controversial (Pope and Bouhoutsos, 1986; Bates and Brodsky, 1989). Even as late as 1977, Virginia Davidson's paper dealing with this issue, which was sardonically entitled 'Psychiatry's problem with no name: therapist–patient sex' (Davidson, 1977), seemed to point to the fact that, for many, the subject-matter remained a taboo topic.

One early published research project, however, presented in the form of a questionnaire distributed to fifty highly experienced therapists, found that 75 per cent of the sample could imagine being in an embrace with clients, 60 per cent acknowledged the possibility of a patient being nude or nearly so during therapy sessions and 50 per cent allowed the possibility of a situation wherein the therapist sexually stimulated the patient or vice versa (Bugenthal, 1963). Masters and Johnson, in their own pioneering research on this topic, were among the first to warn that a far greater number of therapists than had previously been supposed had had sexual relations with their clients and that, in most instances, relations were between male therapists and female clients (Masters and Johnson, 1966, 1970). Some years later, the authors further argued that these contacts should be considered the equivalent of rape and demanded that the establishment of suitable legislation that would make such contacts open to legal action should be made a priority (Szymanska and Palmer, 1993).

But not all early literature on the subject condemned therapist–client sexual relations. Indeed, several physicians and therapists asserted that there were significant *positive* effects for clients (Shepard, 1971). The therapist J. L. McCartney, for instance, claimed to have been in sexual contact with 1,500 of his clients (all of whom were female) who, he argued, had subsequently reported beneficial effects (McCartney, 1966). (Concerned readers should note that McCartney was subsequently expelled from the American Psychiatric Association.)

Most researchers interested in this issue agree that, considered together, all these studies suggest that somewhere between 5 and 11 per cent of therapists engage in sexual contact with their clients and that over 80 per cent of all cases involve male therapists as the perpetrators (Kardener, 1973; Holroyd and Brodsky, 1977; Bouhoutsos, 1985; Gatrell et al, 1986; Pope et al, 1986; Pope, 1990).

Studies of sexually abused clients demonstrate that they are predominantly (92 per cent) female, whose average age is 24.5 years. Further, 60 per cent of the female clients are either unmarried, separated or divorced women, the great majority of whom tend to have low self-esteem and sexual difficulties (Llewelyn, 1992). The average age of male sexually abusive therapists is 43.5 years. Of these, 55 per cent describe themselves as being frightened of intimacy, 60 per cent see themselves as father figures, 55 per cent claim to love their clients, and 80 per cent continue to engage in sexual relations with other clients either simultaneously or subsequently (Llewelyn, 1992).

Related research revealed that while 79 per cent of these therapists were in private practice, 14 per cent practised in an organization. Sexual contacts tended to be initiated in the first few sessions for 30 per cent of the cases, after six months for 22 per cent, and in 4 per cent of the instances under study sexual contact began within three months of termination of the therapy. Finally, 41 per cent of these therapists did go on to consult colleagues with reference to their involvement; repeat offenders, however, were found to be less likely to do so (Llewelyn, 1992; Szymanska and Palmer, 1993).

While it might have been expected that a greater likelihood for sexual relations between therapist and client would emerge in those instances where the type of therapy being practised is particularly intensive and focused on the private psychic life of the client, in fact no evidence linking a particular theoretical orientation or approach to greater frequency of sexual relations weighted towards any particular orientation has emerged (Llewelyn, 1992). Related findings also show that completion of accredited training does not decrease the likelihood of sexual relations occurring between therapists and clients. Indeed, if anything, offenders are more likely to be trained therapists, though this statistic may be partly misleading in that the great majority of American therapists are likely to have undergone training of some type or other (Llewelyn, 1992).

The evidence in favour of the conclusion that therapist–client sexual relations are harmful to clients is overwhelming. In a widely reported study, for example, Bouhoutsos and his associates reported details of 559 clients who had had sexual relations with their therapists while in therapy. Of these, 11 per cent had been subsequently hospitalized, and 34 per cent had suffered a negative impact on their personal and social adjustment (on the basis of increases in the incidence of depression, loss of motivation, higher levels of emotional disturbance, and so forth) (Bouhoutsos, 1985). Apfel and Simon's research both confirmed these findings and pointed to some incidences of clients' psychotic breakdown or attempted suicide (Apfel and Simon, 1985).

A number of published first-hand accounts from clients furnish further testimony of the generally harmful effects of therapist–client sexual contacts as well as providing researchers with information containing greater depth and personal insight (Plasil, 1985; Bates and Brodsky, 1989; Russell, 1993). Needless to say, in all these reports there exists virtually no evidence of progress with the originating issues that had led these clients to therapy in the first place (Apfel and Simon, 1985).

Even so, between 50 and 75 per cent of American clients who have been abused remain unaware that sex between therapists and clients is unethical or actionable, and, among those who are aware, only between 1 and 4 per cent take out proceedings against the offending therapist (Masson, 1988).

This statement serves as an important reminder that *virtually all the studies carried out have been reliant upon data collected from therapists themselves (i.e. the potential offender group).* As such, just as the number of incidences of rape is highly likely to be far greater than the number of incidences of reported rape, so too might it be the case that the agreed-on percentages of between 5 and 11 per cent may be far less than is actually the case. In line with this concern, recent reports have suggested that between 50 and 70 per cent of therapists currently in practice will work with one or more clients who have been abused by a prior therapist (Rutter, 1990; Pope and Vetter, 1991).

Some researchers have drawn parallels between therapeutic abuse and other forms of abusive relationship. Like many child abusers, abusive therapists often deny any harm in their behaviour, tend to rationalize it with statements such as 'I loved her' or 'I tried to help her to learn how to experience a truly loving sexual relationship', and often shift the responsibility for initiating the act on to the client. Finally, just like the abused child, the client is often sworn to secrecy and is allowed to relate in an intimate fashion to the therapist only within the boundaries of a specified place, usually the consulting room (Stone, 1983).

While such provocative and potentially informative parallels and resonances should not be dismissed, it is important to bear in mind that adult clients are *not* children. They may behave or express and experience emotions *as if* they were, but they also retain powers and abilities that children do not possess. This is not to say that abusive therapists are in any way less responsible for their behaviour. I am simply pointing out that, just as there may be many similarities in various forms of abusive relationships, so too are there significant differences between them – just as there are likely to be significant differences in the way in which different clients experience and deal with therapist abuse. It seems to me that there is enough to deal with in focusing upon the issue of abuse in therapy per se, without unnecessarily linking it to other instances of abuse.

Interestingly, some of the later research on this topic seems to suggest the possibility of a *decrease* in the incidence of therapist–client sexual relations, together with a decline in the number of repeat offenders (Pope et al, 1986). While the authors speculate that this may be due to both the increased publicity given to the issue and to the more stringent sanctions and penalties that offending therapists open themselves to, it must also be considered that these decreases may have more to say about therapists' greater unwillingness to reveal – even anonymously – their sexual liaisons with clients than about real changes in their behaviour.

Taken as a whole, then, the research findings on therapist–client sexual relations present a disturbing picture of both the incidence of these relations and their likely effects on clients.

It is important to remind readers that virtually all the above data is American in origin and should not be directly extrapolated as being equally representative of the situation in the UK for a variety of important reasons, including cultural divergences and the various factors associated with these. Even so, initial research focused on UK data, while still limited, does seem to suggest similar patterns of incidence (Russell, 1993). Nevertheless, as I pointed out before, both the UKCP and BAC have taken steps to control, if not prevent, therapists from engaging in sexual relations with their clients. Recently, for example, the BAC has amended its constitution so that it now states that counsellors who engage in sexual activity with current clients or within thirteen weeks of the termination of the counselling relationship (a time-scale derived from American research suggesting that sexual relations with former clients is most likely to occur within three months of ending therapy) are acting unethically and are liable to have their names struck off the BAC membership list either on a temporary or permanent basis. Further, the BAC's code of practice also states that if the counselling relationship has been over an extended period of time, a much longer 'cooling off' period is required and a lifetime prohibition on a future sexual relationship with the client may be more appropriate. While these steps are by no means perfect, they can be seen as sincere and significant attempts to deal with the issue in a pragmatic fashion that both acknowledges the need to protect clients and the diversity of focus and style of working of therapists. Certainly, they are an advance on the current situation in the American Counselling Association which has been unable to adopt a similar stance on the issue because of the diversity of views of its membership.

D. *The Problem with Therapists' Attraction towards Their Clients and a Suggestion on How to Deal with It*

It seems to me that the various attempts to prevent or control the occurrence of sexual relations between therapists and clients, while clearly laudable, fail to address a more fundamental question. For even if it were to be found that a much higher proportion of therapists than has been suggested by research studies engage in sexual relations with their clients, it would still remain likely that a far greater number might be tempted to consider this possibility, even if they elect not to act on it. In other words, we are presented with the issue of *therapists' attraction towards their clients.* This attraction might be specifically sexual or more general in the sense of the therapist being attracted to the personality, personal beliefs, social manner and standing and so forth of the client. It is interesting that whereas there has been almost from the start of modern-day therapy a recognition of the possibility, if not likelihood, of clients' experiencing and expressing feelings of attraction towards their therapists (Smith, 1991), there has been far less written concerning the opposite instance or, indeed, of instances of mutually shared attraction (whether acknowledged or not) between therapist and client.

What statements have been made concerning this issue are usually presented under the jargon of *transference and counter-transference.* I will explore these terms more fully in Part 3, but for the moment I will simply say that these terms lead both the therapist and client to the consideration of other emotionally charged relations (usually from the past – such as with one's parents) as either causes of or catalysts for the currently experienced feelings. But if one does not accept this assumption (even if simply for the sake of argument), this tells us virtually nothing about how one is to understand and deal with the current attraction in and of itself. That the very great proportion of therapists *do* experience attraction towards their clients is beyond doubt. A 1986 report revealed that 95 per cent of male therapists and 76 per cent of female therapists admit to feelings of attraction to clients at some point in the therapeutic relationship, even if the vast majority opt to abstain from any action that might provide for their expression (Pope, Keith-Speigel and Tabachnick, 1986).

How are therapists to deal with these feelings? Are they to treat them as unacceptable or taboo and seek to find ways to avoid their occurrence and expression? Do such feelings reveal unresolved concerns and conflicts that should have been dealt with either during training or in the therapist's own therapy? Are feelings of attraction unprofessional and, hence, open to regulation and directives from the professional bodies? All these questions, and the many more that readers might consider, reveal complexities, both hidden and obvious, which do not facilitate easy, or general, answers.

When I have addressed this issue with my students, they have tended to respond in ways that demand that therapists somehow should be able to eradicate from their thoughts (by means of some form of determined will-power) any and all such feelings and, instead, interact with the client from a neutral, or 'neutrally caring', standpoint. Would that it could be so easy! In the same way as we are far more likely to be overly focused on the colour 'red' if we say to ourselves 'Whatever you do, don't think of the colour red', so too are we likely to be overly focused on our feelings of attraction towards someone if we tell ourselves 'I mustn't think about how attractive I find this person.' It would seem to be another instance of 'sod's law' that the more we tell ourselves not to think of something, or to admit to it, the more likely we are to think it and to remain focused on it to the extent that it might begin to hamper severely any other thought or message that we might offer in its place. If therapists are no different from others, nor better able to cope with such problems than anyone else (and I firmly believe that they are not, and cannot), then how are they to deal with the question of attraction towards their clients?

Firstly, notwithstanding my students' suggestions, I would argue that rather than seek to deny or suppress such feelings, or, alternatively, to 'transform' them or minimize their impact by invoking such terms as 'counter-transference', therapists might do better to *acknowledge* them as being present in their experience of, and relationship with, their client. But, lest I inadvertently mislead the reader from the start of the argument, let me make it clear that 'acknowledgement of feelings' should in no way be misconstrued to mean, or imply, 'acting upon them', either in the form of their direct communication to the client or in terms of allowing them direct expression.

Rather, the initial step of acknowledgement, I believe, actually grants a greater possibility for therapists to *deal with* the attraction in ways that prevent, or at least greatly minimize, the potentials for abuse. As the success of so many self-help groups has demonstrated, no individual can truly choose to act with regard to any issue, be it problematic or not, until he or she has acknowledged the issue's existence.

The typical response given to therapists who find themselves attracted to their clients is that they should take the issue to their supervisor or to their own therapy in order to ascertain what separate and personal meanings and issues this attraction might be expressing in a disguised or symbolic manner. Without denying the possible values in responding in this manner, I want to put forward an alternative suggestion.

Let me begin by supposing that a therapist in this situation were to take the matter up with a supervisor or another therapist and discovered that the attraction was not related to any separate or personal issue, and that, instead, what attraction was being felt towards the client was specific and direct rather than representational. In other words, that the therapist was attracted to the client simply because the client was attractive to the therapist. Stranger things have been known to happen! Then what? Well, then, I would suggest, the therapist has two initial, and obvious, choices. Either he or she must elect to cease therapy, or, alternatively, to choose to surrender his or her personal feelings and desires to the possibilities of the therapeutic relationship. In other words, in both instances, what is being asked of the therapist is *to choose an act of sacrifice*.

Sacrifice is *not* self-denial; rather it is an attempt to place the self in equal context and value to the other. It is a selfish act, to be sure, but it is other-directed selfishness. That is to say, it is an attempt to shift from a hierarchical relationship (where either the self or the other is seen as being more valuable or significant or deserving of greater attention) towards an egalitarian relationship (where self and other share equal value, significance or attention). Put simply, sacrifice is not a question of doing something for my sake, or for your sake, but for *our* sake. In this sense, sacrifice is not principally concerned with giving up but, rather, with embracing, or encountering, self and other as beings who strive to approach mutual responsibility and equality.

This is no easy task for anyone to attempt, much less hope to accomplish. But it seems to me that if there is anything that might distinguish therapy as a special enterprise, it is precisely this willingness and attempt on the part of the therapist to sacrifice that which is typical in relationships and to approach the untypical, or extraordinary. I will return to this point in order to explore it further and in a more general fashion in Part 5 of this text. For now, I simply want to consider it just a little further with regard to the specific issue of attraction.

What I am suggesting is that therapists have, among various choices, the choice of dealing with attraction by first acknowledging it so that they can remain *within* the therapeutic relationship from the standpoint of the sacrifice that comes with the choosing not to focus or act upon something one perceives to be principally for personal benefit, or alternatively for the principal benefit of the client, but, rather, for their mutual benefit as expressed in the therapeutic relationship.

This stance requires of therapists the desire to consider something that is initially experienced as being in some way problematic as being potentially *useful* to the undertaking of remaining with, or 'being there' for, the client. Once again, what is being asked of therapists is nothing more than what is being asked of their clients – that is, the honest acknowledgement of who one is, or what one is thinking and feeling, in the current moment. This very willingness towards honest assessment in itself allows a greater possibility of avoiding the experience of being 'swamped' or overwhelmed by one element of one's experience and, instead, of treating that element more equally as one of several or many elements of current experience. In this way, the experience of attraction, while by no means denied, is nevertheless prevented from distracting or overwhelming their attention to the client.

Perhaps a somewhat silly example will here clarify what is being argued. While researching material for this text, I came across a number of interesting (or 'attractive') issues that I would have liked to have considered more fully. Had I done so, I would have indulged my own personal desires to the detriment not only of my potential readers, but also of myself – since my goal in writing this text is not solely the possible benefits of insight it might allow my audience, but also my own similar and differing benefits. As such, I had to sacrifice some personal desires not by denying them, but by not allowing them to intrude or overwhelm my text-focused attention.

But something else is worth comment. In my choice of retaining my focus on the writing of the text, I might find to my surprise that, as I go along in my writing, a relevant point I wish to clarify or explore more fully might actually become more understandable or enhanced if I employ some aspect of a topic I had previously set aside as not being of mutual interest. In this way, that very topic of personal interest now becomes something that can be utilized for the purpose of mutual benefit and clarification. Once again, however, this insight is only possible if I have not denied or sought to expunge this interest but, rather, have simply not allowed it to distract or overwhelm my chosen focus. Again, placing this point in the context of therapy, I might find that my experience of attraction towards my client, which I have acknowledged and chosen not to pursue (rather than deny), may actually at some point in the encounter prove to be of insightful or clarificatory value to the chosen focused task of engaging in a therapeutic relationship. How might this occur?

For example, I might find that as I listen to my client's account of her experience of herself, she tells me that she feels that people are readily attracted to her physical appearance to the extent that she cannot allow herself, or feels that others will not allow her, to express her other qualities and that, as a consequence, she feels both her own fragmentation and a hatred of others since they 'use' or treat her solely as an object of physical appeal and pleasure. In this way, my sacrificed physical attraction towards her takes on a new and previously unforeseen relevance in that it allows me a more experientially informed means of further exploring and clarifying her views, not from some abstracted or distanced stance but, rather, from one that is able to 'hold' both her experience of herself and of others in a direct or 'lived' fashion. Through this stance all manner of issues, such as her own possible competing attitude towards her appreciation and resentment of her physical appearance, as well as her competing appreciation and resentment of others' physical attraction towards her, may be exposed and examined in ways that approach the issue more accurately with respect to her lived experience.

Although I have employed an example that focuses on heterosexual physical attraction, I want to make it clear that the point being discussed holds just as significantly for any form of attraction towards a client experienced by a therapist. Just as I might be attracted to clients (be they male or female) on a physical level, I might also be attracted to them for their sense of humour, their communicative abilities, their sense of fashion and style, the similarity of their life experience to my own, and so forth. In each case, my inability to prevent what attracts me to them from overwhelming or intruding on my focused task of engaging in a therapeutic relationship with them threatens the possibility of fulfilling that task. Similarly, my willingness to sacrifice personal interests and inclinations focused on my sense of attraction towards the client not only enhances the possibility of our maintaining a therapeutic relationship but also may provide a mutually beneficial means of utilizing those personal interests or desires. Through this sacrifice, that which was previously experienced as being problematic might be transformed into something both appropriate and advantageous to the therapeutic process.

2. THE ISSUE OF POWER IN THE THERAPEUTIC RELATIONSHIP

Both the question of physical and sexual abuse and the more general problem of attraction contain within them an implicit, fundamental concern. This is the question of the therapist's *power* in the therapeutic relationship and the means by which the utilization of such power may, in itself, either inherently contain abusive elements, or, alternatively, lead to various forms of abuse.

A. Against Therapy: Jeffrey Masson on the Imbalance of Power

This issue has been of increasingly greater concern over the last decade. Much of this has been generated by various critics of therapy in general and, more specifically, critics of psychoanalysis – particularly with regard to its early history and development under Sigmund Freud (Thornton, 1983; Masson, 1984; Crews, 1993). Although by no means the first to raise such critiques, I think it would be fair to say that it is largely due to the critical writings of Jeffrey Moussaieff Masson (1984, 1988, 1992) that the concern with therapeutic power, and its potentials for abuse, has come to be seen to be of increasing significance to therapists, clients and critics alike. Masson's stance seems to me both to present the major concerns raised with regard to the question of power in therapy, and to take the most extreme position with regard to the 'solution' to the problems it raises, in that Masson advocates the abolition of therapy on the grounds that *the therapeutic relationship is inherently power-imbalanced in favour of the therapist and to the detriment of clients.* As he himself writes:

> The structure of psychotherapy is such that no matter how kindly a person is, when that person becomes a therapist, he or she is engaged in acts that are bound to diminish the dignity, autonomy, and freedom of the person who comes for help (Masson, 1988:24).

Although Masson's critiques initially focused on Sigmund Freud's renunciation of his 'Seduction Theory' (Masson, 1984), the first signs of his increasingly critical view of therapy in general came in 1986 with the publication of *The Dark Science:*

117

women, sexuality and psychiatry in the 19th century (Masson, 1986). This 'reader of the horrors inflicted on women in the name of "mental health"' (Masson, 1988:28) chronicled the various ways in which nineteenth-century women patients had been abused by the male medical establishment which claimed to help and perhaps understand them and how the models of science they employed became the basis for modern theories of psychiatry.

Then, in 1988, came Masson's well-known attack on the whole of therapy. In *Against Therapy: Emotional Tyranny and the Myth of Psychological Healing*, Masson sought to convince his readers that the very idea of therapy – in whichever form it is practised – is inherently abusive and should be banned (Masson, 1988). Instead of therapy, Masson argues, there should be an egalitarian relationship in some ways akin to friendship, which does not involve the exchange of money, is not a professional business enterprise, addresses various feminist critiques of patri-archically dominated therapy, acknowledges and focuses on the real socio-political issues that are at the root of personal misery and pain, and which allows clients to ask personal questions of their co-investigators while expecting to receive direct and honest answers from them (Masson, 1988, 1992, 1993b).

While admitting that his suggestions remain somewhat vague and insubstantial, Masson has argued that his call for the aboli-tion of therapy is akin to that for the abolition of slavery, such that his point is not to develop a more caring or humane model that seeks to reform therapy, but, rather, to eradicate it from society (Masson, 1993b).

Masson's stance on therapy – and on therapists – has, if anything, grown increasingly negative and strident over the years. In a paper entitled 'The tyranny of psychotherapy', he writes:

> . . . it is not very difficult to unmask therapists, especially if they have achieved any fame. All you have to do is read what they write, and sooner or later you will come across what you need (Masson, 1992:9).

The 'impossible' profession makes demands that simply cannot be met. No therapist can consistently and permanently avoid the temptation to abuse the inevitable and inherent power imbalance. Even the kindest therapist may well experience envy of somebody else's capacity for love, or anger that they are leading a more interesting life, or that they are richer, smarter, better looking, deeper, happier, more amusing, or whatever quality they have and the therapist lacks. We may be tested and tempted by our friends in this same regard in real life, but we have no strangle-hold on them, nothing that is built into the relationships we do or do not form. But in therapy that strangle-hold is pre-ordained (Masson, 1992:18).

A Response to Masson's Critiques

There is no doubt in my mind that most, if not all, of the concerns expressed by Masson in his various books and papers are both highly relevant and deserving of the greatest attention by therapists. I also believe him to be broadly correct when he states that therapy has not given sufficient consideration to these criticisms and, indeed, may even have avoided addressing them to any serious extent prior to his attacks – though it must be said that others prior to him (such as R. D. Laing, 1967; Thomas Szasz, 1978; and Peter Breggin, 1979) had provided either similar or equally significant critiques. I also agree with Masson that important issues such as the extent of the incidence of incest have been 'whitewashed' by therapy and related professions such as psychiatry, and that questions concerning the purpose and value of training therapists have not been sufficiently addressed or clarified (Masson, 1992). Further, Masson's call for a 'consumer's guide' to therapy is both valid and helpful (Masson, 1992) – and some initial steps in this direction have already been taken by the BAC.

Nevertheless, I am at times disturbed by the often polemical tone of Masson's writings which, in many instances, serves only to restrict the possibility of open and non-defensive dialogue to the extent that, as Jeremy Holmes has put it, it becomes 'difficult to show gratitude when someone is spitting in your face' (Holmes, 1992:29). I am also troubled by Masson's single-minded insistence on proving his case to the extent that even when he is forced to acknowledge that at least *some* clients find significant benefit from the enterprise, he must interpret their experience in ways that strike me as being no different nor less defensive (or abusive?) than those of the therapists he criticizes (most recently, by suggesting that such instances reveal a type of sado-masochistic sexual pleasure generated by the (usually female) client's loss of power, and the (usually male) therapist's exercise of it, which is fostered by the structure and process of therapy (Masson, 1993b)). But such qualms would be insignificant if Masson's central premise were shown to be correct. Are Masson's conclusions beyond criticism?

While his examples of some therapists' physical and sexual abuse of clients are deserving of all the invective raised against them, they do not, in themselves, provide sufficient grounds for condemning the practice per se, not least because Masson cannot provide the evidence to show that *most* or even a significant number of therapists behave in these ways towards their clients.

Practically speaking, it is essential that therapists and therapeutic organizations seek to ensure that appropriate measures are taken to protect clients and provide a suitable means for them to address their complaints to a relevant body which is itself empowered to act on their behalf (e.g. deregistration of the offending therapist) and that therapists are themselves more fully aware of their power and how it may become abusive. But all these measures, and any others that might come to mind, need not lead us to conclude, as Masson concludes, that the very *idea* of therapy is wrong. He may be correct in asserting that the greater the power, the greater is the likelihood of its abuse. But 'likelihood' is not the same as 'certainty' and in this difference lie various means of influencing that possibility such that it moves further and further away from its realization.

Masson's principal argument rests on the assumption that *an unequal power relationship is, in and of itself, abusive.* This view strikes me as being singularly naive. What relationship can Masson point to that is *not* unequal in power? In pointing us towards friendships and kind, loving relationships, Masson seems to suggest that these are examples wherein power has been equalized. But this seems patently false. In all such cases, power can be seen to be in disequilibrium, constantly shifting between individuals. Indeed, there exists some research evidence to suggest that his contention that non-professional relationships are *ipso facto* less open to abuse than others is, at best, questionable (Bell, 1989). Any act of involvement, or relationship, excludes neutrality; relationship *is* power in flux.

Masson also raises concerns focused on the *dependency* of the client towards the therapist which is fostered in the therapeutic process, and considers how this can be in keeping with therapy's broad aims of increasing the client's autonomy. In relation to this point, Holmes and Lindley point out that while there may at first appear to be a fundamental paradox in this, it is only so due to the mistaken assumption that autonomy and dependency are in opposition. I agree with their view that

> . . . the capacity to depend and be dependable is an important feature of most successful intimate relationships. Many people seeking psychotherapy suffer from problems concerning dependency. They may feel trapped, and therefore out of control when they form close relationships; or they may be unable to depend on, and get close to others, despite the wish to do so. The opposite of autonomy, therefore, is *not* dependency, but *heteronomy*. This means, roughly, 'not being in control of one's self'. Psychotherapy, often in the setting of secure dependency on a therapist, *reduces* heteronomy by helping the patient to be more aware of, and so less controlled by, experience and feelings which have been suppressed or ignored. This awareness makes it easier to establish relationships based on mature dependency. In this way the dependency of the patient on the therapist does not in itself threaten autonomy (Holmes and Lindley, 1989:5–6).

Power can mean, as Masson insists, the control of the other. But power also has another meaning: the ability to act, to take charge over oneself. In this more complete sense, power – and

121

the imbalance of power – is neither necessarily 'good' nor 'bad'; it is unavoidable.

But, the reader might suppose, perhaps what Masson is suggesting is not simply that therapy involves an imbalanced power relationship, but that, more pertinently, that this imbalance is *always* favourable towards the therapist. This may seem to be a far more appropriate point to consider.

It is certainly the case, as this text has set itself the task of demonstrating, that therapists do hold extensive power which they can misuse or abuse within the therapeutic relationship. Equally, as Petruska Clarkson recently pointed out, it is important to recognize that clients too hold power which they can misuse or abuse within the self-same relationship (Clarkson, 1993). It may be different to the therapist's power, but it need not be seen as being necessarily inferior. Just as therapists may exert their power by setting the time, duration and cost of sessions, or may attempt to impose unwanted and destructive viewpoints or interpretations on their clients, so too may clients seek to deviate from the agreed-on frame, or withhold payments, or simply not show up to sessions, or not return to therapy without providing notice, or heap undeserved verbal or even physical abuse on the therapist.

I do not think it is enough to say that abuse of power in therapy (or in any other instance) is unwanted and if such occurs the relationship must be dissolved or abolished. Rather, it seems to me far more significant to seek to understand what has provoked that abuse and, in so doing, prevent its recurrence. It seems essential to me that therapists be willing to examine their role and therapeutic interventions precisely for these reasons, and it is a stated aim of this text to provoke and assist them in this task. Similarly, it can be argued that one of the principal duties of therapy is to provide the means whereby clients may examine various facets of their experience of abuse – either as recipients or perpetrators – not in order 'to explain away' or to 'forgive and forget', but to better understand and acknowledge it so that it is either less likely to recur, or so they can better deal with it, or both.

Masson's arguments seem to hinge on a desire for perfectionism. If something is not perfect, he seems to tell us, then it should not be allowed to exist. So, for instance, a good deal of his critique of Carl Rogers rests on the argument that

> [n]o real person really does any of the things Rogers prescribes in real life. So if the therapist manages to do so in a session, if he appears to be all-accepting and all-understanding, this is merely artifice; it is not reality (Masson, 1988:232).

Masson seems to be saying that because no person, much less no therapist, has fulfilled such goals then to claim to have done so is at best misleading, if not downright abusive. This may be a valid argument, *if* this is what Rogers claimed. However, my own readings would suggest that Rogers sets forward his necessary and sufficient conditions as *aims* rather than asserting that he – or any other person-centred therapist – has achieved such. That certain aims may be unrealizable in any final, complete or perfect sense does not mean that there is no value in finding the means at least to approach them. All of us, I think, have experienced relationships that are at different points along a continuum that stretches between 'no acceptance' and 'all-accepting', or 'no understanding' and 'all-understanding'. To suggest that there is no significant difference in the variants between these extremes, or to demand an all-or-nothing stance, would suggest to me that what is being wanted is a somewhat unrealistic perfectionism which no relationship can hope to offer.

Therapy is clearly imperfect, but it is, nevertheless, one of the few ways we have found of confronting certain forms of human misery and pain. Yes, ideally, our families or friends or even ourselves should be more than sufficient replacements for therapists. But in the world we inhabit, this is not always the case and, in some instances unfortunately, those self-same persons may be pivotally implicated in the pain and misery we experience.

As the comedian Lenny Bruce used to say:

> People should be taught what is, not what should be. All my humour is based on destruction and despair. If the whole

world were tranquil, without disease and violence, I'd be standing in the breadline – right back of J. Edgar Hoover (Bruce, 1975).

. . . And, one might add, all therapists.

Therapy and Ethics

But, let us be clear, if we reject Masson's conclusion and accept that, however imperfect it may be, therapy still offers at least potential benefits, then we must be prepared to consider its weaknesses and dangers and seek to enhance its beneficial possibilities. If for no other reason, then, therapists should be grateful to Masson, as well as to all other critics, in assisting them in this task. Masson, in particular, has pointed out a number of fundamental dilemmas for therapy to address. However implicitly, he has clarified a number of *ethical* concerns that deserve attention.

Hare (1991) has argued that we tend to see ethical issues from subjective or intuitive standpoints. We tend to believe that we know what is right and wrong. But the many dilemmas we are confronted with throughout life are not principally concerned with questions of right versus wrong but about *the choices* we make between actions that, in themselves, contain elements of both 'right' and 'wrong'. So, for instance, I may find myself in a situation where I am forced to decide between extending my session with a client who is in distress or ending it on the hour so that I can get to my college on time to teach my students. Whatever choice I make is neither completely right nor completely wrong. But *how* I choose is underpinned by an implicit or explicit ethical stance.

Thomas Szasz has emphasized the role of ethics in therapy (Szasz, 1974c, 1992a) and has argued that a principal task for therapy must be the greater acknowledgement and consideration of ethical issues raised in such a relationship. I agree with him entirely on this point. It seems to me to be paramount for therapists to clarify such matters as how *informed* a client is when he or she consents to therapy, whether the therapist's and the client's assumptions as to what their therapeutic relationship is for have been agreed (or at the very least stated), what specific rules and conditions each brings to it, and so forth. The resolution of such issues cannot be entirely generalized nor applied indiscriminately. Nor can the ethical decisions that are arrived at be seen to be 'perfect', but they can be sufficient, or, to employ D. W. Winnicott's now-famous phrase, 'good enough' (Winnicott, 1971).

All these points should not be seen as suggesting that the dangers of physical and sexual abuse in therapy, and the issues surrounding the exercise of power, have been resolved and need no longer concern both clients and therapists. Obviously, this is not so. But it is fair to say that, particularly over the last few years, when these questions have been the focus of so much debate generated by both critical outsiders and concerned insiders, significant steps have been taken to address the issues and seek to prevent their recurrence.

The very fact that, in spite of major theoretical and practical divisions between the various approaches to therapy, organizations such as the BAC and the UKCP have come into existence, and have begun to address these concerns, is an achievement that should not be minimized nor scorned for its imperfections, but, rather, is deserving of continued support. It may be difficult for the general public to understand just how much effort has had to be expended in order to get this far. Until relatively recently in the history of therapy, the consensus has tended to have been one of studied disinterest in, and avoidance of, dialogue between therapists of divergent approaches and theoretical stances. That there now exists increasing evidence to suggest that therapists have developed a greater willingness to address the concerns raised by issues such as the various abusive potentials within therapy is a significant development.

Nevertheless, as a practising therapist, I remain aware, together with many other colleagues, that major, if more subtle, problems remain with regard to the inadvertent misuses of therapy, and it is to these that we must now turn for discussion.

3. THE MISUSE OF POWER IN THE THERAPEUTIC RELATIONSHIP

I mentioned earlier, with regard to the views expressed by Jeffrey Masson, that his concerns first arose when he concluded that Freud had exhibited 'moral cowardice' by rejecting his initial theories concerning childhood sexual abuse and re-interpreting these events as fantasies rather than memories of actual events. This issue has provided a good deal of on-going debate among the critics and adherents of psycho-analysis – debates that have recently resurfaced as a result of a review article of Frederick Crews in the *New York Review of Books* (1993) and in the subsequent responses that have appeared in the *Review*'s letters pages (1994). I want to consider this debate not for its own sake but in order to provide an entry point to a discussion on how *theory-led therapeutic interventions* may, in themselves, provoke potential issues focused on the misuse (and possible abuse) of the therapist's power in therapy.

A.   Freud's Seduction Theory: *An Example of the Misuse of Power*

In 1896, Freud published a series of papers which put forward what has become known as his *Seduction Theory*. In fact, there were really two related, if closely connected, theories being presented. Initially, Freud claimed that the root cause of the hysterical symptoms exhibited by his patients had been sexual abuse perpetrated on them either by adults or older children, including their siblings, nursemaids, members of their family, governesses, servants, and so forth, prior to his patients' tenth birthday. By 1897, however, he amended these views to some degree by arguing that with regard to his female patients (and possibly some male patients) the main (if not sole) abuser had been their father. Indeed, in his letter to his confidant and friend Wilhelm Fliess, dated 3 January 1897, Freud wrote excitedly that he had found clear evidence of paternal abuse and now felt certain that he was on the right track. So strongly did Freud believe in his theory that he began to consider that his own father had abused his (Sigmund's) brother and several of his younger sisters since they too exhibited a number of hysterical symptoms (Hopkins, 1994).

Stated briefly, Freud's seduction theory argued that his patients had repressed their memories of these events but, once puberty had set in, this repressed memory began to express itself in the form of various hysterical symptoms. As such, Freud saw his task as being that of turning the repressed memories of his patients into conscious memories because, he believed, by acknowledging these events his patients would no longer need to express them in the disguised form of their hysterical symptoms (Gay, 1988).

Although he publicly defended these views in spite of their apparent unpopularity, towards the end of 1897 Freud too began privately to express his own doubts as to the validity of his claims and, by 1899, he abandoned this stance in favour of his new theory of infantile fantasies which he eventually began to advocate publicly in 1905 (Gay, 1988). This new theory argued that what Freud had previously thought to be repressed memories were actually *repressed sexual wishes or fantasies* from infancy and early childhood which were principally focused on the patients' parents.

Why did Freud change his views? He tells us that he did so for several reasons, primarily because the evidence for his earlier views did not turn out to be as conclusive as he might have originally imagined and, more significantly, because his patients' hysterical symptoms either persisted or returned in spite of their conscious acknowledgement of their having been abused. Freud's critics, on the other hand, have argued otherwise. Masson, for instance, has argued that Freud abandoned the seduction theory not because it was wrong, but because it was all too correct and Freud could not face the defensive social wrath that his continuing adherence to these views would have provoked. Instead, Masson argues, Freud effectively betrayed his patients by turning the tables on them with his new theory such that those who were once the victims of abuse now became the originators of unconscious sexual fantasies and, equally, those who had previously been the perpetrators of abuse now became the innocent dupes of their children's unconscious fantasies (Masson, 1984).

For many therapists and critics, the evidence seems to be in favour of the latter conclusion as presented by Masson – so much so, in fact, that it has recently resurfaced as the main impetus for some current practices dealing with what has become known as 'Repressed Memory Syndrome'. Similarly, some scholars who are critical of Freud's subsequent theories have reconsidered these early papers as exemplary of Freud's lack of scientific objectivity (Schimek, 1985; Crews, 1993, 1994).

However, an alternative, if no less significant, view can be taken. Firstly, it is important to correct a mistaken assumption that many of Freud's critics have made of this material. Freud did not state that childhood sexual abuse in itself caused hysterical symptoms. It only did so, he argued, *when the memory of this event had been repressed.* As such, Freud's abandonment of his 'seduction theory' is not, per se, an attempt on his part to deny the existence of sexual abuse of children by adults (including their parents). Rather, it is a recantation of the view that hypothesized a causal relationship between repressed memories of sexual abuse and hysteria. While it might be justifiable to argue that Freud and his followers minimized the social reality and significance of sexual abuse in its diverse forms, it is quite a different matter to suggest that it was not acknowledged as existing.

Secondly, and of far greater consequence, Freudian scholars such as David L. Smith (1991) have pointed out that when one reads Freud's papers dealing with the clinical evidence obtained for his early theory, quite a different picture from what has been suggested emerges. For what one discovers is that Freud's own evidence is never direct, but is actually 'indirect, inferential . . . like an unknown language which must be "deciphered and translated" in order to yield "undreamed of information"' (Smith, 1991:8).

What this implies is that Freud's evidence for his theory was inferential rather than directly obtained. Freud writes that the 'scenes' of abuse had been *reproduced* by his patients during their clinical sessions. What Freud meant by the term 'reproduced' is unclear. Jean Schimek, for example, has written that they involved 'visual scenes, often of hallucinatory intensity, accompanied with strong displays of affect, physical sensations and motoric gestures' (Schimek, 1985:943), and Smith concludes that

> Freud makes a point of emphasizing in each of the 1896 papers that his patients did not experience these events as memories (*they have no feeling of remembering the scenes* – Freud, 1896c:204). It was Freud, then, and not his patients, who connected the scenes with hypothetical unconscious memories of sexual abuse. Freud's later statements to the effect that his patients told him that they remembered having been seduced as children are flatly contradicted by the evidence (Smith, 1991:9).

What both Schimek and Smith go on to argue is that Freud's seduction theory was constructed by him in a very selective manner influenced both by his technique and by his own belief in the truth of his theory. At that time, Freud employed a 'pressure technique' that involved his placing a hand on his patient's forehead, applying increasing pressure, and, at the same time, insisting that the patient produce not just memories in general but *those memories that Freud was certain the patient was repressing.* This scenario can be gleaned from Freud's own statements:

> One only succeeds in awakening the psychical trace of a precocious sexual event under the most energetic pressure of the analytic procedure, and against an enormous resistance (Freud, 1896a:153).

> If the first discovered scene is unsatisfactory, we tell our patient that this experience explains nothing, but that behind it, there must be a more significant, earlier experience (Freud, 1896b:195–6).

In addition, Freud also tells his readers that he would inform his clients prior to the start of treatment that certain required 'scenes' would emerge – scenes that he would steer them towards (Freud, 1896b).

All this might begin to strike the reader as all too similar to activities designed to extract confessions from individuals who have been 'judged guilty until proven innocent'. What Freud, however inadvertently, tells his readers is that he began his treatments with a pre-set assumption (i.e. that they *had to have been abused*) and that, lo and behold, with the right amount of physical pressure, insistence, and selective reinforcement he 'proved' this to be the case. As Smith concludes after considering Freud's account of his treatment of a female patient:

> We need to look no further than Freud's interaction with his patient to form a plausible hypothesis about why she 'spontaneously' became preoccupied with issues of seduction, abuse, and exploitation (Smith, 1991:23).

It is important to note that Smith's statement contains added meaning. For it is Smith's contention that this patient's acknowledgement of abuse – in common with similar statements during treatment – was not simply the result of Freud's powerful suggestions, but was a comment on her 'current experience of abuse at the hands of Freud' (Smith, 1991). Smith argues this in order to clarify certain ideas central to the theory of Communicative Psycho-analysis, but we need not follow this particular path in order to understand that Freud's own unwavering belief in the validity of his theory clearly influenced and affected his patients' self-understanding by *imposing* a particular viewpoint (i.e. Freud's) on them.

Smith argues that it is likely that Freud himself came to see this, and it was probably this insight above all others which led him to abandon his seduction theory. However plausible Smith's suggestion may seem (and I personally think it to be plausible enough for Freud scholars to pursue), it remains, nevertheless, speculation, since Freud does not ever state this in any direct manner either in his subsequent papers or in his private letters. However, even if Smith is essentially correct, we are still faced with subsequent evidence from Freud's case studies dealing with aspects of 'psycho-analysis proper' (e.g. the cases of 'Dora' (Freud, 1905) and the 'Wolf Man' (Freud, 1918) as discussed by Crews (1993)) that although Freud changed his theory, his directive behaviour remained pretty much the same. In other words, Freud continued to impose his beliefs on his patients' stories, emphasizing and directing them to those elements in their accounts which 'fitted' his theory and provided him with 'evidential proofs' of its correctness. In the case of the 'Wolf Man' (Freud, 1918), for instance, virtually the whole of Freud's analysis rests on a particular dream which Freud interprets as a disguised recollection of his patient's witnessing his parents engaged in sexual intercourse (Freud, 1918). Not only does the dream consist of a minute amount of the case material that Freud records in his account but, additionally, the 'Wolf Man' himself, many years later, voiced serious doubts as to the likelihood of the 'primal scene' ever having occurred, and suggested that he only went along with Freud's interpretation because Freud so clearly thought it to be of such significance (Obholzer, 1982).

B. Therapist Reliance upon Theory as a Misuse of Power

The issue of Freud's directive, theory-driven behaviour would be of little relevance to most if it were simply historically placed and specific to Freud and possibly his early followers. I have raised it, however, because it seems to me to be of current concern in that a great deal of contemporary therapeutic practice – regardless of the theory espoused – remains theory-led and, as such, can be seen to open therapists to accusations of misuse (however inadvertent) of their therapeutic power.

Virtually all theories of therapy are based to a significant extent on sets of observations of people's behaviour. These observations then become the basis from which views and hypotheses about mental phenomena are inferred and which seek to describe accurately various psychological processes (e.g. thought, memory, emotions, etc.) the influences of which may explain or predict past, present and future behaviour. This, in itself, is neither a unique nor an unusual form of scientifically influenced enquiry. The danger only arises when both the observations and the hypotheses that spring from them come to be seen and employed as truth or dogma. This danger is not specific to therapy since all scientific enterprise remains open to such possibilities, but it is especially problematic to therapy because, unlike established scientific enterprises, therapy is currently made up of many and diverse theories that share little in common – even at the level of the most basic assumptions.

As such, in the current state of things, significantly different, even contradictory, theories share relatively equal value and validity. As we saw in Part 1 of this text, no evidence has as yet been found to demonstrate the superior effectiveness of any one theory-derived approach to therapy over any other. This, in itself, should be warning enough to current therapists not to depend unnecessarily on the validity of their particular theories as sufficient rationale for their interpretations and interventions. Unfortunately, therapists tend not to have heeded this warning. For in presenting the therapeutic process as being special and unique, and in believing that their expertise is derived from their employment of skills and methods that are themselves derived from the theory of mental functioning that they subscribe to, therapists, somewhat unquestioningly, have tended to adapt their patients' 'stories' and conflicts to fit the theory that they (the therapists) believe in, even though they have little basis on which to assert that their theories are based on reliable and valid evidence.

For example, Katharine Mair points out that the very influential cognitive-behavioural therapy of Aaron Beck emerged from his observations of the attitudes of depressed individuals. Mair argues that Beck

> passed off his description of the thinking of depressed people (beefed up with a lot of jargon) as an explanation of depression, which had been validated by 'systematic research'. Even as a description, its validity has been questioned. There is a wealth of experimental data which suggests that depressed people do not have distorted perceptions, and that they may

indeed be rather more accurate than the rest of us in many of their judgments . . . (Mair, 1992:140).

Similarly, if the therapist's original idea relates only to a limited aspect of behaviour, it can be made to sound more general and plausible if it is infused with 'a new jargon and hints of organic underpinnings' (Mair, 1992:141). Terms like 'syndrome' and 'disorder' may also play a role in 'authenticating' a theory. Spanos (1989), for instance, demonstrated that 60 per cent of all the patients in one American clinic were found to be suffering from 'Multiple Personality Disorder', possibly because the therapists in that clinic were firm believers in the disorder – as were, consequently, the patients themselves. In the same way, 'Repressed Memory Syndrome' has 'blossomed' recently in clinics and institutes that subscribe to its existence.

This is not to say that such symptoms and syndromes do not, or cannot, exist. Rather, the point being made is simply that therapists should be more tentative and open to alternative explanatory possibilities before being fully convinced – or fully convincing their clients – of any particular one. Unfortunately, this does not seem to be the case and 'true believers', in their readiness to assert the unequivocal truth of their findings, may be inflicting serious psychological and social damage on their clients (and their families). Indeed, as in the case of Repressed Memory Syndrome, some therapists' diagnostic procedures for determining the symptomatic basis for their conclusions have been questioned with growing alarm since the defining symptoms of the syndrome seem so vague and general that they appear to contain little diagnostic worth. The recent successful case brought against a therapist who had 'assisted' in uncovering his client's 'repressed memories' of having been sexually abused by her father (the plaintiff) has raised further concerns about this approach as a contemporary example of the possible dangers in theory-driven therapeutic intervention.

If therapists remain in general agreement that an important function of their enterprise revolves around the desire and attempt to challenge their clients' world-views so that they become more flexible and realistic, then they must surely ask the same of themselves. Equally, if they are to answer charges of abuse and misuse of their authority and power successfully, they must be prepared to acknowledge that the current status of their theories, and the applications derived from these, is, at best, tentative and requiring of attitudes and practices that recognize and express such.

C. Avoiding Theory-Led Misuse of Power: Some Initial Considerations

All approaches to therapy acknowledge the importance of its relational constituents. But, having done so, the impact of the therapeutic relationship, both at the private or personal level and at the shared or interpersonal level, has tended to have been insufficiently recognized and explored. It seems to me likely that many of the concerns expressed about issues surrounding the abuse and misuse of power in the therapeutic relationship have arisen precisely because the influence and meaning of these relational features have not been generally addressed. Among these features is the issue of therapists' central reliance on their theories as defining boundaries to their investigations of, and attempts to understand, the meaning-world, as perceived and behaviourally enacted, of their clients. But this reliance, if it is expressed or believed in by therapists in an uncritical manner or in a fashion that demands unquestioning subservience to theory-driven 'truths' by both therapists and their clients, creates a relationship the imbalances of which provoke and make far more likely the appearance and experience of varying degrees of abuse.

As an example that should make this point clear, we need only re-examine my own experience as a trainee as described earlier. My therapist's unswerving allegiance to his theoretically derived conclusion that my rebellion at his insistence that I refer to him as 'Daddy' was an expression of my being a 'psychic orphan' produced a relationship that emphasized and demanded a power-focused conflict between us. Equally, within me, it provoked all manner of personal views and reactions that, at the time of the event, could not be explored or examined but only acted on from a fixed perspective. In my case, those views and responses were primarily assertive and dismissive of external authority as embodied by the therapist; in someone else, they might just as easily have been submissive and unquestioningly accepting of that same authority. In the same fashion, although I have no knowledge of what they were, various personal views of my therapist were also sure to have been highlighted and acted on in an equally closed and unwavering fashion. In the end, probably both of us experienced the other as being abusive, experienced ourselves as being the victims of abuse, and, concomitantly, experienced the relationship we had engendered as being blocked, or resistant to insight, or destructive. If, on the other hand, my therapist had been more hesitant or willing to have his theoretical views challenged, then it might have been far more likely that my response, in turn, would have been more open to a consideration of his perspective. More than this, however, in our mutual willingness to contemplate the other's input, the very nature of the relationship we had generated would have altered and would have been more likely to have been experienced by both of us as challenging *and* respectful, and, while still imbued with power, nevertheless constructive and trustworthy rather than debilitating and oppressive. In short, each of us would have been far more willing and capable of *listening* to one another.

What is being suggested is not that therapists (or anyone else, for that matter) should seek to engage with and listen to their clients from a theory-less or 'blank slate' standpoint. It would be the height of naïveté to imagine that this could possibly be achieved. Rather, the point being argued is simply that therapists should treat their theories and assumptions critically, remaining open to their falsifiability, to the uncertainty of the 'truths' they might contain, and to the alternative possibilities with which their encounters with their clients may provide them.

In relation to this point, I am reminded of a lecture I once attended concerning some psychological aspects of the Major and Minor Arcanas in the Tarot deck. In that lecture, it was argued that while each of the four Kings in the Minor Arcana

135

were, on the one hand, the most powerful cards, they were, paradoxically, also the weakest because in mastering the 'element' they represented they had also become slaves to it in that it was *all* they knew or could experience their world through. In their reliance and unquestioning loyalty to a particular model, therapists run the same risk as the Kings in the Tarot deck and, thereby, become both extremely powerful and powerless at one and the same time. Perhaps they might find it worthwhile to consider another point made in that lecture: that true power and mastery emerge out of the attempt to balance faith and doubt.

But, in order to do just that, therapists must be willing to reconsider their most basic and deeply held assumptions. Many of these lie at the heart of their psychologically derived theories and include such issues as the influences of the past on current thought and behaviour, unconscious mechanisms, innate growth of self-actualization tendencies in human beings, and the existence of a fixed, or real, self. It is to these and other such fundamental assumptions, therefore, that we must now turn our attention in order to examine, assess, and, hopefully, demystify.

PART THREE

DEMYSTIFYING
THERAPEUTIC THEORY:
1. THE PSYCHO-ANALYTIC MODEL

The greatest psychopathologist has been Freud. Freud was a hero. He descended to the underworld and there met stark terrors. He carried with him his theory as a medusa's head which turned these terrors to stone. We who follow Freud have the benefit of the knowledge he brought back with him and conveyed to us. He survived. We must see if we now can survive without using a theory which is in some measure an instrument of defence.
– R. D. Laing

The focus throughout this and the next part of the text will be on a number of fundamental assumptions that therapists have derived from their theories. In so doing, it will both examine their meanings and values and consider how therapists' tendencies to accept and believe in them from an unquestioning standpoint may both impede the therapeutic process and open it to the possibility of misuse.

This is not to say that theories themselves are worthless to both the therapist and client; all that is being suggested is that the strength of belief in a particular theory, as well as the manner in which the theories are applied and presented, may well provoke unnecessary and debilitating strains in the participants and in the therapeutic relationship to the extent that the therapy itself may become 'untherapeutic'.

Equally, it is important to be clear that these suggested alternatives will not seek to dismiss nor deny the experience-based origins of the avowed phenomena; rather, the focus for criticism will be on the subsequent theory-based explanations and interpretations that have been provided.

The great majority of theoretical models of therapy encompass three main strands of approach: the *psycho-analytic*, the *cognitive-behavioural* and the *humanistic*. In addition, the humanistic strand also contains subsidiary *transpersonal approaches* that focus on the 'spiritual' or 'over-self' elements that influence both intra- and inter-personal relations. Of course, while nearly all of the large number of current therapies tend to present themselves as being unique in certain ways, in most instances they can be seen to be substantially derived from, or seeking to integrate, various fundamental assumptions that are present in one or more of the three main models.

As I will seek to argue, each of these three main models, while clearly offering important psychological insights the relevance of which to the therapeutic process is obvious, nevertheless contain within them a variety of theoretical assumptions that, as I will endeavour to demonstrate, contain in-built problematic elements that significantly affect and determine both the type and the quality of the therapeutic relationship that is likely to emerge because of their application. I will consider each of these approaches separately and concentrate on those elements that I view as being most significant to the argument being presented.

Before doing so, however, I must confess to my own biased position. There exists what I believe to be a fourth approach – the *existential-phenomenological model* – which, as I have previously mentioned, I personally subscribe to.

One of the reasons I have been drawn to this approach lies in its stance of critical – even sceptical – questioning of the assumptions underlying *all* models and their applications by seeking to maintain a descriptive focus on the experience under consideration or investigation. Simply speaking, it does this by seeking to 'open up' or clarify a given experience rather than 'step behind or beneath' what is presented (Spinelli, 1989).

But in this very attempt, it confronts investigators with all manner of biases and assumptions that they bring into the investigative process in order that they may both acknowledge these factors and attempt to set them aside (or 'bracket' them) as much as possible. This attempt (and I emphasize that it can only be an attempt rather than a fulfilment) at 'pure description' contains a number of important implications for the therapeutic process. One of these implications is precisely the topic under consideration.

Further, the existential-phenomenological model is fundamentally *relational*. As such, its focus on therapeutic relationships centres on various relational variables – including, naturally, the relationship between therapist and client. This emphasis too is deeply relevant to the current topic.

Finally, while the existential-phenomenological model can be seen to be a separate approach which can be contrasted to others, it can also be seen as a model that provides *all* approaches with the means of clarifying and critically examining their various biases and assumptions. In this way, it need not be in competition with other models; rather, it may well be a useful and constructive tool for all approaches as long as they are willing to be open to the analyses it engenders.

It is for these three reasons that I have opted to introduce it into this discussion and into subsequent discussions that will make up the remaining parts of this text, as I believe that it has much of value to contribute to the general aim of demystifying therapy.

1. THE PSYCHO-ANALYTIC MODEL: AN OVERVIEW

The history of modern-day therapy begins with the introduction and application of the psycho-analytic model as formulated by Sigmund Freud. Taking as its most basic premise the idea of a 'talking cure' carried out in a private, one-to-one encounter bounded by various structural, or frame, features such as the duration of each session (the 'fifty-minute hour'), its setting, location and 'ambience' (usually a specified room in the therapist's private dwelling containing comfortable furniture to sit – or lie – on, dimmed lighting, and so forth), and emphasizing the need for the client to speak freely and openly about his or her most private and intimate thoughts and experiences ('free association'), it laid the basic foundations for therapeutic practice as adopted and adapted by the great majority of therapeutic models, and, as such, currently remains the most widely influential model – either in whole or in part – in contemporary therapy.

While this model is made up of a substantial variety of sub-models (e.g. Freudian, Kleinian, Object-Relations, Lacanian, etc.), some of which may be further sub-divided (e.g. British and

American Object-Relations), these distinctive divergences and reformulations of (primarily) Freudian concepts lie beyond the boundaries of this discussion. Similarly, the influences of psycho-analytic theories are extremely wide-ranging, covering virtually all aspects of psychology such as human development, personality, memory, sexuality, and so forth, and providing, as well, a philosophy of human nature, sociological models of group behaviour, culture, religion, and the arts, and a novel means of conducting critical analyses of historical figures, events, and literary material.

For all these reasons, my focus on the psycho-analytic model will, of necessity, restrict itself to specifically therapeutic assumptions which I believe are fundamental to the applied skills of psycho-analytically trained therapists and which, as well, are shared by all of the sub-models. Of these assumptions, I believe that three in particular stand out as being central concepts of psycho-analytic therapy which have a direct effect on the nature of the relationship that is engendered between therapist and client. These are: 1) the notion of hidden or 'unconscious' mental processes; 2) the notion of the past as causal agent of current symptomatic behaviour and current personality-based attitudes and dispositions; and 3) the allied notions of transference and counter-transference which play a pivotal role in the nature of the therapist–client relationship as perceived by the psycho-analytic therapist.

These three assumptions taken together demand of the therapist the trained skills to extract from the plethora of the client's statements and behaviours those elements that reveal all these factors at work, to interpret such, and, where necessary, to note the client's resistances to their interpretations since such point not only to deeply held defences (or patterns of psychic pain reduction) but also to those general stances and attitudes insistently held by the client in spite of their incapacitating consequences. In many cases, such defences are further understood to originate in psychic conflicts usually built around sexual or aggressive desires that the client will not admit to or confront.

2. THE PSYCHO-ANALYTIC UNCONSCIOUS

Quite a few years ago now, during the time in my life when I was most enamoured of psycho-analytic approaches to therapy, I was working with a client, June, who had come to me desperate to rid herself of nightly disturbances that prevented her from maintaining undisturbed sleep for suitably extended periods of time. June explained to me that she had suffered in this way since some time not long after the age of thirteen – she was twenty-two years of age when she began therapy with me – and believed that the problem had to do with the fact that she could not dream.

When I pressed June further on this last point, she stated that each time she began to dream (or, more correctly, each time she *remembered* beginning to dream) she would 'see' an image – the same one each time – that would startle her out of her sleep. What was the image? Oddly enough, it was, she said, a chessboard, or at least part of one, since the whole image consisted of a pattern of dark- and light-coloured squares symmetrically laid out such that they followed one another. That was it. What could be so disturbing about a chessboard? June couldn't say. All she knew was that whenever she saw it, even when talking about it as she was with me, she would begin to feel anxious, scared, dizzy and on the verge of vomiting.

We talked more about June's experience of herself and her inability to sleep for a few sessions and then our weekly meetings settled into something approximating a psycho-analytic encounter in that she was encouraged to 'free associate' (or express her thoughts freely as they came to her) while I mainly listened, interjecting the occasional seemingly apt remark.

Finally, after a relatively brief number of sessions (less than twenty), June began to focus her associations on the image of the chessboard. We worked on this over the subsequent three weeks, but as she was clearly becoming increasingly frustrated in that her associations seemed to be leading her nowhere, I finally urged her just to stay 'tuned' to the image itself in silence and see what happened. She did so, and suddenly, after about ten minutes, her face registered a shocked reaction. She began

143

to cry and continued doing so for about a quarter of an hour, by which time I was desperate to know what she had seen. Finally, brushing aside her tears, she smiled and told me. In the course of her concentration on the image, June had realized that it was not a chessboard at all, but, rather, her family's basement floor which was covered by linoleum patterned with red and white squares. And suddenly she had remembered that a terrifying event had happened to her in that room when she had been thirteen. A male friend of her older brother had been there alone with her and had forced her to fellate him. She had never told anyone of the event and, indeed, had 'forgotten' it until now.

The next time I saw her, June informed me that she had had her first undisturbed sleep in years and had actually managed to dream a proper dream. Our sessions together ended and that was seemingly that.

Here, then, as far as I was concerned, was clear and straightforward evidence of unconscious processes being made conscious. June had *repressed* the event by allowing it only to express itself in consciousness in the disguised and innocuous image of a chessboard – an image that, nevertheless, provoked strong emotional and physical, if seemingly inexplicable, reactions.

But . . . the twist in the tale.

A few weeks following our last session together, June telephoned me and asked if I could see her. I agreed. Was there more repressed material to work through? Had the disturbances begun again? No, she was fine and sleeping well and had come to terms with the assault. But there was something she'd felt the need to tell me. What? 'Well,' June confessed, 'I hadn't *really* forgotten the event. I'd thought of it in a kind of detached way lots of times. But I just hadn't connected to it. It was kind of there and not there in my thoughts. It was like a thought that didn't belong to me.'

I remember June's words as clearly today as I did on the afternoon she first spoke them. They contained a message, an idea, that frightened me at first since its impact had important consequences for my unquestioning belief in the unconscious as

I'd come to understand it. I continued to believe in and employ this notion of the unconscious for a number of years, but I could not shake off the memory of June's statement, until, eventually, I allowed myself to accept that what she had told me applied as much to my own experiences of 'making the unconscious conscious' as it had to hers. For I too had experienced the same phenomenon. Whenever I had remembered a seemingly forgotten event, I'd felt, often immediately, that I'd known it all along. The revelatory material had not been hidden from me; rather, I had somehow *disowned* it by keeping it separate from my phenomenological meaning-world.

In some way, the 'I' who knew the material and the 'I' who defined my sense of who I was had become, seemingly, disassociated. It had only been my insistence on believing in the unconscious which had blocked this insight. But, if this were so, then the key to understanding how I could detach certain memories such that they seemed not to belong to me lay not in any notions of an unconscious but, rather, in consciousness itself.

This phenomenon of 'disowned thoughts and memories' has been shared by such a large number of subsequent clients that I have come to believe that it offers a significant alternative view to phenomena typically associated with the unconscious. Once again, let me stress that it does not call into question or doubt the experience of insight or 'connection' that is usually explained as repressed unconscious material being recalled. What it does question is the adequacy of that explanation. But if that explanation is judged inadequate, what more suitable alternative can be presented? I recently wrote a lengthy paper which attempted to provide a suitable alternative (Spinelli, 1993), but as it was aimed at a specialist audience and entered into detail that would require incursions into several issues outside the immediate focus of this part of the text, I will attempt to reframe some of the more pertinent points raised within it so that the main thrust of my argument will hopefully be both relatively clear and brief.

A. Pre-Psycho-Analytic Theories of the Unconscious

The unconscious was not a new term invented by Freud. It had been around and employed by a substantial number of philosophers, poets, scientists and medical doctors since the eighteenth century (Whyte, 1978). For instance, Henry Maudsley, the great British psychiatrist, wrote in 1867 (a good quarter-century before Freud's own research led him to posit the existence of the unconscious) that the 'most important part of mental action, the essential process on which thinking depends, is unconscious mental activity' (Maudsley, 1867, quoted in Whyte, 1978:162). But how was the unconscious defined by these pre-Freudian thinkers?

Broadly speaking, all who employed the term did so in order to assert the existence – based on their experience – of mental processes that lay outside, or beneath, immediate, or current, awareness. In other words, this view of the unconscious expressed the idea that as well as our conscious awareness there also existed mental activity that took place without our being aware of it. As such, broadly speaking, the unconscious was a term employed to represent all mental activity other than 'those discrete aspects or brief phases which enter awareness as they occur' (Whyte, 1978:21).

So, for example, while I might be consciously aware of the movement of my fingers on my notebook's keyboard and of the words that appear on the screen, this conscious awareness is but a minuscule part of all the other sensory stimuli that my brain interprets and which, in a sense, I am aware of at a non-conscious, or pre-Freudian 'unconscious', level. This view of the 'unconscious' is backed up by a good deal of modern experimental evidence from, among other subject areas, perception studies in psychology. So, for instance, psychologists have carried out tests employing a machine known as a tachistoscope which is capable of 'flashing' images at micro-second speeds such that their subjects are unable consciously to process and be aware of them. However, if they are then presented with an array of images, including the 'flashed', or target, image, they will be able to pick it out even if they cannot explain the reasoning for their choice. Studies such as these, as well as related studies on selective perception or attention, clearly demonstrate that non-conscious mental processing occurs (Spinelli, 1993).

But we can think of this early idea of the unconscious in another way. When we concentrate on, or *attend* to, something, we can only do so because we are 'selecting' it from all other possible 'somethings'. So I am only able to concentrate on my keyboard by *not* concentrating on the images and sounds coming from my street, or my sleeping cat on the armchair beside me, or the grumbling in my stomach, and so forth. In this way, we can see that what we are consciously aware of is but a minute selection of the sum total of possible things we *could be* consciously aware of. But these non-selected items don't just 'disappear'; we remain aware of them in a non-conscious manner.

This phenomenon reveals something else of tremendous importance: consciousness is a *relational* process. It requires both that which we focus on and that which we do not. In order for something to 'stand out' it needs all manner of 'other somethings which are not the focused-upon something' to stand out from. This idea is usually expressed by the term *figure/ ground*. While it is a term most commonly employed in object perception studies, its influence is far greater.

So, for instance, we can only name or describe something not only on the basis of what it is, or what features it possesses, but also by what it is not, or which features it does not possess. We can only name, or describe, ourselves as unique beings, for example, by implicitly or explicitly contrasting ourselves to all other potential selves (i.e. others). And, indeed, our statements only make sense, or are meaningful, because of this contrast. Saying that I am of Italian origin, for instance, is only meaningful if there exist examples of people who are not of Italian origin.

But 'others' can also be internal, or 'intra-psychic', contrasts. So if I say that I am feeling happy, this statement only makes sense because I can contrast my experience of 'being happy' to alternative, or 'non-happy', experiences.

So the pre-Freudian view of the unconscious referred to processes or experiences that, while not currently accessible to consciousness, could become so in a relatively direct fashion.

Equally, this view of the unconscious revealed an inseparable relationship between conscious awareness and unconscious awareness.

B.   The Psycho-Analytic Unconscious

It was Freud, of course, who would extend, if not subvert, this basic idea. While he accepted the inseparable relationship between the conscious and the unconscious, he argued for the existence of a barrier between them, such that that which was unconscious could not be accessed in a direct manner in most circumstances and only expressed itself in an indirect, disguised fashion. He accepted previous views to some extent by positing the idea of the *preconscious* – that is, thoughts, images, wishes, fantasies and so forth that were not currently conscious but could become so – but spoke of the *unconscious proper* as the 'residue' or 'store-house' of thoughts, images, wishes, fantasies, etc. that *could not become conscious* other than by concerted and courageous efforts usually brought about by the use of specific psycho-analytic techniques.

What was so problematic about the Freudian unconscious that it sought to prevent conscious access? The answer to this question lay in Freud's supposition that the unconscious was made up of unacceptable, disturbing, deeply frightening, irrational, even disgusting wishes and fantasies originating from our infancy and childhood which we could not (or, more accurately, would not) allow ourselves consciously to consider because of their unacceptable sexual (or erotic) and aggressive emotional and imaginal content. This material, he argued, had been *repressed*.

Repressed material can be most easily understood as material that we have somehow 'blanked out' from our conscious thoughts by convincing ourselves that it does not, or cannot, exist. And yet it does. And, more, it impinges on, or 'pushes at', our conscious thoughts, demanding our attention. As a result, a compromise of sorts occurs. The unconscious material is allowed expression but in a disguised fashion. We can think of it as material that has been 'censored' in some way so that it becomes consciously palatable or so obscurely expressed that its true meaning becomes vague, distorted, indecipherable.

But there is a psychic price to be paid for this compromise. We all know what it is like to try *not* to think of something. But imagine what it is like to try not to think of something that we have convinced ourselves we are not thinking of in the first place! The result is confusion, befuddlement, anxiety, a loss of control.

Freud's theory of the unconscious was revolutionary. It clearly pointed to, and seemed to explain, all manner of psychic imbalance and conflict. It appeared to clarify experiences we can all 'sense' in ourselves. So the issue it not that Freud pinpointed false or insignificant experiences – quite the opposite, in fact; rather, the question is: Is his explanation the most adequate one? Does it get closer than any other explanation to the lived experience we have of this process?

My view is that it does not.

Nevertheless, before I attempt to convince readers of the greater adequacy of my view, it remains important to acknowledge just how *powerful and fascinating* an idea the notion of the psycho-analytic unconscious is.

A major part of that fascination, of course, lies in the connected idea that, were we to bring to consciousness at least some of the repressed material that remains at the unconscious level, a great many of the mysteries, conflicts and oddities that we encounter in our daily thoughts and actions, oddities that taunt and mystify and disempower us, would be explained, and, through explanation, diminish or disappear altogether. In adopting Freud's early dictum, we come to believe that we suffer mainly from (unremembered) reminiscences.

It is all too easy to understand, even experience, the strength of this idea. 'I want to know my deepest secrets!' most of our clients exclaim. 'And you, the therapist, must help me to uncover them!' Such heartfelt pleas implicitly require the acceptance of the existence of a Freudian-derived unconscious. Or so it would seem. For, if not, what would it reveal to us about our clients? About ourselves? Essentially, that we are liars, that we deceive ourselves, that that which we say has been repressed is, always has been, available to us, and that what is mysterious is not some hidden content, not some missing pieces of the puzzle, but, rather, some mad mechanism that wishes us to *believe in* the existence of hidden and inaccessible material. Such a notion seems absurd, far more absurd than any notion of an unconscious containing repressed material. But is it?

C. Critiques of the Psycho-Analytic Unconscious

As appealing as the idea of the psycho-analytic unconscious may at first appear to be to practitioners and public alike, and as useful as it may be in our attempts to understand ourselves and others, there remain a number of serious problems with the concept. Several major philosophers such as Ludwig Wittgenstein (1982) and Jean-Paul Sartre (1956), for instance, have pointed out a number of logical problems with this idea on the basis that it is a *circular argument*, in that the evidence for the existence of the unconscious, as presented by psycho-analysts, always depends upon the a priori assumption that it exists. In other words, they argue, if during psycho-analysis material is presented which it is claimed was once unconscious, the basis for this claim relies upon the hypothesis of an unconscious, for how else could the material be recognized as once-unconscious material? Clearly, even if we accept the notion of the unconscious, it remains the case that, at best, all we ever directly confront is 'the unconscious made conscious' and never the unconscious itself. But, if this is the case, then we cannot say that the existence of the psycho-analytic unconscious has been proven.

Further, if it cannot be directly proven, how can we ever be certain that the unconscious *has been* made conscious? Could it not also be the case that what has been made conscious is yet one more defensive deception we play upon ourselves? There seems to be no way out of this dilemma. Who could say for certain that the unconscious has been exposed to consciousness?

As Betty Cannon has recently remarked with regard to this question:

> The conscious subject could not, since it has always been out of reach of consciousness. Nor could the complex recognize itself, since Freud tells us that it lacks understanding. Only a subject who both knows and does not know his or her own tendencies and desires could recognize what had previously been hidden. In fact, only such a subject would be able to 'resist' the analyst in bringing this material to light, since only such a subject would know that there is anything to resist or defend against (Cannon, 1991:36–7).

Pursuing this line of argument, Sartre raises concerns about the logical basis for the notion of *repression*, arguing that to repress material we must somehow know and not know it at the same time. While psycho-analysis would respond to this by arguing that while the unconscious knows the conscious mind does not, Sartre's position suggests that the question revolves around the issue of *self-deception*, which would suggest that this 'splitness' or dissonance is an issue to be examined and understood within *consciousness itself* rather than through hypotheses that rely on the notion of an unconscious.

Just as there are philosophical questions raised with regard to the psycho-analytic unconscious, so too is there the lack of any conclusive experimental evidence for either the existence of the psycho-analytic unconscious or for the notion of repression. With regard to the latter, for instance, Matthew Hugh Erdelyi, a cognitive psychologist who accepts the idea of the psycho-analytic unconscious, has critically considered the empirical evidence for repression and has concluded that while there exist numerous experimental studies whose data comply with the phenomena implied by repression (such as the rejection of selective information from consciousness), the mechanism itself remains open to doubt or to alternative theoretical explanations (Erdelyi, 1985).

Lastly, just as a number of important therapists who have been influenced by the writings of Sartre and Heidegger have

151

re-interpreted or rejected the psycho-analytic unconscious (for instance, the Swiss psychotherapist Medard Boss (Condrau, 1993)), so too is it the case, as has already been noted in Part 1 of this text, that there exist a number of therapeutic approaches the beneficial outcomes of which (at least as far as these can be measured) seem to be no less effective than those from psycho-analysis, even though they neither rely on nor make use of hypotheses concerning the unconscious.

Nevertheless, if there were no suitable alternative to the unconscious all these criticisms would be of little practical importance. After all, even if the theory is seen to be imperfect and problematic, as long as it remains the most adequate theory available in so far as it explains otherwise inexplicable phenomena, then better to work with it than reject it outright. But I think a more adequate and suitable explanation for the phenomena associated with the psycho-analytic unconscious *does* exist, and that while it allows a radical re-interpretation of the unconscious, not only does it more adequately attend to, or 'capture', the phenomenology of the experiences associated with the unconscious, it also offers insights that might be of significant general benefit to the practice of therapy.

D. Dissociated Consciousness

Perhaps ironically, Freud himself toyed with the essential idea of this alternative viewpoint. At a key moment of theoretical transition, Freud at first flirted with the notion of advocating the idea of a 'split' (or dual) consciousness (Smith, 1992). He rejected this view in favour of the idea of the unconscious, but a number of his contemporaries continued to explore this notion of *dissociated, or divided, consciousness*.

Among proponents of this alternative view, it was the French psychiatrist, therapist and the most important of Freud's early rivals, Pierre Janet, who first proposed the thesis that certain thoughts, memories, affects, and so forth (usually associated with a traumatic event) could be dissociated, or split off, from one's consciousness and continue to exist as a separate consciousness. Janet employed the term 'subconscious fixed ideas' to represent this secondary, if autonomous, consciousness, and argued that its manifestations included such phenomena as compulsive activities, hallucinations and hysteria (Ellenberger, 1971; Braude, 1991). It is important to note, however, that for Janet the concept of dissociation was solely a phenomenon of psychopathology.

This latter view has changed over time such that current theories of dissociation have turned Janet's original idea on its head in that, whereas Janet saw dissociation as a *failure* in one's capacity to maintain mental unity, contemporary theorists perceive it as a 'widespread human *capacity*, whose manifestations [range] from the normal to the pathological' (Braude, 1991:103). C. A. Ross, for instance, argues that 'dissociation is an ongoing dynamic process in the normal psyche', in that the ability to attend to information requires the ability to dissociate irrelevant sensory input from that which is relevant to one's focus of attention (Ross, 1989:87).

As such, dissociation is seen by researchers in the field as a capacity of the human species to 'split off' or compartmentalize 'volitions, knowledge, memories, dispositions, and sometimes even behavior' (Braude, 1991:97) which, nevertheless, remain 'potentially knowable, recoverable or capable of re-association' (Braude, 1991:98).

In addition, Stephen Braude, in critically discussing the research surrounding dissociation studies, has contributed significantly to the debate by reminding us that there is a subtle but important distinction to be made between 'believing one's state to be one's own and experiencing it as one's own' (Braude, 1991:71). This distinction points out the *epistemological* (i.e. knowledge- or belief-based) aspects and the *phenomenological* (i.e. experiential) aspects of self-awareness. While it is reasonable to suppose that in most cases this distinction is blurred, nevertheless, as examples from certain circumstances such as panic, sexual orgasm or meditation demonstrate, 'one's phenomenological sense of self can be quite vigorous and acute, even though the ordinarily well-developed epistemological sense of self is either non-existent or radically attenuated' (Braude, 1991:74–5).

Generally speaking, what this distinction makes plain is that examples of dissociation may be understood as instances where the usual links between knowledge- or belief-based awareness and experiential 'ownership' of that knowledge have been impaired or 'split off' from one another. This distinction might clarify many confounding examples from both 'everyday' and 'pathological' thought and behaviour where knowledge of something is somehow 'denied' one's experiential awareness.

For instance, in reconsidering the example presented at the start of this discussion, it might be seen that while June knew that sexual abuse had occurred, she had denied this knowledge to her experiential self-awareness. In this way, she succeeded in 'knowing it as if such knowledge belonged to someone else'.

What is implicit in this argument is that *the question of dissociation revolves around an individual's self-concept in that it supposes a dissonance between beliefs about one's self and the experience of one's self.* Bearing this, and the previous points on dissociation, in mind, an alternative theory to that of the psycho-analytic unconscious can now be presented.

An example of dissociated consciousness

Let me begin with an example taken from my therapeutic practice. One of my clients, Rebecca, was a woman who was continually being physically abused by her boyfriend. Although she steadfastedly asserted that she wanted to leave him, and indeed various realistic possibilities for such an act were available to her, nevertheless each week she would return to therapy still living with him.

If we were to take the viewpoint of psycho-analysis, we would be led to the hypothesis that unconscious wishes or demands lay *beneath or behind* Rebecca's stance and that, if these were to be 'made conscious', then she would be freed from their influence and act accordingly. The alternative view being suggested is that her contradictory stance (i.e. I must leave him and

I must stay with him) was meaningful *in itself*, requiring no recourse to unconscious motives for its understanding.

Rebecca's problem suggested that something of significance about herself and her stance in life was being expressed in that 'split' position. Further, its dual meaning could be explored at the conscious level by clarifying its opposing viewpoints so that they could be reflected upon rather than remain unreflected. In doing so, what emerged was the clarification that while Rebecca was deeply miserable in her situation, nevertheless remaining with her boyfriend provided her with something (such as security, status, the escape from loneliness) which, if no longer available to her, would have forced her to face these anxieties. On reflection, Rebecca saw that this latter circumstance had seemed clearly far less tolerable to her than that of continuing to live with the man who brutalized her.

What can be seen immediately is that what it took for Rebecca to make initial sense of her situation was not the uncovering of hidden or repressed (i.e. unconscious) material, but rather the willingness and courage to expose, explore and confront reflectively that which she had allowed to remain unreflected.

But there is much more to the matter. Again, the view being put forward would suggest that her stance revealed an additional 'split'. Through further clarification, it emerged that Rebecca held very fixed, sedimented beliefs about herself. In order to see herself as successful, fulfilled, happy, respectable or, more generally, 'good', she had to prove to herself and the world that she could both enter into and remain in a relationship. To have failed at either would destroy this self-concept and, generally speaking, reinforce the belief that she was 'bad'. Once again, this clarification adds further meaning to her inability to leave the relationship (for to do so would condemn her as a failure, a 'bad' person).

In this way, it might be seen that Rebecca's beliefs about herself (or who she had to be) were held to be of more significance than the awful circumstances she found herself in. Better to remain in some kind of relationship — no matter how abusive — than to be in no relationship at all. Better to be 'good' and suffer physical pain than 'bad' and racked with guilt. My client was split between the knowledge of the intolerability of being in the relationship and the intolerability of not being in the relationship.

Further still, Rebecca's stance could also be understood as an expression of 'disownership'. What she believed to be necessary (remaining in the relationship) forced her to disown the competing knowledge she had about what options lay before her. This was most often expressed in terms such as 'All my friends get beaten up by their husbands' or 'Why should I expect to be treated differently?' This is not to say that Rebecca's statements were necessarily untrue, only that they allowed her to maintain a position of stasis. But similarly, it can also be seen that her disownership was also at a more subtle, if no less significant, level in that it expressed the disownership of her own experience of herself as a woman who could make choices in order that she could maintain her sedimented beliefs about what is required in 'being a good woman'.

This leads us to one final point for consideration. In the course of our encounters, Rebecca admitted to experiencing thoughts, or carrying out actions, that were, somehow, not her own. What did these thoughts and actions express? Basically, they expressed a stance that rebelled against her sedimented belief about 'being a good woman' — a stance that Rebecca insisted she could not — did not — hold. This, then, is a further expression of dissociation. Rebecca experienced a 'split' in her self as well in that when she thought or acted in ways which *did not fit, or were alien to, aspects of her self-concept, such thoughts and actions could only be understood as being not hers nor of her making.* It was as if she had access to, or knowledge of, thoughts and actions that were someone else's, or which just seemed to exist on their own as if 'orphaned' from whoever had generated them.

It is important to be clear that the exploration of these various 'splits' may well have led (as it did, in fact) to the exposure of sedimented attitudes or world-views that Rebecca had held since childhood — but this process would require no need to impose a theoretical structure based on assumptions concerning her unconscious, or aspects of repressed material; whatever meanings or explanations she derived from her confrontation with the 'disownerships' in her life had always been available to her

— rather than repress them, she had, more accurately, avoided reflecting upon them for all manner of meaningful — if debilitating — reasons.

Dissociated consciousness: a summary

If we consider the points just raised in a more general manner, it can be understood that an alternative theory to that of the psycho-analytic unconscious stresses the idea of *consciously unreflected dissociation* rather than repression. In addition, this view argues that whatever the presenting conflict, its meaning lies in the conflict itself (rather than in what may be supposed to exist behind or beneath it) such that it is a direct expression of the conflict rather than a disguised or distorted expression of unconscious processes. Further, it suggests that the exploration of this meaning can be achieved through the clarification and challenging of conscious views and assumptions rather than by interpreting these as obscured 'eruptions' from the unconscious. Finally, it suggests that what has tended to be understood as the process of 'making the unconscious conscious' may be more adequately described as a movement 'from disownership towards ownership' in that it does not involve the uncovering of lost or forgotten material but, rather, the acknowledgement of thoughts, affects, memories and the like as not being somehow alien but, more properly, 'belonging to one's self'.

Put in another way, this view points to the possibility that many, if not all, such dissociations reveal that awareness at a phenomenological level has been somehow dissociated from the epistemological knowledge or beliefs contained in the awareness such that the experiences are not 'owned' or acknowledged as 'belonging to' the experiencer.

Having discussed the principal ideas contained in this alternative view, it becomes important to ask what are the differences between it and that of the psycho-analytic unconscious?

The psycho-analytic unconscious vs dissociated consciousness

Ernest Hilgard's text *Divided Consciousness* (1986) provides the basis for some important distinctions. First, there exist significant *metaphorical* differences in that where psycho-analytic theory suggests *horizontal* barriers between the conscious and the unconscious, wherein unconscious material is presented as though it were 'deeper' or 'residing beneath' consciously accessible material, the alternative view being presented suggests that those barriers are more accurately understood (metaphorically, at least) as being *vertical* 'splits' in consciousness. Secondly, a principal assumption of the psycho-analytic unconscious lies in the idea of an active mental defence principally inhibiting direct access and recall. The alternative model, on the other hand, avoids this idea and, instead, focuses on the phenomenological experience of accessible material as being somehow perceived as 'alien' in that it is recognized as something not belonging to one's own self-related experience. Thirdly, while communication with the psycho-analytic unconscious remains indirect in that the unconscious can only be inferred (through dreams, parapraxes, etc.) and its 'language' is distorted, symbolic, and primitive (primary process thinking), communication with dissociated conscious states, on the other hand, is direct (insofar as any first- or third-person communication can be direct) and requires no assumption of a secondary transformational language such as primary process thinking.

To these three distinctions made by Hilgard, I would add a fourth which is based on a point discussed earlier. That is, whereas the concept of the psycho-analytic unconscious requires the assumption that the meaning of a conflict-provoking event can only be discerned by exposing its hidden (i.e. unconscious) meaning through the therapist's theoretically derived interpretations, the alternate view being put forward requires no such assumption in that the meaning of the event is obtained through the descriptive clarification of the conscious event itself as lived and understood by the client.

Nevertheless, while this alternative approach questions the need to assume the existence of a psycho-analytic unconscious, it does not invalidate any of the consciously experienced phenomena that are said to originate from the unconscious. Even so, it remains to be asked whether the proposed alternative presents a *more adequate* position. Certainly, it avoids the logical inconsistencies of the unconscious as pointed out by its critics. Also, it is more parsimonious in that it requires far fewer assumptions than does the previous model, not least because it jettisons both the very notion of the unconscious as hypothesized by psycho-analysis and the subsidiary hypothesis of repression. On the other hand, some might argue that it does rest on the assumption of a *divided mind* – a problem that the psycho-analytic model does not necessarily impose (Gardner, 1993). But, on consideration, this view is not necessary to the suggested alternative either, since the argument being put forward can be seen to focus not so much on the idea of a divided mind, but rather on the *division in the interpreter's reflections.* This issue, it seems to me, more accurately reveals a problem of belief versus experience rather than being an issue concerned with the unified or partitive nature of the mind. The mind may well be unified even if the person experiences divided or conflicting reflections.

Pulling together the various arguments presented, I believe that I have provided an alternative to the notion of the unconscious that

1. Accommodates all the clinical observations associated with both early and psycho-analytic theories of the unconscious.
2. Accommodates all the experimental data provided by both critics and adherents of theories concerning the psycho-analytic unconscious.
3. Removes the logical inconsistencies and circularities associated with psycho-analytic theories of the unconscious.
4. Removes the necessity of imposing the hypothetical sub- (or super-) structure of an unconscious on consciousness.
5. Removes the tendency to impose a drive- or instinct-based metatheory and, instead
6. Retains its focus on relational issues.

7. Returns the focus of attention to consciousness itself, and
8. Allows for a more parsimonious, adequate, economic and non-deterministic account of psychic conflict.

Dissociated consciousness: the self

Nevertheless, in order to make a decisive case for the argument it must be asked whether there exists more powerful, and direct, evidence for its ideas than might be found for the prior model. I think that a good deal of independent collaborative evidence does exist, and I have discussed some of this evidence elsewhere (Spinelli, 1993). It would be too lengthy a digression for this text to focus on the various forms of evidence available from a wide range of studies, but, in essence, what all such studies point to is that the various forms of dissociation that have been studied – ranging from everyday selective attention to extreme dysfunctions and distortions in individuals' perceptual construction of their body-image (including what parts of one's body are perceived as belonging to an individual, and what the body looks like to, and how it is experienced by, an individual) – reveal a common dissonance factor.

This factor can be most clearly understood as an imposed 'splitness', or 'disownership' of certain experiences – both current and from one's past – on the basis that they do not 'belong to' or 'fit' the 'self' that we have defined ourselves as being. While these 'disowned' experiences are available to our conscious awareness, and can be recalled, nevertheless our awareness of them is from a distanced or alien perspective – we might think certain thoughts, or remember particular memories, but it is as though these belong to someone else and have little emotional impact on or meaningful significance for us. Alternatively, as I will discuss more fully in Part 5, these disowned thoughts may be so pressing that they temporarily 'swamp' the self we regard to be *our* self, and one or several other alien or competing 'selves' (to whom these alien thoughts belong) control or 'possess' us. For most readers, the most obvious examples of such phenomena that will spring to mind will be those that suggest 'split' or 'multiple' personality disorders in certain individuals. These are clearly extreme instances of the mechanism I am suggesting, but my argument is that something very much akin to this phenomenon is experienced by all of us – and, pertinently, is the source of the psycho-analytic theory of the unconscious.

When, for instance, one of my clients, Robert, suddenly 'connected' his current belief that 'instances of great success are always to be followed by a major disaster' with the memory of his father's constant 'put downs' of his childhood achievements, the connection made it possible for him to see that the main task he had made for himself of seeking out a life of limited joy, or neutrality, was an attempt both to express and resolve the conflict contained in his previously disconnected experience. While this insight might be understood in terms of unconscious mechanisms, an alternative viewpoint also emerges. Previous to his connection of phenomena, Robert had always spoken of his father only in the most positive of terms. Did he not feel *any* ill-will toward him? At first, Robert insisted that he did not. So did this mean that they had never argued? Well . . . yes and no. Whenever they *did* argue, Robert did not feel it to be *himself* who was doing the arguing; it was as though 'someone else' took over. And how did this 'someone else' view Robert's father? Oh, as 'a cantankerous, opinionated old bastard who was never satisfied with anything'. What can be seen in this admittedly highly abbreviated case example is precisely the process of dissociation discussed above. Robert 'disowned' those negative feelings that he had about his father. Yet they remained available to him in that rather than having been 'repressed' they had been alienated from Robert's self-awareness and had been 'attached', or made to belong, to an alien entity who sometimes 'possessed' Robert and spoke its – not Robert's – mind about its feelings for Robert's father. But this act of dissociation served a purpose for Robert – it allowed him to maintain or believe in a 'self' that only thought good things about his father. When Robert experienced his relationship with his father as 'good' he 'owned' that experience because it 'fitted' with the self that he believed himself to be. However, when Robert experienced his relationship with his father as 'bad', Robert could not 'own' this experience because it did not fit the self that he believed himself to be

– so the experience had to be disowned by Robert and be made part of the experience of an alien possessing entity.

As I will discuss in Part 5, the issue of dissociation has further significant and revelatory ramifications, all of which hold vital implications for our understanding of a variety of issues surrounding our concepts and experiences of our 'self'. For the moment, however, I will bring this discussion to its close, since I believe that it has served its primary purpose of demonstrating a viable, and more adequate, alternative perspective to the psycho-analytic concept of the unconscious.

By now, some readers may be left wondering: So what? What if a potentially better alternative to the idea of the psycho-analytic unconscious has been presented? Does that have any practical significance? As I will seek to demonstrate later in this section, I believe that it does have major implications both for what therapists perceive their function in the therapeutic encounter to be, and for the wider issue of power in the therapeutic relationship – particularly in the context of therapists' interpretations of either 'unconscious mechanisms' or 'disowned experience'. Before this discussion, however, our attention must first remain on the critical evaluation of further assumptions to be found within the psycho-analytic model – of which the next is that of the influence of the past.

3. THE INFLUENCE OF THE PAST

Perhaps the most widely accepted assumption in the psycho-analytic model (and in a great many other models, come to that) is that of *the past as a causal determinant of current states of both order and disorder in the client's intra-psychic life.* As such, for psycho-analytic therapists, the focus of therapy, at least initially, lies in a backward-moving process that seeks to uncover the causal origins of current client distress with the aim of making such origins clearer, or conscious, to the client. In this way, the hope is that either this awareness will reduce or remove the experientially restraining influence of the past or that it will allow a conscious acceptance of such factors and thereby return to the client a greater degree of control over them and, as a consequence, promote the development of greater flexibility of thought and behaviour.

While some psycho-analytic therapists talk in terms of 'ego-strengthening' as their main therapeutic focus, others concentrate on the 'object-relational' elements that have survived since infancy and which continue to impose unnecessary limitations on the client's current relations both with self and others. In either case, however, such factors are seen to have developed directly from past causes originating in the client's infancy and early childhood (Fine, 1979).

Although I think it would be absurd for me, or anyone else, to seek to argue that 'the past' has no bearing on an individual's current attitudes to life, it is, I believe, altogether quite a different matter to question the idea of the past as assumed and understood by the psycho-analytic model. For, clearly, the psycho-analytic past is conceived to be both *fixed* (that is, that there exists *a* past) and *linearly causal* (i.e. that current issues can be, in theory at least, traced back directly to past unresolved conflicts or traumatic interludes in the client's life). So prevalent are such notions of the past that it must be further acknowledged that many clients themselves hold to such assumptions and perceive the task of the therapist as being that of uncovering the issues and influences of 'their past' on their current lives so that the conflicts and concerns that have arisen from, or which have been aggravated by, the past can be at least partially resolved.

Both these points, I believe, are open to significant criticism which I will endeavour to address. Further, I will present alternative avenues of exploration which, I believe, considerably influence the therapeutic task and the nature of the therapeutic process.

A. *A Critique of Linear Causality*

Linear causality has come to be increasingly seen as the weaker of the two assumptions. Indeed, even as a general concept, it remains deeply problematic. For instance, even in controlled behavioural experiments dealing with various forms of *reinforcement* where variables are artificially manipulated so that an event appears to occur as a consequence of another, there has been a marked avoidance of imposing the notion of causality as an explanatory device. So, as a concrete example of the unwillingness to suggest causality, in the now famous studies demonstrating *positive reinforcement* within the controlled environment of a 'Skinner box', while it is the case that an animal may come to *associate* the pressing of a lever with the appearance of food, it is important to bear in mind that the associated events are not claimed to be causally related. For, after all, which event is 'cause' and which is 'effect'? Does the pressing of the lever 'cause' the food to appear? Or does the appearance of food 'cause' the pressing of the lever? Much to his credit, B. F. Skinner, the most famous advocate of modern behaviourism, studiedly avoided any causal implications in his behaviourally descriptive theory. What Skinner was willing to state was that a stimulus (a) was *associated* with a response (b) through some form of reinforcement. But what elements there may have been that 'led' the rat from a to b (or, possibly, from b to a) remained unknown 'black boxes' that were tied up in all manner of possible variables whose number, variations, degree of influence, and so forth could not be simply understood in terms of 'causality' (Skinner, 1953, 1971). As such, at best we can speak of *correlations*, or of predictive possibilities, but not of causal certainty. Indeed, even Freud, who, to some extent, might be regarded as a determinist who also incorporated notions of causality into his system, acknowledged a multi-causal position, and indeed his 'ultimate causes' (eros and thanatos drives) are so plastic in their defining boundaries that the search for intervening causes becomes deeply problematic.

This issue can perhaps be best understood when we take it away from the realm of psychology and psychotherapy and place it in another context, such as that of history. If we were to ask, for instance (as so many have already done), 'What caused the First World War?', we would find a multitude of competing causal possibilities ranging from the murder of the Archduke

Ferdinand in Sarajevo to the disastrous complexity of European railway timetables.

It is precisely because so many differing 'causes' can be provided to explain a given event that it has become increasingly recognized by most individuals (with the obvious exception of propagandists and a great many politicians) that thinking in terms of 'cause and effect', particularly in a linear or uni-directional manner, tells us very little and can be seen to be of minimal value to our understanding of human thought and behaviour.

As an extreme example that should make this conclusion obvious, consider the case of an individual who insists that the 'cause' of his current behaviour and manner of thought lies in the activities of the 'little green men' that hover over his head and 'make' him do and think what he does. Such a stance may strike most of us as being somewhat absurd since we may not believe in, or accept, his contention regarding the existence of 'little green men'. If we were to argue against this stance by pointing out that we could not see them, our believer might well clarify his view by informing us that they were there but had made themselves invisible to everyone other than himself and that, indeed, their invisibility had caused us to ask our question in the first place.

And so the argument would continue, becoming increasingly complex and circular. For, just as the thesis of 'little green men' would seem to explain everything, it would actually have little, if any, direct explanatory value *unless* we were to begin to clarify what the man's *belief in* the little green men and their powers over him might mean to him.

If we substitute the theory of 'the past as linear cause to our current circumstances' for that of 'little green men' we can see that both lead us into the same 'closed circle' of explanation. Both, after all, are hypothetical agents the existence of which is reliant on the belief in their influences. And, just as the believer in the little green men may be able to enter into a complex discourse regarding their behaviours, powers, appearance, and so forth, so too may that same analysis be carried out with regard to 'the past as cause to the present'. One position only *seems* more absurd than the other because we are generally more willing to believe in the idea of the 'causal past' rather than in 'little green men'.

It is seriously misleading to speak as if there were *one* cause of something as complex as a person's current experience or self-awareness. The assumption that there is tells us more about individuals' beliefs about who they are and how they have come to be than it does about any governing principle of causality. Equally, the belief in this assumption may have much to tell us not only about what is revealed or 'explained' about individuals through its adoption, but also about what it allows to be experientially obscured or 'disowned'.

Chaos theory and causality

It may be the case that part of our difficulty in questioning linear causality lies in the continuing dependence on nineteenth-century physics of many of our assumptions concerning human behaviour. The great success of nineteenth-century physics lies in its ability both to accurately describe and predict certain kinds of behaviour – such as that of the planets in orbit, the swings of pendulums, the motion of balls rolling along a surface – broadly speaking, those movements and behaviours that are orderly and regular. The geometry employed to represent these movements is in the form of linear equations that – to mathematicians at least – are far from complex and easily calculable.

As long as nineteenth-century physics was applied to these orderly and regular movements, its value was unquestionable. However, there exist all manner of other movements – such as the turbulence of water, or changes in the weather – the complexity of which is such that their orderliness and regularity is neither easily describable nor predictable. When the geometry of nineteenth-century physics was applied to these movements, its value was shown to be minimal. The linear equations that physics employed to study such movements were both limited and limiting in that they could only deal with small parts of these complex movements *and* sought to reduce these complex movements to the level of the fairly straightforward, regular movements that it had been so successful in describing.

In the 1960s, a new theory was proposed which sought to deal specifically with complex movements. This theory has become known as *Chaos Theory* (Gleick, 1988). Chaos theory concerns itself precisely with those movements or behaviours the complexity of which is such that they appear to be unpredictable. Further, even dramatic changes in movement of these systems (for instance, as I write this, I note that literally over the past fifteen minutes or so the weather has changed from sunshine to pouring rain, to sleet, and back to bright sunshine) seem to be dependent in a highly sensitive manner on alterations in conditions which are both numerous and subtle. Indeed, so numerous and subtle are they that linear equations have been shown to be both near-valueless and misleading. Chaos theory avoids linear equations and, instead, rests on a far more complex geometrical model known as Fractal geometry.

What is the point of this brief and highly simplified lesson in physics? We have tended to employ notions derived from nineteenth-century physics in order to understand and describe the general behaviour of human beings and to predict it. Our notions of linear causality are expressions of our attempts to predict through this model. But, as has been shown, the value of this model of physics is restricted to regular, ordered behaviour. Does this fit the behaviour of human beings?

Certainly, we would like to *think* so – and linear causality allows us to do so. But *are* we such simplistically ordered creatures? Consider the following example. Let us say that you decided to audio-tape a dinner-time conversation between yourself and a friend. If you were to play this back, you would likely be surprised to note how haphazard were the changes in topic, mood, and general directional ebb and flow of the conversation. Indeed, a transcript of the conversation would be much more 'chaotic' than expected in that it would reveal both the art and artifice in staged and televised encounters between characters.

Now if you and your friend had been asked 'How did your discussion move from topic A to topic B?' the chances are high that some manner of fairly simplistic linearly causal chain of events would be construed in order to explain the movement of the discussion. But the audio-taped record would likely reveal that, far from being so straightforward or linear, the change came about as a result of several factors, which were both obvious and subtle. In fact, it would be hard to argue that one specific factor determined the change; rather, it would make more sense to view the whole complex system and the innumerable and minute changes taking place within it as influencing these 'dramatic' (or noticeable) changes.

The conclusion here is that human beings are much more adequately understandable when placed within a 'chaos' model rather than within a 'linear' model. We may have some resistance to this, however, because, in acknowledging this fact, we would have to admit that changes and movements in our lives are far more haphazard and difficult to predict than we would like – or believe – them to be. With regard to the specific topic of linear causality, we would also have to acknowledge both its limitations and how it imposes a distorted and limited perspective on our experience of ourselves as changing beings.

If nineteenth-century models of causality allow us to maintain the belief that 'If A, then B', Chaos theory models of causality are more akin to the viewpoint expressed by the Algonquin Nation, which is 'If A, then . . . everything.'

As such, it seems very likely that notions of human behaviour which are dependent on linear causality are highly suspect. Nevertheless, during therapy, clients are likely explicitly or implicitly to adopt these notions in order to allow them to make sense of themselves and their relations with others. While it is vital for therapists to respect these causal constructions, their therapeutic value lies in what they reveal about clients' beliefs – *not* whether or not they have made accurate or inaccurate causal connections. The 'causality' we impose on our lives expresses what we believe to have been a necessary factor in our 'becoming as we are'. If psycho-analytic therapists persist in maintaining this questionable assumption, they will only impose limits and distortions both on their model and, more significantly, on the experience of their clients. Linearly causal perspectives *are* important – not because they reveal 'truths' about individuals' development, but rather because they reveal what individuals have come to believe themselves to be and how they explain their becoming.

On further consideration, it can be seen that assumptions of linear causality also rely on the view that *the past is fixed or constant*, in that it does not change either in character or in content. Is *this* contention any more feasible than the previous one?

B. A Critique of the Psycho-Analytic View of the Past

When one goes back to the original ideas presented on this topic, what we discover is that Freud himself reveals in his writings that he held a much more complex position regarding the nature of the past than he is usually given credit for. Indeed, a particularly pertinent paper by Freud entitled 'Constructions in analysis' (Freud, 1937b) has been discussed by Irvin Yalom, who provides the following summary:

> An analyst who is not successful in helping the patient to recollect the past should, Freud suggests, nonetheless give the patient a construction of the past as the analyst sees it. Freud believed that this construction would offer the same therapeutic benefit as would actual recollection of past material (Yalom, 1980:347).

As such, what Freud would seem to be suggesting is that whether the constructed past event is or is not historically 'real' or accurate does not matter; *what is important is the process of construction – not the content itself.* For through construction the client is able to forge meaningful links with a hypothetical past. This is a revolutionary stance for Freud to have taken. In doing so, he opened the way for us to understand our notions of the past as being essentially 'interpretative' rather than historically fixed or real. The past, seen in this light, becomes a 'plastic' or flexible concept open to re-evaluation and re-creation dependent on the current attitude and behaviour of the individual who experiences it.

Let us consider this shift in stance more closely. What is being argued is that we have far greater flexibility in constructing or interpreting the past than we might have previously thought possible. At this point, an example illustrating this contention might prove to be useful.

The fluidity of the past: an example

When I was ten years old, a teacher caught me playing with a pack of 'bubble gum cards' instead of doing the arithmetic exercise that she had set the class. In order to teach me a lesson on obedience, the teacher took the cards away from me and proceeded to rip them up before my eyes. I remember walking home that day in tears since the teacher's deed had destroyed something I held to be of great significance; my whole world had been seemingly irrevocably shattered by that incident. That day, and for several months subsequent to it, I hated that teacher and all she stood for. I saw in her the source of all that was unfair and wicked in the world, and though no adult, my parents included, could understand or accept the great degree of evil that was obviously contained in her act of ripping up my cards, I most certainly could. At the age of ten, the event had been a shattering cataclysm in my experience, one that would seemingly for ever ring in infamy and whose consequences, so I believed at the time, would remain to influence my life for ever.

Of course, looking at that incident today, some three and a half decades later, I experience nothing of the powerful emotions I felt then. Indeed, in the face of all the subsequent 'cataclysms' that have entered my life, the event seems more laughable than life-shattering. In many ways my whole stance towards the event, and the perpetrator of it, has changed dramatically. Indeed, for many years I even forgot the event and its seeming gravity and only 'chanced' upon it a few years back when I was searching for an example dealing with the plasticity of the past.

Now as we can see from this instance, it becomes clear that the remembered past is composed of two main variables: there is the content or story element of the past – what occurred – and there is as well the affective component, that is, the associated feelings and emotions, attitudes, and so forth which imbue the event with its specific meaning – in other words, how the event is experienced. Now it is clear that while I am able to recall the event with some degree of accuracy, and as such we can argue that the 'story' or content element of the past seems to have remained pretty much the same, my stance towards it, that is to say my relationship to it with regard to its emotional meaning and significance, has altered dramatically. Why is this so? Well, it is not simply because other, more 'cataclysmic' circumstances have overwhelmed that one into relative insignificance, but, more importantly, because I, as the person recalling the event, have changed over time, such that my attitude towards the significance of 'bubble gum cards' in my life has shifted greatly − so greatly in fact that the incident has attained a quite different meaning for me than that which it had when I was the ten-year-old child.

Equally, just as the 'bubble-gum card event' may have been presented by me at the age of ten as being a milestone in my life which stood at the forefront of my memory and to which I would likely have given centre stage in the recounting of my history, and, by implication, which I might well have employed as a means of presenting my identity, my sense of self, to both myself and others, today, given this same task of historical construction, I doubt very much that I would even mention it in passing − assuming that I felt it significant enough even to remember. What this point bears out is that *our reconstructed past is always a selective process* − we could not ever begin to recount all the events in our lives, much less their relational significance, simply because the task could never be completed. Indeed, in a way, the task could never truly even begin since just to initiate the description of the sum total of experience that occurred at the start of writing this sentence would take me well beyond my life, possibly even beyond a near-infinity of lives, to complete.

If this last point strikes some readers as a difficult notion to accept or comprehend, the following exercise should clarify things. Let us say that you are asked to write down all you experience at the moment you read the word 'Now!' At first, perhaps naively, you might say that little has occurred. But this seems so because a process of filtering incoming sensory data and interpreting such has occurred. As discussed in the previous section, psychologists tend to refer to this as 'selective attention' in that only a minuscule amount of incoming data is being consciously attended to. A useful, if far more simplistic analogy might be helpful here. Let us say that for some reason you decide to audio-tape an interview with someone else. When you play back the tape you might be highly surprised to hear recorded not only the interview itself but all manner of extraneous noises – such as the sound of cars going by, birds chirping, planes flying overhead, and so forth – noises that you had failed to hear during the interview session itself. The tape recorder picked them up because although it has a basic filtering system in that it picks up noises within its auditory range, this system is nowhere near as complex as that which our brain employs in order to focus on or attend to selected stimuli. Basically, then, at the conscious level, one picks up input stimuli that the brain is capable of picking up and which are deemed relevant to the task at hand (which in this case was conducting the interview). In the same way, the sensory-input material that you remember as being part of the 'now' that you focused on in the given exercise is only a small part of the full range of material that your brain attended to in that instant of time. As such, it is entirely feasible that if we were to have total access to the full range of sensorily available material at the moment of our exercise, it would be so much that we might never hope to record it all.

What are the implications of this with regard to the notion of the past? Clearly, the remembered past also makes up an infinitely small number of sensorily derived events that our brain has picked up over the course of our lives. Further, even within the remembered events themselves, what is consciously recalled is itself a minute selection of all the data contained within that remembered event. As such, we are left with the conclusion that the past – even at the level of its 'content' – is itself a selective interpretation of the complete past content that makes up that memory.

If we think about this further, we are likely to recognize that in a good many instances of remembered events our focus point of recall may well shift significantly such that where once, as in the 'bubble gum card' example, my main focus on the event might have been the images on the cards that my teacher ripped up, in another instance in time the focus might have shifted to the features of the teacher, or on to the title of the mathematical exercise book that I should have been concentrating on, or on the clothes I wore that day, and so forth. In each case, then, *it is not the same past event that I recall.* While in a general sense the basic outline of the story remains the same, in its focused-on details it is a different event that is being created.

The pivotal element, of course, is the very being who recalls the event in question, both in the manner in which the event is related and in terms of the focus points that are emphasized, or which emerge in the reconstruction of the memory. The past, then, can be seen as plastic and open to interpretation in our current life make-up. While it may be the case that we can recall with seeming accuracy any number of past events, even those from the very earliest parts of our lives, the important element determining both what is recalled and how it is recalled is *the being* who recalls.

The past as currently lived and future-directed

This conclusion is crucial to a more adequate understanding of the past for, as it underlines, both the content and meaning of any remembered past event hinge on the current view that the remembering being holds about himself or herself. In this way, it can be seen that rather than influence or 'cause' our current thought and behaviour, the remembered past *reflects the current views we hold about ourselves.* That is to say, our interpretations of the past serve to validate our current understanding of ourselves. We 'manipulate' the past, shape and reshape it, so that it 'fits' who we believe ourselves to be (or who we believe we must/must not, can/cannot be). The past is so tied to the present that it is more accurate to speak of 'the currently lived past' than of the past itself. For, as Freud himself seems to have understood and implied in some of his writings, the past and present are meaningfully associated with, and reinforce, one another, not because of any inherent causally fixed relations but because the being who interprets both the past and the present, and their relationship to one another, is quite literally 'substantiated' (or made real) through those interpretations.

All of us, then, invoke interpretations of the past in order to define who it is that we believe ourselves to be today, and in order to validate our beliefs we further claim that this interpreted past is the causal influence on who and how and why we are (as we experience ourselves to be).

As if this were not complicated enough, further consideration allows us to recognize that as well as the relationship between the interpreted past and the interpreted present, there is also the important matter of the role of *the imagined or desired future* to take into account. For, just as one's current sense of self is validated through the interpreted past, so too does one's self-image contain within it assumptions, goals, purposes and wishes that are directed toward one's future. If the interpreted present 'tells a story' the content of which is the interpreted past, then it is also the case that the story contains elements of intent or purpose which are focused on the future.

Broadly speaking, then, any interpreted past event can be seen to be a means of defining both who one currently believes oneself to be as well as who one might wish to become at some future point in time.

If I return to my remembered 'bubble gum incident', I can ask myself 'What does this remembered event have to say to me about who I believe myself to be now?' Perhaps it expresses my current concerns about power and authority and their potentials for abuse. Perhaps, as well, it seeks to express my concerns about myself as a figure now potentially far more like the teacher in the remembered event than the child of ten. Whatever the case, it can also be seen that the remembered event also expresses something to me about my desired future goals or aspirations or direction in life. 'Look,' it might say, 'now that you've gained some power and authority, however relative, how are you going to employ them? What do you want to do with them?' Or it might reveal some ethically based aspirations. 'Do you want to become like that teacher? No? Then what have you to attend to?'

But let me take the argument further by extending the example. Around two years ago, I learned that the self-same bubble gum cards that my teacher destroyed have now become highly sought-after collectors' items whose worth runs to thousands of dollars in the American bubble-gum card collecting world. What has this new information done to my remembered event? Firstly, it has given it a new form of import. 'If that blasted teacher hadn't destroyed those cards,' I tell myself, 'I might still have saved them to this day, and I would be able to make a substantial amount of money that would allow me to entertain thoughts of the kind of holiday that, given my present financial conditions, I could not otherwise contemplate.'

As such, the remembered incident now has a totally new focus from any I might have had up until the time when this new information became known to me. Not only have I reassessed the incident, I have basically constructed quite a different meaningful past which once again has much more to say about who I believe myself to be today, and the aspirations, goals, and ambitions that I hold for the future, than it does about any linearly causal process initiated by an 'originating' event.

Any remembered past event, then, can be understood to be a crucial indicator not only of one's currently interpreted self, but also of the future-directed aims and purposes that that current self embodies. As such, it is far more adequate to see the past as *the past as currently lived and future-directed* than to conceive of the past as a fixed and unchanging event-laden moment in time.

Therapeutic implications

What implications do these various points have for dealing with accounts of the remembered past in a therapeutic situation?

Clearly, we are faced once more with the realization that the remembered past is not merely, or even principally, concerned with the past per se, but rather is an important means of presenting one's current view of oneself as well as one's view of the being that one imagines one will be (or would like to be, or would like to avoid becoming) at a future point in time.

Equally, this view allows us to understand that the past does not stand in a linearly causal relation to the being we are today, but, rather, informs both therapists and clients as to the current beliefs that clients hold about themselves in the present instance.

175

In this way, therapists can better understand that if there is a 'fixedness' in their clients' remembrances of the past, it is not a fixedness that is about prior events but rather is the means by which clients' current needs to believe that certain characteristics of their self-image have been 'fixed' can be 'proven' correct.

So, for example, if I insist to myself that I can only be a being who cannot learn to do mathematics, then I *require* the existence of past events such as 'the bubble-gum card incident' in order both to confirm my sense of self as one who cannot learn mathematics, and to 'fix' that belief so firmly in that self-construct that it does not readily lend itself to challenge or to re-appraisal. *It is not the past event which has imposed this stance on me; rather, it is my stance about who I believe myself to be which imposes a fixed past memory of the event.*

But what of instances when the past remains impervious to recall? What if, as is not unusual, a client perceives the problem to be that a forgotten past event must somehow hold the key to his or her current conflicts? How is such an event to be understood in the light of what has been argued?

Once again, it is important to recall Freud's own view on this. He tells his followers that finding the actual past event is of far less import than constructing a probable past that the client can accept and, in this way, begin to make sense of his or her current situation (Freud, 1937b). In other words, the therapist's task is not to reconstruct a real, or objective, past, but to allow the client to find a past that 'fits', or makes meaningful, currently lived experience. In this sense, it can be seen that the client's problem is not truly about an unremembered past, but, rather, that the client cannot make sense of issues or conflicts within the current beliefs relevant to his or her present self-construct.

I am in agreement with Freud's analysis, but I also hold deep reservations about his suggestion that the therapist should construct a plausible past event. For this latter decision bestows on the therapist significant, and potentially destructive, powers. What right does a therapist have to impose a past, no matter how plausible, on a client? Unfortunately, many therapists continue to think that they *do* have this right – and the consequences of such arrogance have become increasingly obvious of late as in those instances where the most extreme 'true believers' of 'repressed memory syndrome' appear to have manipulated and persuaded clients of the 'reality' of past traumatic experiences that, upon investigation, appear to have no historical basis.

But, putting aside the ethical issues raised by this, even from a practical, or therapeutic, standpoint, it can be demonstrated that it is far from necessary for the therapist to take such actions. The following example should make this clear.

A client of mine, Alexander, was convinced that his inability to decide whether or not to risk accepting a more challenging, but also more risky, new job had to be linked to an unremembered past event, or series of events, and that if he could but make this conscious, then he would know what the source of his current conflict was and be able to resolve it. Instead of trying to uncover the supposedly forgotten material, I asked Alexander to explore and clarify for himself what it would mean to him either to take the new job or to remain in his current one. In this way, over time, he was able to confront and challenge his beliefs about the sort of person that each job seemed to define for him and consider that in the light of both the person he currently thought he was (or that he believed others saw him as being) and the person he would like to be, and how each job allowed or prevented these aspirations. In doing so, Alexander was able to note and assess not only the gains and losses in his life which each possibility might provoke, but also, and more significantly, he was able to give voice to fears he currently held about how either of these options would force a change in his current self-construct. Alexander's inability to decide, as well as his inability to find the hidden past, were expressions of a meaningful, if unattended, alternative option: namely, that so long as he could remain undecided he would also remain 'himself', or as he was. Alexander was faced with the fear of 'losing himself', and saw that if he were to act upon either option that feared event would become reality. Considered in this light, we can see that his inability to remember an assumed key event was a direct expression of a current conflict concerning his self-construct. To have 'found' that unremembered material, or to have constructed it, as Freud suggested, might have enabled

Alexander to decide whether or not to change his job, but it might also have provoked far more serious psychic conflicts since the issue of whether or not he was prepared to reconstruct his self on the basis of his decision would not have been properly addressed.

As we have seen, then, while there is clearly an importance to be attached to the examination of clients' past experiences, that importance has little to do with the discovery and acknowledgement of past causes as direct sources of their present state. Rather, this examination provides the means to explore what is being expressed about clients' current experiences of, and beliefs about, their present self-construct and its meaning with regard to their future goals and aspirations.

The past is a creation – an important one, to be sure – as it is a vital means of establishing those qualities that make us who we believe ourselves to be, but it is far from the causal source point of such qualities and, in itself, neither holds 'the' truth nor is a fixed point in one's life.

Such conclusions have important implications for the therapeutic process, not least because, as I have stated earlier, many clients believe that the examination of the past is a worthwhile, even necessary, process in the therapeutic relationship. As therapists, we must respect such beliefs and accept that it is important for the client to believe in them – just as it would be necessary, I believe, to accept a client's beliefs in 'little green men'. *In a general sense, it is essential for the therapist to believe that the client believes in such; the only dangers that arise occur when the therapist believes in such assumptions as 'real' truths.* In other words, if the client believes in the past as causal agent, then the therapist must accept that belief system and work with it in order to ascertain both its meaning to the client and its importance in providing the client with a sense of his or her own current self-construct – so long as the therapist understands that what he or she is exploring with the client is a deeply held belief and not necessarily anything other than that.

Taking the stance of becoming the 'discoverers' or 'creators' of clients' pasts prevents therapists from truly listening as adequately as they can to them and, in the course of such, both hampering what therapeutic possibilities may lie in the process and, worse, creating the conditions for theory-led misuse.

4. TRANSFERENCE AND COUNTER-TRANSFERENCE

The related hypotheses of *transference and counter-transference* have been seen by psycho-analytic therapists from Freud himself onwards as necessary consequences of the therapeutic relationship which must be 'worked through' in order for therapy to be both successful and brought to its termination. So prevalent have these notions become that many therapists allied to other models of therapy have either explicitly or implicitly accepted and employed them in their own practice. On the other hand, some therapists have expressed on-going concerns both about the validity of these hypotheses and of their effects on the therapeutic relationship (e.g. Shlien, 1984; Smith, 1991). Ian Owen, for instance, has recently argued that transference and counter-transference provide the means for therapists to disown the real and conscious aspects of the therapeutic relationship. In addition, he has suggested that both terms are allusions to a metaphor that seeks to explain how people misperceive and treat one another and act in an immature and inflexible manner similar to that of a child (Owen, 1993a).

A. Defining Transference and Counter-transference

Freud's original conception of transference and counter-transference posited that both were based on unconscious wishes emanating either from the client (transference) or from the therapist (counter-transference) the meanings of which could only be deduced by psycho-analytic theory.

Transference

When he first introduced the notion of transference in 1895, Freud tried to express the idea that transference was a disruption

. in the relationship between therapist and client brought about by the client's ' "false connection" between the idea appropriate to some past, extra-therapeutic situation and the analyst' (Smith, 1991:26). In this sense, transference was a hypothetical process whereby various emotions and attitudinal reactions from the client's past intruded on the present therapeutic relationship.

Initially, Freud felt that transference interfered with the therapeutic process and had to be removed (Holmes and Lindley, 1989). Over time, however, he changed this view and argued that 'transference contains in a living form the very difficulties in relationships that contributed to the neurosis. He saw too that, alongside positive transference, there are also negative feelings towards the therapist that are equally important to analyse' (Holmes and Lindley, 1989:127).

In its modern-day usage, *transference* has been generally defined as something said to be displaced, projected or transferred on to another from one's past 'prototypes' and includes treating another, particularly the therapist, as one's mother, father, brother or sister. *Counter-transference*, on the other hand, has been defined as any disruption of the therapist's constant attentive attitude and, rather than being restricted to the therapist's unconscious wishes alone (as Freud had originally maintained), has been extended as a term to mean the whole of the analyst's unconscious reactions to the individual analysand – especially to the analysand's own transference (LaPlanche and Pontalis, 1985).

Translated into more readily understandable language, transference refers to an unconscious process in which the client projects on to the therapist both positive and negative qualities belonging to another significant person in the client's life and behaves towards the therapist as if he or she was that person (Shlien, 1984). Transference is generally viewed by psychoanalytic therapists as a necessary 'ingredient' of the profound therapeutic relationship that has been formed.

The importance of transference for psycho-analytic therapists (and, very likely, for a great many other therapists) should not be underestimated. As David L. Smith has argued, it 'is at the very heart of psycho-analytic theory and technique. It is almost universally regarded – within the profession – as an indispensable concept for understanding the analytic process . . . and the analysis of transference is believed to be the most important component of analytic technique' (Smith, 1991:25).

Both the therapist's and the client's feelings of *incongruity* in the relationship are often taken to be the first clue that transference has occurred. Once the meaning of the transference has been deciphered, the therapist can employ the therapeutic relationship to challenge the client's fixed negative interpretations of early experiences by fostering more positive and accepting ones through the transference bond that has come into being. Following this, the therapist can begin to reflect the patterns of behaviour from which the transference originates back to the client so that the insight to analyse and change behaviour is made available.

In this way, it can be seen that the popular view of transference as that of the experience of 'clients falling in love with their therapists' is a serious trivialization of the concept. The theory of transference argues that the currently experienced feelings, thoughts, and behaviours that the client directs toward the therapist 'may be unconsciously influenced, coloured, and distorted by earlier childhood experiences, especially those with parents' (Holmes and Lindley, 1989:116).

Counter-transference

As some readers might have already surmised, *counter-transference* can be understood as a complementary concept to that of transference in that the term seeks to express the idea that during the therapeutic relationship the therapist's feelings, thoughts and behaviours towards the client may also be influenced by unconscious wishes and fantasies originating from the therapist's childhood which now impinge on and distort the therapeutic relationship. However, the concept of counter-transference has also been broadened and generalized to include the therapist's 'blind spots' – or conscious emotional responses – towards the client. In becoming aware of the influence of each of these distortions, psycho-analytic therapists believe that they can be put to good use in aiding them in their understanding of their clients since this awareness allows them to remain sensitive yet neutral towards them (Holmes and Lindley, 1989; Smith, 1991).

General views of counter-transference suggest that it can be distinguished as either *neurotic or non-neurotic* (Holmes and Lindley, 1989). Neurotic counter-transference is initially unconscious, and allows the therapist's personal psychic disturbances to be expressed in various ways, including rivalry and competition with the client, idealized identification with the client, experiencing inexplicable anger or sexual attraction towards a client, and so forth. Non-neurotic counter-transference refers to the therapist's experience of overwhelming empathy (or deep entry into the psychic world of the client) so that the therapist feels or behaves in ways that are foreign to him or her but which accurately reflect, or 'capture', the client's conscious and unconscious experience (Holmes and Lindley, 1989).

Counter-transference makes it evident that the therapeutic relationship can be highly emotionally laden and that therapists must be sufficiently self-aware in order both to note their unnecessary contributions to this and not to be overwhelmed by them so that they may become helpful, rather than debilitating to the client. Counter-transference is viewed as always difficult to deal with, and some psycho-analytic therapists have gone so far as to suggest that a therapist's confrontation with his or her counter-transference is an heroic act since it demands a willing exposure to his or her unruly (even dangerous) unconscious impulses (Strachey, 1934).

Finally, some analysts have argued that both transference and counter-transference are likely to occur in all relationships that become involved, intimate or intense – regardless of whether or not they are desired (Balint and Balint, 1939; Sharpe, 1947).

B. Critiques of Transference and Counter-transference

Although both transference and counter-transference have become generally accepted by a great many therapists, regardless of the model they have allied themselves to, a number of important problems remain concerning these concepts which need to be addressed.

General critiques

Firstly, with regard to transference in particular, it is important to be clear that Freud originally employed the term as a hypothetical unconscious process designed to explain why it was that clients became emotionally aroused by their therapists. As such, he was making an explicit distinction between the observed phenomenon (i.e. the client's emotional arousal) and the hypothetical cause (i.e. transference). But many therapists today seem to have missed this point such that transference appears to have become the equivalent of the observed phenomenon and a confusion, or blurring, of phenomenon and hypothesis has occurred (Smith, 1991). As such, it is necessary to clarify that transference is not 'proven' by the appearance of certain phenomena, only that these phenomena have been connected to, or correlated with, the transference hypothesis.

Secondly, it is necessary to bear in mind that the first hypotheses concerning transference related to its *positive* expression alone. But when Freud began to encounter negative reactions to his words, he saw in these the basis of what he subsequently hypothesized as being *negative* transference. However, his sole basis for arguing the existence of the latter was the evidence of the former and, similarly, it was on the basis of the existence of these latter that Freud claimed the proven basis of the former! If readers conclude that this would seem to be a decidedly strange, and suspiciously circular, argument, they would be right!

Thirdly, transference is commonly understood to be related to, or deal with, clients' inappropriate emotional responses. But this viewpoint assumes that inappropriate emotional responses can be easily distinguished from appropriate ones – an assumption that even some psycho-analysts have questioned. Among them, Louis Chertok has concluded that, while transference is a relevant principle, no current acceptable means exist for distinguishing the responses associated with it from non-transferential responses (Chertok, 1968). So, for instance, when as a trainee I expressed disdain at my therapist's interpretation that I was resisting him because of unresolved conflicts with my father, was this (as he believed) transferential disdain or (as I believed) accurately directed disdain?

In a similar fashion, Otto Fenichel wrote in 1941: 'Not everything is transference that is experienced by the patient . . . If the analysis appears to make no progress, the patient has, in my opinion, the right to be angry, and his anger need not be a transference from childhood – or rather, we will not succeed in demonstrating the transference component in it' (Fenichel, 1941:95).

Fourthly, as D. W. Winnicott observed, the therapeutic relationship places a great deal of strain on therapists, requiring them to avoid attempting to gratify clients' expressed desires towards them and to maintain a professional stance. But one way in which therapists can alleviate this strain is by interpreting these desires as instances of transference (Winnicott, 1965:72). In this way, the invocation of transference may be self-serving to therapists rather than therapeutic for clients.

Shlien's critiques

The above concerns have provoked a number of therapists to raise serious questions about the whole notion of transference. In his important paper 'A countertheory of transference', the person-centred therapist John M. Shlien presented the argument that '[t]ransference is a fiction, invented and maintained by the therapist to protect himself from the consequences of his own behaviour' (Shlien, 1984:153).

At first, this conclusion may strike many readers, especially those who are also therapists, as being somewhat over the top. But if there is any basis to Shlien's assessment (and the quote from D. W. Winnicott given above would suggest that there is), just how *might* the hypothesis of transference serve to protect the therapist?

As an (admittedly extreme, but illuminating) example of how psycho-analytic therapists have employed the hypothesis of transference to protect themselves (or, alternatively, to make fools of themselves), readers might do well to consider the following account taken from Janet Malcolm's *In the Freud Archives* (1984).

An analyst treated an elderly female client during the years before her death. When she died, the client's will revealed that she had altered it so that, in gratitude for the analyst's help, he had been bequeathed a substantial amount of money. Concerned about the ethical issues raised by this, the analyst informed the client's lawyer that he could not accept the money and expressed his desire to have it either returned to the other beneficiaries or donated to charities. However, the husband of a relative of the deceased, whose legacy had been negatively affected by the change of will, and who also, himself, happened to be an analyst, formally objected to the probation of the will and argued that the elderly lady's analyst had exercised undue influence on her through the 'unconscious utilization of the transference' (Malcolm, 1984:73). Having become embroiled in these legal manoeuvres, the lady's analyst now began to experience acute and disturbing embarrassment, and, in dealing with it, 're-interpreted' his client's gesture of gratefulness and affection as 'an expression of her hatred of him – an expression of the negative transference that had never been allowed to emerge during treatment' (Malcolm, 1984:73)!

The absurdity of this situation should not obscure its significance. In order to deal with unpleasant circumstances, both analysts invoked the hypothesis of transference (both positive and negative). But is this invocation not significant evidence for Shlien's contention?

Shlien suggests that what transference may actually be pointing to is the imbalance of power in the therapeutic relationship. For, through its use, the therapist alone becomes the person in the relationship who is able to declare which emotional responses are appropriate and which are inappropriate.

Further, he declares, if the clients found themselves to be in contact for probably the first time in their adult lives with a figure of authority (i.e. the therapist) who expressed respect, concern, and care towards them and who took the time to listen to their life-stories and treat such as being both meaningful and significant, is it *so* surprising that they should experience gratitude, deep trust, affection, love and fear of separation towards that person? And, in the same way, if the clients had come to believe that that figure of authority had offered respect and interest but, in fact, had betrayed them by not believing their accounts, or siding with other versions of the accounts, or misinterpreting them, would it equally be surprising if they responded angrily or violently towards the therapist?

But by invoking terms such as positive or negative transference, therapists are able to distance or exculpate themselves from such criticisms. When one adds to this the fact that, just as nearly all the early therapists were men, so too were the great majority of their clients women, it becomes possible to consider that the reliance on transference may also have served the dual purpose of diluting the 'sexually charged' atmosphere of the sessions and protecting the therapists from accusations of sexual improprieties by their critics as well as serving as a useful means of reining in any 'unprofessional' thoughts or responses they themselves may have had.

Placed in this perspective, it becomes sensible to consider whether there exists a 'climate' *within the psycho-analytic process itself* which might impose on the client various conditions and responses that can then be 'explained' in terms of the transference phenomenon. Perhaps, as one critic has put it, '[t]ransference develops in consequence of the conditions of the analytic situation and the analytic technique' (Waelder, 1956: quoted in Shlien, 1984:165).

When we consider the later addition of the notion of counter-transference, we are presented with a problem concerning transference which psycho-analytic therapists seem to have left unconsidered. For the very ability to *recognize* transference rests on the assumption that the therapist is a kind of 'blank screen' to the clients' expressions of emotional experience. But the hypothesis of counter-transference no longer allows therapists to view themselves in this way. So, once again, how can therapists be certain that their awareness of transference is not, conversely, a misconstrued instance of counter-transference?

Considered in this light, the following statement by Shlien deserves serious attention:

Over many years, I have been perceived in many different ways. Humble and proud, kind and cruel, loyal and unreliable, ugly and handsome, cowardly and brave, to name a few wide-ranging contradictions. Someone must be mistaken? No, they are all true. This sense of my self ... makes me hesitate before characterising someone's perception as distortion (Shlien, 1984:169).

Again, as Shlien argues, 'transference is a shorthand term for qualities and characteristics of human interaction. Any shorthand will fail to represent the particulars of a unique relationship. Rather, the shorthand will obscure (in a somewhat comforting way, to be sure) the realities of the relationship' (Shlien, 1984:170).

Shlien suggests that the psycho-analytic therapeutic process (in the same way as other therapeutic processes) not only permits but encourages 'intimacy, privacy, trust, frequent contact, revelation of precious secrets' (Shlien, 1984:171). In this way both the content of the revelations and the process of revealing is a form of erotic, or erotically charged, activity. Similarly, Shlien argues, the therapist's attempts to understand, or 'enter into', the client's world-view is a form of 'love-making', whether or not the therapist intends it to be such. Just as misunderstanding can be seen as a form of 'hate-making'.

Understanding, or being understood, or feeling that one is understood affects us all in psychological and physiological ways. The sensations *originate* in the situation and through the encounter when it is experienced as being benevolent. It is not transferred or inappropriate. In the same way, experiencing the fact that someone else experiences you as having understood them also generates affects and physiological events that are a direct consequence of this real, immediate encounter (Shlien, 1984:172).

Considered in its totality, Shlien's argument reveals a fundamental illogical assumption in the hypotheses of transference and counter-transference. Both, ultimately, rest on the view that

> any response that duplicates a prior similar response is necessarily replicating it. But similar responses are not always repetitions. They appear to us to be repetitions because, in our effort to comprehend, we look for patterns, try to generalize. There is breathing as a general respiratory pattern, but my most recent breath is not taken because of the previous one: rather for the same reason the previous breath was taken (Shlien, 1984:174).

This last point, it seems to me, is of vital importance. For what Shlien is pointing out (to rephrase his analogy) is that each breath we take, while duplicating in significant ways previous breaths, has its rationale (its meaning, if you will) in its *current* situation. In a similar fashion, the emotional reactions of the client, or of the therapist, while in the therapeutic encounter, may have resonances with past relations, but are meaningful (or 'of') this current encounter. As such, to see them solely as transferential or counter-transferential is, at best, limiting their significance (if not deeply distorting it) because *the meaning of the emotional reaction within the current encounter is being either minimized or obscured simply by imposing the terms transference or counter-transference on it.*

C. Re-interpreting Transference and Counter-transference

It seems to me to be evident from the various points just discussed that a Freudian-derived view of transference and counter-transference cannot distinguish examples of these hypotheses from their non-examples. Even among those who accept these hypotheses, and who argue that they become apparent to therapists through their personal experiences of training analysis, there exist numerous disagreements both at the level of identification of instances of either and at the level of what these instances might mean. These disagreements suggest that the notions of transference and counter-transference reveal entrenched positions (or sedimented perspectives) taken by many therapists which may actually hinder their understanding of their clients, of themselves, and of significant facets of the therapeutic relationship. While therapists may be prepared to qualify and correct the meanings of these hypotheses, they seem to be unwilling or unable to question the basic concept itself. And yet, serious questions are there to be raised. How, then, might one continue to accept and respect the phenomena that are associated with these hypotheses without relying on the hypotheses themselves?

I would suggest that rather than pursue the unsuccessful routes discussed above, therapists might consider that *all encounters always contain elements of transference and counter-transference* in that every encounter expresses similarities or resonances with previous experiences in our lives.

Within the psycho-analytic model itself, there is some partial agreement with this view. Melanie Klein, for example, theorized that transference should be viewed as a component of every act and encounter in a client's life and should not be viewed as a singular outcome of the therapeutic process (Klein, 1952). However, Klein's stance creates more problems than it resolves since she advocates this interpretation of transference in order to validate her own 'brand' of psycho-analysis which hypothesizes a number of innate, fundamental 'unconscious phantasies' which originate during the earliest part of human life and which deal primarily with issues of sexuality, destruction and reparation which the therapist must interpret from the client's conscious statements.

The following example, summarized by David L. Smith from the work of the Kleinian therapist Hanna Segal, should clarify this idea:

Segal recounts how a candidate opened the first session of his training analysis with the announcement that he wished to obtain a psychoanalytic qualification as rapidly as possible. He then went on to mention some digestive troubles that he had been experiencing and then, in a different connection, mentioned cows. Segal promptly interpreted this, informing her analyzand that the cow represented her analyst, and that he wanted to empty her greedily of her 'analysis-milk' in the minimum time possible (Smith, 1991:44).

This is fascinating as an interpretation, but it is also seriously flawed in that it requires an act of faith for anyone to accept its validity. For, as Smith points out, the basis from which the transferential interpretations are made rests on the prior assumption of unconscious fantasies. But these, in turn, are assumptions 'proof' of which is determined through the therapist's interpretations. As such, the theory is circular, self-validating and unfalsifiable (Smith, 1991).

If we pursue the idea that any interaction contains within it the 'echoes' of all other interactions that one has engaged in elsewhere and with others, it becomes evident that therapists would not be able to distinguish certain specific 'echoes' as 'transferential' or 'counter-transferential'. Indeed, any claims to this ability would be open to counter-claims of unnecessary mystification of the therapist's skills and knowledge, and would reveal that such distinctions simply serve the therapist's interests rather than have value or validity for the client. On the whole, therapists seem reluctant even to consider this possibility. Indeed, when I made a similar point at a workshop examining the notion of transference, I was met with immediate protests about the impossibility of my claims and the evidence of an over-sceptical closed-mindedness on my part. And yet I would suggest that, given the unresolved problems with the hypotheses of transference and counter-transference, such a point of view is at least as tenable as those that accept the hypotheses and is deserving of serious consideration simply on grounds of logic.

But what is so special about these hypotheses such that so many therapists of diverse orientations seem unwilling to let go of them? I would argue that it is precisely the demystificatory nature of the suggestion which makes it so difficult for some therapists to consider it seriously. For if they were to allow themselves to ponder this option it would force them to acknowledge the centrality of the current therapeutic encounter and that what is expressed and experienced within it has as much to say about the existing relationship between therapist and client as it does about any other in their, and their clients', past encounters.

Invoking the notion of transference and counter-transference allows a significant shift in the nature of the therapeutic relationship such that the focus of interest and emphasis is moved on to other relationships. In emphasizing these, therapists allow themselves to step aside from the issues within the existent relationship and to minimize their involvement in the on-going process.

What is being suggested is that there is sound logical and therapeutic reason not to allow the correlated past experiences to *swamp* the meanings contained in the current encounter. Rather, what the therapist should seek to maintain is an attitude that gives *equal value and significance to resonating elements* (rather than viewing one as being the substitute of the other) so that a more adequate meaning for the current experience can be gained and understood as an expression of both the client's and the therapist's current relationally construed experience of themselves and each other.

An alternative perspective on transference and counter-transference

In this way, the argument being presented *inverts* the significant aspects of the hypotheses of transference and counter-transference in that the resonating elements originating in past experiences are seen to be significant in that *they clarify the meaning of current experience and the current self-construct – not the other way around.*

Some time ago, a client, Nick, who was himself a trainee in therapy, came to a session and after some twenty minutes started to show increasing signs of tension and discomfort. Eventually, he began to express what was bothering him, and, in doing so, directed some very angry words towards me. I was seeing Nick in my office at home and, as he came for his twice-weekly sessions in the afternoon, when I was usually free, I would be waiting for him at the entrance of the house and, on hearing the sound of the gate being unlatched, I would open the front door in greeting. On this particular day, however, for various reasons, I had had to attend to a number of last-minute matters so that when Nick arrived he was not instantly met by me but, instead, had to ring the door-bell. Now here he was, furious with me for not having enacted our 'ritual' and searching out a significant meaning for this event. Placed within the context of the hypothesis of transference, I, as a therapist, could have taken this to have been an instance of negative transference and sought to assist Nick in refocusing his anger on the 'correct guilty party'. The alternative to this, which was the approach that I pursued with Nick, was to remain focused on his anger as it was being directed towards me and explore it as it was being manifested rather than seek to understand its latent significance. In so doing, through clarification, Nick began to express not only his current feelings as directed towards me, but also those feelings that 'resonated' with his current ones and which had been focused on others in his past (in particular, his mother). As such, a *connection* could be made between his current experience and past experiences, or between his relation to me and his relation to his mother.

But, in doing so, one relation (that of Nick to his mother) was not interpreted as being the 'cause' of his current supposedly transferred feelings towards me, nor was it allowed to 'swamp' the other on the theoretical basis that it was the more significant relationship. Rather, we were able to move back and forth between these relationships, exploring their similarities and differences and their meaning to Nick. By taking this clarificatory stance, I was able to listen to Nick's statements about either relationship (i.e. the one with me and the one with his mother) and challenge him to explore those statements from the standpoint of both relationships. So, for example, when Nick mentioned that his mother had always given the impression that she would do what he asked, but had actually rarely fulfilled his wishes, thereby leaving him with a sense that he could not trust her, I was able to challenge this statement in the light of our relationship by saying: 'And so when I give you the impression that I will be trustworthy by being at the door, and then fail to be there, it leaves you with the feeling that I may not fulfil your wishes either – though I might seem to pretend to.' Equally, when Nick expressed that he'd felt that through my act of omission I was letting him know that I was becoming bored with him and wanted to end our sessions, I was able to challenge this by getting him to clarify whether or not he'd felt that his mother had held similar feelings towards him.

But it is important to be clear that this kind of exploration can only take place if therapists are willing to *engage* with their clients and recognize that their presence is not only as a representative or transferential other, but that *they* are *the other in the current encounter*. And, in being so, *their* words, *their* behaviour, and *their* presence are at least as 'real' and significant as that of any 'other' whom the client brings from his past encounters. Indeed, following the view of the past discussed earlier, it can be argued that the 'others' from the client's past are being employed to express issues concerning clients' experiences of their *current* relationships – including, of course, those with their therapists.

The same process can be seen to account for those instances of counter-transference which therapists may experience during therapy. For example, during my therapeutic encounters with Nick, it became apparent that our lives 'parallelled' one another's in differing ways and that a number of issues and conflicts raised by Nick, and the manner in which he understood them, bore similarities with concerns – both past and current – in my life. While these were, to some degree, useful to me in my attempts to enter Nick's world-view as expressed through these issues, it was equally apparent to me that I must also be cautious in not assuming that our experiences and views were one and the same and, thereby, 'swamping' Nick's world-views with my own.

Instead, what I could – and did – do was to ask myself: 'What is it about this current encounter with Nick that is provoking me to consider and focus upon these parallels *in the particular way I am considering and focusing upon them now?*'

In other words, while acknowledging the 'resonances' being

evoked, rather than perceiving them as instances of 'counter-transference' – which would have led me away from the current encounter and which would have placed Nick in the role of my 'transferential other' – I was able to stay with the current encounter and treat the resonances *as they were being experienced* as being possible insights or cues that emerged from my attempt to 'enter' Nick's world-view and which were, therefore, of potential worth in my gaining a more adequate sense of what might be *implicit* within Nick's explicit statements.

For instance, at one point during a session, Nick began to speak of how grateful he was feeling towards me for having taught him to see certain aspects of himself in a manner that had greatly simplified his understanding of himself and how he related with others. As I attempted to gain a better sense of Nick's experience of himself as he told me this, I was struck by a sudden memory from my childhood. On my first day of school, I was being taught to write the number 8 by drawing two circles that 'met' one another. As it happened, I had already been taught by my parents how to write an 8 properly and I began to do so. When the teacher saw me doing this, her response was not one of praise (as I'd expected) but rather of anger. She wanted me to 'unlearn' what I already knew in order that she could 'teach' me to do something that was more 'primitive' than what I was already capable of doing. The emotions this memory provoked were of deep confusion and resentment. Why did I have to pretend I didn't know something I already knew in order that some idiotic teacher could convince herself that I had learned something from her? Why did I have to please her at the cost of a lessening of my own self-worth? Now, sitting across from Nick, I found myself experiencing a great deal of anger.

Seen from the standpoint of counter-transference, Nick had become my 'counter-transferential other' in that he'd somehow 'represented', through his words, my long-ago nemesis. In doing so, according to this hypothesis, he'd provoked some 'unruly', insufficiently analysed childhood conflicts within me which I should 'take away' and scrutinize. In following this line of thought, my evoked memories had little to do with my current relationship with Nick except insofar as it was through 'Nick

194

as representative of my teacher' that I had been made aware of issues that, while affecting this current relationship, were not really part of it.

The alternative view being proposed would take quite a different perspective which would – did – have significantly different consequences for the current encounter. This view takes into consideration the possibility that my memory was directly relevant to the current encounter in that it might have been my way of conceptualizing that which, in my attempt to 'enter' Nick's world-view, I had grasped as being 'implicit' within Nick's explicit statement to me. In other words, when Nick told me about how grateful he was, was there an aspect to his gratefulness which also revealed a sense of anger similar to what I remembered experiencing from my encounter with my teacher? This is not to say that Nick did *not* feel grateful, but, rather, that he might have felt *both* grateful and angry.

I was able to test this possibility by putting it to Nick that I appreciated his positive statements and also wondered what he was telling himself when he told me how grateful he was. In this instance, Nick's reply was that he was telling himself that he had to be really stupid not to have figured things out for himself rather than have to rely on me. The following brief dialogue took place:

'So, Nick, does that mean that I've had a role in your making yourself feel stupid?'
'Well . . . if you put it that way.'
'Do *you* put it that way?'
'Yeah . . . I guess I do.'
'So, is this something general? "When I feel grateful to people, I make myself feel stupid"?'
'Yeah . . . I guess . . . Well, not all people. Just some people.'
'Which people?'
'People who think they know me better than I do.'
'Ah . . . does that mean that you see me as someone who thinks he knows you better than you know yourself?'
'Yeah . . . Sure you do. You're supposed to, anyway!'
'And if I do . . . What's that say about what's going on here?'

'I don't know . . . It's confusing. Like, sometimes it feels like we're two adults talking about me. And then, sometimes, it feels like you're the adult and I'm a child.'

'And it's when you're feeling like a child that you feel grateful and stupid?'

'Yeah. Sometimes you're just clever and you say something that I hadn't thought of before. Then I just feel grateful. But other times, you get 'clever-clever', you know? And you say things that I know already but I wasn't ready to talk about yet. Then I feel grateful and stupid.'

'And like a child.'

'Yeah.'

'So, when I'm 'clever-clever' and you feel like a child . . . who am I like?'

In this way, that which could have been seen as merely 'counter-transferential' takes on quite a different perspective and allows the focus to remain on the current encounter rather than lead it away from it. Nevertheless, it is evident that there exists a risk in this perspective in that all such 'resonances' must be treated with caution by the therapist and, if presented to the client, must be hesitant or 'invitational'. A further risk must also be mentioned: in order for therapists to adopt this perspective, they must also be willing to accept their clients' statements about them – whether positive or negative – non-defensively in order that they can explore with as much honesty as they will allow themselves those potentially significant 'resonances' which the encounter evokes.

This re-interpretation of the hypotheses of transference and counter-transference promotes a fundamental shift in viewpoint as to the significance of the therapeutic relationship. For if therapists were to let go of the more commonly held assumptions regarding these hypotheses, they would find themselves very much more experientially 'in' the therapeutic relationship. At the same time, the adoption of this stance opens therapists to direct confrontations not only with the strengths and skilful expertise they might bring to the relationship, but also to their weaknesses and failings. Further, it confronts them once again with the power contained in the theories they adopt and employ – and whose main interests that power may serve.

5. INTERPRETATION

A. *The Issue of Interpretation in Therapy*

The previous discussions on the unconscious, the past, and trans-ference/counter-transference serve to demonstrate the implications and consequences that can occur when therapists fail to see beyond their theories, or employ them in ways that emphasize the mystificatory aspects of their role and authority in the therapeutic process.

Equally, all the points discussed implicitly address the important issue of *interpretation* in that all the hypotheses discussed are definitionally reliant on this therapeutic 'skill'. If they have each been found to be problematic or open to differing analyses, then these alternatives arise out of the uncertainties encountered through interpretation. And yet, interpretation is a central therapeutic skill, and not only for the psycho-analytic model. What then can be done with the problem of interpretation?

In the first instance, it must be acknowledged that to assert that a therapist (or anyone else for that matter) can claim to engage in any form of dialogue with a client which is free of interpretative variables would not only be a false claim, but also an absurd one. In an important sense, from a mental standpoint we can do *nothing but* interpret. I have argued this position extensively elsewhere (Spinelli, 1989) and will discuss it more fully in Part 5. This view can be seen to hold great significance in the therapeutic enterprise. For within this specific instance, the therapist's aim of 'entering the world-view of the client' (in order to understand it, 'reflect it', 'interpret it', or whatever) can also be seen to be a project that cannot be fulfilled in any final or complete sense. Therapists, like anyone else, place any number of assumptions and biases (be they personal, socio-cultural, theoretical or whatever else) on their experience or understanding of their clients which cannot be removed or avoided and, as such, they can only hope to arrive at more or less adequate approximations of their clients' experience. *Clearly, then, therapists can do nothing but interpret their clients' inner worlds as expressed through their statements and behaviours.*

This somewhat over-simplified contention should, nevertheless, make clear that the questions and issues surrounding interpretation in therapy do not focus on the argument of *whether* a therapist should or should not interpret, but, rather, are concerned with *how* (or what kind of) interpretations can be made, and which manner of interpreting will be most beneficial and clarificatory both to the client and to the therapist's aim of gaining an increasingly adequate understanding and experience of that client's self-awareness in relation to the issues and conflicts being confronted.

I would suggest that one way of clarifying categories of interpretations lies in determining whether they are *analytically* or *descriptively* focused.

B. Analytic and Descriptive Interpretations

Analytic interpretation

An *analytical interpretation* seeks to go behind or beneath the presented (or 'manifest') material contained in a statement so that its hidden (or 'latent') meaning may be ascertained. For instance, a client's statement that 'I am terrified of rats' may be analytically interpreted as meaning that the client is expressing in a disguised fashion some form of antagonism or revulsion towards a sibling, or even towards the therapist. The 'manifest' statement therefore is understood to be a disguised expression of a 'latent message' which, for any number of reasons, the client is unwilling or unable to express in a direct fashion. Analytical interpretations, therefore, place on therapists the superior knowledge (gained through their training) that allows them to understand the 'true' or 'correct' meaning behind their clients' statements with which, at some point in the course of therapy, they will confront them. In relation to this last point, however, it must be said that some intriguing research evidence drawing on transcripts of analytic sessions from the Tavistock Clinic revealed that it was impossible to arrive at criteria for determining the 'truth value' of particular interpretations offered by analysts (Farrell, 1967).

In any case, this avowed ability to 'see through' clients' manifest statements and motives is characteristic of the psychoanalytic model (and several other models of therapy). And the assumptions contained within the hypotheses of the unconscious, past influences, and transference can be understood to be essential 'tools' for the accomplishment of this task.

At the same time, analytical interpretations place therapists in a position of great power since they rely on their abilities to understand and reveal the hidden meanings in their clients' statements and behaviours before they are consciously acknowledged by the clients themselves. Indeed, the psycho-analytic hypothesis of clients' *resistance* (or unwillingness to accept the truth of the therapist's interpretations) only makes sense when placed within these presuppositions. But all of this also endows therapists with the ability to know 'the truth' and, in this way, they become 'truth bringers' to their clients who, in turn, must rely on and accept their offerings in order to ameliorate their condition.

In this fashion, the therapeutic relationship that is based on analytic interpretations fosters the client's dependence on the therapist and comes to resemble a relationship such as might be seen between parent and child. While psycho-analytic therapists might claim the inevitability of this and thereby argue that their theories have been validated, it remains to be asked whether, instead, what has been done is to set up the conditions for self-fulfilling prophecies to be enacted.

Descriptive interpretation

A *descriptive interpretation*, on the other hand, retains its focus on the manifest material and seeks to extract the meaning of that material to the client by engaging the client in a descriptively focused process of clarification wherein the manifest material may be 'opened up' to mutual investigation. This might be done, for example, by focusing on various elements contained in the manifest material and considering what they express to the client about his or her currently lived experience, what they reveal or imply about his or her self-construct, relations with others, and so forth. In this way, a descriptive interpretation of the statement 'I am terrified of rats' might focus on the clarification of such elements as: what the experience of 'being terrified' is like for the client; what its meaning is in relation to his or her self-construct; what the client thinks and believes about others' views and attitudes towards his or her expression of 'being terrified'; what views and assumptions the client holds towards 'rats'; and so forth. While this descriptive process might well lead to conclusions similar to those derived from analytic interpretations, it might equally guide investigation to quite different ones. For example, it might be discovered through descriptive analysis that the client finds rats to be attractive and lovable creatures and that the issue has more to do with the experience of 'being terrified' of them than it does about the animals themselves. Alternatively, in describing the experience of 'being terrified', the client might clarify that this is a generalized experience in his or her relations with others.

In other words, descriptive interpretations 'stay with' the manifest material. In doing so, they restrain therapists from searching out its hidden meaning from a theory-led standpoint. Nevertheless, it remains the case that interpretations *are* being made by the therapist. Firstly, because the therapist makes decisions about which elements in the client's material seem worthwhile clarifying. And secondly because the therapist must at some point make assumptions about the client's descriptions as being 'good enough' approximations of the client's unique and not fully shareable world-views.

Nevertheless, while it must be acknowledged that descriptive interpretations still place therapists in positions of power, it is a qualitatively different type of power to that assumed by analytical interpreters, not least because they avoid assumptions of therapists' theory-based independent accessibility to the underlying meaning and truth of clients' statements and behaviours.

Rather, such meanings are seen to emerge from the descriptive process and, even then, remain only partially available to therapist and client alike. Indeed, in the descriptive process meanings always remain incomplete and open to further elucidation and are continually placed in the context of current experience rather than being seen as fully revealed and determined regardless of time and circumstance.

While descriptively focused therapists are by no means passive 'reflectors' in their clients' process of elucidation (since it is evident that therapists direct clients to examine and clarify certain selected elements in the manifest material), the rationale for such directions and the manner in which such directions are given reveal a distinctively different focal emphasis to that of analytical interpreters. For while the latter rely on their theoretical assumptions to lead them to the assumed latent material which they will subsequently analyse on the basis of their theoretical formulations, the former's directions are principally governed by their aim of 'entering into' the meaning-world of their clients so that their assumptions and theories concerning their current self/other relational constructs can be more adequately exposed to clarificatory examination.

Nevertheless, it remains the case that while the descriptive model may minimize many potentials for misuse of therapeutic power which are inherent in analytic interpretations, all instances of descriptively focused interpretations place a certain degree of directive power on therapists which cannot be dismissed or disregarded.

This inescapable conclusion clearly demands descriptively oriented therapists to address the basis on which their decisions are being made. Clearly, they respond to certain cues, either from their clients' statements or from the manner in which these statements are made, which they believe might indicate something of import. But this, in itself, would imply that they are active interpreters, and, as such, are pursuing some manner of hypothesis or theory-derived stance in their dialogues with clients, even if these are far more flexible and open to clients' rebuttals or rejections than the theory-led stances of analytically oriented therapists.

It must be concluded, therefore, that all therapeutic encounters, no matter how client-concerned they may be, are open to potential misuse or abusive influences by therapists. I am well aware that this judgement may be employed as 'ammunition' by critics of therapy; nevertheless, it would seem to me to be of greater benefit for therapists and clients alike to acknowledge the 'givens' or limitations of therapeutic encounters and to strive to develop approaches that are more adequate in their recognition of therapists' influences and powers so that they may better avoid inordinate abuses, rather than argue that, until such time that the impossible occurs and a 'perfectly safe' form of therapy comes into being, one should forestall the continuance of 'imperfect' therapeutic encounters regardless of the therapeutic benefits that might be derived from them.

Therapy, like all other investigative approaches, may be incomplete and approximate. But it can, nevertheless, inform and enlighten. The philosopher Martin Heidegger suggested that it is fundamental to the make-up of all human beings that we 'never arrive, but are always only "on the way"' (Heidegger, 1962). This view, taken in a wider context, strikes me as a particularly apt summation of all attempts at human enquiry and clarification – therapy included – in that they, too, 'never arrive, but are always only "on the way".'

This stance, for me, defines the notion of 'more adequate' interpretations in that it stresses the attempt to remain open to increasing possibilities of meaning and significance rather than seeking out a final and fixed 'truth'. It seems to me that all those encounters (therapeutic or otherwise) which strike us as being special and significant to our understanding of ourselves are imbued with an 'openness of interpretative possibilities', just as it is through these encounters that we are reminded that 'whatever we might think, it is more than that'.

That interpretations are expressions of power cannot be disputed, but power is not in itself a problem, just as interpretations are not in themselves problematic. Rather, what problems may arise can be seen to be related to the *manner* in which they are employed. Descriptively oriented interpretations, as employed in therapy, allow a greater possibility for the recognition that both therapists and clients wield power, and while the power each wields may not be the same, or even equal, nevertheless possibilities exist which allow power to be employed to enhance the potentials of therapeutic dialogue. It is this very shift away from competitive and towards more co-operative expressions of power which ultimately distinguishes descriptive interpretations from analytic ones. It is this self-same shift, I would argue, which should be the aim of all therapeutic discourse.

6. CONTRASTING CASE STUDY EXAMPLES

Since the psycho-analytic model of therapy, perhaps more than any other, contains significant issues that permeate much of therapy and, as pertinently, public views of therapy, the discussion of two actual case examples – one psycho-analytic, the other from my own practice – should enable readers to understand in a more concrete fashion how the assumptions discussed and criticisms made of this model provoke quite differing approaches to, and interactions within, the therapeutic encounter.

A. An Analytically Focused Case Study: 'A Child Leads The Way'

I will begin by summarizing a case study by Patrick Casement, a well-known and highly respected psycho-analytic therapist and training analyst, which can be read in its entirety in Casement's text *Further Learning from the Patient* (Casement, 1990). I must also state my indebtedness to one of my students, Ms Imogen Smallwood, for first pointing out this case, and its intriguing implications, to me. I must also state at the outset that my decision to focus on this study is partly based on the high regard I hold for its author, not least because he seems to be far more willing than other psycho-analytic colleagues to expose his approach to therapy to critical analysis both by himself and by others. Although, as will become apparent, I have significant reservations about many of the assumptions and interpretations he brings to the case discussion, I hope that these will be read as constructive attempts to make plain the differences in approach discussed above, rather than as destructive attacks on either the psycho-analytic model or the author of the case study. I am very much in favour of increased dialogue between representatives of differing models and would hope that my comments will be read in this spirit of respectful airing of differences and agreements.

The case

Patrick Casement's case presentation 'A child leads the way' (Casement, 1990) begins with a number of important remarks by the author. He informs his readers that his encounter with the six-and-a-half-year-old girl he names Joy was the first analytic work he undertook and that he wishes to discuss the case because it was through Joy that he learned of the importance of the therapeutic setting as a means of providing clients with the space to verbalize their anxieties, and, as significantly, that he was able to overcome his reluctance to carry out his own analytic interpretations (rather than rely on his assumptions of what other analytic therapists might say) so that Joy could begin to communicate to him her own understanding of what she required. The case presentation itself focuses on the first five weeks of his regular sessions with Joy which, initially, were on a five-times-a-week basis.

Joy was referred to him by her mother's own analyst, who recommended Casement as a 'reading teacher' who could also attend to Joy's 'psychotherapeutic needs'. Although Casement accepted the invitation, he acknowledges his own strong reluctance to take on a therapeutic relationship with Joy on the sensible grounds that he had not been trained to work with child clients. (Nor, it must be said, had he trained as a reading teacher.)

Even so, Casement admits, he had been recently stimulated by his reading of Melanie Klein's analysis of a child client (Klein, 1961). Klein, Casement concluded, had managed to provide the boy 'with a symbolic language through which he could, eventually, communicate deep anxiety or unconscious phantasy with a possibility that this could be understood by the person who had been teaching him this language' (Casement, 1990: 32–3).

This passage holds the key to Casement's approach throughout the case study. Readers should note, however, the circularity of thought in Klein's argument. For if she is *teaching* the language to the child, how could she *not* understand it? Surely the question is more whether the boy had understood it – or, perhaps, that he had understood what his teacher wanted him to understand.

In any case, Casement decides that he will not make any interpretations with Joy and, instead, will allow her to think in a relatively unrestrained manner.

Joy was the middle child of three, and the only daughter. According to what her mother's analyst told Casement, Joy's mother was experiencing problems in accepting and demonstrating affection towards Joy because she was a girl. Soon after her birth, Joy had been passed on to a nanny. Although her mother engaged in minimal physical contact with Joy, she was seen as being over-indulged and was allowed a great deal of freedom to do as she pleased. In contrast to this state of affairs, both Joy's brothers experienced a warm and affectionate relationship with their mother; indeed, the younger child, who was two years old, was under the direct care of his mother.

Casement initially met Joy's parents at their home around a fortnight before Christmas and received further details of Joy's schooling and her reading difficulties. At this same interview, he was informed by Joy's father that she was 'a very sexual child' (ibid: 34) who behaved quite seductively towards him. In order to make Joy feel special, and in order to make up for his being away from the family a good deal of the time owing to his work commitments, Joy's father had begun to take Joy away to the family's seaside home over the weekends – an experience which, he claimed, Joy appreciated a great deal. In addition, Joy's father expressed the hope that Joy would 'fall in love' with Casement and, in so doing, learn to read for him. Finally, the parents informed Casement that the family poodle, Polo, was likely to have puppies in the spring as she had recently been mated with a 'boyfriend poodle'. It was agreed that Casement would meet Joy every weekday morning during the week before Christmas and less frequently following the holidays.

On the morning of their first meeting, Casement is met by Joy's mother who leads him to the drawing room which he describes as 'huge (for purposes of play-therapy) . . . oppressively clean and tidy and respectable' (ibid: 34), but because of the ambiguity of his role he feels unable to ask that their meetings be held in a more suitable room.

At last, left alone with Joy, Casement unpacks his bag and reveals, along with various items of remedial reading material, some coloured felt-tip pens, plasticine of various colours, a scribbling pad, scissors and sticky paper, and informs Joy that although they will eventually get around to playing some reading games, for the present he wants her to play with whatever materials she wishes. Choosing some brown-coloured plasticine, Joy declares that she wants to make a figure of Polo the poodle. At this, she proceeds to shape 'a fat sausage from which she pinches legs, head and tail' (ibid: 35).

Noting that it is a good likeness of a dog, Casement then comments in a somewhat leading manner: 'Polo is rather fat, isn't she?' (ibid: 35). To which Joy responds that of course she is because she went away to stay with Gonzo the boy poodle and Joy's parents have informed her that she will have puppies.

Bored with the poodle, Joy begins to make a model of her older brother who, she declares, is almost as big as Casement. Again, somewhat leadingly, but explaining to his readers that he wished to give Joy 'permission to be more explicit about sexual differences because of the apparent discrimination against her by her mother' (ibid: 35), Casement asks how they (i.e. Joy and Casement) could tell that the figure was a boy, and urges her to show him. In response, Joy makes a long thin sausage, looks at her teacher, then flattens it in a manner that Casement describes as 'mischievous', and, announcing that this is her brother's school cap, she lengthens its peak. At this, Casement replies that her brother has a large peak. Telling him that this is so he can keep the sun out of his eyes, Joy proceeds to make another 'thin sausage' which, after some initial hesitation, she

squashes into the shape of a satchel. Then, repeating her movements, she makes still another 'sausage', looks up and down the
figure's body, and then places it inside the satchel announcing
that this is her brother's 'big pencil'. Finally, shaping a lump of
plasticine, and 'after more hesitation and "knowing looks"'
(ibid: 35), says that this is her brother's ink-pot.

Having now grown bored with playing with plasticine, Joy
begins to draw her mother with Polo beside her. Adding 'rain'
dots to her picture, she then draws her father first with an
umbrella and then with a satchel, followed by a black sun, and,
finally, her brothers. While drawing, she tells Casement that she
will reveal a secret to him which he mustn't reveal to anyone else,
the secret being that she has hidden a telephone under a chair so
that she can ring up a friend of hers without anyone knowing.

Reflecting on the material presented to him in the first session,
Casement concludes that Joy is knowledgable about pregnancy
and the primary sexual differences between males and females
but is frightened to be explicit, that her plasticine creations
reveal various penis symbols, that her comment to him about
her brother being nearly as big as him might be a possible early
indication of transference, that Joy's drawings reveal an ambiva-
lence towards her parents, that Joy wishes to be allowed to be
special in her mother's eyes and that, on the basis of subsequently learned additional information, that Joy has been a
persistent bed-wetter since her mother's last pregnancy, that the
rain in her drawing is an expression of her eneuresis. Finally,
with regard to her sharing her secret with him, Casement writes:
'I felt she sounded conspiratorial in telling me her secret – something that must be kept just between her and me. But we may
also be seeing an unconscious prompt for me to establish boundaries around her contact with me' (ibid: 36).

I have gone into some detail with regard to this first meeting,
not only because it provides readers with a good sense of Casement's approach to his work with Joy but also, and more
importantly, because it encapsulates the whole of the case presentation.

For in spite of his claim that he would abstain from interpretation and allow Joy to express herself, Casement, from the start,

focuses and directs his (and Joy's) attention to what he assumes to be the focus of Joy's disturbances – her sexuality.

All of Casement's subsequent accounts of particular sessions, and his reflections upon them, reveal his single-minded conviction that Joy must address explicitly – to herself and to him – her knowledge and anxieties related to her sexuality.

I will provide some examples of this below, but readers should also note that from this initial encounter the notions of transference and the unconscious have already been introduced, as has the idea that behind Joy's creative manifest material there must lurk significant latent material that is clearly sexual (the penis symbols) and aggressive (Joy's 'squashing' of the symbolic penises). Though Casement does not express his interpretations in a direct manner to Joy, nevertheless he does so indirectly through the leading questions he poses. It should also be noted that while Casement does not wish to interpret and thereby restrict the inner world of his client, he does seem to suggest that he has already understood it. But what is his basis for this? Partly, it is likely to have been shaped by his reading of Klein, but also he seems to have accepted Joy's father's statements about her sexuality and seductiveness with little question, thereby possibly imposing on Joy's expression of her inner world a far more restrictive, if also more subtle, interpretative barrier.

Casement's reliance on his analytic interpretations and the leading manner with which he imposes them on Joy is made even more obvious during the second session when Joy begins to draw a gorilla with large thumbs, followed by three squiggles with a banana on top and then, drawing a banana in the gorilla's hand, states that she likes to take bananas when her mother isn't looking. In response to all this, Casement asks Joy to show him that the gorilla is a man on the grounds that she has indicated her jealousy towards her brothers, and perhaps towards her father, because they are allowed to have what she would like to have. She had to steal bananas whereas the man gorilla had a banana all to himself. But readers should note how subtly Casement has turned *his* supposition that the gorilla was a man into a proven statement on the basis that 'the phallic symbolism of the big thumbs, and the banana, seemed obvious' (ibid: 37).

Equally, he seems to pay no consideration to the events as they occurred in that Joy was not 'responding' to the fact that the gorilla had a banana, she willingly *gave* him one by drawing it.

The influence of Casement's analytical stance on both the content and manner of his interpretations becomes even more apparent during the third session. While drawing, Casement inadvertently rubs one of his eyes, to which Joy says: 'I should have told you – you mustn't rub an itch, because although at first it feels nice it soon begins to hurt' (ibid: 38). Not surprisingly, Casement takes her words to be an allusion to masturbation, but, for the moment at least, elects to remain silent. Later in the session, when Joy draws a complex picture involving, among other images, a man dangling from a crane (whom she says is Casement himself) trying to go down into a treasure cave which is guarded by Polo and Gonzo, Casement produces an interpretation that suggests that the picture is rather like the dogs mating and that the man has to enter the cave so that later a baby will emerge from it. Joy rejects this interpretation outright, reminding Casement that the dogs are not where he says they are. It is only when Casement alters his suggestion to something more acceptable ('Well, perhaps it is like you having secrets which have to be guarded carefully, and you won't let anyone except me in to know about them' (ibid: 39)) that Joy expresses happiness at his attempts to interpret. Nevertheless, Casement feels sufficiently justified to stick with his first interpretation because, as he tells his readers: 'I had made these comments so that she knew she was allowed to speak about sexual matters, which I could tell – from what I knew about her and from her play – were evidently preoccupying her' (ibid: 39).

When the sessions begin again, following the Christmas break, Joy is initially restless and difficult to control. In his reflections, Casement wonders whether Joy may have been angry with him for not having come to see her. This seems a reasonable explanation, but even here Casement interprets it in a somewhat grandiose manner by suggesting that Joy 'might have . . . felt obliterated' (ibid: 40) by his absence.

The extent of Casement's uncritical belief in the accuracy of his interpretations and his pushing of them on Joy are further

DEMYSTIFYING THERAPY

clarified during session eight. Noticing that Joy has been drawing
a large number of images of sharp teeth and dismembered limbs,
Casement comments:

'You've been drawing a lot of teeth today. Does that mean
that you want to bite people because you are angry?' She
replied: 'No.' I continued: 'Well, I have noticed that you do
draw teeth when you've been angry with me over the reading.'
She seemed to accept this but she made no actual reply (ibid:
43).

And so the sessions continue until session twelve when, for
Casement, a significant shift occurs. Casement presents Joy with
a reading game wherein he selects a series of letters – PA PE PI
PO PU – and adds a T to each of them to make a word. Joy
seems interested in this reading game and makes her own word,
NIT, which is her 'favourite' word of the day, and then follows
this with other words made up with Casement's assistance. In
his reflections on this session, Casement writes that an important
moment has occurred in that Joy made the game her own and
that a real sense of sharing had been felt by both of them. I
agree with Casement on this point. But could it be that this
sharing experience came about because Casement has, for the
moment at least, *ceased* interpreting and placed himself 'in' the
relationship with Joy, allowing her to express herself without
the imposition of his theoretical perspective? Interestingly, it
might be worth considering that Casement is not as entirely free
of his biases as he thinks. For, on reflection, some of the letters
he selects, when read aloud, sound like infantile excretory language (PI, PO, PU). In any case, a significant shift in the process
has occurred and its influence on Joy is as immediate as it is
obvious – perhaps not least because they are finally engaged in
the activity that Joy has been led to believe is the rationale for
Casement's presence (i.e. he is helping her to read).

However, Casement the analytical interpreter soon returns
with a vengeance. Bringing a torch into the room at the start of
session sixteen, Joy states that this is her gun and then begins
to burrow around the cushions on the settee. Having created a

210

'secret passage', she begins to climb into and out of it. Casement writes:

> I responded to this reference to 'secret passage' and said to her that it was rather like being born. She wasn't too sure about this, but she had so far always rejected such comments from me. (Joy had a rich capacity for phantasy and imagery in her own terms. Interpretations still seemed to be experienced by her as an intrusion into her private world.) (ibid: 52).

Not that these acknowledged rejections seem to bother Casement a great deal. Noting that Joy has placed the lit torch under her jumper while saying that no one will know where it is, he supposes (to himself)

> that she was wanting to boast of an obvious penis-like protrusion that I couldn't fail to notice. But, as I didn't know what she called a penis (or if she had any word for it at all), I tried to interpret this more vaguely by saying 'It makes you look like a boy.' She wouldn't accept this. 'What do you mean?' she asked. I replied lamely: 'You know what I mean.' . . . (ibid: 52).

Having decided that he has been too inhibited in interpreting the sexual allusions in Joy's statements to her, Casement now embarks on a series of encounters which seeks to remedy this situation. In the very same session, for example, he interprets Joy's emphatic unwillingness to accept his statement that she wonders what her parents do together in their bed by suggesting to her 'that she had denied this so strongly because she really wanted to know very much' (ibid: 53). Similarly, during session seventeen, Joy draws what she first calls a cow, then a bull. When Casement asks her to show him that it is a bull, she draws horns on the image. But Casement is not satisfied by this and asks 'what it had underneath that made it a bull' (ibid: 54). Once again, however, Joy will not play along, and she replies that she's never looked underneath a bull.

Finally taking the bull by the horns, so to speak, during session twenty-one, Casement makes a figurine of a man 'with a very obvious penis' (ibid: 55). Joy's reaction to this image is to remind her teacher that a man doesn't have three legs. Now unwilling to avoid direct verbal references to sexual differences, Casement tells her 'that she knew very well that it wasn't a third leg, but that it was what her brother . . . has and calls "a penis"' (ibid: 59). However, as Joy does not seem to understand this word, Casement translates it into the infantile word 'winkle'. Joy finds this hilarious and begins to recite: 'Winkle, twinkle, little star; how I wonder what you are!' (ibid: 59) and removes the figure's penis, leaving Casement to ponder, somewhat ruefully (and honestly), that he, his words, and the plasticine penis have all become very much the butt of her humour. Even so, he remains convinced of the value of his interpretations and thinks it to be 'extraordinary how explicitly Joy had been illustrating her need for me to interpret her sexual curiosity and anxieties about it' (ibid: 59).

From session nineteen on, the frequency of sessions is reduced to four times per week. Parallelling this change, Joy's behaviour becomes increasingly messy and uncontrollable to the point where Casement finally finds it necessary to confront Joy's mother and request a room change. This is duly granted and the setting for the sessions is moved to the children's play-room. However, on the very next day following this decision, Joy is taken ill and Casement doesn't see her again for five days. It doesn't seem to occur to him that Joy's behaviour may have had something to do with the changes in their relationship. Rather, he interprets her unruly behaviour as a demand on her part to be provided with the right environment for her to express her 'messy thoughts' and, subsequently – contradicting this interpretation – wonders whether her illness is connected to Joy's feelings about his seeing her mother.

Whatever the case, sessions twenty-one to twenty-three, which are the last on which Casement provides detailed commentary, seem to have been quite significant for the therapeutic relationship. For instance, during session twenty-two, Casement explicitly informs Joy that the hole that she has just poked through a sheet of paper with a pen 'was pushing a penis into a baby-hole' (ibid: 60) and was an expression of her desire to have a penis like her brother's. No longer resistant, Joy accepts this. Indeed, later, when Joy pushes a pencil in and out of Casement's hair, she tells him that it is a penis. Similarly, when she makes a plasticine man, she provides him with a 'huge and unmistakable penis' (ibid: 60). And again, during session twenty-three, when pondering the difference between 'h' and 'n', Casement tells Joy that the 'n' has had its tail cut off. Understanding, Joy answers that the 'n' has had its penis removed.

Casement's sessions with Joy continue for another fifteen months, during which time Joy's bed-wetting diminishes and subsequently disappears. Finally, and not least significantly, her reading improves and Joy begins to find pleasure in its worth.

For Casement, the eventual success of this case lay in Joy's recognition of her own worth as a female which became expressed in her improved reading abilities and the cessation of her eneuresis. But all this rested on her being allowed to address her unmet needs to discuss sexual issues in a direct fashion which 'helped her to understand the hidden things about herself as a girl' (ibid: 62). He concludes:

> we have an opportunity to witness a child repeatedly giving active cues for me to respond to her most pressing needs. And, by following these leads (as I gradually developed the courage to respond to them), I eventually began to grapple with those key issues.
> The naivety of this untrained approach highlights what Joy needed from a therapeutic relationship. Persistently, and with increasing clarity, the process of her unconscious search showed me where she needed to go. I had to learn to follow (ibid: 64).

The case discussion

In considering this case, it is important to recall that it is, as Casement tells us, the first in his career as a psycho-analyst and that, as such, it would be unfair to emphasize particular points of clumsiness or inconsistency. On the other hand, the fact that

Casement had elected to present this case not as a trainee but as a well-established and respected analyst would suggest that he is not entirely ill at ease with it. Equally, in a spirit of fair-mindedness, it is necessary to acknowledge that he is quite critical of himself throughout the presentation and, indeed, makes much of his clumsiness in order to make the case for the valuable lessons that clients can teach to their therapists. I am in whole-hearted agreement with this viewpoint. The question that must be asked, however, is whether Casement is correct in his conclusion. *Did* a child lead the way? Or is it the case that she was *led in a* particular direction by her therapist? I would suggest that, on the basis of what is stated in the presentation, the latter view is the more likely.

Throughout the discussion, Casement's interactions with Joy are riddled with theory-led assumptions which are clearly expressed in his interpretations – both 'timorous' and direct – which attempt to impose a specific 'sub-text' on Joy's statements and behaviours. With these assumptions in mind, Casement analyses the 'movement' in the therapy as being one that shifts from 'veiled allusions' to Joy's sexual concerns (though I am not as convinced as he is that these allusions are, indeed, quite so 'veiled') to the direct acknowledgement of them on the part of the therapist.

Now it may well be that Joy *does* hold these concerns; but the question that is of importance to us is whether they are the ones she is attempting to express to Casement and whether it is the clarification of these, through Casement's interpretations, which is the key to her eventual improvement.

We must recall that the issue of Joy's sexual curiosity is something that is raised by Joy's father, not Joy herself. This is, itself, a curious circumstance. For while Casement seems to accept the father's statement as true, I suspect that I am not the only person reading the case to have wondered about the remark itself and what it might mean for Joy's father to have volunteered it quite so readily to someone who, after all, was supposedly there to teach her to improve her reading abilities. Perhaps Joy's father knew of Casement's double role, but, if so, this is not made clear. In any case, what *does* seem clear is that Joy is very much the 'outsider' in the family. Her mother's relationship with her is obviously different to that with Joy's brothers. Could it not be as likely that just the fact that Joy is allowed to engage in a special relationship with Casement, wherein she is permitted (even encouraged) to play and express herself *in the presence of someone else*, might, in itself, promote the improvements that Casement subsequently notes?

In the same way, while Casement seems convinced that these are due to his new-found willingness to address Joy's sexuality directly, is it not also of possible significance that these changes occur exactly at the point when Casement finally finds himself able to stand up to Joy's mother and convince her to change the setting for his sessions with Joy? Could it not be from this event in itself (which Casement tells us Joy was a partial witness to) that Joy might have been convinced that Casement's allegiance was to *her* and not to her mother and that it was this realization that provoked her change of stance towards him (and towards herself)? Prior to this, Joy seems to have alluded to her uncertainty about Casement (e.g. he was 'a clown' who was also 'a spy'), but once she became convinced that he was there for her, she began to 'reward' him – and herself.

As to the sexually leading interpretations that Casement makes throughout, is it also not possible that rather than being 'on the mark' (as he believes them to be), these might have been seen by Joy initially to be odd and confusing, possibly even amusing and curiosity-arousing? And, in the end, perhaps she came to see that in order to 'please' him, or just keep him coming back and maintaining his relationship with her, she would have to accept and learn to play within the 'rules of the game' as set by him? In other words, Joy, like possibly all other children, learned to adapt to the (often) odd demands of this particular adult so that she could gain the benefits of his attention, affection, concern, and so forth, and, in turn, be allowed to express the same towards him and towards herself.

Of course, we cannot ever know whether these alternative viewpoints might have promoted the kind of beneficial changes in Joy which Casement notes at the conclusion of his paper. But they seem to me to be worth serious consideration. In Part 1 of this text, I pointed out that research with clients indicates that the aspects of therapy which they most value have little to do with the theories held and expressed to them by their therapists, but rather emphasize more 'mundane' elements such as the ability to express themselves, to be listened to, to be in a relationship with someone, and so forth. It is as though clients seem to be saying: 'So long as I am allowed all these, I'll put up with the "mumbo-jumbo" that you (the therapist) seem to find so important.' Might not Joy have concluded the same?

So, did she lead or was she led? As in most other circumstances, probably both. I would suggest that Joy was clearly led by Casement with regard to her having to accept the 'rules of the game' as expressed in his analytic interpretations and their reliance on the theoretical assumptions espoused by him. In this way, I believe that he is deluding himself in thinking that it was Joy who led him to make such interpretations in an increasingly direct manner. On the other hand, I would suggest that, having learned the rules, Joy was able to lead Casement into a relationship that, if still imbalanced and power-based, nevertheless provided her with the means to express and experience various significantly human aspects of encounter which seemed to be sorely lacking in her other experiences with adults.

What is illuminating is that even a therapist as concerned with clients' experiences and as willing to learn from them as Casement undoubtedly is completely fails to consider these possibilities. Led as he is by his theories and by his analytic attitude towards interpretation, he imposes assumptions on the encounter which may have little therapeutic value and which greatly mystify the relationship.

But are there any suitable alternatives? How might an attempt to remain at a descriptive level of interpretation promote a therapeutic relationship that retains the process and outcome benefits just discussed but which also avoids the interpretative impositions required of analytic approaches? Hopefully, the following example, drawn from my own work, will provide some initial clarification.

B. A Descriptively Focused Case Study: 'Sex, Death and the Whole Damned Thing: the case of Stephen R'

The case

When he first introduced himself to me, Stephen R believed himself to be on the brink of committing suicide. I was, he stated emphatically, his last real hope. Just turned thirty years of age, some eight years earlier Stephen R had set himself a 'life-plan', or schedule, which demanded that he be already married and a father by the age of twenty-nine, and was upset by what he saw as his failure to fulfil this goal. Stephen R was a bright, fit and handsome young man who was already highly successful in his job where he held a position of significant authority in a middle-sized management firm. His income approached £40,000 per annum and included various additional perks such as an expensive company car. He enjoyed and felt stimulated by the demands of his work, and was, as far as he perceived it, well liked, admired and respected by his colleagues and administrative staff. Similarly, by his own admission, Stephen R had no difficulties in forming strong, open relationships with women, and had had, over the years, numerous short-term, intensely emotional and sexual relationships with various partners and was currently in a relationship that had begun some six months earlier. Although he professed himself to be bisexual and had 'experimented' sexually with several men, he now yearned to remain in the current monogamous relationship he was in with the woman who, he believed, would 'become the mother of his children'.

His most pressing problem, he admitted, was an unusual one, at least as far as he was concerned. Bluntly, with little sign of embarrassment, he explained that although he wished to marry his partner, and that this desire was shared by her, one major obstacle stood in the way of their mutual yearning to have a child: he could not bring himself to ejaculate while engaged in penile–vaginal intercourse. He explained that while he had no difficulty in achieving and maintaining penile erection, and enjoyed penile–vaginal intercourse, once he felt himself to be on the verge of ejaculation he found it necessary to withdraw and to ejaculate on his partner's body. My request for clarification on this point provided the added information that, once he'd ejaculated, Stephen R then felt compelled to lick up and swallow his semen and that, indeed, it was only once he'd fulfilled this task that he could fully experience the psychological pleasure of orgasm. In the early months of their sexual relationship, his partner had not been disturbed by this behaviour (or so Stephen R believed), especially as its compulsive nature had been obscured by the non-appearance of this reaction during other forms of sexual intercourse (mainly mutual masturbation and anal intercourse), although, on reflection, Stephen R realized that while he had not prevented his partner from swallowing his sperm during oral intercourse, he did not enjoy this act a great deal and had usually found ways of ensuring that he'd disengaged his penis from his partner's mouth before ejaculation. When I queried his rationale for this, he explained that he believed that women didn't really enjoy swallowing sperm. Following several moments of mutual silence, he added that another reason might be because as a teenager he'd been told by a friend that some women had been known to become pregnant as a result of swallowing sperm. When I asked Stephen R whether he still believed this information to be correct, he blushed for the first time in our dialogue and admitted that, although in one sense he knew of the impossibility of such an eventuality, nevertheless he could not truly dismiss this information.

'Stranger things are possible,' he joked. 'Wasn't Christ supposed to have been conceived via some jiggery-pokery through Mary's ear?'

'Perhaps so,' I concurred, 'but that conception is supposed to have been somewhat unique. Are you suggesting that any conception that you and your partner may bring about would have to occur under similar circumstances?'

'If I don't resolve the problem, it looks like it might have to!' he joked once more.

The remainder of our session yielded the following information: Stephen R's problem was not a new one in his life, nor was it specifically related to his current relationship. It had been present since his first sexual encounter with a woman and, perhaps unsurprisingly, had been the stated cause of the break-up of at least three previous significant relationships. It had also been the spur to his 'experimentation' with sexual relations with men, since for a period of time his own ruminations and attempts to understand this behaviour had led him to consider the possibility that he 'might be gay'. However, although he had enjoyed his period of 'homosexuality', he had discovered that he preferred intimate contact with women. While he had been somewhat relieved by this knowledge, the significance and mystery of his problem had intensified over the years and had now reached crisis point. Although he had not discussed this issue with any of his friends, nor any of his sexual partners (including his current partner), he had taken steps to read up on sexuality and had concluded that he required the services of a sex therapist.

When I informed him that, while I was more than willing to explore sexual problems with clients, I was not a specialist in sex therapy, he became somewhat dejected and asked whether I could supply him with names of sex therapists. I responded that I was willing to provide him with suitable organizational addresses which he could then follow up. Several minutes of silence ensued, at the end of which Stephen R said: 'Well, seeing as I've started this with you, perhaps I should stay on for a while and see what you have to offer.'

I repeated that I was willing to work with him but added that I could only 'offer' to explore with him what he was willing to bring into the dialogue. I don't know what he understood from this statement, but, nevertheless, he replied that he wished to work with me. The remainder of the session was devoted to the clarification of practical and 'frame'-related issues leading to a verbal contract between us.

We met once a week and during the following five weeks the focus of our dialogue, set by Stephen R, was the exploration of his sexuality. One issue that I sought to clarify quite early on in these sessions was related to his use or non-use of a condom during intercourse and what effect this had, if any, on his inability to achieve intra-vaginal ejaculation. Surprised with

219

himself, Stephen R admitted that he had not considered this before, but, considering it now, he realized that, while he still avoided attempting intra-vaginal ejaculation even while wearing a condom, he could think of at least a couple of instances in the past when he had, indeed, ejaculated during vaginal penetration. 'But I hated myself for it afterwards,' he added. In any case, even if he'd been able somehow to 'do it' while wearing a condom in the past, this option was no longer available since he and his partner, having agreed to maintain a monogamous relationship some two months earlier, had ceased taking any precautions. It was also during this time that Stephen R informed me that he experienced his greatest sexual pleasure while masturbating in private and that even when he was in an on-going sexual relationship his masturbation ritual was still regularly enacted. This ritual required him to angle his body in such a way, and to practise a version of the *stop-start technique* devised by Masters and Johnson, so that, on ejaculation, he could catch the jet of sperm with his mouth and swallow it. The swallowing of his own sperm was *the* essential element to the ritual and his failure to do so, as happened on occasion, led to strong feelings of dejection and the compulsive need to repeat the act, once sufficient time had elapsed, until he succeeded.

I asked him to explore and describe his experience of dejection further but, although he showed every sign of attempting to vocalize his experience, he soon gave up, stating that nothing he could verbalize occurred to him. I suggested that he stay with this experience of *nothingness* and explore that. What did it feel like to him to come up with nothing? What did he associate with this experience? Much to Stephen R's surprise, he found that the first related thought brought him, once more, to the remembered experience of those few occasions in his life when he had been too aroused to prevent himself from ejaculating while his penis was still inside his partner's vagina. On such occasions, he had experienced an instantaneous 'low' that he'd tried, but usually failed, to conceal from his partners. And how had he eventually rid himself of this unpleasant feeling? There was only one way: an extended session of 'successful' solitary masturbation.

We also explored the meaning and significance of his homo-sexual relationships. What emerged from these discussions was Stephen R's contention that, although he had 'ceased being a homosexual', nevertheless he looked back on his sexual experiences during this time in his life as being second in intensity only to his masturbation rituals. Clarification of this point led to the awareness that, for reasons he could not pin down, he had felt particularly free and relaxed in his sexual encounters with other men. How so? Was it because of their activities? Did these avoid any form of penile penetration, for instance? No. Anal intercourse was commonly practised, and enjoyed, by Stephen R. Was it the experience of being protected with a condom that allowed the pleasure? No, he confessed; although he and his partners had tended to use condoms, there had been a number of occasions when they had risked anal sex without them. Now, looking back on this, it surprised him to discover that the use or not of a condom had had no significant effect whatsoever on his ability to ejaculate during penetrative intercourse with men. This realization provoked a great deal of contemplation and, initially at least, confusion.

It was during the eighth session that Stephen R announced that he was beginning to get bored with his exclusive focus on sexuality and wished to talk about other matters.

'What would you like to talk about?' I enquired.
'I suppose you want me to talk about my past.'
'Do you want to talk about your past?'
'Christ, no!'
'All right, then, what do you want to talk about?'
'This is just a way to get me to talk about my past, isn't it?'
'Do you want to talk about your past?'
'I knew it! Well, I'm going to call your bluff and talk about something else!'
'Fine. What do you want to talk about?'
Stephen R laughed loudly. 'Okay, smart arse. I'm not going to give in to this! I'll talk to you about my favourite author! How's that grab you?'

'Tell me what you want to say about your favourite author.'

So, grudgingly, not quite sure whether he'd 'won' the argument or not, Stephen R told me that his favourite author was the American writer Norman Mailer. He'd just recently finished reading his novel *Ancient Evenings*, Mailer's re-interpretation of *The Egyptian Book of the Dead*, and prior to that he'd read *The Executioner's Song*, a 'novelization' of the life and execution of Gary Gilmore. He asked me if I'd read these books as well. I answered that I had.

He then stated that the first of Mailer's books that he'd ever read had been *An American Dream*, that it was still his favourite, and that he now intended to reread it.

'What was it that impressed you about that particular book?' I asked.

'Its style. The way it's written. The main character . . .' He paused. 'Mostly, it was that scene where Roark kills his wife.'

I remembered the scene as well; it's difficult to forget. In it, Mailer describes in detail a woman's desperate attempts to escape death by strangulation, her failure to do so, and the involuntary release of her urine and faeces at the moment of her death.

'Put yourself in the woman's place for a moment,' I suggested. 'What do you see happening to you?'

Stephen R shuddered at the thought. 'I wonder what it must feel like,' he half whispered.

'What's the "it"?'

'All that crap and piss coming out of you.' (Long, silent pause.) 'I suppose I'd be squirting "cum" all over the place as well.'

'And what does that thought leave you with?'

Stephen R laughed. 'I guess I'm wondering what that would feel like!'

'What would it feel like?'

'I don't know. Horrible, I suppose. But then again, who knows?' He paused, smiled once more. 'I read somewhere that some people do that to themselves, nearly hang themselves just to "come" like that. It's supposed to be the ultimate "come".'

'Do you think it might be?' I asked.

Still considering his last statement, Stephen R paid no attention to mine. He produced a sudden smile. 'We've got back to sex again,' he laughed.

'Via death,' I challenged.

'Yeah, well, they're connected, aren't they?'

'How do you connect them?' I asked.

Much to my surprise, tears started to flow out of his eyes. He cried for the rest of the session.

During the ninth and tenth sessions, Stephen R chose to return to the exploration of immediate concerns in his life, primarily the increasing degree of tension that had been developing between his fiancée and himself. As I'd never heard him use the word 'fiancée' before, I enquired as to whether there had been a recent decision made concerning their relationship. Indeed there had. A day or so following the events of the eighth session, Stephen R and his fiancée had decided to marry as soon as reasonably possible and 'get on with the business of producing offspring.'

'And how is "the business" progressing?' I enquired.

Perhaps not surprisingly, Stephen R's reply was to confess that he'd been working so hard lately that the frequency of their love-making had declined somewhat dramatically over the last two weeks. And what of the frequency of his masturbatory ritual? That had remained the same; indeed, it might even have increased a little. I then asked whether he saw any relationship between the decline in frequency of sexual intercourse and the increased tension between the couple. He did. And had they talked about it? They had. And? The discussion had been going well until his fiancée had wondered aloud whether Stephen R really did want to have children. After that it had turned into a slanging match that had still to be fully resolved. I asked him whether he'd thought that his fiancée's question had been justified or not. His anger obvious by the grimace on his face, Stephen R shouted back at me: 'Of course not! I *do* want to

have kids! It's just this bloody problem that gets in the way!'
He paused, then added: 'I don't know. You don't seem to be
able to help. We just keep going around and around in circles.
Maybe I should have gone to see a sex therapist in the first
place!'

'I can understand your concern,' I replied. 'You took a chance
in staying on with me and, right now, you're not sure whether
this was the right decision for you to have made.'

'I don't know, do I?' he said. 'It's just that . . . Oh, I don't
know!'

In spite of this statement, at the completion of our session
Stephen R said 'I'll see you next week' as he left the room.

From the very start of the eleventh session, he seemed particularly agitated. With a strong emotional tone to his voice, and
his body shaking in uncontrolled spasms, he sat down. For some
minutes he remained silent, avoiding looking me in the eyes.
Finally, sighing deeply, he stated that he wanted to tell me
something.

'I've been thinking things over,' he began. 'There's something I need to let you in on.'

I made a gesture with my head, attempting to convey the
message that I was 'with him'.

'Something you said a few weeks ago has stayed with me.
In fact, I can't stop thinking about it.'

'Something I said,' I repeated.

'Yes. About death.'

'What about death?'

'It was in connection with Mailer's books.'

'Yes, I remember that. What did that say to you?'

'Well, I remembered later that I read somewhere that
orgasm used to be referred to as "the little death" or something like that.'

'You see a connection between orgasm and death,' I
ventured.

'I'm not sure. I want to explore this with you.'

'Okay. Let me just throw something out, then. I remember
a phrase out of some book I read once that goes: "Death is

the price we pay for sex." Does that link in to your own thoughts at all?'

Initially, the phrase struck Stephen R as being odd, but he seemed intrigued enough by it to want to clarify its meaning. Though he asked what I thought it meant, I responded that, while I was willing to share my interpretation with him, I would first appreciate knowing what the phrase meant to him.

'I don't know,' he replied. 'It seems a bit screwy. That's why I wanted to know what you made of it.'

'Okay. Then let me ask you this: what do you think the phrase means to me?'

For the first time that day, Stephen R smiled. 'You want to know what I think that you think?' he chuckled. 'That's crazy!'

'Humour me,' I said.

He paused, considered the request once more, then began. 'I guess that to you it might mean that since we all die, then sex is the only thing we have to make us want to stay alive for as long as possible.'

'Do you mean it's the thing that makes life worth living?'

'Yeah.'

'Anything else?'

'Like what?'

'I don't know. Put it within the context of your problem. Does anything come up?'

'Having kids?'

'Yeah. Reproduction.'

'The only thing that comes to mind is another question.'

'Which is?'

'Well, if we didn't have to die maybe we wouldn't be so worried about having kids.'

'If I didn't have to die, I wouldn't have to worry about reproduction,' I re-phrased.

'Yeah.'

'Let's play with that a little bit. What if we change a couple of words around? "If I didn't have to reproduce—"'

'I wouldn't have to worry about death,' Stephen R completed.

Mere seconds later, Stephen R's facial appearance altered dramatically. His face turned pale, his jaw, quite literally, dropped. 'That's what I was trying to put into words earlier, but I couldn't then! That sums it up exactly!' he exclaimed.

'Good. So let's explore this one.'

We did precisely that for the remainder of that session and the following two. These explorations proved useful to Stephen R since they led him to an initial clarification of his personal views and anxieties concerning his eventual death. Further, they opened up discussion concerning the death of his father some six years earlier. In turn, these led to his concerns about the noticeable ageing process he'd observed in his mother. Finally, they led him to the remembrance of an incident from his childhood when, aged seven, he'd seen his father cry at his father's (Stephen R's grandfather's) funeral. This had been the first 'real' experience of death that he'd encountered and it had frightened him to the extent that he remembered having nightmares about it for several weeks afterwards. Most significant, for Stephen R, was the connected memory of his father saying to someone (Stephen R? Stephen R's mother? He could not recall) during this time: 'At least he had children to cry for him! I can't imagine dying all alone, without any of your own kids there.'

Repeating this phrase out loud to himself, as much as to me, Stephen R now saw a double meaning to it. Could he, making sense of it as a child, have construed it to mean that death itself was impossible so long as one's offspring had not yet come into being?

Perhaps. Whatever the case, of far greater significance to Stephen R was the fact that, parallel to these explorations, his relationship with his fiancée had begun to improve and the frequency of their love-making had once again returned to its previous level. More significant than its quantity, however, had been its improved quality. For the first time in his sexual life, Stephen R found himself 'really giving himself to someone'.

With all this in mind, Stephen R and I were now able to reconsider his 'problem', and aspects of his sexuality in general, in a new light. This activity led him to the insight that all his actions had been expressions of his divided, yet connected, views on reproduction and death. If he did not make the possibility of his fatherhood more likely through intra-vaginal orgasm, he was, in some way, prolonging his own life, almost making himself 'immortal'. Considering his sexual relations with men and women, he began to wonder whether his greater enjoyment of homosexual encounters was related to the fact that he knew in all certainty that no childbirth was possible in such relations, whereas with women there was always the uncertain possibility, the superstitious thought, that pregnancy might just somehow occur even in the strangest of circumstances. Perhaps the very fact that he could engage in, and enjoy, anal intercourse with men leading to penetrative orgasm, whether he used a condom or not, further revealed that the crux of the issue lay in his concern that virtually any variant of sexual intercourse with a woman (regardless of whether he used a condom or not) might, somehow, lead to her pregnancy and, by implication, set up the mechanism initiating his eventual death.

Similarly, when we explored both his masturbation ritual and his compulsive need to lick up his sperm from his partners' bodies, Stephen R now interpreted this as an act whose meaning lay in the self-same quest to cheat death. For in taking back into himself the very substance that was necessary for another's life to begin, it was as though he were 'erasing' the life-endangering aspects of the sexual act. After all, if the potential for life was being returned to him, then no quantity of substance (or of 'life-time') was lost.

In his own way, Stephen R had found the means to refute the quotation I had offered him. Indeed, he must have arrived at the essence of that quote long before he'd ever heard it from me and had been living a good part of his life as a challenge to its meaning. That had been acceptable, or at least often adequate, as long as the idea of becoming a father remained simply that. Once presented with a real possibility of reproduction, this world-view had been threatened to its foundations. To take part in a successful attempt at reproduction would pave the way to his own eventual death.

This explanation seemed to be particularly worthwhile to Stephen R in that it opened up to him various ways both to reassess the fundamental premises on which he'd built up the 'meaning' of his sexuality and how this, in turn, had dictated the limits to its expression. More specifically, it allowed him to begin to deal directly with his 'problem'. This task took further time and exploration, but during our seventeenth session he proudly announced that he had managed to achieve orgasm during penile–vaginal intercourse. Not that he'd greatly enjoyed the act, but at least he'd done it! And more, he realized that what had allowed him to do so was the thought he'd maintained during the act that now, at last, he knew without doubt that he really did want to have children, even if death was the price required of him.

Our sessions together came to an end in the twenty-sixth week. By then, Stephen R's ability to achieve orgasm during penile–vaginal intercourse seemed no longer to be an issue for him; indeed, he claimed to have begun enjoying the act for its own sake. Interestingly, the frequency of his masturbation ritual had not declined. For Stephen R it remained something deeply private, personal and important.

Case discussion

Although this case is by no means a typical example of my practice owing to the brevity of its duration and, to a lesser degree, to the specificity of its concern, I believe that it provides a fairly accurate representation of my style of working and, more significantly, of an approach that seeks to avoid the imposition of unnecessary theory-led assumptions and which attempts to remain at a descriptive level of interpretation as was discussed in the previous section.

Firstly, it seems to me that the fundamental premise of the stance I adopted was that of accepting and working with the material provided by Stephen R without, from the start of the enterprise, seeking to impose on it my preconceived theories and assumptions concerning the meaning and aetiology of the presented problem. Instead, the interventions made attempted to be invitations to explore and clarify the meanings of Stephen R's statements as perceived and understood by him. This attempt required a great deal of willingness on my part both to confront and seek to set aside, or 'bracket', the plethora of personally held views, opinions, and meaning-biases concerning the issues being disclosed and explored by Stephen R. This was by no means an easy, or always possible, requirement to fulfil, and part of my rationale for providing brief snippets of dialogue in the case discussion was to allow readers to see how my responses and interventions sought to adhere to this form of *descriptive challenging*.

So long as I attempted to stay with, and respect, the content of Stephen R's disclosure, my challenges took the form of silence, or clarificatory questioning, or even the introduction of new, if still directly related, material (such as, for example, my disclosure of the quotation concerning sex and death). All these challenges may have been 'risky', in that they may have misunderstood what he was attempting to express, but I believe that they provided the means to a more open, effective and less artificial dialogue between us. At the same time, they allowed Stephen R to indicate on several occasions that he was entitled to reject particular challenges without having such responses interpreted by me as forms of 'resistance'.

Nevertheless, it is important to make clear that the approach I employed *did* depend on the assumption that all the issues raised by Stephen R were meaning-derived in that their presence, or their problematic nature, reflected assumptions or world-views held by him. As such, while it remained my task to challenge such world-views through descriptive interpretation, the relative effectiveness of these challenges could be evaluated on the basis of whether Stephen R's responses indicated that I had adequately described and clarified his world-view. Put simply, what I attempted was to 'enter' his meaning-world, and to experience and interpret it in a manner akin to his experience. It is in doing so that I, in my 'otherness', was able to assist him in confronting, exposing and challenging the (often unstated) assumptions, limitations, and 'sedimented perspectives' held by him. To attempt do so required me to try to accept Stephen R's meaning-system, however irrational it might have appeared to me to be, and, rather than dispute it by means of any other alternative meaning-systems, to seek to expose and challenge whatever inconsistencies, gaps, unstated assumptions and so forth I had perceived to exist in his meaning-system. Obviously, I could only begin to achieve this if Stephen R's meaning-system *had* been sufficiently understood, and, as importantly, if Stephen R felt me to be trustworthy enough to allow me access to it.

This approach also turned my task away from symptom removal (i.e. 'curing' Stephen R) and towards a refocusing on symptom exploration and clarification. Again, I must acknowledge an assumption here that the symptoms expressed were themselves 'clues' or representations of Stephen R's world-view. While, obviously, symptoms may diminish or cease to exist (as in Stephen R's case) because of the therapeutic encounter, a severe limitation would have been imposed on what ability I had to attend to and challenge the client if I'd made the removal of symptoms the principal goal of our therapeutic dialogue.

Readers may have also noted that throughout the case discussion no reference was made to 'unconscious' factors or mechanisms. I believe that the case demonstrates how it may be that significant insight into the conscious meaning-world of the client, allowing extensive shifts in psychic orientation, is both possible and, dare I say, sufficient, without the imposition of any theoretical assumption concerning an unconscious mechanism.

Similarly, while Stephen R's perception of his past was employed in order to clarify aspects of his current experience, the past as discussed can be seen to be, more accurately, an exploration of the 'past as currently lived and future-focused' rather than 'the past as it really was' or 'the past as fixed in time and meaning'. Nor was there any assumption of the past as a 'linearly causal' element in Stephen R's current experience. While it remained his ultimate right to choose to impose causality on his world-views if he so wished (and, in this case, it is implicit that this is what Stephen R elected to do), I would argue that I, as the therapist, did not need to assume such, and, indeed, that whatever ability I demonstrated in remaining open to the myriad of alternative possibilities as to the 'why' of his current world-views or experience allowed a greater adequacy in my ability to 'hear' him. Finally, the approach avoided any reliance on the hypotheses of 'transference' and 'counter-transference' and, instead, presented an alternative stance that was in keeping with the one discussed previously.

If, by this point in the discussion, some readers have begun to think that this approach to psychotherapy is somewhat easier to apply than other approaches, it remains my duty to dissuade them of this conclusion. The abdication of a position of authority or superior knowledge is no simple task at the best of times; it becomes even more problematic when, not unusually, one's clients seem to demand such of the therapist. I have included an obvious example of this in the case summary (Stephen R's query as to whether he had done the right thing in continuing to work with me). My response, whatever its value, attempted to 'stay with' his concern *as expressed* rather than to adopt a defensive stance which, for instance, might have sought to interpret the statement as an expression of 'negative transference', or might have tried to convince him that his initial decision had been the right one, or might have attempted to mollify his implicit demands by providing information or theoretical explanations designed to demonstrate my superior knowledge and authority. I can assure the reader that the temptation to adopt any of these latter positions retains its strength over time (or, at least, it does for me!) regardless of what value there might be in keeping it in check. My own view on this is that the strength of the temptation is related to the personal difficulty I experience in attending to the material being expressed.

Perhaps more than any other, this approach exposes therapists to their own biases, prejudices, and sedimented outlooks and challenges them to find the strength (at times, even the courage) not to allow them to interfere with the process of listening. For example, the case discussed brought up for me difficult, often painful, personal material surrounding the issue of reproduction. In this instance, I felt able to 'bracket' it sufficiently; though I can assure readers that this is not always the case.

231

In a similar vein, when I step back from the case itself, and my relationship to Stephen R, I can see that, in a more abstract sense, his concerns might well be understood in terms of theoretical outlooks that posit the existence of a fundamentally human 'death anxiety'. However, while it may be useful to view and discuss it from this perspective, it seems to me that all the points I have made in this discussion would be seriously weakened had I, in some way, *imposed* this theoretical perspective on my dialogue with Stephen R. As far as I can judge it, the critical reader might take issue with me in one instance alone – namely, on the occasion when, following Stephen R's résumés of Norman Mailer's books, and his declaration that we had returned to the subject of sex, I made the statement: 'Via death.' I was well aware of the risk in this challenge, and, perhaps more pertinently, that I might be stretching the boundaries of descriptive interpretation too far. And yet it seemed a proper statement to make at that moment on the grounds that the focus of Stephen R's descriptions of Mailer's books had been the themes of the death journey, reincarnation, death by execution, and murder. Further, had Stephen R dismissed my challenge, I would not have pressed him on it. While it is true that he arrived at conclusions in line with those suggested by the hypothesis of 'death anxiety', and while I cannot ever be entirely certain that my own theoretical leanings did not, in some subtle way, impose themselves on our dialogue through my challenges, thereby influencing his clarifications of his world-views, nevertheless, as I hope the case summary clearly shows, no overt references to 'death anxiety' were made at any point in the therapy.

Once again, it seems to me that if 'death anxiety' is, indeed, a fundamental aspect of the human condition, then clients can and should be expected to discover it for themselves without the theory-based assistance of the therapist. I believe that Stephen R did confront aspects of his 'death anxiety', and that he was better able to do so through the quality of our dialogue, but I am also reasonably convinced that he did so without my having to 'guide' him towards it.

In a similar fashion, Stephen R was able to express his sense of the relationship and how it did or did not fulfil his needs in various way, not least through his decision to end therapy at a time he thought opportune. My own preference would have been for him to have continued in therapy somewhat longer, since I felt that there was more – indeed, most likely much more – for us to explore. But whatever my feelings on this matter, I believe it more important that Stephen R's (or any other client's) decision should take precedence and, in doing so, establish that whatever power exists in the relationship does not belong solely to the therapist.

Most significantly, I hope that the case presented has allowed readers to gain a sense of the fundamental importance of the *therapeutic relationship* itself. For, far more significant than any theoretical views or their various applications, it seems to me that whatever was made possible in a beneficial sense for Stephen R emerged through the quality and respectful openness of the dialogue we engaged in. In this sense, the case as presented could only convey a small part of that encounter and, even then, what was conveyed was itself a very limited expression of the manner in which the sessions were conducted. I will have more to say about this question in Part 5 of this text, but for now I hope that my attempt to demonstrate to readers that the possibilities of descriptively oriented interpretations are by no means limited and can provide clients with as valid and sufficient an insight as might be obtained from the psycho-analytic model while, at the same time, remaining less open to the dangers and difficulties contained within the latter.

But the alternatives presented are by no means the only ones that have been forthcoming or which have taken a critical perspective on the numerous assumptions contained within the psycho-analytic model. Both the cognitive-behavioural and the humanistic models arose partly in response to many of these same assumptions, and each has become a major therapeutic model in its own right. Equally, as Part 4 will seek to demonstrate, each has also raised novel concerns for therapists which require critical attention.

PART FOUR

DEMYSTIFYING THERAPEUTIC THEORY: 2. COGNITIVE-BEHAVIOURAL AND HUMANISTIC MODELS

It is easy to love a perfect being. The real test is to love a being who is also imperfect.

– Anonymous

Part 3 of this text discussed a number of fundamental assumptions contained within the psycho-analytic model and considered their implications with regard to the practice of therapy in general and the issue of therapist power in particular. While the psycho-analytic model has had – and continues to have – a vast influence on both therapeutic theory and practice, it would be misleading to suggest that it is the dominant model in contemporary therapeutic thought. From around the middle of this century, two other models rose to prominence, both of which have had a major impact on our understanding of therapy and each of which, in its particular fashion, has advanced both its theory and practice. As in Part 3, Part 4 will discuss these two models – the cognitive-behavioural model and the humanistic model – and appraise a number of fundamental assumptions on which each theory rests. Equally, as in Part 3, it will focus particular attention on the implications of these assumptions with regard to the overall issue of power in the therapeutic relationship.

1. THE COGNITIVE-BEHAVIOURAL MODEL

A. *An Overview*

The *cognitive-behavioural model* of therapy focuses on *action-oriented* approaches aimed at altering particular patterns of individual thought and behaviour which have been classified as debilitating or irrational. The various techniques that make up this model share a common emphasis in that they are founded on an *experimentally derived scientific view* of human behaviour and, as such, their specific procedures rely heavily on experimental data analyses as the primary means of confirming their reliability and validity.

In turn, the results obtained from experimental work also provide the means for practitioners to amend or significantly alter their current procedures. In this way, therapeutic techniques that have adopted the cognitive-behavioural model can claim verification for its assumptions through extensive quantitative research, where primary attention rests on the testing and measurement of therapeutic outcomes and the statistical analysis of the efficacy of the procedures employed. The emphasis on on-going experimental research is both a central defining characteristic of this model and remains the most important means of designing and refining systematic applications of cognitive-behavioural therapy to presented problems.

The cognitive-behavioural model assumes a fundamental relationship between individuals and their environment which is both interactive and co-productive (Bandura, 1986). To this extent, it argues that just as individuals act on, or shape, their environment, so too are they shaped by it. However, whereas in the past, when solely behavioural models were applied to therapy, the current model emphasizes the cognitive elements in human behaviour so that the examination of clients' *beliefs and biases* is a central concern of the cognitive-behavioural therapist (Ellis and Whiteley, 1979).

Equally, the cognitive-behavioural model focuses on clients' current issues or problems and the immediate factors influencing these rather than concern with the analysis of their possible originating determinants. Therapists' interventions are designed to be *instructive*, or broadly educational, so that specific skills can be learned, practised, and generalized to meet the particular needs and conditions of individual clients (Corey, 1991). In doing so, specific and concrete *outcome goals* are designed. These are negotiated with clients on the basis of such factors as how realistic the goals may be and what advantages and disadvantages in terms of the client's lifestyle and world-view their fulfilment may elicit.

Similarly, cognitive-behavioural therapists' interventions focus on the clarification of *how* a client experiences a particular problem or maladaptive condition and *what the client does* in response to this cognitively construed experience.

For example, if a client's presenting problem is stated as being 'depression', the cognitive-behavioural therapist will initially seek to understand what the specific elements of the experience that are contained in the client's definition of 'depression' may be, and will then go on to clarify with the client what consequent behaviours are enacted both to express and attempt to deal with the condition. In doing so, the cognitive-behavioural therapist might uncover various *irrational beliefs or assumptions* held by the client (such as the view that 'I am not allowed to make mistakes') which in themselves may be provoking the experience of 'depression'. Alternatively, the therapist may discover that the client's response to the experience of depression is to take himself to bed and sleep for hours, which, while temporarily alleviating the condition, subsequently aggravates it owing to the various inter-personal consequences of this act and *their* reinforcement of the conditions that led to the initial assessment of 'depression'. So, for instance, having taken himself to bed, the client fails to appear at work, which leads to his superiors being angry with him, which further provokes and reinforces the belief that 'I am not allowed to make mistakes', which in turn sets off the depression once again.

In negotiating a concrete goal with the client, the cognitive-behavioural therapist may find that the initially desired goal is unrealistic (e.g. 'I never want to make mistakes again') and that a more realistic goal must be set (e.g. 'I must find more suitable ways of dealing with my making mistakes'). In doing so, the therapist may have to challenge underlying fundamental assumptions and beliefs held by the client (e.g. 'I am not allowed to make mistakes') by pointing out their inappropriateness or irrationality (e.g. 'My mistakes may be irritating, but are an allowable fact of life'). Equally, the therapist may seek to teach the client more rational ways of dealing with the presenting problem (e.g. 'When beginning to feel depressed, find something to do which re-affirms various positively held values and beliefs about yourself').

In some cognitive-behavioural approaches, various *relaxation or desensitizing techniques* will he taught (Jacobson, 1938; Wolpe, 1969); in others, the cognitive-behavioural therapist will engage in dialogue with the client which aims to diminish or remove the irrational belief and replace it with a more rational one (Ellis and Whiteley, 1979). Alternatively, some cognitive-behavioural therapists will utilize the relationship itself as a means of promoting the therapist as a *model* for the client to observe, imitate and learn from (Bandura, 1986). Various popular *assertiveness training* procedures, for instance, employ any one or combinations of these techniques.

B.   *Rational-Emotive Behaviour Therapy (REBT)*

One of the most influential of the approaches using a cognitive-behavioural model is *Rational-Emotive Behaviour Therapy (REBT)*, which was developed by Albert Ellis (Ellis and Whiteley, 1979). A key assumption of REBT is that human beings have a biological tendency to think irrationally (or 'crookedly'). Equally, however, human beings also have 'the capacity to change their cognitive, emotive, and behavioral processes . . . and train themselves so that they can eventually remain minimally disturbed for the rest of their life' (Corey, 1991:329). REBT argues that these irrational assumptions tend to be expressed in terms of *deeply ingrained demands* that people either make of themselves or of the world (e.g. 'I/the world *must/should/ought to be*' . . .) which act to impede severely individuals' constructive experiences of life.

Ellis's REBT model basically focuses on the *irrational beliefs* that follow an activating event and which give rise to particular behavioural and emotional consequences. The task of the REBT therapist is to *dispute* these beliefs so that more rational ones may be accepted and, therefore, provide a new attitude towards subsequent activating events and (implicitly) provoke novel, and rational, behavioural and emotional responses. So, for instance, a client enters REBT because she feels that 'life is no longer worth living'. A recent event that has provoked this conclusion may be that she attended the wedding ceremony of her last single friend and now she finds herself to be the one remaining single person in her circle. Further, in response to this activating event, she feels shunned, lonely and unattractive and, looking back on her life, has concluded that there is something wrong with her, that her previous relationships were both intermittent and unsatisfactory, that her job is unrewarding, and that the future is likely to hold no significant positive changes. When asked to describe the beliefs and assumptions she holds about this general stance, she answers that 'life is unfair, I am a hopeless failure, and I am an awful and boring person who deserves what she's getting'.

The REBT therapist, following Ellis's approach, would seek to challenge her beliefs by demonstrating to her that she has turned a number of desirable outcomes into '*must*urbatory needs', and that she is irrationally 'awfulizing' both the conditions of her life and herself. Further, the therapist might attempt to convince her that she is capable of adopting other, more rational, viewpoints, and that she could *do* things to change at least some of the conditions of her life. For instance, she could join clubs or societies where she might meet suitable partners, or she might consider what she can do to improve her job or find a more interesting one.

In addition, and as a way of putting these suggestions into practice, the REBT therapist would be likely to set her weekly 'homework' exercises designed to help her achieve some of these goals in a more systematic fashion. At the same time, REBT theory assumes that the act of carrying out these exercises itself challenges and weakens the client's irrationally held beliefs.

In general, the REBT therapist attempts to re-educate her, not only in a behavioural sense, but in an attitudinal sense, by trying to shake her out of the pattern of beliefs she has adopted. Nevertheless, some of these beliefs may be so deeply held and ingrained that they go back to childhood and her early relations with 'significant others' such as her parents, siblings and teachers. The therapist focuses on these and, again, seeks to demonstrate to her that her beliefs concerning these can be reconsidered and reassessed.

In the course of this interaction, the REBT therapist, together with the client, might uncover further related assumptions and beliefs that strengthen her irrational stance towards the world. For instance, the therapist and client might find that, as a child, she had developed the belief that her role in the family was to be the 'carer' of others and that, whenever she attempted to fulfil her own needs, this upset other members of her family because they did not receive her whole-hearted attention. The therapist might then dispute the client's underlying assumption that she was *responsible* for her family's upset by wanting or doing something other than what they expected by attempting to demonstrate to her, through *disputational dialogue*, that the others' responses were of their own making and, hence, their responsibility rather than hers.

Throughout, the REBT therapist works from the assumption that, 'in order to bring about a philosophical change' (Corey, 1991:335), the client must accept

1. The reality that she has largely created her own disturbances and has the ability significantly to change them.
2. That her problems stem mainly from irrational beliefs and demands.
3. That she must learn to identify and dispute these beliefs and replace them with rational alternatives.
4. That she must be willing to commit herself to practising the adoption of a new and rational philosophy through the use of the cognitive, emotive and behavioural skills she has learned in therapy (Dryden and Ellis, 1988).

In order to achieve this, the REBT therapist must be sufficiently skilful both in discerning the irrational beliefs held by the client and in arguing the case for rational alternatives. Further, the therapist must be sufficiently empathic towards the client for her to be willing to address and reconsider her beliefs while in dialogue with the therapist. To this end, the therapist must be recognized as being both trustworthy and intelligent enough to earn her attention and respect in a manner similar to that of a good teacher. Finally, the therapist must be sufficiently practised in a variety of skills that include: the disputation of irrational beliefs, the setting of suitably realistic and relevant homework, and the training of the client to change or make more precise her own 'inner' language, or to develop a technique of mental imagery designed to remove irrational emotional patterns and replace them with rational ones. More recently, REBT therapists have begun to employ role-playing techniques and 'shame-attacking exercises', as well as to develop the use of both humour and forceful debate in order to facilitate the movement from intellectual to emotional insight (Corey, 1991).

While all these assumptions and techniques are specific to REBT, nevertheless variations of most, or all, of them can be found in the various approaches that fall within the cognitive-behavioural model.

C. Critiques of the Cognitive-Behavioural Model

As can be deduced from this brief summary, the hypotheses and assumptions contained in the cognitive-behavioural model stand in significant contrast to those that are to be found in the psycho-analytic model. On the whole, they avoid reliance on hypothetical systems such as the unconscious, are more present-oriented, and while the relationship between therapist and client is considered to be an important element, it is primarily the 'instructional quality' of the relationship, rather than its 'transferential basis', which is considered to be essential. As an additional contrast to the psycho-analytic model, cognitive-behavioural therapy is principally derived from, or supported by, experimental data, and the cognitive-behavioural model prides itself (with some justification) on its scientific foundations which allow it to remain flexible and accepting of reformulations of its techniques on the basis of the on-going research carried out by its practitioners and theorists.

The question of the therapist's superior knowledge

At the same time, while clearly different in significant ways to the psycho-analytic model, the cognitive-behavioural model nevertheless shares a fundamental assumption with the former. For both models emphasize the therapist's superior knowledge and ability – even if the manner in which this superiority is understood and applied is different. This common strand within both models can be traced back to the therapist's virtually unquestioning belief in, and adherence to, the theoretical assumptions underlying the chosen approach. In this way, any failures of therapeutic intervention can be blamed either on the client's 'resistance' (in the psycho-analytic model) or the client's misapplication of (or unwillingness to apply) the specified instructions presented by the therapist. While the cognitive-behavioural model claims to be the most flexible in its on-going reassessment of its theory and its applications based on the 'results' engendered, nevertheless it must be asked if these results reflect the qualitative experience of the client and are valid within that experiential framework. That clients who have worked within the cognitive-behavioural model are as likely to experience dissatisfaction with its effects as they are with any other model, and go on to other forms of therapy just as frequently as do other clients, would suggest that there exists a significant weakness within the model. My own view is that this weakness lies in the assumption of 'objectivity' – an assumption, among several, which I will discuss more fully below.

The values and limitations of a scientific model

The cognitive-behavioural model has come to be widely employed in a number of therapeutic settings, particularly within clinical and educational establishments, where its action-oriented focus on process and outcome is particularly valued. While clearly concerned with presenting itself as a model that is based on clear, scientifically derived principles that are open to experimental verification, at the same time the cognitive-behavioural model contains a number of biases and assumptions that require some clarificatory examination.

While its emphasis on scientific principles and experimental design is obviously a great strength of the cognitive-behavioural model, it may also, somewhat perversely, be seen as a weakness of some potential significance. The roots of cognitive-behavioural therapy lie in developments that have occurred in academic, experimentally oriented psychology over the last thirty years. Once deeply steeped in the behaviourist theories of John Watson and B. F. Skinner, which avoided all inferences of unobservable, hypothesized mental processes and which basically expunged terms like 'consciousness', 'mind', 'will', and so forth from the psychological dictionary, contemporary academic psychology has undergone what has become known as the *cognitive revolution*. Owing to inherent weaknesses in the strict behavioural models that, in a variety of instances, were shown to be insufficient in themselves to explain human faculties such as memory, linguistic ability, abstract thought, and the like, and whose own experimental findings in these areas revealed flaws and contradictions in the theories themselves, growing numbers of psychologists became increasingly dissatisfied with behaviourism and began to develop *cognitive* approaches that focused on intermediary, or mediating, processes that, while not directly observable, could be inferred from experimental findings.

In this way, previously 'taboo' terminology (e.g. 'mental acts', 'feeling', even 'consciousness' itself) began to be re-introduced as proper subject-matter for psychologists to study and examine. Soon enough, the findings obtained from these new approaches began to be applied in various ways – not least in therapy, thereby giving rise to the cognitive-behavioural model in its diverse approaches.

However, while these changes provided the basis for significant theoretical and applied developments, theorists and practitioners have retained their allegiance to their behaviourist 'roots' by remaining firmly bound to experimental procedures geared towards the study and analysis of *quantitative* (or statistically measurable) variables. This is, in itself, nothing to be derided. However, it has become increasingly a matter of concern and debate that this quantitatively oriented method-ology may be, at best, limited in its scope of enquiry. With particular reference to its applications in areas such as therapy, it has been argued that this 'quantitative exclusivity' may be methodologically unable to address and examine a number of relational and process variables that are increasingly acknowl-edged as being central to analyses of therapy.

As was discussed in Part 1 of this text, most experimental studies of therapy are focused on 'outcome', but far fewer have examined 'process' variables (Reason and Rowan, 1981; Kline, 1992). Put another way, while quantitatively based experimental studies may be very useful, and necessary, for the analysis of certain measurable changes that may result from therapy, they are severely restricted in studying those variables that appear within the relationship (i.e. relational variables) which are pri-marily *qualitative* rather than quantitative. As such, while the cognitive-behavioural model emphasizes *what* has occurred as a result of therapy, it says very little about *how* the therapeutic relationship is experienced, or, indeed, how the relationship itself influences outcomes.

The status of the emotions

In the specific context of the approaches discussed above, it can be seen that 'the "feelings" or emotions of clients are paid scant attention other than in terms of their cognitive or behavioural content' (Corey, 1991:327). These *experiential* factors seem to me to be of substantial importance, not least because they serve as significant guides for the therapist in seeking accurately to 'enter into' the client's world-view. If they are minimized, the therapist is less likely to gain a suitable understanding of the client's experience. In the cognitive-behavioural model, the emphasis placed on problem-solving, goal-setting and condition treatment, while in itself valid and laudable, may well prove to be counter-productive if the features being stressed as important by the therapist are not 'in tune' with the client's experience.

So, for instance, to return to the second example discussed above, what is being argued is that it is of importance for the therapist to gain an understanding of what it is like, or what it means to the client to feel 'shunned' or 'unattractive' or 'different to her friends'. For, surely, it is through the exploration of this 'felt experience' that the therapist may better understand what is problematic or unacceptable to the client about herself or her relations with others. But the cognitive-behavioural therapist, in avoiding this exploration, *imposes assumptions on this felt experience* on the basis that the therapist somehow already knows what it is, and what it is like for the client. And, further, as a result of this assumption, the 'problem', the goal-plan, and the treatment may not truly express or represent the client's issues. In this way, while the client's beliefs and behaviours may change with regard to the problem as defined by the therapist, the underlying, or 'felt', issues may well remain and provoke 'new' problems.

The question of symptom substitution

While some critics of the cognitive-behavioural model have incorrectly suggested that clients will eventually 'transfer' or substitute one set of symptoms for another (so, for instance, a client who is successfully treated for a phobic reaction towards dogs will come to substitute something else such as dust or cars for the anxieties once associated with dogs), what I am arguing is that the issue is not one of 'symptom substitution' but that, rather, the underlying conflict being expressed symptomatically has not been sufficiently understood and addressed by the therapist so that it remains even though its associated symptoms may have been treated successfully. My own experience with clients who have previously been in therapy with cognitive-behavioural therapists is that rather than 'substitute' symptoms, they increasingly 'internalize' them such that they become more diffuse and general rather than focused on a specific thing or event. In this way, an important question arises as to whether they have really been helped by therapy or whether the therapy has exacerbated the problem by dissociating it from its symptomatic focus.

The question of objectivity

This issue leads directly on to the question of the role of the cognitive-behavioural therapist as a directive instructor or teacher. The assumption of this stance places a good deal of power and authority on therapists in that it is assumed that not only do therapists 'know' their clients' issues and concerns as specifically experienced by them (the clients), but, just as significantly, that therapists know *better* than their clients how to deal with them on the basis that they (the therapists) are more able to be 'objective' about them. It is this assumption of the *objectivity of the therapist* that now needs to be addressed.

Once again, it is understandable on the basis of the history and development of the cognitive-behavioural model that the notion of objectivity should be greatly stressed. After all, a primary characteristic of the model is its emphasis on 'objective measurement' by means of quantitative experimental studies. The problem with this view, however, is that the notion of a truly objective investigator, observer, or experimenter has been sufficiently cast into doubt by developments within science itself. As I discussed earlier, it is more accurate to speak in terms of *interpretational* investigations rather than objective analyses. This is particularly relevant to the specific 'investigations' that can be carried out in the therapeutic process since the therapist is *interpretationally involved* in the process. While it is fair enough to say that the therapist may provide viewpoints that clarify or add new meaning to the client's world-view, and in this way may be seen as being broadly educational or instructive, the cognitive-behavioural model takes this view several steps further when it suggests that the therapist is being objective. For this latter stance implies that the therapist can distinguish the 'real' from the 'unreal' – a position that would be difficult to maintain. If the cognitive-behavioural model were to argue that therapists challenged contradictions and illogical assumptions *within* the client's world-view, there would be little argument, but by invoking the assumption of the therapist's objectivity, the model bestows unnecessary and potentially abusive power on the therapist.

Normative influences

Nevertheless, the evidence that exists as to the efficacy of outcomes resulting from cognitive-behavioural interventions must be acknowledged. In a broad sense, the cognitive-behavioural model 'works'. But the question must be raised: *Who does it work for?* The cognitive-behavioural model places the therapist in a position of a *normative judge* whose principal *raison d'être* is to define and attempt to remove those client beliefs and behaviours that have been deemed to be irrational or debilitating. But in doing so, it is implicit that it is the therapist who makes the initial assumption – on grounds that are culturally influenced and culturally desirable – as to which attitudes and behaviours are 'irrational' or detrimental to the client's psychological well-being. In this way, the therapist becomes a broadly libertarian representative of the *norms and codes of conduct of the society of which both the therapist and client are members.* But such socio-cultural norms and codes are not in themselves 'objective'. In this way, the cognitive-behavioural model opens itself to criticisms of therapy as a means of controlling alternative or dissenting views that may be seen as being disturbing, unacceptable or dangerous by a particular society.

Clearly, all of us must in some way deal with the dilemmas of conflicting personal and socio-cultural attitudes and desires, and therapy is an important means of confronting such dilemmas, but if therapists base their interventions on the stance that, in being objective, they have somehow resolved these dilemmas and are in some way better able or better informed than the client as to what is true, good, and right for the client, then they run the risk of imposing a socially conformist ideology on the client.

For instance, if we consider the example of the client who no longer feels that life is worth living which was discussed earlier, the 'objective' stance taken by the therapist assumes that her conclusion is wrong and steps must be taken to deal with it. But this view adopted by the client may be seen as not merely something that originates from 'within' the client, and is personal to her alone, but also as a 'response' to attitudes and assumptions that are dominant within her society concerning the undesirability of 'being single'. From the therapist's response to the issue we can see that such attitudes and assumptions are held by the therapist as well, and that the goals set and the interventions made result from these assumptions and attitudes. Does this suggest that the client should be 'doomed' to remain feeling the worthlessness of her own life? Not at all. But until the assumptions are exposed and challenged so that their possible meaning and influence on the client's own world-view are clarified, the therapist cannot assume a knowledge or understanding of the client's experience of worthlessness.

Rational and irrational beliefs

This issue also raises questions with regard to the cognitive-behavioural model's distinction between *rational and irrational beliefs*. Once again, it is only by assuming the ability to maintain an objective stance that therapists can impose such distinctions from an external perspective. Just how 'irrational' is the client's belief that her life is worthless and meaningless? Given the very real demands that society makes on her, which she has not been able to fulfil, her conclusion may be saddening or upsetting, but not necessarily 'irrational'. Once again, it is not just a view that has somehow come to her because of some internal psychic malfunction, but, rather, through her *relations* with others. If there is 'irrationality' it is an irrationality that has as much to do with her society's assumptions and views as with hers. Would it not make more sense for the therapist to work from a stance that *accepts* her conclusion, rather than disputes it, and seeks to clarify just what it is about this conclusion which the client finds difficult to cope with, rather than assume its 'inherent irrationality'? Perhaps, in doing so, the therapist might discover that the problem is not that she is single in a world of couples but that she believes that her willingness to remain single is a sign of abnormality and, hence, her conclusion as to her 'worthlessness' is a consequence of this. Whatever the case, the therapist cannot begin to uncover the source of her conflict if its consequence is immediately understood as being 'irrational'.

The therapeutic relationship

Further, while there is some acknowledgement of the significance of the relationship between client and therapist, nevertheless its importance tends to be stressed as a means to an end
(which is the client's willingness to learn from the therapist and
apply the learning-based goals that have been set) rather than
being of value in and of itself. This emphasis on a tutor–pupil
orientation creates a very different and goal-oriented dialogue
which limits the nature of the encounter in a manner that minimizes, if not excludes, the possibility of any significant learning
(other than on the level of skills amelioration) on the part of
the therapist. The very scientific attitude taken towards the task
of therapy seeks to emphasize the 'curative' aspects of therapy
and, as such, it is of little surprise that cognitive-behavioural
approaches are those that are most strongly concerned with the
analysis of the success of therapy – such success being mainly
statistically focused and to a large extent defined and determined
by the therapist's parameters of concern.

This conclusion, in turn, reveals a fundamental assumption
within the cognitive-behavioural model that the process of
therapy is one where primarily one individual (the therapist)
'does something to' another individual (the client) on the basis
of the assumptions the former has as to the nature of psychic
disturbance and the superiority of one form of behaviour and
mental attitude over another. As such, the investigation of the
client's meaning-world, while clearly relevant to cognitive-
behavioural therapists, has a much more specific and defined
purpose than that of clarification and challenge, since it is
focused on finding the means whereby the therapist can determine the best means of inducing beneficial change in the client.
There is a strong, if implicit, medical stance in this approach –
a stance that suggests that, as with a visit to one's GP, it is the
task of the therapist to employ specialist knowledge in order to
ascertain the nature of the disturbance, to impart only as much
knowledge of this to the client as is deemed necessary and relevant, and to set out particular tasks (in the form of 'homework')
which, if they are followed according to the specific instructions

laid down by the therapist, should ameliorate or remove the disturbing symptoms.

While cognitive-behavioural therapists clearly challenge their clients' views, they do so in a limited sense in that the challenged views are only those that are deemed by the therapist to be relevant to the specific goals set in the initial consultation with the client. In addition, the form of challenge is disputational in that the therapist does not seek to 'enter into' the client's world-view but rather *to attack it* from the onset in order to rid it of its inconsistencies and irrationalities, and to present an alternative position that is the therapist's and is deemed to be both rational and more beneficial for the client to adopt. But, in all such cases, the distinction between that which is 'irrational' or 'unbeneficial' and that which is 'rational' or 'beneficial' is made by the therapists themselves on the basis of their authority. Gerald Corey, among many others, has expressed his concern about the implications of this, particularly with regard to REBT.

> [C]lients can easily acquiesce in a therapist's power and authority by readily accepting the therapist's views without really challenging them or without internalizing ideas. As a precaution it seems essential for therapists to know themselves well and to take care not to merely impose their own philosophy of life on their clients (Corey, 1991: 360).

The issue of what constitutes rational behavior is central here. In line with this concern, I would point to a further crucial issue that has not been suitably considered by cognitive behavioural therapists. So long as this model emphasizes the exploration of client's *goals* in order that they may be analysed as 'realistic' or 'unrealistic', it places significant interpretational power in the hands of therapists. But, on consideration, the issue is less about client's goals than it is about *the means by which clients seek to achieve them*. If cognitive behavioural therapists retained their principal focus upon the clarificatory challenge of such means (i.e. the process) rather than whether their desired outcome is realistic or not, they would continue to attend to their clients without opening themselves to the concerns expressed by their critics.

The issue of successful outcomes

The cognitive-behavioural model claims to have provided the necessary data to demonstrate the superior efficacy of its approach to therapy over all other models. This 'proven' efficacy has helped substantially in determining the extensive adherence to this approach in the majority of clinical, educational and institutional settings on the basis of its success rate and relative brevity. However, what the cognitive-behavioural model appears to have failed to consider is that just as there may be other, less directly quantitative measurements for determining success, so too may it be the case that its definition of success, which of necessity must be a quantitatively measurable definition, may in itself be significantly limited and limiting. That is to say, in failing to give due consideration to clients' less easily quantifiable (or even unquantifiable) responses, such statistical analyses are able to provide only a partial representation of success, which, in turn, is heavily skewed in favour of the model. It may be all too easy to 'prove' success on the basis of statistics – not necessarily because one is 'cooking the books' but, more importantly, because statistical 'language' restricts the 'meaningfulness' of analyses to measurable elements and fails (or is unable) to say anything about other elements which, if considered, might produce a radically different conclusion. Statistics need not necessarily be 'damned lies' to be seen as incomplete – or even inadequate – measurements of success. We need look no further than to Parliament where, for years, the ruling Conservative Party has been producing statistics 'proving' that we are all so much better off. Even if we were to agree that these data have not been 'fudged', the limitations of these claims, at the lived level of most citizens' experience, remain all too obvious. This is not to deny what success *has* been achieved by the cognitive-behavioural model, only to clarify that 'success', in its terms, is a restricted concept.

Change

The emphasis on quantitative measurement raises one final, important issue. This emphasis assumes the all-pervasive importance of *change* as a result of therapeutic intervention. For, otherwise, the quantitative measurements would be of little value. But this assumption is itself open to question. Is therapy *necessarily* about observable and quantifiable change? Should therapists equate the evidence (or lack of such) of change in their clients as *the* determinant for effective therapy? It would appear to be the case that many therapists (and non-therapists) do. But does this *have* to be the case? I will explore this issue more fully below when considering the humanistic model, since perhaps more than any other model it appears to insist on this assumption. But it should be noted that the critical observations made therein apply equally to the cognitive-behavioural model.

D. Conclusions

From this brief synopsis, it should be clear that the cognitive-behavioural model avoids many of the assumptions of the psycho-analytic model of therapy, in that it minimizes, if not dismisses, notions of the unconscious, the determinist influences of the past, and the importance (if not existence) of transference and counter-transference, and seeks to avoid interpretations intended to expose hidden or symbolic meanings. Indeed, the emphasis placed on the clarification and descriptive analysis of currently experienced issues, and the focus on the unique experience of the client, would initially suggest that a good deal of convergence (both actual and potential) exists between the cognitive-behavioural model and the descriptively focused model I have presented in various parts of the text (and which will be discussed more fully in Part 5) as a source for alternative perspectives with regard to various therapy-related issues under discussion.

At the same time, however, as I have attempted to demonstrate, a number of significant divergences remain. Principally, these revolve around the cognitive-behavioural model's assumptions of objectivity, its inability to consider the client's 'feelings' other than as cognitive indicators of rationality or irrationality, its superficial examination of the therapeutic encounter per se, and its emphasis on the directive instructional role of the therapist. While I am of the belief that constructive dialogue between these two models would be both relevant and useful, and would personally welcome this, nevertheless it is of some importance to remain clear as to what these current divergences are and to consider their significance and impact on the therapeutic process.

2. THE HUMANISTIC MODEL

A. *An Overview*

The *humanistic model*, like the psycho-analytic and cognitive-behavioural models, has had a major influence on therapy and is today the most widely employed model within the British counselling movement. Characterized by its emphasis on the exploration of current subjective experience, its promotion of qualitative factors such as compassion, acceptance and tolerance as essential characteristics of the humanistic therapist, and its accentuation of those positive, constructive capacities and potentials for growth and development which it assumes to be present in all human beings, it remains steeped in a humane and libertarian philosophy that is often at odds with the currently dominant competitively oriented and punitive ethos of contemporary British society.

The humanistic model of therapy has its immediate origins in the humanistic and 'human potential' movements in psychology which flowered principally in North America and in Britain between the mid-1960s and early 1970s. This psychological 'revolt', which became characterized as the 'Third Force' in psychology, rejected the reductionistic orientations of both psychoanalysis and behaviourism as being 'de-humanizing' and argued that psychology's tendency to 'study human beings by dividing them up into various parts' not only produced limited know-ledge but, more significantly, succeeded in removing from indi-viduals their experience of themselves as whole, autonomous beings. In place of these approaches to psychology, humanistic psychologists emphasized the study of conscious experience (rather than the study of the unconscious or of behaviour per se), and presented a view of human beings which emphasized their wholeness, integrity, freedom of choice, autonomy, unique-ness and ultimate undefinability (Shaffer, 1978). Equally, it took as fundamental the view that all human beings have an innate tendency to *self-actualize* (Maslow, 1968). These assumptions, in turn, led to the development of a number of applied tech-niques designed to promote subjective exploration which would allow a realization of these human potentials. Humanistic therapy emerged from these developments as a unique model focused on self-actualization through the exploration of current subjective experience in a constructive and accepting environment.

Given the diversity of its influences and the unique emphases of influential practitioners and theorists such as Abraham Mas-low, Carl Rogers, and Frederick (Fritz) and Laura Perls, the humanistic model in therapy represents a wide range of approaches and techniques among which the most well known include *Person-Centred Therapy*, *Gestalt Therapy* and *Trans-actional Analysis (TA)*. While each of these differs significantly in a variety of ways from the others, nevertheless all share a number of fundamental *attitudes* concerning therapy. Broadly stated, these attitudes emphasize the following features:

Firstly, the humanistic model argues that the focus of therapy should be on the client's currently lived experience, rather than on the past influences that may have led up to, or which might explain, this present position. In this way, the humanistic model is *experientially focused on the 'now' of experience*. In order to remain at the level of exploration that emphasizes current experience, humanistic therapists focus on descriptive question-ing and clarification (which, broadly speaking, focuses on issues concerned with the 'what' and 'how' of experience) and avoid analytic questioning (which, in its implicit and explicit causal assumptions, emphasizes the uncovering of past events through its focus on the 'why' of experience).

Secondly, the humanistic model concentrates on the 'totality' of the client rather than emphasizing the client's presenting problem. In this way, it is not oriented towards problem-solving, but, rather, concerns itself with the examination of issues and concerns within the client's experience which give rise to, or are expressed as, problems. The therapeutic relationship, therefore, provides 'the necessary freedom to explore areas of . . . life that are now denied to awareness or distorted' (Corey, 1991:210).

Thirdly, the humanistic model places the task of understanding or interpreting the client's experience on the client rather than on the therapist. In this way, the therapist must be willing to set aside theoretically based assumptions, biases and generalizations about human experience so that the client can be viewed as a unique being who generates distinctive, singularly applicable meanings and world-views.

Following this last point, the fourth feature of the humanistic approach lies in its emphasis on the client's *freedom and ability to choose how to 'be' and what meanings to live by*. In this way, the humanistic model restrains therapists from assuming or presenting themselves as being more capable than clients of discerning or interpreting their experiences.

The fifth general characteristic of the humanistic model is that it promotes an *egalitarian relationship between therapist and client*. In furtherance of this stance, the therapist is equally free to choose to disclose personal attitudes, feelings or conflicts that arise from the encounter.

The sixth feature is that the humanistic model views the curative or positive benefits of therapy as arising from *within the therapeutic process itself*. More specifically, it argues that these potentials can be realized once the therapist adopts an *accepting and caring stance towards the client*, expresses *congruent or genuine attitudes*, and is able *accurately to reflect the subjective experience of the client* so that it is opened up to non-defensive exploration. While this view is most apparent in Person-Centred Therapy which emphasizes the above 'being', or attitudinal, attributes as both necessary and sufficient for a beneficial therapeutic encounter, nevertheless, even when various other human-istic approaches, such as Gestalt Therapy, do employ a number of skills-based techniques designed to promote self-challenge or emotional discharge, they continue to emphasize the therapist's 'being qualities' as essential constituents of the process which provide the necessary qualitative variables for the techniques to be both appropriate and successful.

The seventh characteristic of the humanistic model argues that the problems or presenting symptoms that clients bring to therapy reveal an underlying experience of *incongruence at the level of the self-concept*. As such, clients' own awareness of themselves is understood as being fundamentally divided in a variety of ways, all of which are focused on the self. So, for instance, clients may experience incongruence between the current view they hold of themselves and their ideal self, or between the self they believe 'must' be as opposed to the self that 'is' (Person-Centred Therapy); or between assumed 'ego states' representing child, adult and parental stances and values within the self (Transactional Analysis); or they may have 'disowned', dissociated or depersonalized unacceptable, painful or contradictory aspects of their self (Gestalt Therapy). Seen in this way, the task of humanistic therapy becomes that of *integration*, either by providing the means for increased self-congruence, or self-acceptance and validation, or a greater willingness and ability to 'own' one's experience.

Underlying these characteristics, the humanistic model contains a number of fundamental assumptions or viewpoints about human nature. Deeply influenced, not surprisingly, by philosophical attitudes rooted in humanism, it emphasizes human beings' capacity for *transcendence or self-actualization*. It argues that all individuals can develop a clearer and more integrated awareness of their personal and species-shared values, of the choice and responsibility they are capable of acknowledging, and of their experiential uniqueness, through the exploration of their *human potentials*.

As such, the humanistic model assumes that human beings have an innate tendency to grow, or develop, in a positive, life-affirming manner regardless of the disabling conditions present in their environment. It is this fundamental assumption ✗ which is the source of humanistic therapists' rejection of the role of 'the authority who knows best what is right for the client', and which infuses their belief that clients have the 'inherent capacity to move away from maladjustment toward psychological health' (Corey, 1991:208). For instance, Carl Rogers, the founder of Person-Centred Therapy, has argued that all human beings share a number of fundamental values (including sincerity, self-knowledge, sensitivity to one's own and others' feelings, and so forth) and that these will express themselves in a relationship that is experienced as being accepting, open and non-threatening, thereby allowing the individual to develop in a manner that is both positive and naturally directed towards the realization of their full potential (Kirschenbaum and Henderson, 1990a).

These views, in turn, reveal the humanistic model's assumption that human beings have an *innately positive nature* which may be impeded or twisted by negative environmental influences that place conditions or demands on the individual's capacity for actualization. '[I]t is cultural influences which are the major factors in our evil behaviour . . . I see members of the human species . . . as essentially constructive in their fundamental nature but damaged by their experience' (Rogers, in Kirschenbaum and Henderson, 1990b:238). Nevertheless, no matter how damaged their condition, individuals remain capable of expressing their positive nature.

> When an individual's negative feelings have been quite fully expressed, they are followed by faint and tentative expressions of the positive impulses which make for growth . . . the more violent and deep the negative expressions (provided they are accepted and recognized), the more certain are the positive expressions of love, social impulses of fundamental respect and of a desire to be mature (Rogers, in Kirschenbaum and Henderson, 1990a:71–2).

Finally, the humanistic model assumes the existence of a *core,* ✗ *unitary self* which is the source point for individual development and actualization directed towards becoming 'the self which most truly is' (Rogers, 1961). Once again, this assumption clarifies the humanistic therapist's dual emphasis on both the exploration of *incongruence* within the client as a way of eliciting the existing discrepancies between lived experience and the self-concept and on the therapist's own ability to remain 'real' or congruent in the therapeutic encounter. In maintaining both emphases, it is argued, the client becomes more able and willing to *accept and integrate* aspects of lived experience that did not previously 'fit' the self-concept and, through this acceptance, is put in touch with the core self.

B. Critiques of the Humanistic Model

Each of these assumptions requires some critical examination. However, before going on to consider what I believe to be crucial areas of concern within the humanistic model, it is important to address one of its most distinctive features, namely the value it places on the therapist's willingness to *self-disclose* during therapy.

Self-disclosure

Clients often question therapists' unwillingness to reveal aspects of their lives to them, or to state their personal views on particular issues. This one-sided stance seems at the very least artificial and unnerving to clients, and is likely to be the source of a good deal of irritation directed towards the therapist. The psychoanalytic model set the standard view on therapist self-disclosure by arguing that therapists' self-disclosures impinged on the transference relationship and were, therefore, to be strictly avoided. By and large, subsequent therapeutic models have adopted this position to varying extents, although a number of therapists, R. D. Laing for instance, have argued that in some cases at least it is therapeutically counter-productive for the therapist to avoid self-disclosure (Laing, 1960). In a similar fashion, critics of therapy such as Jeffrey Masson have pointed to therapists' unwillingness to disclose their views as a further means of maintaining an imbalance of power that is heavily weighted in favour of the therapist (Masson, 1988).

Various approaches within the humanistic model have argued for the importance of therapist self-disclosure since it makes clear the therapist's willingness to be 'real' or congruent in the encounter and, by extension, promotes the establishment of a real encounter within the artificial confines of the therapeutic process.

While this view should not be dismissed as insignificant, it remains possible to consider instances where therapist self-disclosure, regardless of circumstance, may be as counter-productive as the unwillingness to self-disclose. For instance, a number of humanistic practitioners have tended to interpret the notion of therapist 'transparency' or 'congruence' as being the equivalent of their right to express feelings or attitudes currently experienced towards the client. These might include interest, boredom, irritation, relief, anger, love, and so forth. While such terms may certainly reveal the therapist's current attitude towards the client, and so present an image of 'congruence', it is easy to see that in a great many circumstances they might well be experienced as abusive by the client in that they might be interpreted as *statements of demand or lack of acceptance of the client's current way of being*. So, for example, if a client is informed that the therapist 'is bored', is it not likely that what will be understood by this statement is: 'You are not allowed to be boring; you must change'?

At the same time, humanistic therapists might well point out that not to have disclosed their experience would have promoted the continuation of a 'false' encounter and that their feedback to their clients, while possibly experienced as painful or con-frontative, would nevertheless reveal their willingness to engage with clients on an egalitarian level that does not seek to protect or infantilize them.

Both views seem to me to have some merit. Nevertheless, even if one were to accept the humanistic stance and engage in self-disclosure, it would appear sensible to consider both *what* to self-disclose and *how* to express that self-disclosure. In the first instance, therapists should ask themselves whether their intended disclosure is principally for the purposes of serving the therapist's personal interests or those of the client. So, to return to the previous example, if the disclosure of boredom is primarily to give vent to rising frustration with the client, then it is unlikely that the disclosure will be of much therapeutic benefit; better for the therapist to attend to the experience and consider what it might be saying about the current state of the therapeutic relationship rather than seek to change it. On the other hand, there might be some relational benefit in addressing the experience of boredom; but here too it becomes important to consider how it might be addressed. The statement made by the therapist might be presented as demanding ('I am bored') or as invitational ('Look, I don't know if it's just me, but I'm experiencing a growing sense of boredom. Is this anything like what you're experiencing?') While the former implicitly places the emphasis or source of the experience on the client (therapists do not 'naturally' get bored, so if boredom is being experienced it must have something to do with the client), the latter acknowledges the therapist's interpretational role in the experience and allows the client to challenge it.

In one sense, therapists, however unwilling they may be to do so, cannot do other than self-disclose. How they dress, their appearance, their posture, their gestures and mannerisms, the language they employ, their accent, the environmental features of their consultation room, all these factors and many more 'reveal' them – as, indeed, does the very fact that they invest so much significance in their anonymity. Equally, when a client asks the kind of question that requires some degree of self-disclosure, it might be wise to enquire of the client what meaning this question has to the client – but it might be just as important to offer to answer it directly.

My own experience has been that clients want very few self-disclosures from me and that when they ask for them they are not just giving way to their curiosity, nor are they seeking to assert their power, nor are they revealing some transferential issues, but, rather, they are likely to be expressing something about our on-going encounter with one another. And if I address their question or statement in this light, it does not compromise my anonymity but is a revelation both to myself and to them that I am willing to engage myself in their world-view.

As such, the humanistic model's attitude towards therapist self-disclosure is integral to its general stance and assumptions concerning the nature of therapeutic discourse and, in this sense, is valid. At the same time, the way self-disclosure is interpreted and how it is expressed suggest an underlying assumption concerning its view about the 'self' and 'self/other' relations which requires further attention. First, however, several other, if related, fundamental assumptions within the humanistic model need to be considered.

Self-actualization

When addressing the issue of the innate capacity to grow or actualize, humanistic therapists often invoke analogies in the plant and animal kingdoms. They might refer, for instance, to the analogy of an acorn which is innately predisposed to grow into an oak tree (Corey, 1991) or, more commonly, they point out that potatoes placed in the unnatural environment of a basement will still, quite naturally, sprout roots that direct themselves towards distant window-light (Thorne, 1992). These analogies serve to convey the experiences of human beings who, in spite of the adverse conditions of their environment, will nevertheless struggle to express their potential. While such analogies are, at best, metaphorical, they are also, more significantly, limited. For, on consideration, these examples, while making the point that all living things struggle to remain alive and may survive to some degree under the most difficult of circumstances, have nothing really to say about self-actualization.

Equally, what is omitted from such analogies is the fact that in a great number of environmental conditions acorns will simply not grow and potatoes will just rot away. As to the 'natural' direction of growth and development, it is difficult to see how a distinction can be made between 'natural' and 'unnatural' conditions for growth. If we remain at the level of analogy, the development of cross-breeding techniques in plants and animals has demonstrated that the capability of living things to survive rests on their capacity to mutate in response to various changes in the environment (be they artificially induced or in response to uncontrolled variations in such factors as weather and temperature), such that these mutated species may differ significantly from the original. But can we say that one is 'natural' and the other is not? In this way, the direction of growth is not governed by 'the thing itself' but by its *relations with the environment*. In the same way, human beings develop in such myriad directions that it is more sensible to speak of this process as one of *interactive disclosure* rather than 'upwardly directed growth'.

In other words, while it might make sense to speak of human beings as expressing themselves within set conditions and, in turn, through their presence, influencing those conditions so that 'all and everything' is in a state of continuing flux, it is somewhat naive and narrow-minded to assume that, ideally, 'naturally directed' growth would occur in a condition of stasis.

Change

Underlying this stance is the notion of *change* itself. Some humanistic therapists – like so many other individuals – may speak somewhat glibly in terms such as 'life is change' and will therefore focus on 'change' as being central to the therapeutic enterprise. Now while there is a fundamental sense in this assertion, since one of the 'givens' or invariants of human experience is its plasticity or on-going changing process, it is important to be clear that the 'changes' that humanistic therapists emphasize are those that are in some way or other 'directed towards growth'. This is a much more limited and limiting notion of change than that invoked by phrases such as 'life is change' since it focuses on a particular aspect of change which has been interpreted as being 'natural' or 'good' or 'valid' because it is seen as being 'self-actualizing'.

In humanistic therapy, it can be seen that therapists 'value' their clients because of their assumed ability to change in a self-actualizing direction. But what if this assumption were to be questioned and all that could be said of change were that 'it is' and that, as such, human beings change in so many ways and so continuously that no particular direction can be inferred as 'natural'?

Conditional unconditionality

Such a conclusion raises an unforeseen yet significant problem for the humanistic model. For while all humanistic therapists seek to maintain and provide their clients with qualities or conditions such as acceptance and accurate empathic understanding from an 'unconditional' standpoint, it must be asked: *How conditional on the assumption of innate positively directed growth is this 'unconditionality'?* In other words, if this assumption were to be removed or presented as doubtful, would humanistic therapists still offer those qualities? My own questioning of a number of humanistic therapists on this very point suggests that at the very least they would find it extremely difficult to maintain an accepting attitude towards their clients and, in some cases, would seriously question their basic rationale for providing therapy.

If the basis for the provision of acceptance, empathy and so forth rests on the assumption of an underlying inherent 'goodness' or 'positively directed development', then it would be the case that such assumptions, however worthy or humanly desirable they might be, would have been shown to be *implicit demands or conditions set by the therapist for the client to accept and demonstrate.* Such demands may be far more subtle than any other that clients may have experienced in their lives, but they remain demands nonetheless, and clients, once they have ascertained them to be such, are likely to respond to them as conditions for their way of being which must be fulfilled in order that they may be accepted or deserving of the attention being given.

Such subtle guidelines require acknowledgement from humanistic therapists for they reveal that rather than being unconditionally accepting 'reflectors' of clients' subjective experiences of themselves, they are actually *directive* and impose a stance

265

for clients to adhere to. Rollo May has argued this same point by noting that in his observations of person-centred therapists working with clients at the Veteran's Hospital in Madison, Wisconsin he found that the therapists did not acknowledge clients' expressions of hostile feelings that were both generally directed and focused on the therapists themselves. May suggested that this unwillingness on the part of the therapists acted as an impediment to the clients' expression of self-autonomy (May, in Kirschenbaum and Henderson, 1990b). Interestingly, in his response to May, Carl Rogers, while regretting this evidence and emphasizing the need for therapists to accept *all* expressions of feelings, nevertheless characterized the clients' feelings as 'negative' – but why should this additional label be attached to these feelings unless, however implicitly, they are to be discouraged?

In a similar fashion, such directives may prove to be far more problematic and difficult for clients to contend with than any of the explicitly stated conditions presented by cognitive-behavioural therapists. For clients are likely to wish to accept the assumptions of humanistic theory and desire to see themselves as growth-oriented, innately good beings. But what happens when clients cannot see the evidence of this assumption, or worse, see its 'evil' contradiction in the thought or behaviours they engender? In such circumstances, are clients not likely to conclude that something far more seriously problematic exists which in some way defines them as being fundamentally flawed and somehow less than human? Rather than provide them with a sense of experiential choice and responsibility, does it not invoke the experience of passive victimization to external influences?

Given this, it would seem to me far wiser to adopt the position argued by the existential philosopher and psychotherapist Emmy van Deurzen-Smith, that 'people may evolve in any direction, good or bad, and that only reflection on what constitutes good and bad makes it possible to exercise one's choice in the matter' (van Deurzen-Smith, 1988:56–7).

Further, the emphasis placed by humanistic therapists on the therapeutic relationship itself reveals a hidden agenda above and beyond the establishment and maintenance of the relationship itself in that it contains the implicit goal of nurturing the positive growth and goodness of the client. But why should humanistic therapists insist on this unless it is something that is more for their benefit than it might seemingly be for their clients? If humanistic therapists require such an assumption, does it not seem worthwhile for them to examine this demand in order to clarify in what ways it might be influencing or directing their ability and willingness to listen to their clients in as flexible and attending a manner as possible?

Perhaps even more importantly, the humanistic model's contention that those attitudes and behaviours that are termed 'negative' or destructive result from the 'twisted influences' of environment need further examination. As well as suggesting a form of determinism that runs counter to the humanistic model's fundamental stance, this view places the person *outside* the environment. Once again, as Rollo May has pointed out, this assumption ignores the influence that all of us have in interpreting, perpetuating or altering the cultural environment we exist in and define ourselves through. 'Culture is not something that is made up by fate and foisted upon us' (May, in Kirschenbaum and Henderson, 1990b:241). Rather, human beings and their cultures *co-constitute* each other; that is to say, each defines, and is itself defined through, the other. This relational definition places each of us, or *implicates* each of us, within our culture – *not* outside it – just as our culture is implicated within each of us.

While the humanistic model initially seems to suggest, or articulate, this viewpoint, on analysis what is revealed is that its assumption of the separateness of 'self and society' is a *required* stance for it to hold. This conclusion is made explicit in Rogers' response to May when, presented with experimental evidence disputing this humanistic assumption, all he is able to state is that 'there is much I don't understand about some evil behaviors. The experiments . . . are a shocking puzzle to me . . .' (Rogers, in Kirschenbaum and Henderson, 1990b:254), for which he can supply no adequate explanations.

The self

The humanistic model's emphasis on *the self as a distinct and separate entity* opens it to further significant criticism in that this stance contains an inherently *solipsistic (or self-aggrandizing) attitude* the implications of which for the self–other relationship are as pertinent as they are profound.

The humanistic model has for many years been criticized, and satirized, for its implicit disregard for others' subjective realm on the basis that each of us is solely, and separately, responsible for the interpretation we give to our experience. An extreme example of this view would be the so-called *Gestalt Prayer*:

> I do my thing, and you do your thing.
> I am not in this world to live up to your expectations.
> And you are not in this world to live up to mine.
> You are you, and I am I,
> And if by chance we find each other, it's beautiful.
> If not, it can't be helped (Perls, 1976:4).

While it would be unfair to suggest that this extremity of solipsistic absurdity has continued to dominate humanistic thinking, nevertheless what does remain is the false logic on which such self-centred stances are based. For while there is a validity in suggesting that our experience of the world is an interpretational process, what is missing from this stance is the recognition that the 'self' that interprets is *itself* an outcome of reflective interpretation derived from a fundamental relational 'given' of being. In this way, self and other (however each is defined) co-constitute, or derive their definitional meanings from, one another. As such, rather than suggest, or allow (or even, as Perls's 'prayer' makes explicit, celebrate and exult in) a real and verifiable distinction between self and other, this view presents us with the very opposite conclusion in pointing out the inextricable nature of self–other as relational foci within the co-constituted reality within which each is perceived to exist.

That, over time, the humanistic model may have significantly re-appraised its stance on the self is beyond doubt, but that many of its practitioners still insist on notions of the self which do not make its relational context explicit is also a current reality. The very title of one of the main humanistic journals, *Self and Society*, exemplifies the issue through its ambiguity of meaning. For while on the one hand the title may be read to mean that humanistic thought recognizes the lack of any real division between self and society, it can also be read as a statement that acknowledges the exact opposite viewpoint.

The 'real' self

The humanistic model's approach to the self raises a further area of concern in that it expresses the virtually universal assumption among humanistic theorists and practitioners of the existence of a fundamental or *real self* that is the source point and means of expression of the positive growth properties and innate natural goodness of any individual. Indeed, it can be seen that it is precisely this stance on the 'real self' that allows humanistic therapists to retain their assumptions concerning positively directed growth and change. Each view *requires* the other in order to be meaningful.

Further, it is the maintenance of this view of the fixed and fundamental existence of a 'real self' which allows a distinction to be made between the 'real self' and all expressions of 'false selves' that clients may manifest. In upholding this view, humanistic therapists are able to focus on the assumed manifestations of positively directed growth in their clients as expressions of the 'real self' that continues to exist and exert its influence in spite of all the 'false selves' (that is, the destructive, growth-preventative, 'bad' attitudes and behaviours) that clients exhibit.

But, once again, it must be asked how humanistic therapists are able to distinguish the 'real self' from the 'false selves' other than by relying on the assumptions they hold concerning the nature of human beings. In this way, the humanistic model's notion of the 'real self' reveals an inherent circularity of argument that itself relies on the unfalsifiability of its assumptions (that is to say, if one initiates all investigations on the basis that a 'real self' exists, then all the accumulated evidence can do nothing but 'reveal' the 'correctness' of this assumption).

This stance also reveals the significant interpretative power that humanistic therapists bestow on themselves in that, however explicitly or subtly, it is they who, in the encounter, direct their clients towards the recognition of their 'real self', influence their movement towards closer identification with such, and point out or reinforce the gains and rewards available once this assumption has been accepted. Far from assisting humanistic therapists in remaining 'unconditional' or accepting of the client's experience, the notion of a 'real self' promotes conditionality and lack of acceptance since any manifestation of a 'false self' (however defined) is at best tolerated, rather than accepted, by the therapist, and even then only because this toleration will better enable the client to change in ways that will promote ('real') self-actualization.

It is surprising to me that therapists as astute as Carl Rogers appear to have failed to see, much less seriously considered, the directive and potentially abusive features contained in their stance concerning the 'real self'. In not doing so, they have, however inadvertently, promoted the development of one more model that limits the client's possibilities of being and which lumbers important aspects of humanist philosophy with an assumption that is difficult to defend. This is particularly galling given the oft-stated claims of humanistic theorists such as Rogers and Perls that their models are founded on existential phenomenology (Shaffer, 1978; Corey, 1991). Perhaps they are partly so, but if such authors had given serious consideration to the relevant aspects of existential-phenomenological thinking, they would have realized that the notion of self that emerges is one that emphasizes as fundamental the view of 'self-in-relation' and self as 'plastic' constituent of reflection (van Deurzen-Smith, 1988; Spinelli, 1989, 1993).

Gerald Corey has succinctly expressed this important divergence between humanist and existential-phenomenological thought:

[E]xistentialists take the position that we are faced with the anxiety of choosing to create a never secure identity in a world that lacks intrinsic meaning. The humanists, in contrast, take the somewhat less anxiety-evoking position that each of us has within us a nature and potential that we can actualize and through which we can find meaning . . . for the existentialist there is nothing that we 'are', no internal 'nature' we can count on . . . (Corey, 1991:206).

Placed in this perspective, we can begin to see that statements concerning 'real' and 'false' selves become limiting, if not absurd, notions to maintain.

A case example

As in the previous critiques of other therapeutic models under discussion, it seems worthwhile to consider the points just raised from the concrete standpoint of a case presentation. The following summarized example, taken from the person-centred approach to therapy advocated by Carl Rogers (Rogers, in Kirschenbaum and Henderson, 1990a:135–52), should clarify a number of the issues under discussion.

At the age of eighty, Rogers gave a thirty-minute demonstration of his person-centred approach in front of six hundred workshop participants in South Africa. In spite of its brevity and therapeutic limitations, Rogers felt that it illustrated 'several aspects of the therapeutic process as it occurs in the changing relationship between therapist and client' (Rogers, in Kirschenbaum and Henderson, 1990a:138).

Rogers' volunteer client was a thirty-five-year-old woman named Jan who presented him with two problematic fears which she wanted to explore. These were: her fear of marriage and children, and her fear of ageing. As Jan expressed it: 'It's very difficult to look into the future, and I find it very frightening' (ibid: 139).

When Rogers asked which of these fears she would prefer to look at first, Jan selected the problem of ageing. Asked to clarify this fear, she noted that she had only five years left before turning forty, that this concern had been affecting her self-confidence and that the feelings had only begun some eighteen months to

271

two years earlier. When asked whether anything significant had happened during this time which she might have associated with the onset of the fear, Jan at first replied that she couldn't think of anything and then added that her mother, whom Jan saw as being youthful and intelligent, had died at the age of fifty-three. On further reflection, Jan disclosed that her mother had been a talented woman but that 'unfortunately, towards the end, [she] became a bitter woman. The world owed her a living . . . I *do* feel that what happened to my mother is happening to me' (ibid: 141).

As the encounter progressed, Jan refocused her attention on the second issue – her fear of marriage. Initially, her words suggested that the concern involved an underlying fear of commitment. With further clarification, the issue was seen not to be about commitment in general, since Jan claimed to be able and willing to commit herself to her work and her friends. It was her specific inability to commit herself to marriage and children which was the problem. Then, following a long silence, Jan stated:

> . . . My love is for the arts, right? I'm very much involved with music and dancing. I'd like to be able to just throw everything up and devote my life to music and dancing. But unfortunately the society that we live in today forces one to work and live up to a social standard. It's not something I regret. It's something I miss, something I really want to do . . . I'm getting older and I keep turning around and running back (ibid: 142).

On further reflection, Jan expressed her fear of being trapped. This experience seemed to be something that went unnoticed by everyone but herself, since others glibly pointed out to her that she was 'in her prime' and that she 'had everything going for her'. With this, Rogers suggested to her that while others' views were accurate reflections of Jan as she was 'on the outside', she was quite a different person 'inside'. In response, Jan revealed that she enjoyed playing 'the naughty little girl' since it allowed her to get away with things.

Following this, Jan spoke of her frustration at not having someone else to believe in her and provide her with the necessary confidence she felt she lacked. Rogers' subsequent response to this is illuminating:

> Somebody you can relate to. And I guess that – this may seem like a silly idea, but – I wish that one of those friends could be that naughty little girl. I don't know whether that makes any sense to you or not, but if that kind of sprightly, naughty little girl that lives inside could accompany you from the light into the dark – as I say, that may not make any sense to you at all. [Puzzled by his words, Jan asked Rogers to elaborate.] Simply that maybe one of your best friends is the you that you hide inside, the fearful little girl, the naughty little girl, the real you that doesn't come out very much in the open (ibid: 148).

Finally, as the session drew to its close, both Jan and Rogers joked about their mutual ability still to be 'naughty little children' in spite of their chronological ages.

This encounter is fascinating on a number of counts. Firstly, it manages to convey the essentials of Rogers' person-centred approach (and, more broadly, of several key assumptions within the humanistic model), including his willingness to accept the client, his ability to reflect her statements accurately and sensitively, and his openness in disclosing aspects of his experience of himself to Jan. At the same time, however, it also reveals Rogers' (and the humanistic model's) underlying assumptions and how these sometimes lead him to step out of a 'reflecting mode' and into a directive one. Most obviously, this occurs when Rogers chooses to return to the theme of 'the naughty little girl' – a theme that Rogers re-introduces spontaneously quite some time after Jan has mentioned it and then moved on from it. Rogers' rationale for this is that it 'was the kind of intuitive response that I have learned to trust. The expression just formed itself within me and wanted to be said' (ibid: 148). However, in doing so, Rogers seems to remain unwilling to acknowledge it as a directive interpretation on his part and, rather, mystifies it as an 'intuitive response'. More pertinently, however, Rogers' own words with regard to this reveal his theoretical belief in the 'real self' – a belief that Jan eventually seems to come to accept, work with, and gain insight from.

While I have no criticism of Rogers' decision to express his hunches (in this, it is he who is being implicitly critical of his own approach), I do take issue with his assumption that 'the naughty little girl' is the *real* Jan and that the 'adult', fearful Jan is somehow an aspect of an 'unreal self'. Could they not *both* be experientially 'real' in the same way as Rogers can be 'real' being the eighty-year-old man and 'the naughty little boy'? In ascribing 'reality' to one and not to the other, Rogers is being led by his theory and, in being led, is possibly missing a vital feature of Jan's problem.

For Jan herself expresses herself as being torn between opposing demands. She tells us that she wants to be free to be committed to her artistic development but feels that she should be doing what is socially acceptable for a woman of her age – like being married and having children perhaps? She presents this initially by speaking of her mother who was talented but became a bitter woman – perhaps because she did the 'socially acceptable' thing and married, raised children and did not put her talents to any great use? Could it not be that Jan's dilemma lies in the issue of having to choose the direction of her life and *not* whether she is being 'real' or not? Both options are 'real', just as the Jan who will emerge from either choice will be 'real'.

The issue does not seem to me to be one of 'reality' versus 'unreality' but, rather, that of Jan's experience of anxiety in choosing a direction in her life and her expression of that anxiety through her fears and her unwillingness to acknowledge the choice she has (however limited) by invoking 'societal demands'. Given this position, it would have been useful, perhaps even essential, to have explored Jan's experience of, and the meanings she gives to, her *relations* with others and with herself and how these relations are expressed in the 'self' that she has constructed. But none of these views and strategies is open to Rogers. Firstly, because he believes in the 'wisdom of the organism' (ibid: 151) to direct itself towards self-actualization and this belief prevents him from acknowledging that several, and incompatible, directions are possible. Secondly, because he views the organism, and the 'correct' or 'real' direction it will take, as being 'set' rather than disclosed through and within its relations with the world that contains it.

Would these opposing views have any significance for Jan? Rogers tells us that, following her encounter with him, Jan stated: 'I realize that to face life as a whole person, I need to find those missing parts of me' (ibid: 152). But what parts were missing? This conclusion suggests that, in her quest for integration, Jan might still be putting off making choices and, in her internal quest, will remain cut off from her relations with others, or possibly even experience herself as a victim of them. Jan, in accepting Rogers' views, now seeks to fill that 'gap' through a form of self-development or growth that is internalized so that a greater self-awareness and integrity will be achieved.

The alternative view being put forward might instead ask Jan to consider what it would be like for her if she were to have to go on living with that gap for the rest of her life. In so doing, it would allow Jan to remain focused on her current experience as it is being lived rather than both introducing and emphasizing a hypothetical option that may never be realized. At the same time, in attending to Jan's lived experience of herself, this alternative perspective would allow Jan to explore her divided stances on the possible directions that her life might take, and the gains and losses contained within each perspective, from a relationally based standpoint.

The limitations of the humanistic model

The critical points just discussed both abstractly and through the case presentation presented above should clarify what I believe to be significant problems within the humanistic model. Nevertheless, it must be said that there is much contained within the humanist orientation that avoids many of the issues raised by the psycho-analytic and cognitive-behavioural models of therapy, and which promotes a number of attitudes on the part of the therapist which reduce the likelihood of misuse or abuse of the therapeutic encounter.

Significant among these are the therapist's respect for the experiential meaning-world of the client; the therapist's willingness to consider that the exploration of this meaning-world in itself will cultivate the client's capacity to examine and clarify his or her issues and stances so that they may be placed within the context of choice and responsibility; the therapist's avoidance of being led by theory or skills and, in contrast, the significance placed on the therapist's expression of attitudinal qualities such as concern, care, openness and acceptance as the essential means of encouraging the client to recognize and acknowledge these same qualities in himself or herself; and the emphasis placed on the therapeutic relationship itself as a safe yet challenging arena for self-expression and self-exploration.

All these points, I would suggest, while to some extent implicit or potential within the previous models, are made explicit within the humanistic model and, in being so, provide its most prominent, and by no means insubstantial, distinguishing characteristics. At the same time, however, while emphasizing the important implications of relationship within therapy, the humanistic model's adherence to views of 'the self', as discussed above, opens it to serious charges of philosophical naïveté which place the therapist in the position of willing collaborator in potential extra-therapeutic misuse and abuse of self-elevating attitudes and behaviours that the client might adopt in various social relations.

I believe that this last point, sadly, has not been sufficiently considered by the majority of humanistic therapists. Nevertheless, it strikes me as being of central ethical importance.

When I first began to explore the possibilities of therapy, I initially embraced humanistic approaches since they seemed to provide the most open and accepting attitude towards the exploration of the possibilities of experience within a therapeutic relationship. However, not long after I had begun to immerse myself in such approaches, I was perplexed to discover that they seemed to engender the most prominent abuses of therapeutic power I had yet encountered. Some of this abusive power lay in the 'guru-like' qualities that many trainees tended to attribute to their trainers and, in a more general sense, on the originators of the particular approach within the humanistic model they were training in. While this was not, in itself, an unusual development within any training process, it seemed odd to me that it should be so obvious within humanistic circles. Far worse, however, it soon became blatantly evident that the originators and trainers themselves seemed both eager and willing to allow and encourage such stances in their trainees, and seemingly revelled in the power bestowed on them.

Such stances, which have now been exposed by critics and historians of these approaches (Masson, 1988), involved all manner of abuses – including sexual and financial abuses – which were allowed to continue unchallenged. The elevation and quasi-adoration of the founder bordered on, and sometimes even surpassed, that of devotees of one of the many 'gods' and 'enlightened beings' who arose in the 1970s – and who often adopted the techniques and language of a variety of humanistic approaches (as, for instance, was the case with Werner Erhard, the founder of *est* (Rosen, 1979)). Indeed, as I began to practise, I noted my own promotion and encouragement of similar attitudes in my clients towards me. For reasons that I could not then make sense of, the very approach that seemed to offer a more egalitarian and caring relationship between therapist and client actually provided the means of the development of something that in many ways was the exact opposite of that being promulgated.

On consideration, I believe that such a situation evolved precisely because of the elevation of the self that permeated, however subtly or blatantly, the humanistic stance. While preaching co-operation, such approaches actually glorified competition between beings – a competition that stressed the self as separate and non-relational – which was exemplified in the dictum: *If it feels good, do it.* Under such conditions, an individual could elevate his or her desires as being the only ones of import, and if the enactment of such desires provoked misery or harm in others, well, so be it; these other 'selves' had simply not learned how to assert their wishes and demands adequately or in a manner that allowed their dominance and superiority.

It was on the basis of such stances that the so-called 'Me Decade' that characterized the latter half of the 1970s in the West took hold. This in turn, I believe, allowed the development of the brutalizing and inhumane socio-economic ethos of 'Reaganism' and 'Thatcherism' which dominated the 1980s. For while it might seem initially that the humanistic approaches of the 1970s and the 'monetarist philosophies' of the 1980s stood at opposite ends of the spectrum (and, indeed, each side viewed the other as its 'Satan'), it can be seen that in their shared adoption of a competitive ideology they were both expressions of the same principle: namely, the elevation of the individual as being responsible only for his or her own self-interests – be they psychological or economic – regardless of the impact these may have had on others.

Transpersonal approaches

While it is the case that this emphasis and view of the self which has dominated the humanistic model has been criticized by theorists and practitioners representing other models of therapy, it would be misleading to suggest that there has been no internal criticism. For instance, while Rogers tended to write about the self from the generally accepted standpoint, it is also clear that he emphasized the relational elements of the self in a number of his writings and seemed to be aware of the inherent dangers in the elevation of the self (Kirschenbaum and Henderson, 1990a, 1990b).

At the same time, the growth of interest in *transpersonal models* within humanistic approaches can be seen to be a significant attempt to deal with solipsistic tendencies apparent within humanistic approaches in that, through their additional concentration on the 'beyond, across, or through self elements' of the psyche (Valle, 1989), these models allow the analysis of the psyche from a less egotistical stance that delves into the underlying spiritual or idealistic concerns and experiences of individuals.

Transpersonal approaches are framed within a stance that emphasizes the individual's aspirations and potentials within the wider context of the world in general, as well as the spiritual or ideal dimensions of experience. In this way, they focus on those elements of experience that are 'beyond the level of personal self-awareness . . . in which identity is not confined to the individual mind or more limited sense of self' (Valle, 1989:262). While such experiences are often associated with the spiritual dimensions of being, this need not be the case in that they point to those aspects of human interaction which call into question the usual boundaries that one imposes between self and other. Perhaps an example from my own life will clarify what is being argued.

Some years ago, I found myself sitting on the lawns of the University of Surrey. It was a bright, sunny early summer day, I had just eaten my first bowl of fresh strawberries of the year, and I was feeling relaxed and contented. As I sat and watched people go by, I drifted into a non-focused state of awareness that seemed to treat all sensory stimuli as being equal in significance. While in that state, my very sense of 'I' or self seemed to 'blend' into the stimuli such that my consciousness of them did not impose a subject—object split. Rather, consciousness seemed unitary and inter-connected; I was not aware *of* the perceived stimuli, I *was* the perceived stimuli to the extent that *I* could not be distinguished from them. In fact, it was only when a distinction was forced back into my awareness by the thought 'I must be experiencing satori' that the unified experience ended and 'I' was once again a separate, bounded being able to distinguish my self from other beings.

This experience captures, I believe, the essential concerns of transpersonal enquiry. It was, for me, neither a spiritual nor a religious experience, but it did extend the possibilities of meaning that I had placed on my understanding of my 'self'. It was not experienced as a loss of self, but rather as an extension of self that called into question both the boundaries I had imposed on my 'self' and the 'reality' of distinction between self and other.

Such experiences are not uncommon. Many of us may have gained a sense of them through sexual relations, prayer, meditation, drugs, extreme tiredness, illness, or even through gardening. It may even be the case that as infants and young children, prior to having built up a fairly clear and fixed self-construct, such experiences are commonplace. Whatever the case, as they appear to be part of our experiential 'make-up' as human beings, and as mention of them can be found in all cultures dating back to our earliest civilizations, they are as deserving of enquiry as any other experience. While studies of such experiences have been a subject of interest to psychologists since the beginnings of modern psychology (James, 1890), it has only been in recent years that transpersonal studies have developed as a specific field of psychological enquiry (Tart, 1975).

While transpersonal approaches present views of the self that are implicitly critical of those underlying the humanistic model, nevertheless the tendency to replace such with the assertion 'of a greater trans-personal . . . self or one (i.e. pure consciousness without subject or object)' (Valle, 1989:261) opens them to significant criticism.

Rollo May, for instance, has criticized this assertion on the grounds that 'it is a contradiction in terms to think one can make a psychology by throwing out or "leaping across" . . . the person' (May, 1986:87). According to May, such assumptions can lead to the avoidance or minimization of consideration of aspects of human experience such as cruelty, anxiety and suffering, and promulgate a confusion between psychology and religion by 'taking a point of view which goes beyond humanness' (May, 1986:89). Equally, it can be argued that many transpersonal studies seem to suggest conclusions that treat these transpersonal experiences as pointing to evidence for the extra-experiential, or objective, reality of a spiritual or super-natural dimension. In other words, there is a danger of imposing a meaning or 'reality' on such experiences which elevates them in a manner all too similar to the humanistic model's elevation of the self as a 'reality' that is separate and non-relational.

At the same time, responses to these criticisms argue that transpersonal studies focus on radical shifts in one's reflection of the relational possibilities of experience and of the plasticity of boundaries within the self-construct and that these bring into question such matters as the general lack of psychological distinction between 'mind' and 'consciousness' (Valle, 1989). On the other hand, it seems to me that critics are not as concerned about the idea of exploring these possible distinctions as they are about the tendency on the part of transpersonal theorists and practitioners to *assume and assert them.*

Nevertheless, it should be evident that there is much to be gained in allowing the therapeutic process to acknowledge and address the 'experience of duality dissolving', not least because it may form part of the concerns that individuals bring to therapy and, therefore, should be treated with the acceptance and respect that therapists would be expected to provide towards any meaning or belief that the client presents. Equally, however, it would also be expected in these circumstances, as in any other, that therapists would seek to clarify the specific meaning of this experience to the client and to challenge the contradictions or unreflected assumptions contained within the presented meaning.

Even so, while it remains ethically questionable for therapists to reject or seek to overturn the spiritual beliefs of clients simply because they are beliefs that do not form their own world-views, in the same way it would be an abuse of the therapeutic relationship if therapists sought to impose their spiritual or transpersonal beliefs on their clients. This conclusion would, I think, be shared by most therapists, regardless of the model they represented. But another, more problematic possibility exists. What if it were to be the case that *both* the therapist and the client shared the view that the transpersonal elements of experience pointed to a transpersonal reality? This possibility would not be difficult to imagine. In such instances, the therapist's willingness and ability to clarify the meaning of the client's beliefs may be seriously compromised in its effectiveness since it would be as much of a challenge to the position adopted by the therapist as it would be to that held by the client.

This is certainly not an impossible situation for the therapist to face or deal with, nor would it by any stretch of the imagination be specific to transpersonal therapists or to transpersonal issues raised during therapy. Nevertheless, it must be asked, if some therapists opt to label themselves as 'transpersonal', or present themselves as allied to transpersonal approaches, what influences do these terms have on the therapeutic relationship in general and on the exploration of transpersonal beliefs and experiences in particular?

As such, transpersonal approaches, while important in that they provide the humanistic model with a potentially significant palliative to excessively solipsistic assumptions concerning the self, and focus on aspects of human experience that have tended to be neglected or dismissed by other therapeutic models, also contain some cause for concern since, by their very emphasis on the transpersonal realms of experience, they too remain open to tendencies bordering more on religious conviction than on therapeutic encounter.

3. GENERAL CONCLUSIONS

Throughout the whole of the discussion in Parts 3 and 4 of this text, I have attempted to argue that the various existent approaches that have significantly influenced therapeutic encounters all contain a number of theoretically derived assumptions that may well work against the very enterprise that therapists set for themselves. Further, I have tried to demonstrate how these self-same assumptions impose themselves in diverse ways on the therapeutic encounter such that they both limit therapists' ability to listen and attend to their clients and make more likely the possibility of misuse and abuse of therapists' power.

At the same time, while it must be acknowledged that these forms of power reveal dilemmas that cannot be fully resolved since all are based on various questions of interpretation (which is itself a 'given' of human encounter), I have also sought to demonstrate alternative possibilities that, while remaining respectful of the lived experience of clients and the meanings they have derived from them, nevertheless allow therapists to adopt a descriptively focused approach to the therapeutic relationship which provides sufficient means to clarify and challenge clients' experiences.

However, in adopting this alternative model, it becomes evident that therapists open *themselves* to a number of significant challenges. Among them are those challenges that confront therapists with a number of power-based issues that are derived from the particular *relationship* with their clients that their therapeutic model will allow or promote. Similarly, a number of challenges arise from the fundamental act of labelling oneself as a therapist.

In exploring such issues, a number of basic premises held by particular models of therapy, or either implicitly or explicitly shared by all of them, have been considered and criticized. These criticisms have focused on problems of logic or evidence as well as on their impact on the therapeutic relationship. I have sought to keep these criticisms constructive in that alternative possibilities have been presented which acknowledge the phenomena associated with the assumptions under consideration while at the same time providing what I believe to be more adequate interpretative analyses.

With regard to the specific issues discussed concerning aspects of the therapeutic process, all the points raised broadly emphasize the possibilities that emerge when therapists avoid seeking to impose their own theory-led views in order that they remain better able to suspend their theoretical judgement as to the nature and basis of their clients' issues in the same way as most therapists are willing to attempt to suspend as far as possible their personal judgements of their clients. I have attempted to demonstrate that what obstacles stand in the way of this suspension are mainly derived from therapists' reliance on their theories and their skills-based applications.

In the light of this, I have suggested that these various obstacles can be partially dealt with through various forms of clarificatory challenge that seek to remain at a descriptive level of interpretation and which, in doing so, may expose unreflected assumptions, biases, stances and approaches to living that the client himself or herself can begin to question and/or reconsider in a manner that leads to a more reflected-on form of acceptance or allows the possibilities of change. But it should also be clear that such challenges rely far less on therapists' skills or theoretical knowledge (though clearly these are irrefutable elements in any form of interpretative task) than they do on the nature of the relationship that has been engendered.

But the development and maintenance of such a relationship does not rest solely on clients' willingness and courage to clarify and assess their experience of life. Nor does it depend on the specialist skills the therapist brings to the encounter. Nor on a combination of the above. Rather, as I will argue in Part 5, the central features revolve around a number of '*being-based*' attitudes or qualities which seem to me to lie at the heart of the therapeutic process and its possibilities.

PART FIVE

DEMYSTIFYING THE THERAPEUTIC RELATIONSHIP

The technique of treatment must be in yourself.
— Alfred Adler

Virtually all therapeutic models are in agreement that the *relationship* within the therapeutic process is of central significance. Similarly, as was discussed in Part 1, research focused on various aspects of the therapeutic process has demonstrated that the therapeutic relationship is one of the very few recurring variables extracted from the principal studies – whether they are process- or outcome-oriented – to be singled out by both therapists and clients as being essential to the success of therapy (however 'success' might be measured). And yet, what there might be about this particular relationship which is so significant – or, indeed, 'particular' – remains largely unclear.

Some clues from research studies suggest that its importance and uniqueness lie in the therapist's ability and willingness to listen to and 'be with' the client. But these terms also remain somewhat vague, and if they are to be helpful they must be clarified further. Analyses of therapeutic models have also noted two distinct emphases, or tendencies, within therapists' understanding of the relationship – tendencies that stress either the 'doing' or the 'being' elements or qualities that therapists bring to the relationship and how the emphasis on one or the other significantly affects not only the structure of the therapeutic process but also the direction it is likely to take and the specific exploratory possibilities it will allow to both the client and the therapist.

The final part of this text proposes the view that whatever it may be that can be said to remain unique or special or of

287

potential benefit about the very enterprise of therapy is principally dependent on the establishment and maintenance of a
relationship that both expresses and promotes the exploration
of the possibilities of *being*.

Unsurprisingly perhaps, it is the existential-phenomenological
model which has pursued this same focus of exploration and,
indeed, has taken the questions surrounding the meaning-
possibilities of 'being' to be its primary defining characteristic.
As such, some initial discussion concerning relevant aspects of
this model would seem warranted.

1. AN OVERVIEW OF THE EXISTENTIAL-PHENOMENOLOGICAL MODEL

A. Basic Theoretical Assumptions

As has already been noted in previous parts of this text, the
existential-phenomenological model assumes an *inter-subjective*
basis to all mental activity. In other words, it argues that everything that we are, or can be, aware of, all that we reflect on,
define or distinguish, is relationally derived.

The very experience of 'being', for instance, is only opened
to conscious reflection when it is placed in the contextual
relationship of *being-in-the-world*. In this way, the reflecting
being and the focus, or object, of reflection are each fundamentally defined, or *co-constituted*, through one another.

Intentionality

The structural tendency, or 'given', through which relations
emerge has been termed *intentionality*. Intentionality refers to
the fundamental relational act whereby 'consciousness' reaches
out, or extends to the 'stimuli' of the world in order to 'bring
them back to itself' – or interpret them – as 'meaningful things'.
This idea may initially be difficult for many readers to take in,
so I propose to approach it from another angle which should
be easier to understand.

Jean Piaget, the most influential developmental psychologist of this century, argued that all human beings (indeed, all species) inherit two 'invariant functions', or 'givens', of existence: the tendencies towards *organization and adaptation*.

Organization refers to our tendency to systematize, integrate or make coherent the structures of our experience. This tendency towards 'meaningfulness' (as existential-phenomenological theory interprets this 'given') will be discussed below.

Adaptation, as the term suggests, refers to our species' ability to adapt to the environment (or 'the world'). According to Piaget, we do so by means of two complementary processes: *accommodation and assimilation*. For example, my three-month-old niece, Christina, became attracted to the 'trackball mouse' device I'd placed next to my notebook computer. As I held it up for her, she tried to grasp it. But, whereas she had learned to grasp various other objects, she had never grasped this 'mouse' before. As such, she had to *accommodate* her previously learned grasping 'structures' to suit the particular shape, features and contours of the 'mouse'.

At the same time, however, Christina's attempts to grasp the 'mouse' revealed her efforts to *assimilate* this novel object into her already learned grasping structure. In other words, she approached it as *if it were the same as those things that she already had the 'structures' to grasp*.

This combined process of accommodation and assimilation allowed Christina's grasping structure to adapt to a novel environmental (or 'world') stimulus through the complementary acts of approaching the 'mouse' from the standpoint of its similarity to previous objects (assimilation) and by 're-structuring' itself to suit the difference, or novelty, of the 'mouse' (accommodation).

Piaget argued that both processes are simultaneously present in every act (be it physical or mental) and are the essential 'building blocks' of intellectual development (Ginsburg and Opper, 1969).

Now if we return to the question of *intentionality*, it is possible to argue that intentionality refers to this same tendency to adaptation (as it does to that of organization) through complementary processes akin to accommodation and assimilation.

So, when existential-phenomenologists argue that 'consciousness extends itself, or reaches out, to the world', they are referring to the fact that 'consciousness' and 'the world' are in simultaneous and inseparable relationship one to the other. We only 'know' the world through our conscious relation to it. But our developing relations with the world rest on the self-same processes of accommodation and assimilation. So, if 'the world' presents me with a novel 'thing' I try both to identify it on the basis of how it is *similar* (in shape, feature, possible function, etc.) to those 'things' I already 'know', and also how it is *different* to them. In this way, my intentional relation with this newly interpreted object *enfolds* it into my previous relations but, equally, *extends* those previous relations into this 'novel-thing world' and thereby *reconstructs* them in the light of this 'novel thing'.

Once again, this may sound complex as an explanation, but an example should clarify what is being argued. During my first few years of life, we had a family dog, Dianella, and my 'knowledge' of dogs was initially shaped through my relationship with her. As time went on, I was introduced to other dogs. This forced my previous knowledge of Dianella to attempt to 'enfold' my current, novel relations with dogs (i.e. acknowledge their similarities) and 'extend' my previous relations to include the new dogs (i.e. acknowledge their differences) and thereby 'reconstruct' the whole of my relations with dogs (i.e. 'broaden' the meaning-possibilities of my experience of dogs). So, for instance, while Dianella was a particularly friendly and affable dog who allowed me to pull her tail and pick her up with barely a grumble, I was soon introduced to dogs who were less tolerant and, indeed, to a dog who responded to my attempt to pick him up by biting my right leg. These various relations, focused on the similarities and differences of the dogs encountered in my world, altered the *whole* of my relations with dogs. With each new dog I encountered, my relational stance with regard to the meaning-possibilities of dogs was reconstructed (so that, for example, once I'd been bitten, dogs were not just usually friendly, subservient creatures, they were also capable of hurting me).

So intentionality refers to this fundamental structure whereby our 'reality' is shaped, or interpreted, through our relations, and whereby each new relation, while reliant on previous ones, nevertheless extends or reconstructs the structure or 'meaning' of the previous relations in order that the newly emerging structure can 'enfold' the new relation. This viewpoint is the basis for the existential-phenomenological critique of 'the past', as was discussed in Part 3, in that our current remembrance of the past is not of 'the past as it was then' but of 'the past reconstructed in order that it may enfold current experience'.

The same fundamental tendency of intentionality reveals that through the process of reconstructing the meaning-possibilities of those 'things' that we are in relation with, *we also reconstruct the meaning-possibilities of the 'thing-constructing' being*. So if I return to my example of the dogs in my early life, while my relations with the different dogs reconstructed the meaning-possibilities of the 'being' of dogs, it also extended the meaning-possibilities of my own 'being'. Just as my earliest relations allowed me to formulate my sense of my 'self' as a being who loved dogs and enjoyed playing with them, my later relations reconstructed the meaning of my 'being' to that of a being who loved dogs and enjoyed playing with them, *and* who also feared and hated them.

As such, intentionality, considered from the standpoint of 'being', reveals that both 'self' and 'other' (or 'the world') are made meaningful, or 'come into being', through their interdependent relations, so that it can be said that they 'co-constitute' one another. Equally, through intentionality, the meanings of 'self and other' are revealed as plastic, or unfixed in meaning, in that each new relation presents both 'self and other' with novel meaning-possibilities that allow the on-going, perpetual extension of their meaning.

However, for reasons I will discuss below, the intentional relationship is most often experienced in such a way that the outcome of relations, rather than seeming to extend the meaning-possibilities of the 'being', actually appear to *sediment the meaning of the 'being'*, such that the novel, potentially meaning-extending experience is 'split off' or 'disowned'.

For example, as a child, I learned to tell the time by playing with my father's wristwatch. He would teach me the notion of hours and minutes and seconds and then test my knowledge by getting me to set particular times on his watch. As I learned to do this quite easily and well, it became an important means for me to experience myself as being 'good and intelligent' through my father's statements to that effect. One morning, however, I began to play with his watch by myself and, unhappily, the winding mechanism fell apart. When my father saw what I had done, his words of anger provoked the experience of myself as being 'bad and stupid'. So, through my intentional relation with my father's watch, I had reconstructed my meaning of myself to be that of 'good and intelligent' *and* 'bad and stupid'. However, this extension was *rejected* for various reasons, so that my 'being' could maintain a sense of 'self' that was *sedimented in the perspective that I was* only *'good and intelligent'*. The novel meaning-possibility ('bad and stupid') could not be enfolded within this sedimented self-structure and therefore had to be 'disowned' in some manner or other so that the sedimented perspective could be upheld.

Therefore, while intentionality at the 'being' level reveals the co-constitutional basis of 'self and other', it must be borne in mind that our experience of this may, in some ways, be rejected or denied.

Intersubjectivity

One of the important consequences of this argument is that each of us is actively involved, or *implicated*, in construing, or attempting to make meaningful, our experience of the world – which includes our experience of ourselves, of others, and all those features, objects and mental processes that make up our lived reality. In this way, the existential-phenomenological model argues that we can never properly speak in terms that suggest a real distinction between subjective and objective, or 'internal' and 'external' (e.g. 'in my thoughts' or 'out there'), since all these terms remove us from the interpretative relationship that is at the basis of our experience.

This can be a deeply unsettling perspective to adopt since, in one stroke, it places us in an uncertain, relativistic realm of being. Whatever meaning we may 'find' for ourselves, for instance, is seen to have no independent, or external, basis; rather, it is 'meaningful' only in an interdependent sense. Experientially speaking, nothing 'is' other than in terms of relation.

As a species, human beings are bounded by the 'givens' of our psycho-biological make-up. We experience 'reality' not as it is, but as it *appears to us to be*. In this way, each of us, while sharing the 'givens' of our species, also brings into our experience of reality all manner of biases and assumptions which are derived from our *unique* standpoint. As such, while, for instance, it appears to be a 'given' of our species to perceive reality in a 'thing'-like fashion, the specifically labelled, or named, 'thing' that each of us experiences, and the manner or mode in which we experience it, is dependent on various linguistic, socio-culturally derived influences as well as influences from our own personal experience that dispose, or bias, us to perceive it in the way we do.

As a 'thing-interpreting' species, we perceive our world (and ourselves) to be 'thing-like' or 'object-based'. Further, from a particular linguistic and socio-cultural background we label, or define 'things' (which is to say, we provide them – or ourselves – with meaning). Equally, from each of our own personal experiences of 'things', we further define 'things' in terms of their relational meanings built up from our unique experiences of – and in – the world. Given these various combinations of interpretative acts, all of which are present in any experience, it can be seen that, fundamentally, our experience is always unique.

If we consider this conclusion further, however, we can understand that, as well as being unique, our experience is also *never fully shareable*. So you could never fully experience any 'thing' as I do, nor could I ever fully experience any 'thing' as you do, or as anyone else does. In order to do so, we would have to have complete access to each other's sum total of past and current personal experience. At best, I might make attempts to provide you with some *sense* of my experience of 'things', just as you might, but our attempts, though they might be increasingly *adequate*, would never be total or complete.

From the standpoint of our 'being' or existence, it can be concluded that each of us is *alone* in our experience. And yet, paradoxically, this 'aloneness' emerges precisely because we are *in relation* to one another. That is to say, 'aloneness' is itself dependent on a prior relational distinction that has been made – namely, that of 'self' and 'other'.

'I' am only unique because 'I' exist, or have come into being. But 'I' only exist, in a manner that I can describe, distinguish, or experience, because of the prior act of separating my 'self' from your 'self' or, as the existential-phenomenological model would have it, the act of distinguishing 'I' from 'not I'. At some point in our early development, each of us becomes 'self-aware'. But to do so requires us to define, or make ourselves 'meaningful', by distinguishing that which is 'I' from that which is 'not-I' (or distinguishing 'self' from 'other').

However, as has already been discussed, *our experience of 'I' is by no means 'fixed'*. Rather, it is a 'plastic' relationally based experience. Even our past, which is the major means by which we maintain our sense of 'I', is experienced selectively on the basis of such factors as our current circumstance and our future-directed goals and aspirations.

Interpreted reality

Not surprisingly, if we attempt to take in the full impact of all these ideas, we are confronted with the *meaninglessness* of it all. This meaninglessness refers to the idea that nothing – not you, nor I, nor any 'thing' – has intrinsic or independent or static meaning. If things are 'meaningful', then they are so only because they have been interpreted as being so. In this way, 'meaning' too is a relative and plastic concept. Each of us, if we follow this line of argument, does not inhabit an independently 'meaningful' world – rather, we, as a species, as cultures, and as individuals in relation to one another, *shape or create the various expressions of meaningfulness that we experience and believe in.*

Our need to make things meaningful (by defining, or distinguishing, or 'bounding' them) appears to be another 'given' of our species. Our intolerance of meaninglessness seems to be deep-rooted, even fundamental, in our make-up. Meaninglessness instils in us *anxiety* – something seemingly meaningless disturbs us, such that we refuse to accept it and attempt to find ways to make it meaningful. We might do so by *likening* it to another object whose meaning is known to us and with which the foreign object seems to share some characteristics, or we might impose some sort of functional purpose on the foreign object which, again, places it in a 'meaningful' context derived from our experience. Looked at in this way, it may be argued that much of our success as a species in dominating our planet has been due to our 'quest' for meaning.

But meaning also has its price. If I conclude that my meaning – my identity, let us say – is defined by certain fixed characteristics, attitudes, patterns of thought, and so forth, then when I am experientially confronted with evidence to the contrary, or which expands the 'meaning' I have given myself, I must either accept the evidence and reshape or extend my meaning of myself, or I must reject, or disown, the evidence in order to maintain my fixed meaning.

The former option provokes anxiety because my meaning is now more flexible – and, hence, tends towards greater plasticity which, in turn, is directed towards meaninglessness. The latter option, on the other hand, forces me to *deceive* myself because I pretend to not experience that which I *do* experience. As Taoist philosophy reminds us: *In either case, it will hurt.*

Choice

One important means that we have at our disposal to combat this experience of 'hurt' is to deny the possibilities of *choice* that we may have available to us. In this way, even if the anxieties and deceptions in our lives remain, at least the added hurt of our own active role in their 'being' can be allayed.

The existential-phenomenological idea of choice has often been misunderstood to suggest that we possess unlimited freedom to choose how and what 'to be'. This view, quite simply, is wrong. The choices that we are free to make arise within a 'bounded world'. Ours is a *situated freedom*, which is to say that it is a freedom whose boundaries lie within the intentional relationship through which each of us, as a 'being-in-the-world', is co-constituted. In this way, we are not 'free to choose what we want' but, rather, free to choose how to respond to the 'stimuli' of the world. In fact, more accurately speaking, we are *condemned* to choose. A stanza from a song by Bob Dylan captures this idea most vividly:

> Ah, my friends from the prison, they ask unto me,
> 'How good, how good does it feel to be free?'
> And I answer them most mysteriously,
> 'Are birds free from the chains of the skyway?'
>   (Dylan, 1964).

As such, our choice is not *interpretational* at the event – or stimulus – level. The stimuli in our lives may be determined by or based on pure chance; we cannot choose them, only, at best, seek to predict them. What choice we possess is at the level of what meaning we bestow on them and how we respond to that meaning.

Equally, choice is not to be understood as being solely at the level of 'choosing between optional stimuli' or even between 'optional meanings of stimuli'. For reasons that will be discussed more fully below, we may have *sedimented* particular meanings so that no optional alternative seems available. Even then, however, we can choose to acknowledge or accept that one sedimented meaning or choose to deny that we have chosen it.

This last point may initially strike some readers as being a trick of logic in order to maintain the view that we always choose. Far from it. Many of the problems and issues that clients bring to therapy originate through this self-same 'unwillingness to choose the one choice available'. In this stance of unwillingness, clients are forced to place themselves in the position of 'passive victims of circumstance'. The one choice may remain the same regardless of the position I adopt towards it, but the experience of 'being' varies significantly depending on whether I choose to accept its presence in my relational world or whether

I deceive myself by denying its presence (and, at times, further deceive myself by believing that another choice option is available).

B. An Overview of the Therapeutic Implications of Existential-Phenomenological Theory

Therapy, from an existential-phenomenological standpoint, involves a relationship between therapist and client which explores and clarifies the experience of being of the client with the purpose of examining those anxieties and those deceptions (as uniquely expressed or derived) which 'hurt' or stultify the client's experience of being-in-the-world.

Bracketing

Existential-phenomenological therapists attempt to explore their clients' experience of being-in-the-world by seeking to 'enter into' their world-view. The main means by which they undertake this is the process of *bracketing* those views, biases, assumptions, theoretically derived or lived perspectives from their own personal experience so that they may open themselves to the experience of the client as it is being lived. I will discuss this attempt more fully below, as it has significant implications for therapists' expressed 'being qualities' and 'ability to listen'. But for the moment, I want to stress that the process of bracketing remains *an attempt* rather than suggest the idea that a therapist can *fully* bracket personal experience. In the same way, the therapist's 'entry' into the world-view of the client is also *an attempt that may be more or less adequate but* never *complete* for reasons relating to the notion of 'aloneness', discussed above.

In adopting this stance, existential-phenomenological theory categorically rejects the postulate that anyone, even the most empathic of therapists, possesses the ability to observe the subjective experience of another person precisely as it actually is. Instead, what is being suggested is that while this experience remains inaccessible in any complete sense, the *approximation*

297

of another's experience is certainly possible to increasing levels of adequacy which approach, if never reach, precision. Equally, while the aim requires therapists to attempt to bracket their own personal biases, assumptions, and so forth, nevertheless, if paradoxically, all that they (or anyone else) can know, even approximately, about their clients' conscious experience of 'being' is dependent on their own awareness of their personal experience.

In the attempt to 'enter' their clients' world-views, existential-phenomenological therapists employ descriptively focused interpretations that are designed to attend to clients' statements concerning their experience, to open them to clarificatory examination, and to challenge those assumptions that remain at the implicit level of the statement. Readers will recall that I examined these ideas more fully in Part 3.

Encounter

Most significantly, the existential-phenomenological model bestows on the *relationship between therapist and client* an undisputed centrality because it is through this relationship itself that the client's issues are manifested or 'brought forth' for examination. In other words, the therapeutic relationship is seen to be the 'microcosm' through which the 'macrocosm' of the client's lived reality is expressed and opened to enquiry.

But, equally, in order for this enquiry to reflect 'microcosmically' the 'macrocosmic' experience of the client in a suitably adequate, or 'good enough', fashion, the therapist must be both willing and able to 'place' himself or herself into the relationship. This notion of *encounter* requires *both* therapist and client to 'be there'. From the standpoint of the therapist, this 'being there encounter', as we shall see, contains significant and specific ramifications.

2. AN EXISTENTIAL-PHENOMENOLOGICAL MODEL OF THERAPY

From the ideas just discussed, the focus of therapy can be seen to be the exploration of the meanings and significances that clients place on the various relationships they engage in. But this act of exploration itself emerges out of the current relationship between therapist and client which, itself, must be acknowledged as being 'meaningful' not simply as a result of what is 'done' within it, but, more to the point, because of the 'experience of being' that it engenders.

In its recognition that therapist and client are engaged in an *interdependently disclosing process*, the existential-phenomenological model emphasizes the notion of *encounter*. In this way, therapists cannot 'step aside' or 'be objective' when listening and responding to the client's statements; rather, they acknowledge their involvement and engagement within the existing therapeutic relationship.

While the meaning and function of 'relationship' within the therapeutic process remains somewhat vague, what research evidence exists (as discussed in Part 1) has tended to dispel 'common sense' views (at least as far as therapists can be said to hold such!) that factors like the theoretical model being employed, specialist skills applied, or the extent of their training are the significant relationship-based variables that will increase the likelihood of beneficially experienced therapy of quantifiable 'successful' outcomes. But if these are not the 'essential ingredients' or necessary abilities that might help to define 'good' therapists or distinguish them from 'bad' ones, what might they be?

A. *Being vs Doing*

During my first few meetings with trainee therapists, I often pose two questions for them to consider: 'Who do you think you are being when you say that you are being a therapist?' and 'What do you think you are doing when you say that you are doing therapy?'

These questions usually provoke initial consternation in my trainees since many of them find that either they have never asked themselves such questions before and, now confronted with them, seek to provide sufficiently suitable answers to reassure themselves (and their tutor) that they have the necessary qualifications to have earned them their place on the training programme, or else they assume that the answers would appear to them to be so obvious that there must be some hidden 'trick' or angle to my queries. But my rationale in asking such questions does not lie in either of these concerns. Rather, my queries are designed to expose and confront the many and varied underlying, or unstated, assumptions that trainees hold concerning therapy's aims, goals and defining characteristics and of their own similar assumptions with regard to their perceived stances and attitudes towards themselves as trainee therapists.

Most often, the answers provided revolve around two broad axes. In response to the first question, trainees often reply with statements that seek to delve into, or define, a variety of skills or specific knowledge bases that they assume to be part and parcel of the training requirements of a therapist (these might include or emphasize the therapist's role as 'interpreter', 'solver of life's puzzles', 'provider of unconditional positive regard', and so forth, which trainees believe they already possess or expect to develop at some point during their training). With regard to the second question, trainees tend to come up with a wide variety of skills such as those they are likely to have been taught at a foundation-level course, or which they may have observed being applied by their own therapists whose functions appear to serve the purpose of alleviation of 'distress', and of promoting 'cures', 'growth', 'strengthening of the ego', 'beneficial change' or any combination of the above (and similarly related) aims.

As might have been already noted, in most instances the answers given to the first question would seem to be either interchangeable with those of the second query (and vice versa), or are so closely related to them that a distinction would appear to be impossible and one single statement would suffice in blending together both the questions and their 'proper' answers. So, for instance, just as trainees might believe that their primary defining characteristics of 'being a therapist' involve the necessary knowledge to interpret the client's statements in such a way as to expose the unconscious wishes or motivations behind them, or in order that their statements might be considered in the light of the client's early life experiences and relations with 'significant others' such as their parents, in a similar fashion they will assume that the ability to provide accurate interpretations of a client's statements or behaviours is a primary skill or a central feature of what they do (or will learn to do) as therapists.

What this process reveals in part is that trainees tend to make little distinction (or perhaps, more accurately, tend to find it difficult to provide a distinction) between *who they are* and *what they do*. Now while this, at first, might seem an issue particular to the concerns of therapy, on further consideration it would appear that this difficulty, if not inability, to distinguish 'being' from 'doing' is far more widespread and extends to all aspects of one's attempts to define oneself. For any number of reasons, many of them undoubtedly culturally based, it seems sensible for us to think of ourselves in terms of what we do. Readers can test this contention for themselves. Just ask yourself 'Who am I?' and see what you are able to give as a response to this question. The chances are that your answers will principally focus on a variety of 'doing' qualities or aspects concerning various features and characteristics of your life. Now on further consideration, while one's own answers might appear to be suitable, consider how you might feel if someone other than yourself, asked for some reason or other to 'sum you up', were to give the self-same responses. While not incorrect, the statements might well seem unsatisfactory. 'But I'm not *just* those things!' each of us might well retort. 'Who I am is much more than that!'

But if asked to expand on this sense of dissatisfaction, in order to provide the additional missing defining qualities that would give a more competent version of who one is, the task might lead to a disquieting conclusion. Much of what we can define about ourselves clearly revolves around the things we do, or which interest us, or which represent ideals or convictions we hold and might attempt to put into practice as defining 'values' around which to guide and focus our lives.

However, no matter how exhaustive a survey of such characteristics might be, still a sense of incompleteness is likely to remain. Such things would certainly 'fit' with the definitions we provide for ourselves, but they fail to 'capture' us.

Perhaps this concern is a fanciful and self-elevating illusion that many, if not all, of us harbour about ourselves. The well-known behavioural psychologist B. F. Skinner, for instance, in his text *Beyond Freedom and Dignity* (1971), argued forcefully for reconsidering deeply held, even fundamental, assumptions we are likely to hold about our 'specialness' as human beings. This is a valid point, I think, and one that many therapists, particularly those whose allegiance lies within the humanistic model, should be more aware of. It seems to me to be often the case that approaches inviting a 'celebration' of being human unnecessarily also involve, or at least suggest, a questionable, even dangerous, elevation of the individual or the species such that 'special' often becomes synonymous with 'superior' – a highly suspect connection. So we must be careful: the inability fully to define our 'being' is not in itself a statement of elevation. Rather, one might put it more correctly as a statement of acceptance, a recognition of uniqueness that extends equally, if diversely, throughout all humanity.

Some time ago, I overheard a new company president remind his staff that they needed to remember that they were all replaceable, that no one was to think that the company could not get by, survive, and prosper without them. While there is some validity in his argument in that it warns against the false assumptions that engender attitudes of misguided self-aggrandizement, and, similarly, points out that nothing *done* by any one of us cannot, with very few exceptions, be achieved as successfully by someone else, nevertheless there remains a fundamental error in the contention.

This error, not surprisingly, stands revealed precisely because of the *being factors* that underlie our behaviour. These factors may not be in any way easily open to statistical or quantitative measurement in any complete sense, but their effects can be dramatic. For while the actions or activities of any one individual can, in themselves, be duplicated from mechanical standpoints that might well be observable and measurable, there still remain all manner of qualitative factors that invest, perhaps even in some odd way 'fuel', the behaviour and which remain unique to each individual. In this way, no one person is truly replaceable in any complete or final sense. Again, one need look no further than to the world of business and industry for examples of this; there are a good many accounts of successful companies which, having been bought out or taken over by new management which has replaced the original staff with its own, equally – or even more highly – skilled work-force, find that their success and profits quickly diminish. These companies, once profitable, subsequently find themselves in serious financial difficulties which, as often as not, lead to bankruptcy (Peters, 1992).

Let me stress that such situations rarely involve factors such as lesser expertise or other quantifiable variables. Rather, they reveal the influence or far less definable 'being qualities' or 'attitudinal factors' that might, for instance, generate a particular ethos or level of commitment that imbues the company with its particular and unique 'being-in-the-world'. For reasons that remain incomprehensible to me, a great many 'captains of industry' (and a great many more 'would-be captains') continue to remain oblivious to such factors and, instead, go on to insist that all members of the work-force (save themselves, perhaps) are replaceable. Only in recent years, for instance, has it been the case that a focus on issues and features dealing with factors designated as 'the human environment' and the influences of such on the day-to-day running, and success, of a company has been treated with any degree of seriousness by the business community. Indeed, a great many 'troubleshooting' companies have come into existence whose expertise revolves around 'human environment influences' and who provide specialist consultants whose task is to analyse and mobilize a company's 'human environment' principally through the application of techniques derived from various off-shoots of the 'Human Potential Movement' (such as 'encounter groups' or 'est') which arose in the heyday of the humanistic psychologies of the late 1960s and early 1970s.

Now while it may not be entirely surprising that business and industry have been slow to recognize and acknowledge the influences of such 'being factors' in the work environment, it does come as something of a shock to realize that the world of therapy also contains major gaps both in its language and theories with regard to these self-same issues.

A number of years ago, as a workshop participant at the annual conference of the British Psychological Society Special Group in Counselling Psychology, I was involved in an exercise that very neatly illuminates this point. The session group was given two tasks. In the first, we were asked to note down the main qualities and factors that would guide and influence our decision in appointing a new member to our hypothetical team of therapists. In the second task, we were asked to note down the main qualities and factors that would determine our decision in selecting a therapist for our own personal therapy. The results of the exercises were then discussed and, needless to say, they revealed significant variations. For while the vast majority of participants tended to focus on such factors as the type, duration and standing of training, and the skills-based knowledge and expertise that a candidate obtained from it (in general, the 'doing qualities' of job candidates) with regard to the first task, when it came to considering the qualities we would be looking for and attached great significance to in our own personal therapist, the emphases lay in personality factors, the therapist's willingness and ability to listen accurately and non-judgementally, his or her 'caring' concerns, and so forth – in other words, those general 'being qualities' that seem so difficult to pinpoint but which, nevertheless, were deemed by us to be essential.

But what was it that provoked such differing emphases in our two tasks?

It would seem to me that the main elements responsible for producing such disparate results are precisely the factors considered in Part 1 of this text. That is to say, when confronted with a task that puts into focus qualities or skills which it is assumed are pertinent in seeking to clarify the nature and identity of therapeutic enterprises, therapists will turn to the skills-based or 'doing qualities' that would appear to provide or add substance to their claims of professional uniqueness, theoretical allegiance and training-derived expertise. At the same time, when confronted with their interests and desires as individuals seeking therapy for personal reasons (as opposed to training requirements or purposes), they (like many others) are likely to minimize such factors and, instead, focus (quite correctly, I believe) on the personal characteristics and 'being qualities' they would hope to encounter in an individual whose principal concerns would lie in his or her ability and willingness to *attend to or accept them.*

But such a result quite naturally begs an obvious question: Would not the various clients coming to therapists, or to their practice, be more likely to seek out and emphasize those very same 'being qualities' rather than determine their choice principally on the basis of those qualities centred on the therapist's theoretical orientation, training and skills? And, if so, would it not be more sensible to seek to hire individuals who fulfilled the 'being qualities' satisfactorily rather than base one's decisions primarily on 'doing qualities'?

If readers recall the summary of findings dealing with clients' values and expectations of their therapists provided in Part 1, the answer to these questions would appear to be resoundingly affirmative.

Clearly, the situation is not necessarily an 'either/or' one. Ideally, one would hope to find in one's therapist *both* sufficient professional expertise and personal qualities that would allow suitable attendance. Indeed, it would be absurd to claim that the 'being qualities' most desired do not involve some element of skill that might have been either learned or enhanced through suitable training. But, if so, should one not expect the emphases in training programmes to be clearly (though not necessarily exclusively) focused on those 'being qualities'? As one theorist has put it:

> It seems to me that what is important . . . is not so much what the analyst says as what he is. It is precisely what he is in the depths of himself – his real availability, his receptivity and his authentic acceptance of what the other is – which gives value, pungency and effectiveness to what he says . . . (Nacht, 1969:40).

In keeping with this view, most training programmes do *appear* to acknowledge the importance of these qualities by insisting that their trainees undergo personal therapy of suitable duration.

But are these sufficient and clear indicators of trainees' development of their 'being qualities'? Unfortunately, this is not necessarily the case. For in a great many training programmes the importance of personal therapy is not specifically for such purposes but, rather, is a primary means of demonstrating to trainees, or convincing them of, the 'truth' and effectiveness of the training institute's theoretical assumptions and derived practices. While the personal benefit of 'training therapy' may be valued by the institute, nevertheless trainees are in many cases vetted by their institutes as to their suitability as representative practitioners of a particular approach by means of their training therapy. Indeed, it is not uncommon for the trainees' personal therapists to be closely involved in the decisions governing candidate suitability to practise as a representative of the approach in question and, in order even to be considered a suitable 'training therapist' for an institute, training therapists must *themselves* subscribe to the theoretical assumptions (some might say ideology) of the training organization.

Now this would make perfect sense if it were the case that the knowledge of particular theoretical stances and their applications had been shown to be necessary or more efficacious to successful therapy. But the evidence for such, as has been demonstrated in Part 1, is sorely lacking. Indeed, what has emerged from a great variety of research analyses on this issue is that the factors likely to allow for the experience of successful therapy are minimally dependent on the theoretical approach advocated by the therapist, or by the type or extent of training that he or she has undergone. Rather, the data have suggested something quite different: in studies focused on those cases where therapy is experienced as being the least successful, the tendency has been for the therapist to be overly strict or 'fixed' in adhering to the tenets and practices of theory that he or she has trained in.

This is not to say that therapists should adopt a *laissez-faire* attitude towards their theoretical models – rather, it suggests that it is not merely the model alone, or in itself, which increases the likelihood of beneficial therapeutic outcomes, but, rather, that the particular relationship between the model and its representative (i.e. the therapist) is the key factor. What might research tell us about this relationship?

While there exists some evidence to suggest that therapists' consistency in adopting and staying with a certain model correlates positively with beneficial outcomes (Malan, 1959, 1963; Luborsky et al, 1975), the case remains that research studies are consistent in their failure to verify the beneficial superiority of any one of the major models of therapy over any other (Luborsky et al, 1975; Mair, 1992). On the other hand, research has been able to indicate significant differences between different *therapists* with regard to their effectiveness – regardless of the model they have adopted (Luborsky et al, 1975). And, further, there exists some suggestive research evidence that indicates that there is a positive correlation between beneficial therapeutic outcomes and therapists' *democratic, non-authoritarian attitudes* (Lerner, 1972). Readers will also recall the question of 'non-specific factors' in therapy which emphasize the personal qualities of therapists, regardless of the model being adopted, as predominant factors in beneficial outcome (Aebi, 1993). Lastly, I remind readers of the 'Dumbo Effect' which would suggest that it is therapists' *beliefs* in their models as being valid or superior, rather than the 'natural' superiority of the models themselves, which provide them with the 'magical' means to fulfil the conditions required for beneficial therapy.

Considering these various factors together, it seems clear that models, in themselves, cannot be said to be the key factor. Yet they are important with regard to what they may provide the therapist at a 'belief' level. I would suggest that the issue here lies precisely in the kind of relationship that any particular therapist will have with his or her model. If the model overwhelms the therapist, in that he or she seeks merely to 'accommodate' to it, and practises therapy 'by the book', then this will be expressed in various ways that impose a 'rigidity' and fixedness of outlook on the therapist which, in turn, will restrict the therapist's ability to 'be' in the relationship with the client as anything other than as servant to the theoretical model. If, on the other hand, the therapist not only accommodates to the theory but also 'assimilates' it to his or her 'being' structures, then the theory will have become a direct expression of the therapist's 'being', thereby allowing the relationship with the client to be one where the therapist 'is there' as one who 'owns' the theory in that it 'captures' or 'embodies' who the therapist 'is'. An example of the significance of this change in emphasis can be found in Patrick Casement's case study 'A child leads the way', which was summarized in Part 3. Readers will recall that, for Casement, the significant beneficial shift in the therapeutic relationship came when he ceased doing therapy as he imagined expert therapists would and allowed himself to become the therapist. Although I have expressed a number of reservations about Casement's particular theoretical assumptions, nevertheless it is plain that once Casement ceased being a 'slave' to his theory and instead allowed himself to express it in his way, the therapeutic relationship altered in a qualitatively significant manner.

Again, the issue here is not principally the validity or reliability of one theory over another, but, rather, the greater likelihood that an extreme adherent of any one approach is more likely to take a more mechanistic, 'doing-based' stance towards therapeutic encounters – a stance that, conversely, is likely to minimize the 'being qualities' of both the therapist and client.

This conclusion raises another important concern with regard to the training of therapists. For the great majority of trainees, who have usually invested a great deal of time, energy and income in order to train, an issue of primary importance would be that all these efforts are not in vain and that their training leads to a successful conclusion. But if success is measured to a significant extent by the trainee's ability to understand, accept and apply the specific theoretical assumptions of the training institute, then it becomes more likely that they will be placed in the position of compromising their concerns, critiques, innovative hypotheses, and, perhaps most importantly, the unique qualities they possess as individuals, in order to comply more closely with the beliefs and assumptions of their trainers, supervisors and therapists. At worst, they run the risk of allowing themselves to be 'indoctrinated' by the training institute. The most vociferous and severe opponents and critics of therapy have emphasized this very possibility and, while it might be argued that their stances are unnecessarily extreme, nevertheless they cannot be entirely dismissed.

Our concerns with 'doing' reveal an emphasis that is probably culture-bound. But might it not be the case that a great many of the psychological problems that our clients present us with are in themselves in some way linked with this self-same assumption? Clients, not surprisingly, are likely to think that the sources of their problems lie in their lack of knowledge or lack of success in 'doing the right thing'. Such viewpoints reveal a mechanization of thought and being that a great many philosophers and psychologists have pointed out as being part and parcel of the fundamental crises in our societies (Fromm, 1976; May, 1983). For when we are only able to distinguish or define ourselves through what we do, we place ourselves in an orientation of thought that equates us with machines – which, of course, are replaceable objects, quantifiable in value and, however complex, likely to malfunction or run down over time.

In 1979, as a member of the Edale Research Group, an independent collective interested in the analysis and exploration of the explosion of new 'cults' that had arisen throughout the 1970s, I became a participant in one of the *est* training sessions in London. One of the exercises that the three hundred-odd people carried out over the two weekend sessions struck me then, as it still does today, as a very powerful expression of just what can occur when our 'being qualities' are disregarded or else are equated entirely with our 'doing skills'.

The exercise was of seeming simplicity. The group was divided so that it formed lines of about twenty individuals. One by one the lines were required to walk up to the raised stage at the front of the hall where the training took place and simply stand there and look out over the remaining members of the group. We were instructed to do nothing, just stand still and look out over the group impassively, not seeking to gain anyone's attention or interest through any gestures, smiles, prolonged eye contact, and so forth. When the mechanics of the exercise were first presented, I recall thinking to myself, naively, 'What is the point of this?' I couldn't imagine a less self-confrontative or dangerous game to play. It did not take me long to discover just how wrong I was. Within a minute or so of the first line ascending the stage, I witnessed various individuals in that line-up begin to cry, faint, become dizzy, feel sick, and wail in psychic pain. These same effects were repeated line after line, time and time again. Now while I am not condoning the many potentially manipulative or otherwise problematic practices that took place during the *est* training, I simply wish to point out that this experience was a particularly powerful example of what can occur to people when they are stripped of the many 'doing defences' they have learned to apply when presenting themselves to others (and to them-selves).

I spoke to a number of people in the break following this exer-cise and asked them about its meaning for them. Many reported the deep sense of unease they had experienced during the brief time they had stood on stage. Some stated that they had felt com-pletely empty, transparent, open for all to see. Others pointed to their sense of discomfort, even disgust, with themselves as 'beings with nothing to do'. Some claimed that the experience had led them to confront 'the games' that made up their lives, their insecurities, their fears, their deepest anxieties. One person, a teacher by training, revealed that while he had thought that the exercise would be 'a cinch' since he was used to being the focus of attention in a group and had never felt any nervousness or unease in this position, it had been the most difficult and painful of all the exercises we had done and, indeed, he had fainted within seconds of his being up on stage. When I asked him to clarify his statements a little further, he said:

> It was like people could really look into me, see who was there behind all the bullshit façade. It was as if my deepest being was being revealed and I couldn't stand it. Worse, though, I was seeing myself in this way for the first time. I was just this living thing that had nothing to offer except my aliveness – and it didn't seem enough. What did I have to offer? What could I say in my own defence for existing? Sure, there are things I can DO. But those had been taken away from me. I had no excuses. I wanted to cry: 'Why me? What's

so goddamn special about me that I'm alive and breathing?'
(Spinelli, 1979).

This person's statements ring true, I suspect, for a great many
of us. We have swallowed the idea that our meaning and reason
for living lie in the acts that we carry out. But more than this,
I would suggest, such views point to the difficulty we have in
clarifying the distinctions between 'being' and 'doing'; indeed,
we rarely consider the very possibility of such distinctions so
that our 'being' *is* our 'doing'.

One theorist and therapist who emphasized these very same
points much more clearly and powerfully than I will ever be
able to was R. D. Laing. Throughout his writings, Laing argued
that varieties of severe mental distress and disturbance such as
'schizophrenia', rather than being primarily a form of 'illness'
best dealt with by means of medical models of treatment, could
be more adequately understood as expressions of deep *ontological insecurity* – that is to say, serious 'dis-ease', conflict and
fragmentation of various facets of one's experience of one's own
being as expressed through one's relations with oneself and with
others (Laing, 1960). Further, Laing, together with his colleague
Aaron Esterson, argued the case that ontological insecurity
arises precisely when the distinction between who one is and
what one does (or must/mustn't be or do) remains unclear or
indistinguishable through one's relations with self and others
(Laing and Esterson, 1965).

Many of my trainees are initially mystified, if not angered,
when, early on in their training, I urge them to consider their
assumptions concerning the function of therapy and assert that
any assumptions that place at the forefront of thought ideas
such as 'helping', 'curing' or even 'changing' the client are worth
investigating, not only with regard to their impact on the therapeutic encounter, but also for the possible dangers that such
views may provoke for both their clients and themselves.
Further, I ask them to consider what it might be like for them
and their relationship with their clients if they could set aside,
or 'bracket', such aims and assumptions. Invariably, one or more
of my trainees will respond: 'But if we are not there to do any

of those things, then just what are we there for? What can we offer our clients?'

When I respond that perhaps all we can offer, at least initially, is our 'being there' or 'presence', I am usually met with looks of concern, confusion and sometimes even scorn. Can our presence be enough? Surely not!

And yet, it is not unusual for anyone who has practised therapy to think of instances when whole sessions have passed by with no interjection or interpretation or request for clarification – indeed, where no comment whatsoever from the therapist has been forthcoming or has been asked for by the client – and yet the client will assert at the end of the session that he or she has experienced tremendous insight, benefit, relief, catharsis – in short, a whole gamut of positively experienced changes in outlook and awareness which he or she will then proceed to thank the therapist for having prompted (or even 'made' happen).

During my first few years working as a therapist, I found such statements to be far more unnerving and troublesome than any deviant or disturbing behaviours or experiences that clients acted out or related to me about various problematic aspects of their lives. Truth to tell, when they made these comments, I felt that I had conned them in some way or other, that I had not 'earned' the fee paid me since, when it came down to it, I had done nothing throughout that whole session which I could label a 'therapeutic act'. I confess that, on occasions, in spite of the evident satisfaction, relief, joy or sadness in my client's demeanour, I convinced myself that they were fooling me in some way or other. I hated it when these circumstances arose because clients had done something seemingly on their own – they had not allowed me to 'help' them by way of my expert interventions but had, rather, gone ahead and done something for themselves! They had not allowed me to put to use the years' worth of knowledge and skills I had accumulated and invested so much time and energy in acquiring. Indeed, when I went on to confront such feelings and thoughts (for I was at least aware of their absurdity), I also noted (as I previously mentioned in Part 1) that similar emotions arose in me when clients told me of insights or profound developments in their thinking and behaviour that had occurred *outside* our sessions together when they had been talking in an open and honest way with others – family, friends, even relative acquaintances or strangers. What was my anger and discomfort about?

I suspect that it had largely to do with my desire and commitment 'to be a good therapist' which, more accurately stated, meant 'my belief in my own specialist abilities and powers, and my expertise'. But if clients could achieve significant beneficial insight without my employment of any of these skills, or (perhaps worse) when other 'amateurs' usurped my role, then what did this say about such vaunted abilities?

I can assure the reader that it is painfully embarrassing to reveal this, but it is also my belief that these feelings and thoughts were not specific to my own particular 'neuroses'; rather, through discussions with colleagues and trainees, I have come to accept that they are far from uncommon. Instead, they seem to me to be direct outcomes of those attitudes and positions that place 'doing' at the forefront of the therapeutic process. For, if this is the case, then it becomes a vexing, and disheartening, question to ask how it can be that clients can claim substantial benefit from therapy when the therapist has done absolutely nothing. But, if nothing has been done, then it becomes sensible to question whether a focus that prioritizes these 'doing' elements is *always* proper. And if this line of questioning is pursued, then it becomes both valid and necessary to consider what may be some of the differences and possibilities in the therapeutic encounter when the 'being qualities' expressed by therapists are emphasized over the 'doing' skills that they may have learned to employ.

One of the first variations that this re-orientation forces therapists to reconsider is the notion of expertise. If therapists are specialists, what are they specialists in?

In very broad terms, most, probably all, therapists and clients would agree that individuals who have engaged in a beneficial therapeutic process will have discovered novel possibilities of understanding and, often, changing various disturbing and debilitating patterns of thought and behaviour. I would suggest that in addition to the above – and perhaps more significantly – such individuals will have found, or expanded, various means whereby they can acknowledge and express their current stance or experience through the relationships they engage in with the world both with regard to their *internal, or world-as-self, relations* and their *relations with others* (including other people, living organisms, and the physical and socio-cultural environment). That is to say that therapy can allow a more experientially adequate means of acknowledging and examining who one is and how one is, relationally speaking, in a given moment of experienced time.

This view may be seen as being reminiscent of Freud's profound statement regarding the possibilities of analysis providing the means to enhance the potential to love and work (Freud, 1940). While some have tended to read this conclusion as an expression of Freud's limited – even pessimistic – hopes for therapeutic interventions, it seems to me to be, instead, an admirably realistic, responsible and humanly respectful stance for therapists to adopt.

The experience of living presents one with constant and uncontrollable vagaries of change. It has become a truism or homily to state that 'life is change', yet the accuracy of this statement cannot be lightly dismissed. Nevertheless, it is also the case that as often as we may mouth this view, our tendency is to act in ways that suppose that we can in some manner offset this 'rule'. We present ourselves to ourselves and to others as though we have conquered change. Indeed, we make all manner of attempts to build up a model of ourselves and our world that promotes the opposite notion – which is that 'life remains the same' and, by implication, that *we* remain the same.

B. *Being with and Being for the Client*

An important implication of a 'being' focus in therapy is that it allows therapists to acknowledge themselves as changing beings whose current manner of existence is expressed through their interactive relationship with their clients. As such, it concedes to therapists a far greater range of possibilities of relating to clients in differing, if apposite, ways. This in itself is a freeing process that would be far less possible if therapists were to emphasize 'doing skills' that, in contrast, would more likely demand the maintenance of a similar stance or 'way of being' regardless of the situation or relationship encountered. Does this mean that a 'being' focus allows a *laissez-faire* attitude to the therapeutic process? Certainly not. For being, in the therapeutic process, requires therapists to uphold a stance that is both that of *being with* and also of *being for* the client. While closely related, and mutually inclusive, these two stances point out emphases the implications of which are worth more detailed consideration.

Being with

Firstly, in *being with* the client, therapists acknowledge the interdependence in the therapeutic relationship, and place an emphasis on those qualities of being that seek to promote an attitude that does not, initially at least, seek to confirm the 'objective truth' of the client's statements, or whose aim is to present disconfirmations, rebuttals, contradictions, alternative possibilities, and so forth, but, rather, which *stays with the experienced truths of the client as they are being related* in order that they, and whatever implications such truths may hold, may be exposed to further investigation and clarification by both the therapist and the client. In this way, the process of 'being with' the client allows the focus of the relationship to remain firmly on the client's experientially based statements (be they verbal or non-verbal) so that they can be 'opened up' with regard to the meaning or meanings that the client (not the therapist) perceives them to hold. The following example should clarify this argument.

A prospective client, Rose, once telephoned me to make arrangements for our first meeting. Towards the end of our discussion, having set the time and date of our appointment, Rose expressed the need to inform me that I should know in advance that she had a particularly unsightly facial disfigurement about which she was deeply embarrassed. Prepared (as far as I could be) to be confronted by what I imagined to be my client's gruesome appearance, I was surprised to meet a particularly attractive (to me, at least) middle-aged woman whose facial features showed no sign of any obvious blemish. Sitting down, she immediately launched into an account of how her life had been marred by her disfigurement to the extent that she avoided unnecessary contact with others lest she experience their repulsion towards her. As Rose described her experiences, it slowly dawned on me that the source of her anguish was a tiny, nearly imperceptible mole on her left cheek. This, then, was 'the terrible scar' that had so burdened her life!

I am convinced that had I pointed out to her then and there what seemed so obviously to me (and probably to anyone else except her) to be an absurd concern on her part, I would never have seen Rose again. Instead, I found the means to acknowledge her reality and began to explore with her her experience of herself as a 'scarred' being. It was only much later in the therapy, when Rose felt herself to have been sufficiently understood by me, that the question of how others (myself included) saw and reacted to her disfigurement was confronted. Without going into unnecessary details about this encounter, it is sufficient to state that Rose had always been aware that others did not see the mole *as she did*, and while she could understand their viewpoint, she could not accept their insistence that she, like they, should acknowledge it as being insignificant. Indeed, the mole had come to stand for, or represent to Rose, her sense of her uniqueness and independence from what she perceived to be the powerful demands of others for her to 'fall into line' with their accepted ways of thinking and behaving.

In this way, the mole was not only Rose's 'problem in life', it was also her primary means of 'salvation', since it allowed her the means of asserting and identifying herself as a separate and unique being. All of this, and the subsequent insights that emerged for her throughout our time together, would have been highly unlikely had I not attempted to 'be with' Rose's experience of herself. While it is possible that immediate confrontation might have led us to similar clarifications, it might just as well have prevented any possibility of this and, worse, Rose's experience of therapy may have been labelled, with some justification, as abusive.

Being for

Being for the client enjoins to remind therapists that for the duration of each session they have agreed to attempt a process of encounter whereby they will seek to inhabit the experiential world of the client for the sole sake of allowing the client a form of 'reflecting self' encounter with *another who seeks to be the self.* Such a process once again subverts the possibility of the therapist's task being that of 'truth-bringer', 'healer' or 'helper' in any purposive or direct manner. All such may be experienced by the client, of course, as would be the case if any one of us were to be in a situation where we were willing to confront our concerns, stances, fundamental assumptions, fears and anxieties in a manner that was as open and honest as we might allow ourselves.

The notion of 'being for' the client urges therapists to 'attend to the client', as R. D. Laing put it (Evans, 1976). In other words, it urges therapists *neither to lead the client* in various directions that they think to be of import, *nor to be led by the client* into avenues of thought or affect that remain unclear or disconnected to both or either participants, *but to seek to keep up with them side by side* (to pursue the analogy) so that the client's path becomes the therapist's path and an approximate symmetry of thought and assumption becomes possible.

The distinction between 'being with' and 'being for' is subtle yet significant. For while the former focuses on therapists' willingness to *acknowledge the lived reality of the client*, the latter further asks therapists to *attempt to enter the client's lived reality* in order that they may experience that reality in a manner that approaches the client's way of being.

So, for instance, just as my example concerning my client, Rose, sought to clarify the notion of 'being with' in that it expressed my *willingness* to consider Rose's view of her lived reality as experientially valid, so, too, can it provide a concrete example of 'being for' the client in that, through such willingness, I, as the therapist, was able to contemplate what it might be like to live reality *as Rose did* and, hence, to *partially enter into her way of being* so that my comments, clarifications and challenges sought to be *parallel reflections* of Rose's stance in life *rather than impose alternative or competing stances.*

In this attitude of 'being for' my client, then, I was able to approximate Rose's reality to the extent that I could 'live' it and, in so doing, perceive and provide a voice for the meanings, assumptions, implications, paradoxes, possibilities and limitations with which that reality was imbued not from a distanced, abstract, or 'other-focused' standpoint, but from a standpoint that approached hers. In this way, for example, I was able to guess that if, as Rose, I was able to see the mole not only as others saw it, but also in a manner that others could not, then the mole might contain a meaning that was not only specific to itself but also general to Rose's meaning of self in relation to others. In my attempt to 'be for' Rose, I could grasp that, like the mole, Rose was seemingly like she believed others insisted she be (i.e. insignificant), but experientially she was of major significance (even if she was the only one to be aware of this).

The injunction to 'be for' the client is by no means an easy one for therapists to adhere to, nor is it ever fully possible for them to achieve because, as I suggested earlier, no one is ever fully able to experience or interpret the world in exactly the same manner as another. Nevertheless, perhaps during brief moments in an encounter, therapists may experience a sense of the *uncanny* in that they may feel themselves to be temporarily 'lost' or 'swallowed up' in the client's world. Not surprisingly, this experience may often be characterized as unpleasant or disturbing and, sometimes, even frightening. Conversely, this may also happen to clients if they are led too forcefully or quickly into an experience of exploring the meaning of their issues from the theoretical standpoint adhered to by their therapist. Once again, Laing's work with deeply disturbed and fragmented beings provides vivid examples of what may occur both when a therapist seeks to 'be with' and 'be for' a client as well as, alternatively, what further fragmentation may occur when therapists, adopting a more objective model, impose their – or 'consensus' – reality on their clients (Laing, 1960, 1967, 1982).

The experience of the client's lived reality

The experience of the other – even at an approximate and incomplete level – is often disorientating and may be deeply unnerving. The very 'strangeness' of the lived experience of the other and, perhaps as commonly, the recognition that it may bring forth similarly shared, if unreflected, assumptions in one's own life, may be good reasons in themselves for therapists to seek to establish rationales that avoid making this their aim. Nevertheless, to address and understand these issues from standpoints such as 'transference' or 'counter-transference' (as was criticized in Part 3) seems to me to miss the point of what is being argued. Indeed, it becomes more understandable why some therapists have criticized these terms in that, rather than point out important areas of unconscious conflict in either the client or the therapist, the difficulties encountered may more accurately reflect an unwillingness to engage in this kind of 'being' encounter and may be in themselves defensive and protective barriers or obstacles that serve to distance both the therapist and the client from the acknowledgement and exploration of the direct experience each has of the other and of themselves in relation to the other.

It would not be surprising, since more than any therapist (other than Laing perhaps) it was Carl Rogers who sought to emphasize and distil the 'being qualities' essential to therapy, if readers have begun to suspect that what I have been attempting to communicate is a rehash of Rogers' notion of 'mirroring' or 'reflecting back' (Kirschenbaum and Henderson, 1990a). But this too would be an erroneous assumption. While there are certainly some points of similarity, I would contend that my argument contains several significant points of deviation from, or perhaps more accurately can be understood as being an extension of, Rogers' ideas.

Firstly, the points I have been making do not seek to suggest or pretend that therapists (even if this were possible) should seek to 'erase' themselves such that the client is presented with a blank reflective screen for inspection and analysis. While Rogers clearly seems to have made such suggestions, other comments of his make clear that he did not by any means fully adopt or seek to adhere to this naive position. Unfortunately, quite a substantial number of person-centred therapists I have encountered do, on the other hand, seem to believe themselves capable of such magical feats and are convinced that their 'reflecting back' of the client's statements is bereft of interpretation or of their own being. This stance is patently absurd since the very fact that they choose to reflect back certain statements and leave others unreflected (a necessity in any form of encounter) itself reveals their input and presence. As such, I am not arguing here a case for 'mirroring' in any ordinary sense of the word. If there is any 'mirroring' suggested in my comments, it is more along the lines of a somewhat distorted mirror or, better yet, the kind of 'black mirror' that was alleged to have been employed by alchemists and practitioners of the arcane arts the properties of which were claimed to lie in its ability to reflect back that which is only implied by the surface features of the reflecting object.

Secondly, unlike person-centred therapists who avoid the direct questioning and challenging of clients' statements but whose art lies in making the reflection itself the challenge, so that the impression is given that they have added nothing to their clients' utterances, I would suggest that the emphasis on 'being qualities', while similarly urging therapists to avoid adding anything to their statements which seeks to impose analytical or 'rational' interpretations originating from their theoretical or personal biases and assumptions, nevertheless acknowledges therapists' own input into the relationship and therefore allows (indeed, insists) that therapists urge clarification of clients' experience by means of the *descriptively focused interpretations* that were discussed in Part 3.

Thirdly, the attitude being advocated makes clear that therapists are not being asked to 'be themselves' as Rogers and a number of his followers seem to advocate. The 'self' that the therapist is being asked to attempt to be is a *self-in-relation whose focus resides in 'the other' (i.e. the client)*. This injunction is not entirely unlike the task required of actors who have trained in the 'Method' school founded by Lee Strasberg and whose essential aim revolves around 'immersing' themselves or 'entering into' a specific character or object. As such, in order to seek to achieve this task, the 'self' that they are being, while always invested with 'the self' of the actor, nevertheless expresses itself and 'is' in the world in a much more complex and divergent manner than that suggested by the term 'being oneself'.

Once again, this attempt makes clear that while one cannot ever fully expect to be 'the other' in any complete sense (in the same way that each method actor will 'be' a unique Hamlet or Blanche DuBois through his or her 'living interpretation' of such characters, which will evoke differing qualities and emphases in the interpretation), nevertheless one can focus one's sense of being such that it seeks to 'reside in' the interpreted experiential realm of the client.

The enterprise of 'being with and for' the client serves, among other things, to diminish the likelihood of the therapeutic encounter becoming unnecessarily mechanistic or solely focused on what the therapist is able to *do*. At the same time, while it by no means dismisses the value of learned skills or knowledge on the part of the therapist, it does place these within a perspective that emphasizes *'doing' as an extension of, and not a substitute for, the therapist's being in the relation.* As such, what therapists 'do' should always be understandable within, and an expression of, their attempts to acknowledge and enter into the client's world-view rather than being the means of emphasizing their 'taking charge' of the therapeutic encounter in order to promote cure, symptom alleviation, growth, or change.

I am personally convinced that, however paradoxically, such worthy aims become more likely, or at least may be achieved with the client's greater willingness and co-operation, precisely when therapists give up all assumptions of having the power, the professional credentials and skills, and (perhaps most importantly) the personal need to achieve such. In this sense, the willingness and attempt 'to be with and for the client' may be seen as an act of courage on the part of therapists (just as it is an act of courage for clients to be willing to confront their attitudes to various aspects of their lives) and may well be an essential element of the 'specialness' that is claimed for therapy.

C. Listening

The concentration on this focus in a training situation also provides a worthwhile means of discerning which 'doing skills' are perceived as being fundamental to therapy regardless of the theoretical orientation one trains in or wishes to espouse. A skill that arises continually and which all trainees whom I have taught acknowledge as being both fundamental and of unexpected difficulty and complexity is that of *listening*. It would seem both useful and informative, therefore, to consider this skill both in itself and in the light of the points I have made with regard to the question of 'being qualities'.

Listening skills seem at first so basic and fundamental to trainees and lay persons alike that it appears initially absurd even to consider them as specialist skills. 'Everyone knows how to listen!' might be a common claim, but, as I hope to demonstrate, this view may be somewhat naive.

If pressed to think of an example from their lives, most people are likely to be able to name someone who is 'a good listener'. What do people mean by this phrase? On consideration, the definition of a 'good listener' centrally involves someone who will allow them to voice concerns, experiences, affective circumstances and so forth without the kind of intrusion that would imply any form of judgement or bias; who will avoid advice-giving or suggestions either completely or at least until such a time as these might seem appropriate or welcome; who will comment in such a way as to reveal that they have heard 'the core message' contained within an account; and whose challenges, calls for clarification, or even interpretations flow directly from the statements or experiences recounted. Similarly, 'a good listener' is someone who can 'hold' the speaker in that he or she appears to provide a sense of openness, a willingness or even encouragement to hear the full story and its emotional content without a sense of disinterest or a desire to hurry one along in the recounting of events and their emotional impact on the speaker; who will acknowledge and allow one to express a variety of emotional behaviours such as grief, anger, joy, confusion, rage or hilarity without a sense of the listener's own discomfort or embarrassment; and who, in this way, fulfils such notions as 'empathy', 'congruence' and 'concerned respect'.

All of us, I am sure, have at some time or other in our lives yearned to be in the presence of 'a good listener' in order that we might pour out our tales of woe, misery, frustration, confusion and even joy. We may have found such a person among our family, friends, teachers, representatives of our religion, or even complete strangers encountered serendipitously. Some of us may have engaged the services of a professional such as a specialist adviser or, of course, a therapist. And many more, I suspect, may have looked in vain among any or all of these possibilities and failed to find the person who would qualify in terms of the criteria required of 'a good listener'. Clearly, then, although it would seem initially the case that 'good listening' is a straightforward process requiring little, if any, expertise, there appears to be a particular ingredient, or set of ingredients, which, while not initially obvious, nevertheless reveal themselves as being essential once their absence is recognized.

As it is claimed to be by nearly all authors and practitioners of therapy as an essential, or foundational, skill for the development, maintenance of, and (at least partial) fulfilment of the inherent possibilities in the therapeutic relationship, 'good listening' would seem to be a skill that is worthwhile examining. And, indeed, as might be expected, a wide array of training texts focus on the development of 'good listening' skills by means of useful exercises and lessons focusing on concrete examples designed to assist the trainee in the development of his or her own skills. Gerard Egan's widely employed text *The Skilled Helper* (1982), for example, provides a practically focused analysis of listening skills emphasizing the value of listening to client statements from the standpoint of their *content* and *specificity* and in terms of the client's *focus on specific experiences, behaviours and feelings and emotions* in particular situations. In addition, Egan endeavours to clarify how the trainee may learn to listen out for both the *overt and covert* messages contained in a client's remarks (Egan, 1982).

While there is much of value in such analyses and their related exercises, particularly for training purposes, at the same time I would argue that such 'doing' skills are in and of themselves at best of limited value if they are not in some way reflections or behavioural expressions of the person who enacts them. We are all likely to have had first-hand experience of someone (even ourselves) who might say and do all the right things and yet with whom we still feel a good deal of distrust or sense of unease.

Sartre's now-famous example of the overly solicitous waiter comes to mind as someone who fulfils this scenario – since in this illustration we are presented with someone who is, in many ways, the perfect waiter, and yet there exists in him something totally lifeless, empty, somehow more android-like than human (Sartre, 1956). Relevant to this, the novelist Philip K. Dick, author of many masterpieces of speculative fiction, has suggested that one of the principal qualities that distinguishes a human being from an android is the human's ability *to balk at carrying out certain acts* (Rickman, 1988). An extension of this point would suggest, I believe, that our very humanity rests upon such characteristics as our *unpredictability and imperfection*. Which is to say that human beings possess the acknowledged capacity to alter their thinking and behaviour (e.g. they can elect to do something in a manner that is different from usual) in ways that can both surprise and shock in part due to their unexpectedness.

Predictability and perfectionism

Although both the more behaviourally focused and analytic approaches to therapy tend to concentrate (in admittedly different ways and for differing reasons) on the predictability of human behaviour, as, indeed, do all theories to varying degrees, it seems to me to be equally pertinent for those who make it their task to investigate human experience also to consider our unpredictability.

Why should this point be of significance in the current discussion? The neglect, or avoidance, of the possibility of the unpredictable implicitly leads us to the desire or aim for *perfectionism*. The machine-based android and Sartre's overly obsequious waiter both seek out forms of perfectionism to the extent that change or divergence from their typically complex but highly regulated and patterned forms of behaviour become intolerable and near-impossible.

One of my clients, Tania, a teenage student terrified of sitting her A-level exams, expressed the notion of perfectionism when she stated: 'What's the point of sitting an exam if I don't know if I will pass it?' As well as revealing her intolerability of failure, this viewpoint expresses an implicit demand for the predictable, to know pretty much before anything happens what its outcome will be. As understandable as this desire may be, what is rarely acknowledged is the restriction on our experience of life which predictability imposes. While the unpredictable may be anxiety-provoking, it is also the source of a great many experiences that are both invaluable and deeply meaningful to us all. As much as we might yearn for the predictable, when our lives become overly imbued with it they appear to be far less 'life-filled' and increasingly insignificant.

Over time, I have observed this attempt to avoid uncertainty and to build up a predictable and protective experiential environment to be a widespread feature in the lives of many of my clients. For somehow, in having constructed their lives in such a regulated manner, they seem to have entrapped themselves into ways of relating to the world that severely restrict the possibility of deviation from thought and deed both at the everyday level and at levels that are perceived by them as being of utmost importance. In such circumstances, the very individuals and events (such as their spouses, children, lifestyles) that were once valued because they were construed as providing the means for security and the avoidance of uncertainty have themselves become the 'problematic focus' of lives experienced as restricted and unfulfilling. In their own words, such clients see themselves, in these instances, as beings 'going through the motions' or 'pretending to be human' or 'no longer experiencing and expressing feelings of love, worth and concern'.

But therapists too, in their attempts to be 'experts who always do and say the right thing', need to consider how much of their relationship with their clients (not to mention themselves) is restricted when it rests on assumptions that are similar, and similarly limiting, to those likely to be experienced by their clients. For instance, an activity such as listening, when confined by therapists' devout allegiance either to a theoretical framework or to various learned skills, can also become equally restricted and restricting since not only will therapists, in all likelihood, listen out principally for those parts of what is being said that are either explained, implied or predicted by the theory they advocate and represent, and thereby will minimize the value of other statements made by the client, but they will also listen even to these 'highlighted' sections of discourse in a manner that will allow them to 'feed it back' to their clients through the utilization of specifically learned communication skills that, typically, are designed to focus concentration on those areas deemed significant by therapists. In a similar manner, therapists may come to believe that by following such directives they will approach therapeutic 'perfection' in that the anxiety of the unforeseen or the incorrect will be allayed. In these ways, although therapists might seek to give the impression that they are listening as adequately as possible to their clients' statements, and might believe that they have found ways of promoting themselves as caring, empathic listeners, they might in fact subtly (and sometimes not so subtly) and inadvertently be revealing the 'mechanism' of their listening such that although clients may not be able to point to anything that is incorrect in their therapist's listening, they may nevertheless feel themselves to be unheard or unacknowledged at a 'human' level.

As such, therapists' reliance on a fundamental skill such as listening as something which expresses first and foremost their desire and attempt to be seen as experts, who through the accurate employment of learned training skills express (or, more humbly, approach) the 'perfect embodiment of listening', paradoxically increases their clients' doubts that they will ever be truly heard. *Or, in other words, therapists might hear all the right things, yet still have failed to listen.*

How can therapists avoid this situation? It would seem that a necessary step is for them to accept the 'unknown possibilities' within every act of listening, or, more generally, within every encounter, by acknowledging that their own involvement within it is not at the 'perfectionist android' level but at a human level which, while aiming for the best that one can offer, can also embrace uncertainty, insecurity and error. Considered within a more concrete perspective, this view urges therapists to avoid restricting their listening such that it focuses *solely* on and adheres to their specific theoretical and personal perspectives. To do so does not mean that they must forsake, or pretend not to hold, such outlooks, but, rather, that they should concede that their perspectives can form only *part* of the listening process.

What other parts are there to this process? Broadly speaking, they involve therapists' capacity and willingness *to listen from the perspective of the client*. In their attempt to achieve this, therapists are more likely to shift from *self-focused listening* towards (at least partial) *other-focused listening*. That is to say, 'good listening' occurs when the listener attempts to listen *as if the listener were also the speaker*.

Other-focused listening

Acknowledging this frees therapists to listen not just to the statements originating from 'someone else' (i.e. clients) but also to the statements that originate from within 'the being who is seeking to be the other' (i.e. the therapist). These latter statements may be perceived as hunches or 'niggling concerns' that appear to insist on being attended to. While acknowledging that there may be some danger in expressing these, or that they may be completely off-track, I would personally advocate their acceptance and, in some instances, even their introduction into the dialogue, as long as they are presented in a manner that makes clear therapists' 'ownership' of them, as well as their acknowledgement that they may have no bearing whatsoever on the client's issues and may be rejected by the client with no fear that this will be interpreted as a form of 'resistance', or that they reveal a 'hidden truth' that only therapists' superior knowledge or expertise with regard to the client's mental realm has revealed. Presented in this manner, clients will not only be much more willing to hear such statements and allow them into the dialogue, far more importantly (and paradoxically) they will increase the likelihood of clients experiencing their therapists as good – and human – listeners.

A brief if perhaps somewhat 'eerie' example might clarify what is being suggested here. About four years ago, I had become interested in exploring the possibilities of being involved in a television documentary on the life and work of the afore-mentioned American writer, Philip K. Dick. Just prior to my seeing the client discussed in this example, my agent phoned me to say that there had been some unexpected interest shown in the project and that he would set up some initial meetings with a potential producer. When my session with my client, Lawrence, began, he immediately started to talk about a dream he'd had two nights before that was disturbing him. When I asked him what he wanted to tell me about the dream, Lawrence explained that it involved a friend from his adolescence, named Dick, whom he'd not thought of for many years (certainly, he'd never before mentioned this person in any of our previous sessions). I enquired as to what Lawrence thought the significance of Dick's appearance in his dream might be, and he immediately responded that, it was funny, but all he could tell me was that he'd found it odd that Dick should be in the dream by himself. Who else should have been with Dick? As it transpired, for a period of some years during his teens, my client had had two very close friends who had always seemed to be linked to one another until they'd had a major row over a girlfriend and, as a consequence, had ended their friendship, each vowing never again to be seen in the other's presence. In spite of this, Lawrence, who subsequently moved to London and lost contact with both of these friends, realized that he had maintained a mental link between Philip (the other friend) and Dick.

The correspondence between the two friends' names and the author's name struck me as being both amusing and uncanny – so much so, in fact, that I could not immediately set it aside. Nevertheless, I asked Lawrence to tell me about his relationship with his two friends and he began to explain that, in many ways, they had been exact opposites. And had he 'held them together', so to speak? Yes, in fact they'd often used him as a kind of go-between. Such statements only added to my inability to let go of 'my' Philip Dick. For, both in his life and in his writings, he had expressed and explored an on-going sense of 'splitness' to such an extent that in a number of his later novels he made this splitness explicit by placing himself directly in his stories not as a single character but as two characters who could only be 'made whole' if they could find or recognize each other (Dick, 1981, 1987).

As I continued listening to my client, the interweaving themes of 'splitness', separation and acting as 'go-between' led me to consider that just as Philip Dick, the author, had invented two characters in order to express his splitness, so might it be the case that my client's two friends 'splitting apart from each other' might be reflections of his own sense of personal (and seemingly irreconcilable) splitness. As such, I said to him: 'Look, this might be totally off the wall and irrelevant, but I keep getting a picture of these two friends of yours, who are such opposite characters, as saying something about you – the way you feel about yourself being sometimes more like one, sometimes more like the other. And just as you were the "glue" that held your two friends together, maybe in doing so you were kind of holding yourself together as well. But when that "glue" failed externally in the case of your friends, maybe it also failed at an internal level as well . . . Is there anything at all in this for you?'

As it happened there was and, in this instance at least, my hunch – which was derived from my having combined Lawrence's material with 'my' material on the basis of their possible resonance – proved useful to him and to my ability to gain a more adequate understanding of his experiential world. But I could also have been totally wrong in my supposition. And yet, in listening to Lawrence as though I were the speaker, I could not deny the coincidence or the possibility that the coincidence informed my listening. As such, I took a risk based on what I was hearing from both of us. But, in doing so, I had to acknowledge this in my statement and allow the option of error.

Listening, then, requires *acceptance*. But this acceptance is not just at the level of accepting what the speaker is saying but also of what the listener is hearing, not just from the client but also from 'within'. It is not an issue of 'technique', but of 'being'.

If therapists are willing to 'be in relationship with' or *encoun-*

ter their clients, then they must accept that it is not merely their theories or skills which they bring to the relationship, *it is themselves*. But to accept this requires their acknowledgement of uncertainty as to what this encounter might reveal, what they might bring to it that is of value to the client, and which direction it may take at any given point in time.

With this view in mind, it should now become clear why I encourage my trainees to set aside all ideas of cure, help, promotion of growth, positive change, and so forth when engaged in a therapeutic encounter, since all these direct and restrict the encounter and impose on both the client and the therapist a focus on 'doing' rather than one on 'being'.

In promoting this view, I am in full agreement with Rogers' emphasis on therapists aiming towards 'transparency' and 'congruence'. And, like Rogers, I would argue that this is possible only once therapists recognize the primacy of their 'being qualities' as opposed to the 'doing skills' available to them, so that what they 'do' extends and reflects – rather than mechanizes and obscures – who they are. This form of 'disclosure' on the part of therapists has little to do with what they may or may not reveal about the personal events and relationships in their lives; rather, it points out that they cannot remain 'anonymous' *within* the encounter in that they bring their experience of themselves as participants into it. In line with this thinking, the following statement by Martin Buber, while focused on his view of the process of teaching, has much to say about therapy:

> The teacher who wants to help the pupil to realise his best potentialities must . . . know him not as a mere sum of qualities, aspirations, and inhibitions; he must apprehend him, and affirm him, as a whole . . . this he can only do if he encounters him as a partner in a bipolar situation . . . (Buber, 1970:78).

D. *Encounter*

In shifting the emphasis of therapy on to the realm of 'being', therapists are led to acknowledge the centrality of the encounter which contains within it the willingness on the part of both participants to seek to engage with one another in a manner that recognizes and utilizes the specialness and uniqueness of the on-going relationship. Such a stance brings into focus the realm of possibilities contained within the notion of an *interactive encounter*.

Existential-phenomenological theory argues that such encounters are occurring in an inter-subjective realm through which one's experience of 'being' does not occur *within* each participant but, rather, is co-constituted *between* them. It is this 'middle ground', or 'space' between the engaging beings, which allows an accepting dialogue to occur. At the same time, what can be taken as being 'special' within the therapeutic relationship is that the individuals have agreed to engage with one another in such a way that their disclosures share the common purpose of remaining focused on the examination and clarification of the experience of being of one of the participants – the client.

Nevertheless, because this common focus is relational, both therapist and client experience themselves-in-relation, the other-in-relation, and each-other-in-relation.

Realms of encounter

These 'three focal points' in the therapeutic encounter are rarely made explicit in theories of therapy. Yet it seems to me that recognition of each is essential if one is to approach therapy from a 'being' standpoint. As such, if we consider this view from the perspective of the therapist, what is being argued is the following: In the first realm of relation, I, as therapist, experience my 'self' in that relation and am able to note and consider what I bring to the relationship (this would include my knowledge, my skills, my expertise, the personal and theory-based views, opinions and biases that I attempt to bracket, and my sense of my own being, as well as the particular focus I place on listening to the client). Equally, at the second realm of relation, I, as therapist, experience the client as 'the other' and note and consider that I interpret what he or she brings to the relationship (this would include my understanding of the issues and concerns expressed, their affective components (i.e. those emotions, atti-

331

tudes and values associated with the issues being expressed), and what is implied about the other's sense of his or her own being through these). At the third realm of relation, I, as therapist, experience my 'self-being-in-relation-with-the-other' and note what 'emerges' or is disclosed through the interaction *between* the first two realms – which is the 'material' expressed in this third realm of relation.

In the same way, the client experiences the therapeutic encounter from these three 'focal points' – which is to say:

1. The client's experience of 'self' in the relation.
2. The client's experience of other (the therapist) in the relation.
3. The client's experience of 'self-being-in-relation-with-the-other'.

My view of therapy is that its particular 'specialness' lies in the exploration of the various *conjunctions or points of contact* between both participants' relational realms. While most therapeutic models emphasize and work with either the first or second (or both the first and second) relational realms, they rarely attend to the third, or indeed to the conjunction between the therapist's and client's experience of 'self-being-in-relation-with-the-other'. Yet it is precisely this third realm which existential-phenomenological theory, as applied to therapy, illuminates and provides with its unique 'take' on therapy. In this way, it argues that it is through the exploration and clarification of this 'being realm of between-ness' that the remaining two realms are more adequately disclosed to clarificatory challenge.

A concrete example should make my point clearer. A client, Annie, came to me for therapy because she could not understand how it could be that she had felt, and continued to feel, no grief whatsoever over the recent death of her mother. She had always felt that she had loved her at least as much as any other daughter would love her mother. As far as Annie was concerned, they'd had a good, caring relationship. They saw each other regularly and had not had any significant rows. As she lived nearby, her mother often 'baby-sat' Annie's children and this had allowed

Annie and her husband to go out and have some time to them-selves for an evening most weeks. In many ways, Annie felt, her relationship with her mother had been good – indeed, in her own words, 'as good as anyone had a right to expect'. And yet, now that her mother had died, Annie felt nothing; indeed, she'd felt more sadness when reading about the death of a movie star than she had about her mother's. Why could she feel no grief?

In considering this from the standpoint of the relational views I have been discussing, I, as therapist, would seek to enter Annie's experiential world by 'immersing' myself in the account she has given me so that I might attempt to experience these events as she does. I might ask myself: 'What and how would I be like if I were Annie?; what might "I-as-Annie" experience of myself as I relate this experience?; what and how might "I-as-Annie" imagine that others would experience "me" as being?; what and how might "I-as-Annie" imagine the experience of others (including the "other" who is her therapist) being in response to what "I-as-Annie" have stated?'

In other words, I would be attempting to 'be' like Annie in her relations both to herself and to others. In doing do, my attempts would rely on both my own personal experiential responses to Annie's statements and to the experiential responses I might imagine were I to be Annie. In each instance, my attempts would include, however cautiously or sceptically, whatever theories, assumptions, biases, and 'resonances' her statements provoked 'in' me, since these would be the *interpretative basis* from which I could extract a sense of the 'relational meanings' contained in Annie's statements about her experience. In asking Annie to describe and clarify her experience further, I would be putting my interpretational understanding to the test, so that, hopefully, I would gain an increasingly adequate awareness of Annie's experience. As I did so, I might challenge Annie with descriptively focused statements or questions that sought to express my attempt at 'entering' her world-view.

These would serve a dual function: firstly, they might confirm for Annie that I had understood what she had stated at an *explicit* level; and secondly, they might confirm for Annie that

I had understood the *experiential implications* of these explicit statements.

So, for example, in clarifying Annie's statement that she had loved her mother yet could feel no grief over her dying, the following dialogue emerged:

'Annie, what's it like to know that you love your mother and yet not be able to express that in the form of grieving?'

'It makes me wonder if I really love her.'

'So . . . because I can't grieve, perhaps I didn't love.'

'Yes . . . that's how it feels to me.'

'So, when you were at the funeral and saw your sister and brothers crying, they were expressing their love for your mother.'

'Yes. Well, I guess so. At least they were crying.'

'And there *you* were, not crying.'

'I just couldn't feel anything!'

'Well . . . Would I be right in saying that it wasn't that you weren't feeling anything, but that you were feeling that you *should* be feeling grief but weren't able to feel or express it?'

'I wanted to!'

'Yes. And as much as you wanted to, still you couldn't.'

'I wanted to desperately! She was my mother, after all! But I just couldn't!'

'What was it like for you to be in this "I want to, but I can't" stage?'

'It's awful! I don't feel in control.'

'Tell me what that's like for you: to "not feel in control".'

'It's awful. It's like I don't know who I am any more. I know what the right thing to do is, but when I try to do it, it just doesn't happen. And so I'm there trying to convince myself to do what I want, but it's almost like I'm trying to convince someone else who doesn't want to hear what I'm saying or who does hear it, but refuses to go along with me. It's like I've been pushed aside inside my own body.'

'And this other "being" who's pushed you aside, what are you trying to tell it?'

'To listen to me! To just get out so that I can do what I want.'

'You want to cry, but "it" doesn't.'

'Yes.'

'Okay . . . now, what I'm wondering is: this "I-it" thing. Is it unusual for you to experience this or is it that you usually feel "I-it" and "it" usually does what you want "it" to do and then, sometimes, like in this instance, "it" rebels?'

'No. "It's" not me. When I want something, and I do it, it's me who's doing it. But when I want something and I don't do it, it's "it" that stops it from happening.'

'I see. So you're only aware of "it" when you can't do what you want to do.'

'Yes.'

'So, who, or what, do you think this "it" is?'

'I wish to God I knew!'

'So do I. But, look: we began this exploration with my asking you what it was like to love your mother and yet not be able to express grief at her dying. And you answered that it makes you wonder whether you really did love your mother. But now, you tell me that it's not you who can't cry, it's "it" that won't let you. Now, maybe "it" doesn't love your mother, but that's no reason to suppose that *you* don't – you're just not in charge. And yet, that's what you are wondering: maybe I don't love my mother because I'm not grieving. Does that mean that "it" isn't as separate from you as you seem to be suggesting?'

'I don't know. I'm confused now. Are you saying that I'm "it"?'

'If I were staying that, what then?'

'I suppose that I wouldn't be in touch with myself. My real feelings. I'd be trying to make myself cry when I didn't want to cry.' [Annie begins to cry.]

'You're crying now.'

'I feel awful! You must think I'm awful!'

'For crying?'

'No! For not crying at my mother's funeral!'

'Is that what makes you feel awful – that I, or anyone else, might think you were awful?'

'They'd certainly wonder if I *did* love Mum!'

'Ah . . . So, if I don't cry at Mum's funeral, the others will wonder whether or not I really did love her. But if I do cry, then they will know that I do love her.'

'Yes . . . But, just as you said that, what I wanted to say was that it's none of their bloody business! What do they know about me and Mum?'

'What *do* they know?'

'My sister said that I was Mum's "favourite". That she cared a lot more for me than she ever did for her or any of my brothers. But it wasn't like that! It's just that we lived nearer each other and saw more of each other than my mum saw of my sister and brothers. They could have made more contact. Just because I did and they didn't, is that something to blame me for? They're crying now and saying how much they'll miss her, but when she was alive they didn't seem to miss her all that much. They didn't have her round for Sunday dinner or ring her up every other day . . .'

'But you did. And they're crying, and you're not.'

'They're crying for themselves, not for Mum!'

'And you're *not* crying.'

'They'd love it to see me cry. They'd love it. Then they'd be able to say to themselves that it was all right for them to care so little for Mum, because she got all the care and attention she needed from Annie. They wouldn't feel guilty . . . I know how Mum felt about it. She'd ask why the others didn't come to visit her as often as they could. They really hurt her.'

'Annie, let me see if I've understood what you're saying because this seems important. That question you began with: "Do I really love Mum?" I have the feeling that it's a question that you want the others to be asking because if they were to, then they might start to feel more guilty for having paid your mum so little attention before she died. Am I right so far?'

'Yes. And it makes me think how they could be so two-faced, sitting there crying their eyes out when they didn't really care all that much.'

'So . . . Are you saying that their crying expressed their *lack* of care?'

'Yes.'

'And if they'd seen *you* cry, that would have helped them to maintain this pose?'

'Oh! I see what you're saying: I wouldn't let myself cry in front of them because if I did, then they would be let off the hook.'

'Is this what *you're* saying?'

'Yes. I can see that.'

'Okay, well . . . this makes me wonder about that "it" that wouldn't do what you wanted it to do. Maybe "it" *was* doing what you wanted it to do all along.'

'Yes. But I also wanted to cry.'

'For Mum. Not for them.'

'I wish they'd never come to the funeral! Is that awful of me to wish that? But I do wish it!'

'If they'd not come, you would have grieved?' [Annie begins to cry again.]

'Are you crying for her now?' [Annie nods in agreement and continues to cry for several minutes. Finally she wipes her eyes and sighs deeply.]

'Thank you. I needed to do that.'

'You can cry for Mum when you want to, even though I'm here as well.'

'*You're* not being two-faced and pretending to be upset about Mum.'

'Unlike your brothers and sisters.'

'Why should I give a damn about them? I do, though! I make their feelings more important than my feeling for Mum! I couldn't let myself cry for her. Not even when I was alone and they couldn't see me. Maybe I didn't love Mum after all.'

After all her questioning, Annie seems to have come full circle and returned to the starting point of our encounter. Even so, this extract should serve to clarify some of the points being made above.

Readers may have noticed that my initial comments and queries were designed to clarify Annie's experience as it was being related. In some instances, these attempts remained at the level of 'rephrasing' or 'reflecting' what had been said. On some occasions, however, in order to clarify her experience, it was necessary to expose a possible contradiction in Annie's statement such as when she stated that she'd felt nothing and I queried whether what she meant was that she felt she *should* feel something. This clarification was as much for me, in that whatever her response it would have given me a clearer sense of her experience, as much as it might have been for Annie. In seeking to clarify this, and several other points made by Annie, I attempted to stay with her experience as she saw it, both from the standpoint of her relation to herself (which was suggested during the 'I-It' discussion) and her relation to others (which, in this extract, focused on her relation to her brothers and sister and, to a much lesser degree, on her relation to her mother). But, in order to gain an understanding that suitably approximated Annie's experience, I also had to gain a sense of how Annie experienced others and how she supposed others experienced her. Only by considering all these relations from a perspective that approached Annie's could I gain a more adequate overall 'feel' for her.

Empathy

I believe that this point is of some importance since it presents the notion of 'empathy' from a significantly different perspective. For many therapists, the expression of empathy focuses on the client's experience in a manner that isolates and refocuses it within the therapist's experiential realm. In terms of the case extract just discussed, for instance, a therapist might empathize with Annie's experience of not being able to express her grief by focusing on the experience itself, linking it to a similar personal experience and, thereby, gaining an experiential sense of what it is like 'to want to but be unable to express a feeling'. While valid and valuable, this attempt at empathy is also limited in that while it may succeed in 'capturing' the experience in isolation, it fails to grasp it within its relational context to the being (i.e. Annie) who experiences.

The level of empathy I am suggesting is one wherein the therapist attempts to 'capture' the experience *within the experiential realm of the client*. In other words, it requires the therapist to empathize first with the client's experience of himself or herself and *then* consider how this being would experience the particular feeling. As such, I, as therapist, first had to gain an adequate sense of Annie's experience of herself in relation to herself and others and then ask how 'I-as-Annie' would experience 'wanting but being unable to express my grief'. Empathy at this level may be deeply unsettling but also of substantial importance since in this specific attempt at empathy I might also gain a *broader, or more overall* empathic sense of a client's experience. While, of necessity, requiring the therapist to treat this broader sense of empathy with caution and flexibility, nevertheless it may allow the therapist *to clarify the potential meaningful connections between what is stated explicitly and what is implied more generally within the explicit statement.*

So, for instance, towards the end of the dialogue with Annie, I responded to her statement 'I wish they'd never come to the funeral! Is that awful of me to wish that? But I do wish it!' with: 'If they'd not come, you would have grieved?' This clarificatory challenge relied on a broader sense of empathy that I felt I had with Annie. The statement does not reflect Annie's explicit comment but, rather, focuses on what seemed to me to have been implicit both within it and, in a wider sense, within Annie's general experience of herself as viewed by her brothers and sister. It is clearly an interpretation on my part, and it could well have been an erroneous interpretation, but it was one that emerged out of my attempt to empathize with Annie and, in so doing, to hear her statement as if 'I-as-Annie' were speaking it. In attempting this, I was also able to hear/speak what I took to be the implicit meaning that expressed itself through her words.

It is following this challenge that the then-current encounter between Annie and myself was brought into focus. Prior to this, the encounter had maintained its explicit focus on the first two 'realms' (i.e. the experience of self-in-relation and the experience of other-in-relation). Now we were able to encounter 'each-other-in-relation' by bringing Annie's act of crying into the current encounter and exploring its possible implications. For me, as therapist, it allowed me to further my understanding of Annie's relational issues with 'others' by both explicitly being the current significant 'other' in Annie's experience and by attempting to 'enter into' Annie's experience of myself as current other. Equally, from Annie's standpoint, the encounter at this third 'realm' allowed her to bring me into her experience of 'significant' others, *both as a representative and as an exception to her 'rule'* concerning her view of 'significant others'. In this way, her experience was both illuminated (or clarified) and challenged and proved to be a key moment in her further exploration of her experience.

Broadly speaking, through the exploration of these 'realms of encounter', both therapist and client bring into focus their experience of themselves, their experiences of the other, and their experience of themselves-in-relation-with-each-other. My personal conviction is that in making these relations explicit and open to clarification, the therapist challenges the client to explore the self–self, self–other and self-with-other relations whose meanings 'contextualize' the client's experience of 'being-in-the-world'. At the same time, it is precisely because the client's 'being-in-the-world' is disclosed within the accepting framework of the therapeutic encounter that the possibility of recontextualization (experienced as 'change') can occur.

Therapist encounter

But this process is not solely directly towards the client. If the therapist is truly engaged in this encounter, then a similar challenge and possibility emerges *for the therapist*. It is for this reason that therapy, within the existential-phenomenological model, contains therapeutic potentials for both participants, not solely for one. In acknowledging this, the therapist is led into a stance of being that itself aims at openness and clarification. In a broad sense, it can be seen as a 'process of disclosure' for both.

It would not be surprising, then, to consider that therapists' willingness to disclose themselves as beings-in-encounter may itself provide the client not only with the example of the possibilities of disclosure but also with the courage to attempt such an enterprise. One of the strengths of the humanistic model in therapy lies precisely in this acknowledgement on the part of the therapist. Nevertheless, such a stance also contains within it possible obstacles or dangers, since it is essential for therapists to be clear as to both what is disclosed and how this disclosure is presented to the client.

The humanistic model emphasizes the therapist's 'transparency', but on closer investigation what this 'transparency' typically turns out to be is a form of disclosure that is focused on the first two realms of relation – which is to say the therapist's experience of 'self-in-relation' and of the 'other-in-relation'. Disclosure at this level allows the therapist to express his or her current experience (e.g. 'I am feeling irritated') or his or her experience of the other (e.g. 'I feel you are being evasive'). The existential-phenomenological model, on the other hand, would seek to avoid therapist disclosure at these first two realms and, instead, emphasize those therapist disclosures that remain at the third relational realm (i.e. that of 'self-being-in-relation-with-the-other'). In simple terms, it would focus disclosure on the therapist's experience of that 'in-between realm' in the relationship rather than on the disclosure of self or other. In other words, disclosure at this level would examine how the current 'microcosmic' relationship *both reveals and challenges* the client's 'macrocosmic' relations with self and other. *It is this insight, through encounter, which I believe provides therapy with its 'specialness' and potential for beneficial outcome.*

In order to clarify this last point further, we must turn our attention to the issue of 'self and other' as experiential ramifications of 'being'.

E. The Self-Construct

The issues discussed so far bring to light a highly significant area of concern: namely, the notion of 'self' as understood by the existential-phenomenological model. While I have already provided some general comments on this in the critique of the humanist model's view of the self in Part 4, it is now necessary to examine the existential-phenomenological position regarding the 'self' with particular emphasis on the therapeutic process.

On initial consideration, the existential-phenomenological model's view of 'the self' may strike many readers as being either odd or absurd. For this model argues that the question of whether or not a 'self' exists, in the sense that each of us 'has' a self that is real (as opposed to 'unreal selves'), fixed or (relatively) stable, and which seeks to express, or actualize, itself, is, at best, open to doubt. Instead, this model prefers to view the self as a focal point in relation and, as such, speaks only of 'the-self-in-relation' rather than 'the self' as a separate, fixed and complete 'entity'. This is not merely an abstract distinction; as I hope to demonstrate, this view has significant implications both at a general 'lived' level and for the 'self' in the therapeutic relationship.

While Western thought tends to conceive of the self as the source, or originator, of an individual's experience, existential-phenomenological theory proposes that the self is the *product of*, or that which emerges from, relational experience. In other words, it views the self as being indefinable other than in a relational sense.

As I have stated before, in order for me to say anything about 'who I am', I am also implicitly expressing 'who I am not'. If I say that I am 'male', for instance, this statement about myself only has meaning because I equally hold to be meaningful the existence of 'females' (or, to be more precise, if somewhat sexist, of 'non-males'). As was suggested earlier in this text, our notion of 'the self' is a partial, or selective, reflectively derived interpretation that is dependent on a series of relational 'deductions' based on aspects of current experience, selected elements drawn from past experience which both 'resonate with' and give some validity to our current sense of 'self', and certain future-oriented goals or aspirations which direct the 'self' forward in time. In this way, the 'self' is more properly speaking a *relational construct* and, as such, if, for the sake of simplicity and Western bias, we insist on speaking of a 'self', we should at least acknowledge our bias by referring to the *self-construct*.

Put another way, our constructions of the self rely on the previously discussed perceptual notion of *figure/ground*, wherein the 'figure' focus on this relation is the self-construct and the 'ground' focus is 'that which is not currently perceived to be the self' (that is, 'the construed other'). The advantage of understanding the self-construct in this way is that in its flexibility of boundaries it provides a more adequate 'fit' with a number of experientially derived illustrations that point to the plasticity of our experience of our 'selves-in-the-world'. I have discussed this plasticity of the self-construct elsewhere, pointing to a number of instances that reveal how our experience of our 'selves' undergoes constant (often subtle, sometimes radical) re-interpretation (Spinelli, 1989, 1993). Among such instances, I want to focus on one that, while admittedly radical and unusual, should nevertheless make clear the central concerns being discussed.

Proprioceptive dysfunctions is a term employed to point out a number of disorders in the recognition of one's body definitions and boundaries which may arise from severe illness or from psychological disorders such as depression. Jonathan Miller provides a telling example of variations in proprioception in a number of stroke victims who *disowned* parts of their bodies – usually their limbs (Miller, 1978). In other words, while they continued to recognize the existence of, let us say, their left arm, they did not experience or accept this limb as being theirs. It had somehow become alien, or belonging to another. In order to explain this seemingly attached appendage to their bodies, they produced the most outlandish explanations to account for the 'alien' limb, going so far, in some cases, as to argue that it belonged to someone else who was standing behind them and pretending that his arm was attached to them and, as consequence, they kept 'sneaking looks' behind them in order to catch the prankster at his game. They could not easily be dissuaded from their vociferous denial of the ownership of this limb, and it often took long periods of time before they began to 'reconstruct' their body image in order to incorporate the alien limb. The clinical neurologist Oliver Sacks has also presented a number of even more extreme instances of these dysfunctions in his illuminating text *The Man Who Mistook His Wife for a Hat* (Sacks, 1985).

Similarly, readers may be more familiar with the equally disturbing, if experientially opposite, instance of *phantom limbs*, wherein patients who have had a limb amputated will initially insist, because their experience tells them so, that the missing limb is not, in fact, missing at all. In a similar fashion, it is only after a fairly lengthy period of time that the perception of this 'phantom limb' dissipates and the patients can gain a new body image sans limb.

Now what have these dysfunctions to do with the self-construct? Clearly, one means that we have of defining our 'self' is in terms of the body that the 'self' inhabits or expresses itself through. Indeed, for some of us, our bodies *are* our selves. In either case, studies of proprioceptive dysfunctions reveal that the 'self' constructed from our body image does not necessarily have to fit the actual boundaries of the physical body. We may exclude parts of our body from our body image, or we may include non-existent parts of our body in our body image.

With this idea in mind, let us turn to the self-construct. Existential-phenomenological theory proposes that a similarly 'plastic' process occurs with regard to our construction of our selves. In some instances the self-construct appears to alter so that it *includes* much more than it might ordinarily do in its self-definition. For instance, while in the throes of sexual ecstasy, the self might be experienced as 'blending into' the 'self' of one's sexual partner such that the normally 'separate' selves seem to become 'one self'. Equally, during instances of meditation, or deep relaxation, 'the self' might appear virtually to disappear or become 'indistinguishably connected' to 'all and everything'. This same 'disappearance' of the self may occur when we are deeply *immersed in an activity* such as long-distance running, driving a car, or gardening.

What is paradoxically intriguing about these instances is that rather than being undesirable or unrewarding from a 'self-focused' standpoint, in fact they usually provoke deep 'self-satisfaction' or are seen as significant, rewarding, or highly meaningful experiences in our lives.

Perhaps more commonly, however, we experience the plasticity of the self-construct when aspects of it are denied or *disowned*. In these instances, we are confronted with thoughts, emotions, or behaviours that (seemingly) cannot possibly be 'self-generated' or arising from our 'self'. For example, having injured someone or smashed an object against a wall in anger, we might ask ourselves: 'Whatever possessed me to do that?' Such a question contains the implicit assumption or statement that it was not one's 'self' who originated the act, but that, rather, it was initiated by someone, or something, other than our 'self'. These circumstances point to aspects of *dissociation* or experienced division in the 'self', which, as I argued in Part 3, might provide us with a more adequate alternative to the concept of 'the unconscious'.

Indeed, as I discussed in my alternative to 'the unconscious', these dissociations point to a 'splitness' between experience and belief. These same distinctions between phenomenology and epistemology seem to me to be key features for our understanding of the self-construct. So, for instance, one of my clients, Clive, who was a fundamentalist lay preacher, experienced sexual arousal when in the presence of certain female members in his religious commune. But Clive's belief that he had 'overcome the temptations of the flesh' required him to explain his experience as that of 'temporary possession by Satan'.

Dissociation and sedimentation

Placed in the context of this discussion, this example allows us to distinguish dissociation, or 'splitness' between experience and belief, from a self-construct standpoint. Clive's self-construct included the belief that he (or his 'self') no longer felt sexual arousal and so had to disown or *dissociate* those experiences that did not fit this self-construct. But, in order to explain the experience of sexual arousal, he had to invoke the existence of an alien 'other' (in this case, a supernatural 'other' in the form of Satan). The importance of this explanation was that it allowed Clive to retain his belief in his constructed self. Its price, however, was the invocation of an alien entity that, at times, overwhelmed or possessed Clive's acceptable, constructed self. As I argued in Part 3, it seems to me that such instances might be better understood, and therapeutically challenged, by viewing them as aspects of conscious self-deception derived from a fixed belief in one's self-construct rather than as examples of uncontrolled unconscious impulses.

But we need not go to the extremes presented in the above example to recognize that all of us, to varying degrees, carry out similar forms of dissociation or disownership in order to maintain a self-construct that will appear to convince us of the 'fixedness', stability and reality of the 'self' rather than view it as a relationally disclosing construct.

It was Carl Rogers who first focused on the self from a standpoint that he demarcated as *the self concept* so as to provide the central explanatory feature for the psychotherapeutic understanding and alleviation of psychic dissonance and disturbance (Kirschenbaum and Henderson, 1990a, 1990b). Rogers further proposed the concept of *the ideal self* as a therapeutically useful means of exploring clients' aspirations for growth or actualization. At the same time, however, the ideal self might equally be the basis for psychic disturbance and dissonance since it might be so restrictive and intolerant in its ideals that the 'current self' could be experienced as 'never quite good enough'.

Rogers' stance can be understood as a re-interpretation of the psycho-analytic model's hypothesis of the relationship and conflict between the *ego and the super-ego*. The super-ego, as the internalized unconscious 'moral principle', expresses itself consciously as our conscience which both 'rewards' those thoughts and deeds that fulfil its demands and 'punishes' those thoughts and deeds that violate its injunctions (as such we speak in terms of having a good, or clear, conscience or having a guilty conscience).

While these hypotheses are important in that each resonates with peoples' experiences to a substantial extent, there remain significant conceptual and logical problems within them which qualify their usefulness. With regard to the psycho-analytic model's notion of the super-ego, it can be seen that this concept depends on the assumption of the Freudian-derived unconscious – which, as I sought to demonstrate in Part 3, itself contains significant problems. In the case of Rogers' hypothesis, on the other hand, the problems encountered are derived from his assumption of a 'real and permanent self' which, in turn, forced him to invoke the existence of 'false selves'. The difficulties raised by this stance were discussed in Part 4.

As an alternative to these problematic viewpoints, existential-phenomenological theory argues that while such hypotheses validly express the experience of dissonance and are therapeutically helpful in that they provide various means of exploring clients' experiences of 'splitness', their key flaws can be removed only once we consider the 'self' to be an impermanent, plastic construct that exists only as an outcome of relational factors. As such, the self-construct is 'grounded' in relation and can only be said to be 'real' insofar as it is *that which reflects and is reflected on in any given experience.*

In other words, the self-construct reveals *the self that is being experienced when it is being experienced.*

If this view of the self-construct provides a more adequate perspective for the understanding of our experience of our selves, it must be asked how it explains the phenomenon of 'splitness' or disownership of experiences that would appear to 'belong' to the 'self'. How, for instance, would this approach understand Clive's divided experience?

In order to address this question, readers should recall the examples presented when the phenomenon of proprioceptive dysfunctions was discussed above. In such instances, the problem lay in the patients' deeply held *beliefs* concerning their body image. These beliefs were so strong or fundamental to their body image that they disregarded the evidence of their own perceptions. Such strong, fundamental beliefs have been labelled in existential-phenomenological theory as *sedimented*. Sedimented beliefs, then, are those that insist on the primacy, or correctness, of one particular perspective over all others. However limiting or distorted or irrational they may be, it will take a great deal to override their interpretative power.

Racist or sexist attitudes readily come to mind as examples of sedimented beliefs that are far from easily broken or dispelled. Why might this be so? One suggestion, again derived from existential-phenomenological analysis, is that these beliefs 'hold together' the self-construct of the believer. In other words, *sedimented beliefs are the foundational 'building blocks' of our constructed self*. As such, to give them up forces individuals to fundamentally reconstruct, or redefine, themselves in their self/other relations. As much as they might limit or distort experience, they also serve to *maintain or allow* self-defining viewpoints. For example, the belief that women are 'inferior' to men maintains or allows the belief that I, as a man, am superior. If I change my views concerning the inferiority of women, I not only change my relationship to women, as 'others', I also change my relationship to myself in that I can no longer consider myself as superior in the way I did before. This novel perspective may be deeply disturbing or anxiety-provoking in that it calls into question my very sense of 'self', or 'who I am'.

In such ways, sedimented beliefs allow me to maintain a fixed, possibly even secure, stance or 'sense of my own being' regardless of how distorted or limiting that sense may be.

Further, as well as being personally derived, sedimented beliefs may also be, more broadly speaking, socio-culturally derived or influenced in that they reveal a particular culture's or society's sense of itself. In many ways, these culturally sedimented perspectives *define* the culture or society in that they allow it (and its members) to appear or present itself (or themselves) as distinct from other cultures or societies.

Following this line of argument, existential-phenomenological theory suggests that the belief in a permanent, fixed, relatively stable and on-going 'self' is *itself* both a personally and culturally sedimented belief. This is not to say that such beliefs are necessarily 'wrong'. For instance, if this line of argument is correct, we can see that without certain fundamental sedimented beliefs we would hardly be able to distinguish our most basic defining characteristics such as our name, where we lived, what work we did, who our friends and family were, and so forth. It would seem that a 'given' of human experience is that we hold sedimented beliefs. As such, the question that needs to be asked is not whether or not we should hold sedimented beliefs but, rather, whether certain of our sedimented beliefs define us too restrictively or impose unnecessary limitations on our self-construct.

At the same time, however, it must be recognized that, however restrictive, all sedimented beliefs *serve to define the self-construct* and, as such, in most instances, the challenging of these beliefs is highly likely to be met with serious resistance *because a challenge to any part of the self-construct also challenges the whole of it.*

With these points in mind, we can now return to the example of my client, Clive. We can understand that Clive's quandary was one that expressed a conflict between his *beliefs* about himself (I have overcome the temptations of the flesh) and his *experience* (I am sexually aroused). To have acknowledged his experience in a direct, or straightforward, manner would have forced Clive to reassess his beliefs and call them into question. But to have done so would have, in turn, forced him to reassess and call into question certain aspects of his sedimented self-construct. Had Clive done so, he might have been able to accept, or 'own', his experience of being aroused. *But* the 'price' of this acceptance would have been the experience of anxiety-laden uncertainty (perhaps overwhelming uncertainty) about his very sense of 'self', or who he was.

Rather than risk this, Clive's alternative was to retain that security by 'disowning' his experience of arousal. In doing so, he was able to maintain his sedimented belief about his self-construct. The price of this strategy, however, was the experience of temporary 'alien possession' (in this case, supernatural possession by Satan).

Either choice presents a quandary. While each offers something (i.e. the movement towards 'authenticity' through the 'ownership' of experience *or* the secure maintenance of a sedimented self-structure), each also has its price (i.e. the increase of uncertainty and anxiety provoked by a partially de-sedimented sense of self *or* the 'disownership' of certain experiences). To invert Jean-Paul Sartre's famous epigram that, as human beings, 'we are condemned to choose' (Sartre, 1956), we can conclude that 'either choice condemns who we are.'

This quandary reflects the general conflict of ontology (or 'being'). This can be most easily understood when considering this conflict as expressed in questions concerning identity (who one is). For to know who I am (or must be, or can be, or ought to be, and so forth), I must also know who I am not. But, if so, then what am I to do with (or how am I to explain) those circumstances when I experience myself as being not who I am (or, more accurately, who I believe myself to be) but, rather, who I am not (or who I believe I must not be, or cannot be, or ought not to be)? Clearly, I have only two principal options: either to alter or extend my notion of who I am so that I can 'own' or 'integrate' those previously 'alien' experiences; or to find some means of 'disowning' the experience (such as by seemingly 'forgetting', or not attending to – that is, avoiding reflection – or by invoking internal or external physical, biological, socio-cultural, psychical and/or supernatural agencies that temporarily 'possess' me into becoming who I am not) in order that I may maintain my previously held beliefs concerning my identity.

For any number of reasons, principally having to do with the maintenance of a sedimented self-construct, it is the second option which appears to be the one we most commonly choose since, through it, a certain set of defining characteristics, behaviours, attitudinal factors, and traits emerge which define our self-construct and demarcate and limit its meaning-possibilities. In addition, the second option, while demanding a form of self-deception, nevertheless allows an abdication of our experiential responsibility not only with regard to the responsibility contained within our relations with the world as expressed through our actions and their consequences, but also with regard to the responsibility inherent in our human ability to *reflect on such*.

But it remains important to be clear that the self-deception being referred to here is not one that leads, as Rogers suggests, to a contrast between a 'real self' and one or more 'false selves'. Rather, it expresses a conflict, or dissonance, *between the current self-construct as it is believed to be in terms of sedimented assumptions and the currently experienced self-construct which, in part, does not conform to the restrictions imposed by these sedimented beliefs.*

The self-construct: therapeutic implications

When these views are applied to the realm of therapy, what emerges as typical in clients' concerns and conflicts is that they have tended to adopt a number of deeply sedimented beliefs and perspectives concerning their self-construct whose limiting features, usually expressed in terms of who one 'can only be' (or must/must not be, or should/should not be), are experienced as problematic and the source of deep misery and psychic pain. This division between clients' beliefs in their self-construct and their experiences which bring into question the validity of this self-construct lead them to 'disown' experiences that the believed-in self-construct cannot accommodate without risking the breakdown of its defining characteristics – and, therefore, of itself.

In this way, clients are *divided beings* not only in terms of the dissonance between their beliefs and experiences concerning their self-construct, but, just as importantly, in terms of their desire to break down the sedimented beliefs that have given rise to this dissonance and the opposing desire to *retain* these sedimented beliefs. *Stated simply, they want to change yet remain essentially the same.*

It seems to me that many therapists are not sufficiently aware of these 'divided loyalties' and of their significance to the client. For if they were to take the courageous 'leap of faith' that would allow them to challenge their sedimented beliefs, clients would put at risk their very sense of their constructed self. Since the sedimented beliefs provide the foundations on which their self-construct (no matter how limiting or distorted it may be) has been built up, any 'weakening' of these beliefs through thera-

351

peutic challenge *threatens the maintenance of the entire self-construct.*

One cannot change 'bits' or parts of the sedimented self-construct without its effects being felt by the whole of it; to remove one sedimented aspect alters the entire structure. So, for instance, to employ an initially trivial, but relevant, example, if I were to change my hairstyle, it is not just my hairstyle that is altered; rather my whole sense of 'self' is changed – sometimes to the extent that I not only 'feel' myself to be 'a new me', but the very way I think about myself, or how I move, or the attitudes and aspirations I hold about my 'self', undergoes (sometimes dramatic) alteration.

But, as was discussed earlier, personal sedimented beliefs do not arise in isolation. Rather, they are constructed through relations with others (either at the level of personal interaction with family, friends, acquaintances, and so forth, or at the broader socio-cultural level). In this way, it must also be borne in mind that *any challenges to the sedimented beliefs of a particular individual also challenge the sedimented beliefs pertaining to that individual's relations with others both at the level of personal and socio-cultural interaction (e.g. how the individual views, understands, accepts, or rejects these others).*

These challenges, in turn, dispute the sedimented beliefs not only of the personal and socio-cultural others' relations with the individual (e.g. how the personal and socio-cultural others view, understand, accept or reject the individual), but also of the others' relations with themselves since their own sedimented beliefs are in part reliant on their relation with that individual.

So, for instance, let us say that Clive's sedimented beliefs are so challenged that he begins to 'own' his sexual arousal rather than 'disown' it by explaining it in terms of Satanic possession. Let us first consider the significance of this with regard to his relations with personal or immediate others. Clive's newly emergent self-construct now needs to decide how to deal with sexual arousal and may, for instance, begin to express it more openly towards his friends in the community on the basis that it is important for him now to be honest with them about his sexual feelings. Already, then, a significant relational change between Clive and his friends occurs in that he now views, or constructs, them in a different manner. At the same time, Clive's friends' previous sedimented beliefs about him as a 'morally upright' individual may be challenged such that they now begin to relate to him as a 'changed' or 'sinful' or 'possessed' man. Equally, however, Clive's friends' sedimented beliefs about themselves are also challenged in that they might begin to question their own sexuality or whether the spiritual beliefs they have adopted through the influence of Clive's sermons are as worthy or morally sound as they had once thought them to be.

Significant relational changes can also be seen to occur at the socio-cultural level. Again, Clive, having now accepted his experiences of sexual arousal, may begin to question his previously sedimented beliefs about the 'truth' of the God and Satan on which his community is founded. Equally, his community may begin to question whether it can tolerate such an individual, or may begin to re-interpret Clive as a new prophet worthy of reverence. Furthermore, the community may begin to question its own sedimented beliefs in terms of its moral codes and either strive to re-assert them by 'purifying' itself of heretics like Clive or 'liberalize' its canons by allowing a greater degree of moral flexibility.

What is important here is the recognition that a challenge to the sedimented perspectives held by any one individual not only opens that individual's entire self-structure to question, but also has implications for both that individual's sense of meaning of others (both at the immediate personal level and at the socio-cultural level) as well as those others' sense of meaning of that individual and of themselves and of their relations between one another. These interconnected relations are all to some degree defined and upheld through sedimented perspectives that allow the 'self' (whether personal or socio-cultural) to maintain its identity.

As was discussed earlier, these same concerns present themselves in the therapeutic process through the relational realms of encounter. As such, therapists must be much more aware of the risks that clients take when they decide to enter therapy and, equally, must be far more wary of their own explicit and implicit demands for clients to change. As such, therapists' challenges to the sedimented beliefs of clients must be clear and direct, but also cautious and invitational to clients' consideration. It must also be borne in mind that clients' resistance to the challenging of sedimented beliefs, while usually originating in the constructed self, may also come from others (either significant individuals in clients' lives or, more broadly, from clients' socio-cultural backgrounds) who have in various ways imposed their own sedimented beliefs on those of the client.

If clients' self-constructs change through therapy, then such changes have their repercussions throughout the whole of clients' relational realms.

It would seem necessary, then, for therapists to be clear about these ramifications so that they may be considered within the course of therapy. All too often, however, therapists, somewhat naively, focus solely on change, and its effects, at the level of clients' self-relations as though these have no impact on their wider relations with others. While, obviously, therapists' concerns must remain focused on their clients, nevertheless the recognition that clients are not beings in isolation allows therapists to explore with them the various realms of relation through which the self is constructed and the implications that change in the client's self-construct may have on those self–other relations.

The problems that arise when this view is not considered are plentiful. All too often, clients, having altered their self-construct, are prone to 'disowning' their previous construct and the relations with others that that construct identified with. It is hardly surprising, then, to find as a consequence of this that clients' 'disownership' of their past lives includes the disowner-ship of those 'others' (such as their spouses, families, friends, colleagues, jobs and lifestyles) who are most closely identified with the 'disowned' self. In many of these cases, such instances of 'change' seem to me to be questionable since what has occurred is that one 'disowning' self-construct has been replaced by another *such that while what is being disowned is different, the very issue of disownership has not been properly challenged.*

A concrete example of this can be seen in many cases of

'mid-life crisis' where an individual undergoes an alteration of self-construct which merely replaces one set of disowned relations with another, rather then promote a greater willingness to 'own'.

F.   The Therapist as Other

One important means by which therapists can assist clients in such explorations emerges precisely through their willingness and ability to place themselves in the encounter. In doing so, they become the microcosmic representative of the 'others' in the client's macrocosmic self–other relations. In this way, while they may be able to assist the client in challenging his or her current self-construct, they also allow the client to 'test out' the implications for any newly emerging self-construct's relations with both self and others.

It can be seen that in adopting this stance, therapists are better able to address the various *ethical and value-laden implications within the therapeutic enterprise* – implications that critics (both pro- and anti-therapy) have rightly addressed (Szasz, 1974a; Masson, 1988; Holmes and Lindley, 1989) and which have recently resurfaced in the UK and elsewhere through the critical examination of therapy by abused clients, families and friends of clients, and by the media.

In addition, this issue appears to me to be particularly pertinent to concerns expressed about the practice of therapy within a broader multi-cultural perspective. In following the conclusions derived from the above argument, it becomes imperative for therapists (whether they share the same socio-cultural views and biases as their clients or whether they and their clients are representative of differing socio-cultural backgrounds) to consider seriously the value-laden assumptions they bring into the encounter as 'representative others'. In either case, various concerns will arise which therapists would be wise to consider. In particular, the arising issues will reveal attitudes or biases held by the therapist with regard to the relationship between self and other as perceived by the therapist as 'representative other' of either the same, or similar, socio-cultural background as that of the client, or of a different socio-cultural background to that of the client. In each instance, the degree to which these biases may be influencing the therapist's own stance with regard to both the desires of the individual client and the normative power of the client's socio-cultural background requires the therapist's attention.

For instance, consider the scenario where a client from a culture that holds strict observances regarding some moral code of conduct not held by the therapist's culture expresses in therapy the desire to break away from this moral code. While the therapist's alliance is with the client, the significance of the client's desire to break the taboo needs to be explored not only with regard to what this means to the client as an individual, but also to what it means to the client as a representative of his or her cultural background. The private exploration of the therapist's own attitudes and biases towards the issue itself, the therapist's understanding of the client's experience of the issue, and the relationship of the client's self-construct towards the issue would seem to be obvious areas for clarification. But, in addition, the exploration of the client's perception of his or her culture's stance towards the issue and the implications for the client's self–other relations (both at the 'immediate other' and 'broader cultural other' levels) with respect to the client's potential choices would also seem essential *regardless of whether the therapist comes from the same or a different socio-cultural background*. This would be all the more pertinent if the therapist held particularly strong views regarding the issue under question.

While it might initially be thought that the sharing of a socio-cultural background would be more desirable since the therapist would be better able to understand or 'relate to' the various self–other implications, on reflection it can also be seen that this need not necessarily be the case and that, depending on the strength of the views concerning the issue held by the therapist, his or her identification with that culture – or personal rejection of certain viewpoints held by that culture – may influence the client in a manner that would reveal the misuse or abuse of the therapist's power in the therapeutic relationship.

But this issue need not be seen to be restricted to concerns at a socio-cultural level. All manner of issues related to gender, sexual orientation, religion, moral dilemmas, and so forth reveal the difficulty of the therapist seeking to adopt a *neutral position.*

And yet, while it must be acknowledged that the attainment of neutrality *regardless of the presenting issue* cannot be fulfilled, how does it remain possible for the therapist at least to attempt to approach it more adequately?

Though it may come as a surprise to some readers, my suggested response brings us back to the issue of the sedimented self-construct.

In my prior discussion of the sedimented self-construct, I purposely restricted my focus to issues concerning the client's self-construct and its implications for the therapeutic encounter. But, as I have argued throughout, the existential-phenomenological model's view of encounter *implicates* the therapist. As such, it would seem both obvious and necessary to consider the question of the sedimented self-construct from the standpoint of *the therapist* and consider *its* implications for the therapeutic encounter.

As I argued earlier, therapists' willingness and ability to '*be with and for*' the client requires not only the attempt to accept the client's relational world-view as it is expressed, but also necessitates the attempt on their part to 'enter into' that world-view and seek to experience it *as if* it were theirs. But, in order to do so, therapists must be both willing and able to 'be' from a framework of a *flexible self-construct.* For if therapists' own self-constructs are overly sedimented there is no possible way they can begin to attempt 'entry' into their clients' experiential world.

The question of therapists 'being' in the encounter in a manner that discloses their flexibility of self-construct can be considered from the standpoint of *sacrifice*, as was discussed in Part 2.

In the same way that therapists are capable of sacrificing their emotional or sexual attraction towards their clients by *acknowledging the attraction* (rather than seeking to suppress it, or 'transform' it through the use of such terms as 'countertransference'), in order that it will not intrude unnecessarily or overwhelm the encounter, so too can they, more generally, acknowledge those aspects of their sedimented self-structure that incapacitate their attempt to 'enter' their clients' experiential world.

The sacrifice involved here is that which asks of therapists to attempt nothing more than they ask of their clients, which is to clarify and challenge aspects of their sedimented self-structure and to consider the 'being' possibilities that emerge. *But in their attempts to 'be' flexible, therapists must be prepared to challenge not only their personal biases, assumptions and viewpoints which place their sedimented self-construct in competition with that of their clients in a general sense, but also those aspects of their sedimented self-construct in the particular sense of self-as-therapist which provide them with the power and mystique that will allow their personal assumptions and biases to compete with, and, more often than not, succeed in reshaping their clients' self-constructs so that they reflect their (i.e. therapists') own.*

The very act of calling oneself a therapist invokes power. Even if therapists seek to divest themselves of such, it remains likely that their clients will wish to bestow power on them. Part of this desire, I suspect, is that in investing their therapists with power and authority clients will maintain those very facets of their sedimented self-constructs that are most problematic to them. If so, the greatest misuse or abuse of therapists' power can be seen to be that which seeks to resolve clients' conflicts in a manner that fails to consider their standpoint, or world-view, as reflected in the problematic issue and which, instead, reflects the therapists' world-views.

On the other hand, in adopting the stance of sacrifice, therapists enable themselves to move out of a competitive 'being' relation with their clients, which is based on the wishes and assumptions that fuel their self-construct, and instead seek to co-operate with, or encounter, their clients in a way that expresses therapists' willingness to acknowledge and 'enter into' their self-constructed perspectives.

It would not be surprising to find that this willingness on the part of therapists to present their 'selves' to their clients from a stance that *allows* the clients' self-constructs to 'be' – regardless of how bound they may be to their sedimentations – and, more, which values them enough to seek to 'be like' them in order to better reflect and clarify and understand, in itself provides clients not only with the example of the 'being' possibilities available through the expression of a more flexible self-construct but also enables them to attempt such an enterprise.

Equally, in sacrificing their own sedimented perspectives, therapists are likely to challenge their clients' sedimented perspectives with regard to their 'being' relations with others. For the chances are high that clients' previous encounters with others were competitive in that they experienced others as being disdainful of, or threatening towards, or as the demanding architects of, their self-structure. In this way, therapists, as the 'other' in their clients' current relational experience, present a novel 'other' who accepts rather than competes with the client's self-construct, who clarifies it rather than attempts to threaten or reshape it from the 'other's' construed perspective, and who presents challenges from within the client's self-constructed experience rather than from outside it. Once again, this novel other, simply in its very 'being', allows an encounter to occur which opens the client to the examination of possibilities of 'being-in-relation' which itself allows the questioning of the necessity of the client's maintenance of the current problematically experienced sedimented self-structure.

In the light of the comments and concerns I have expressed, it would seem to me that if there is any significant value in therapeutic training it rests precisely in the challenging of as many of the trainee's sedimented perspectives in as many ways as might be found both viable and ethically possible in order that trainees may learn to challenge their sedimented self-structure so that their 'being' in the encounter is as flexible as they can allow it to be. This, to me at least, is the value of the different models and approaches to therapy. It is not because they 'work', or that one 'works' better than any other, or that they contain 'truths', *but because each challenges our sedimented self-constructs.*

As such, while it remains sensible to some degree for trainees to wish to specialize in a particular model, such specialization should occur only following initial training from a multi-modular standpoint. But, in order to accomplish this, training institutions' own 'sedimented self-constructs' require challenging – and this may not be an easy goal to achieve as long as such institutions persist in maintaining unquestioning, sedimented beliefs about the model they advocate.

G. *Conclusion*

In summary, the existential-phenomenological model provides therapists with a significantly different attitudinal and methodological approach, which is focused on their 'being qualities', to their encounter with clients. In its advocacy of this stance it allows for the focus of therapy to remain on the descriptively focused exploration of the current, conscious experience of clients (whose meaning is partly bounded by 'the-past-as-currently-experienced-and-future-directed) and it emphasizes the therapist's attempt to 'enter' the meaning-world of the client in order to interpret it in a descriptively focused manner so that such interpretations approximate the client's experience rather than impose the therapist's theoretically derived interpretations.

From the above perspective, the therapeutic process focuses on this conflict between 'self-as-experienced-in-relation' and sedimentations in the self-construct in order to clarify the meaning of such dissociations from the standpoint of the client's anxieties of 'being' within the realms of self–self, self–other and self-and-other relations so that it brings into focus the client's current experiences of conflict, anxiety and denial in terms of how they both express and protect aspects of the client's sedimented self-construct.

Further, the above explorations allow the clarification of the client's experience in terms of his or her possibilities, limits and denials of situated freedom and choice. Equally, they also clarify the client's current meaning-world such that the unstated, unreflected, distorted, or previously unidentified aspects of current experience may be considered and challenged in terms of their influence on the client's experience of 'being-in-the-world'.

Most importantly, this model emphasizes the notion of the encounter between therapist and client as expressing in microcosm the client's macrocosmic 'being' relations with self and other. In a similar fashion, it stresses the 'being qualities' of the therapist with regard to the therapist's willingness and ability to 'be with' and 'be for' the client, to listen and respond to the client in a manner that approximates the client's relational experiences, and to be implicated as a 'being-in-relation'.

Through this realignment, the tendency on the part of the therapist to seek to cure, change, help, or promote the growth of the client is 'bracketed'; so that the encounter may foster the client's experience of acceptance of and by self and other through which genuine clarification and challenge of debilitating beliefs and behaviours may occur.

Finally, in its broadest sense, the sceptical stance it advocates brings to light implicit assumptions and sedimented beliefs contained in all models of therapy so that they may be clarified and challenged. In this way, while it can stand as a coherent, systematic and rigorous model in its own right, the existential-phenomenological model provides *all therapists* with a methodological stance that not only removes from them much of their professional mystique, and a good deal of the power that comes with this, but also continually confronts and challenges their theoretical and personal beliefs, their sedimented stances towards themselves and others in their lives, and their ability to attend to clients whose 'material' may provoke all too painful reminders of their own deceits and anxieties. At the same time, the willingness to encounter another in this fashion may also remind therapists of the immeasurable wonder and joy that are possible when beings encounter themselves through one another.

For therapy, along the lines suggested, is not directed solely towards clients; rather, encounter directs itself and involves both therapist and client. If therapy, as some have suggested, is akin to a play, then it is surely a play of mystery and suspense where important clues may be revealed but no final solution is forthcoming.

In such a play, the therapist is neither its director, nor its critic, nor its audience, but its co-writer.

CONCLUSIONS

Pain sure brings out the best in people, doesn't it?
— Bob Dylan

1996 marks the official centenary of therapy in its modern-day form. During its first one hundred years, therapy has progressed from being a controversial, either critically reviled or lauded 'talking cure' to an increasingly accepted, even indispensable, form of care. The availability of therapy in the UK has increased dramatically over the last decade and is set to grow at an even more unprecedented rate during the remaining years of the twentieth century.

During this time, an enormous diversity of therapeutic approaches has arisen, attracting proponents and detractors, critics and 'true believers'. In many instances, the experience of therapy's clientèle has been positive — or at least not negative. Owing largely to its popularization in cinema, novels, theatrical productions, radio, magazine 'agony columns', and popular psychology self-improvement manuals and techniques, therapy is no longer widely viewed as something to be associated with either the very 'sick' or the very rich. Increasingly, people have tended to view it as something probably anyone could benefit from at some point in their lives.

Along with its growth and availability have emerged successive concerns about its risks, its efficacy, its potentials for misuse and abuse, its investment of power in the therapist, its mystique. Similarly, questions have arisen concerning the training background, qualifications and expertise of therapists and how these may influence or affect both the process and outcomes of therapy.

Partly in response to such concerns, and partly as a means of being recognized as the competent UK authorities to speak on matters pertaining to therapy in the European Community, both the UKCP and the BAC maintain publicly available voluntary registers of psychotherapists and counsellors. In addition, both organizations have established regular, on-going dialogue with one another as well as with the British Psychological Society and the Royal College of Psychiatrists.

With the growth in authority of the UKCP and the BAC as the increasingly recognized 'host' bodies of psychotherapy and counselling in the UK, therapy has begun its inevitable movement towards regulated registration which, if nothing else, will help to safeguard the general public from physical, psychological, sexual and financial abuse by professionally recognized therapists.

All these achievements indicate that therapy as a whole is currently undergoing an internal evolution whose significance is already apparent. At the same time, however, as with all evolutions-in-progress, formidable issues and problems remain for therapists to face. Among them, as I have discussed throughout this text, are such questions as the purpose of training, the significant theoretical divergences of the major therapeutic models, the efficacy of therapeutic intervention, and what constitutes 'good' therapy and 'good' therapists.

It should by now be clear to the reader that my views on therapy demand the consideration of each therapist as a living embodiment of the therapy being provided and that the emphasis of therapeutic encounter should not be solely, or even principally, focused on the 'doing' skills of the therapist but rather on the 'being qualities' he or she is able to express in the course of therapeutic interaction. Further, I have attempted to argue that the 'specialness' of therapy, for me at least, lies in each specific and unique *encounter* that occurs between the therapist and the client. As such, while I am broadly in sympathy with the current movement towards regulation, I remain uneasy that, in this movement, the focus of regulatory attention will be principally, if not solely, on the 'doing' elements of therapy, since these are open to standardization, measurement and training criteria, and that therapists' 'being qualities' will continue to be seen as 'addenda' or outcomes of the proper utilization of 'doing' skills.

My concern is exacerbated by the dearth of research evidence that can point to valid and reliable evidence to demonstrate that either the 'doing' skills or the theoretical models of therapy *in themselves* provide successful or beneficial therapeutic outcomes. *If this text has hoped to convince the reader of anything it is that such conclusions are inappropriate and that, if anything, it is the attention given to the 'being qualities' of therapists that requires serious and methodical investigation.*

To claim that 'doing skills' and the learning of theoretical models (and, more usually, *a* theoretical model) can alone be the hallmarks of training seems to me to be highly questionable. 'But,' you might respond, 'at least this stance does no harm.' On the contrary, as I have sought to argue, over-dependence on 'doing' skills and debatable theoretical assumptions opens therapy to a number of mystifications that elevate the power and authority of therapists and, in so doing, increase the potentials for their misuse and abuse.

My aim, throughout the text, has been to confront a number of these mystifications by questioning various fundamental assumptions that either all of therapy, or particular models of therapy, have adopted. I have done so not because I have 'an axe to grind' against therapy, but because, as it is my own profession, I believe that such confrontations provide a valuable means for clarifying one's stance as a therapist and for challenging the mystificatory assumptions that one may bring to therapy or place on oneself. It is my hope that such analyses have been of value both to therapists and potential clients alike. For the former, it was not my aim to disable or undermine their attempts to care and assist, but, rather, to strengthen those possibilities and to fortify their sense of their own capacity as human beings for enriching the lives of clients and of themselves. For the latter, I hope that my stated concerns have been of assistance in enabling them to be aware of the possibilities and limitations of therapy so that if and when they choose to enter therapy they will be clearer about what it may offer and that, should they so choose, that their choice will focus more on the therapist than on the model that he or she represents.

I am well aware of what I have not found the space to discuss in this text. Perhaps most of all, I recognize that a significant feature of my experience of therapy has remained unmentioned: this is the occurrence and value of *humour and laughter* during the therapeutic encounter. It seems strange to me that something that seems so significant to both client and therapist, and to their relationship with one another, has been so rarely mentioned, much less studied by therapists. Perhaps the acknowledgement of the power of laughter would prove too threatening to therapy's mystique. Still, I think that there is much to be gained by considering its place and potential.

While I share the view held by most of my colleagues that therapy has much to provide that is both unique and valuable, I am also greatly sceptical of many of the inordinate claims that have been made regarding its inherent superiority and solitary effectiveness over all other attempts to confront our 'inner demons'. Over the years, I find myself increasingly 'underwhelmed' by tales of therapists' courageous journeys into their personal underworld through which they have emerged 'cleansed' and singularly capable of providing for the 'treatment' of others.

There is, I'm afraid, a great deal about the doing of therapy that is somewhat of a conceit. But . . . through one's encounters with one's clients, it is also a great privilege. And if I have expressed my concerns about the former, I hope that I have also demonstrated my appreciation of the latter.

In line with this last point, I remind readers that all the issues that were stressed throughout Part 5 suggest that the very 'specialness' of, and beneficial possibilities in, therapy are expressed through the various features of *the encounter itself* and of those 'being qualities' that emerge through the meeting between therapist and client. Considered in this light, the value of therapy does not lie in the things that are 'done' within it by both the therapist and the client, but by the 'charged' relationship they have with one another which expresses itself through what they 'do' and who they allow themselves to 'be' within it.

In this way, the relational 'realms' focusing on the experience of self-in-relation, the experience of the other-in-relation, and the experience of self-in-relation-with-the-other, are opened to descriptively focused clarification and challenge. While the object of focus must obviously be the client's experienced relations, nevertheless the therapist cannot be excluded since the therapist 'is' in relation. In this way, the therapist is both the client's (or self's) relational 'other' and is 'the-other-attempting-to-be-the-self' in the relation. In that meeting point of all the various relational realms, the client is able to confront the sedimented perspectives, anxieties, contradictions and denials of 'being-in-the-world' which such perspectives both express and defend against. In 'owning' these, the client may begin to examine them from the stance of choice which allows both acceptance and the exploration of the possibility and implications of change.

Therein, for me, lies the power and value of therapy. Acknowledging all of its imperfections, its limitations, its potentials for misuse and abuse, and its unnecessary mystifications, it remains, nevertheless, one of the very few means available to us for encountering ourselves openly and honestly in the presence of another and thereby regaining not only a sense of our own worth, but of the worth of others.

Yes, of course, therapy can help us to solve our problems, to find more happiness and peace, to rid us of our 'neuroses', to 'put us in charge', to integrate, to change and cure us. But, then again, it might not. Indeed, put in this context, it might well be fair to argue that therapy has itself invented a great many of the discontents and 'dis-eases' that it proposes to alleviate or remove.

But therapy, as I have suggested, when it is 'being'-focused, can be far more than a mere palliative that seeks to excuse or exonerate us from our anxiety or deceit or guilt. Rather, it can confront us with our possibilities or, to paraphrase Abraham Maslow, 'with all that one knows one could do with one's life.' In this, therapy allows us a means of acknowledging that we are co-constituted beings 'in-the-world' whose relations with 'others' both reflect, and are reflected in, our relations with ourselves.

The Upanishads of Sanskrit philosophy teach us, in their wisdom, that 'when there is another, fear (or anxiety) arises.' In a different, if related fashion, one of the aphorisms of the *Code d'Amour Provençale* states: 'He who loves is always full of fear.' And Freud, to his great credit, pointed out that the development and maintenance of social systems always contain a conflict of interest between the individual and the community (or the other) which requires some form of personal sacrifice of one's individualistic desires.

Many have tended to read each or all of these statements as being deeply pessimistic, requiring the individual to abdicate or deny some part of his or her 'being' for the 'good' of others. I believe such conclusions to be, at best, misleading. Certainly, there is a sacrifice, and, as both the above statements and existential-phenomenological theory suggest, its price may well be irresolvable anxiety. But it is only through the step of acknowledging anxiety that novel possibilities of 'being-in-relation' emerge – possibilities that allow us to accept – even cherish – the price of sacrifice. If 'others' provoke our fears, then they also provoke our ability to accept and love not only others, but ourselves as well.

The great error of our age has been the attempt to construct social systems that emphasize our fears of relationship. We have elevated either the individual or the community and set them off one against the other, as if they were natural antagonists. And we all know far too well the destructive consequences of both philosophies.

Here in Britain, for instance, we have recently lived through a period that emphasized individual advancement and success and denied the very existence of society – a view that the Institute of Economic Affairs, the very same free-market 'think tank' that provided the ideological basis of Mrs Thatcher's monetarist policies, has now reappraised and revoked in favour of the philosophy that individuals need to take personal responsibility for the maintenance of social institutions (*Guardian*, 1993).

In a similar, if oppositely focused manner, ideologies at the other extreme, which emphasized the community over the individual rights of its members, have engendered equally antagonistic tendencies. The breakdown of Soviet communism, for example, has provoked a response wherein the Russian community now finds itself at the mercy of black-market profiteers who manifest the worst tendencies of uncontained capitalism.

It may well be that the unprecedented growth in the demand for therapy in the UK over the last decade reflects the influence of an ideology of rampant individualism. Just as the growing signs of 'backlash' against therapy may reflect the realization of the damage done to social relations of every kind by the adoption of and belief in that self-same ideology.

Whatever the case, it is, I think, fair to say that the issues presented by clients in the therapeutic encounter embody the competing tendencies contained within these divisive philosophies and reveal these same consequences at a microcosmic level.

If therapists merely seek to 'repair' the individual, they perpetuate these ideologies and maintain that divided and antagonistic experience that requires 'self' or 'other' to appear to 'win' and yet always 'lose'.

But therapy *can* provide an alternative. In the microcosmic encounter that places the therapist in the position of the 'other', newly experienced possibilities of relation can emerge. The 'self' that is the client can recontextualize his or her relational experience of self-to-self, self-to-other, and self-with-other. And while it is the case that the 'other' in this particular instance may be 'special' or unusual and far from representative of all the 'others' in the client's experience, let us not be too hasty in minimizing the influence of this unique encounter.

The fractal geometry of Chaos Theory has revealed a most remarkable parallel in the movements of complex systems, such that if one were to compare the movement of the system as a whole with that of a minute part of the system, the features and observable changes in either would be virtually the same (Gleick, 1988). Recall, as well, that the view of causality within Chaos Theory argues that changes in movement at a minute, seemingly insignificant level affect and alter the whole of the complex mechanism.

371

Therapy too, taken from the existential-phenomenological perspective discussed in part five, argues that, if focused on the experience and expression of 'being', the encounter between therapist and client can be seen as a microcosmic parallel to the client's macroscopic 'being' relations. And if the client's experience and expression of 'being' is clarified and challenged from a therapeutic stance that accepts that being as it experiences and expresses itself through the therapist's attempts to 'enter' the client's experiential world-view, then could it not be that the consequences of those clarifications and challenges at the microcosmic level of encounter will resonate at the macrocosmic level?

The term *symmetry* expresses the idea of beauty resulting from balance, congruity, or harmony between two or more parts of an underlying whole. It is my belief that therapy, once shorn of its trappings of unnecessary power and mystique, can reveal itself as a valid and unique form of encounter whose potential can provide individuals with the means of regaining some experience of symmetry between 'self and other'.

A 'fearful symmetry' to be sure, as William Blake wrote; but a symmetry none the less.

BIBLIOGRAPHY

ADORNO, T., *The Jargon of Authenticity*. (Routledge and Kegan Paul, London 1964)

AEBI, J., 'Nonspecific and specific factors in therapeutic change among different approaches to counselling', *Counselling Psychology Review*, 8, 3:19–32, 1993

ANON., *Counselling: definition of terms in use with expansion and rationale* (amended version) (British Association for Counselling, Rugby 1991)

ANON., 'Think-tank rounds on Thatcherism', *Guardian*, 27 September 1993:3

ANON., *BAC Code of Ethics and Practice for Counsellors* (amended version) (British Association for Counselling, Rugby 1993)

APFEL, R. AND SIMON, B., 'Patient–therapist sexual contact', *Psychotherapy and Psychodynamics*, 43:57–68, 1985

AXLINE, V., *Dibs: in search of self.* (Penguin, Harmondsworth 1964)

BALINT, M. AND BALINT, A., 'On transference and counter-transference', *Primary and Psycho-Analytic Technique* (M. Balint, ed.). (Liveright (1965), NY 1939)

BANDURA, A., *Social Foundations of Thought and Action: a social cognitive theory.* (Prentice-Hall, Englewood Cliffs, NJ 1986)

BARTLETT, J., 'First Off', *Ms London*, 21 March 1994:3

BATES, C. AND BRODSKY, A. M., *Sex in the Therapy Hour: a case of professional incest.* (Guildford Press, London 1989)

BECK, A. T., *Cognitive Therapy and the Emotional Disorders.* (International Universities Press, NY 1976)

BELL, L., 'Psychotherapy and user empowerment', *Clinical Psychology Forum* 23:12–14, 1989

BERMAN, J. S. AND NORTON, N. C., 'Does professional training make a therapist more effective?', *Psychological Bulletin* 98:401–7, 1985

BETTELHEIM, B., *Freud and Man's Soul.* (Chatto and Windus, London 1983)

BETTELHEIM, B. AND ROSENFELD, A. A., *The Art of the Obvious: developing insight for psychotherapy and everyday life.* (Thames and Hudson, London 1993)

BEUTLER, L. E., 'Toward specific psychological therapies', *Journal of Consulting and Clinical Psychology* 47:882–97, 1979

BILLEN, A., 'Freudians' slips are showing', *Observer*, 30 January 1994:21

BLOCH, S., AND CHODOFF, P. (EDS.), *Psychiatric Ethics* (2nd ed.). (Oxford University Press, Oxford 1991)

BOHM, D. AND HILEY, B. J., *The Undivided Universe: an ontological interpretation of quantum theory.* (Routledge, London 1993)

BOORSTIN, D. J., *The Discoverers: a history of man's search to know his world and himself.* (Random House, NY 1985)

BORDIN, E. S., 'The generalizability of the psychoanalytic concept of the working alliance', *Psychotherapy: Theory, Research and Practice* 16:252–60, 1979

BORYS, D. S. AND POPE, K. S., 'Dual relationships between therapist and client: a national study of psychologists, psychiatrists and social workers', *Professional Psychology: Research and Practice* 20:283–93, 1989

BOSS, M., *Psychoanalysis and Daseinsanalysis* (trans. L. Lefebre). (Basic Books, NY 1963)

—— *Existential Foundations of Medicine and Psychology.* (Aronson, NY 1979)

—— 'The unconscious – what is it?', *Readings in Existential Psychology and Psychiatry* (K. Hoeller, ed.). (REPP, Seattle 1990)

BOUHOUTSOS, J., 'Therapist–client sexual involvement: a

challenge for mental health professionals and educators', *American Journal of Orthopsychiatry* 55:177–82, 1985

BRAUDE, S. E., *First Person Plural: multiple personality and the philosophy of mind.* (Routledge, London 1991)

BREGGIN, P., *Electroshock: its brain-disabling effects.* (Springer, NY 1979)

—— *Toxic Psychiatry.* (Fontana, London 1993)

BROADBENT, J., DAY, A., KHALEELEE, O., MILLER, E. AND PYM, D., *Psychotherapists and the Process of Profession-Building.* (OPUS, London 1983)

BRUCE, L., *The Essential Lenny Bruce.* (Panther, London 1975)

BUBER, M., *I And Thou* (trans. W. Kaufmann). (T. & T. Clarke Ltd (1987), Edinburgh 1970)

BUGENTHAL, J. F. T., *American Psychologist* 18:563–7, 1963

—— *Psychotherapy and Process: the fundamentals of an existential-humanistic approach.* (McGraw-Hill, NY 1978)

CALESTRO, K., 'Psychotherapy, faith healing and suggestion', *International Journal of Psychiatry* 10:83–113, 1972

CANNON, B., *Sartre & Psychoanalysis: an existentialist challenge to clinical metatheory.* (University Press of Kansas, Lawrence, Kansas 1991)

CASEMENT, P., *Further Learning from the Patient.* (Routledge, London 1990)

CHASSEGUET-SMIRGEL, J. AND GRUNBERGER, B., *Freud or Reich? Psychoanalysis and illusion.* (Free Association Books, London 1986)

CHAYTOR, D. (ED)., *Training in Counselling and Psychotherapy* (9th ed.). (British Association for Counselling, Rugby 1992)

CHERTOK, L., 'The discovery of the transference: toward an epistemological interpretation', *International Journal of Psycho-Analysis* 49:560–76, 1968

CLARKSON, P., Comments made at the 6th Annual Conference of the *Society for Existential Analysis*, 20 November 1993

CONDRAU, G., 'Dream analysis: do we need the unconscious?', *Journal of the Society for Existential Analysis* 4:1–12, 1993

CONKLING, M., 'Sartre's refutation of the Freudian Unconscious', *Readings in Existential Psychology and Psychiatry* (K. Hoeller, ed.). (REPP, Seattle 1990)

COOPER, D., *Psychiatry And Anti-Psychiatry*. (Barnes & Noble, NY 1967)

COREY, G., *Theory and Practice of Counselling and Psychotherapy* (4th ed.). (Brooks/Cole, Pacific Grove, California 1991)

CREWS, F., 'The unknown Freud', *The New York Review of Books*, 40, 19:55–66, 1993

CREWS, F. ET AL, 'The unknown Freud: an exchange', *The New York Review of Books*, 41, 3:34–43, 1994

DAVENHILL, R. AND OSBORNE, J., 'What relevance psychotherapy?', *The Psychologist* 2:56–60, 1991

DAVIDSON, V., 'Psychiatry's problem with no name: therapist–patient sex', *The American Journal of Psychoanalysis* 37:43–50, 1977

DEURZEN-SMITH, E. VAN, *Existential Counselling in Practice*. (Sage, London 1988)

—— 'Ontological insecurity revisited', *Journal of the Society for Existential Analysis* 2:38–48, 1991

DICK, P. K., *Valis*. (Corgi, London 1981)

—— *Radio Free Albemuth*. (Grafton, London 1987)

DINNAGE, R., *One to One: experiences of psychotherapy*. (Viking, London 1989)

DIXON, N. F., *Subliminal Perception: the nature of a controversy*. (McGraw-Hill, London 1971)

—— *Preconscious Processing*. (Wiley, NY 1981)

DRYDEN, W. (ED.), *Individual Therapy: a handbook*. (Open University Press, Milton Keynes 1990)

DRYDEN W. AND ELLIS, A., 'Rational-Emotive Therapy', *Handbook of Cognitive Behavioural Therapies* (K. S. Dobson, ed.). (Guilford Press, NY, 1988)

DYLAN, B., 'Ballad in Plain D', *Another Side of Bob Dylan*. (M. Witmark & Sons, NY 1964)

EDELSON, M., *Hypothesis and Evidence in Psychoanalysis*. (University of Chicago Press, London 1984)

EGAN, G., *The Skilled Helper*. (Brooks/Cole, Monterey, California 1982)

EINZIG, H., *Counselling and Psychotherapy: Is It for Me?* (British Association for Counselling pamphlet 1991)

ELLENBERGER, H. F., *The Discovery of the Unconscious.* (Basic Books, NY 1971)

ELLIS, A. AND WHITELEY, J. M. (EDS.), *Theoretical and Empirical Foundations of Rational-Emotive Therapy.* (Brooks/Cole, Pacific Grove, California 1979)

ERDELYI, M. H., *Psychoanalysis: Freud's cognitive psychology.* (W. H. Freeman and Company, NY 1985)

EVANS, R. I., *Dialogue with R. D. Laing.* (Praeger (1981), NY 1976)

EYSENCK, H. J., 'The effects of psychotherapy: an evaluation', *Journal of Consulting Psychology* 16:319–24, 1952

—— 'An analysis of psychotherapy versus placebo studies', *Behaviour and Brain Studies* 6:275–310, 1983

EYSENCK, H. J. AND WILSON, G. D. (EDS.), *The Experimental Study of Freudian Theories.* (Paladin, London 1973)

FARRELL, B. A., 'The criteria for a psycho-analytic interpretation', *Essays in Philosophical Psychology* (D. F. Gustafson, ed.). (Macmillan, London 1967)

—— *The Standing of Psychoanalysis.* (Oxford University Press, Oxford 1981)

FEIFEL, H. AND EELLS, J., 'Patients and therapists assess the same psychotherapy', *Journal of Consulting Psychology* 27:310–18, 1963

FENICHEL, O., *Problems of Psychoanalytic Technique.* (The Psychoanalytic Quarterly, Inc., Albany, NY 1941)

FINE, R., *A History of Psychoanalysis.* (Columbia University Press, NY 1979)

FONAGY, P., 'What is scientific about psychotherapy', *The British Psychological Society Psychotherapy Section Newsletter* 11:18–29, 1991

—— 'How can we ensure that there will be psychoanalytic psychotherapy in the year 2003?', paper delivered to the *Annual Conference of the British Psychological Society Psychotherapy Section.* (London, January 1993)

FOUCAULT, M., *Madness and Civilization.* (Penguin, Harmondsworth 1961)

FRANCE, A., *Consuming Psychotherapy.* (Free Association Books, London 1988)

FRANK, J. D., *Persuasion and Healing* (2nd ed.). (Johns Hopkins University Press, Baltimore 1973)

—— 'Non-specific aspects of treatment: the view of a psychotherapist', *Non-Specific Aspects of Treatment* (M. Shepherd and N. Sartorius, eds.). (Hans Huber, Toronto 1989)

FREELY, M., 'A suitable case for treatment', *Guardian*, 9 February 1994:44.

FREUD, E. L. AND MENG, H., *Psycho-Analysis and Faith: the letters of Sigmund Freud and Oskar Pfister* (trans. E. Mosmacher). (Basic Books, NY 1963)

FREUD, S., *Project for a Scientific Psychology*, in *The Standard Edition of the Collected Works of Sigmund Freud* 1:281–397. (Hogarth Press, London 1895)

—— 'Heredity and the aetiology of the neuroses', in *The Standard Edition of the Collected Works of Sigmund Freud* 3:142–56. (Hogarth Press, London 1896a)

—— 'The aetiology of hysteria', in *The Standard Edition of the Collected Works of Sigmund Freud* 3:189–221. (Hogarth Press, London 1896b)

—— *The Interpretation of Dreams*, in *The Standard Edition of the Collected Works of Sigmund Freud* 4, 5. (Hogarth Press, London 1900)

—— 'Fragment of an analysis of a case of hysteria', in *The Standard Edition of the Collected Works of Sigmund Freud* 7:3–122. (Hogarth Press, London 1905)

—— *Introductory Lectures on Psychoanalysis*, in *The Standard Edition of the Collected Works of Sigmund Freud*, 15, 16. (Hogarth Press, London 1917)

—— 'From the history of an infantile neurosis', in *The Standard Edition of the Collected Works of Sigmund Freud* 17:3–122. (Hogarth Press, London 1918)

—— *The Ego and the Id*, in *The Standard Edition of the Collected Works of Sigmund Freud* 19:3–59. (Hogarth Press, London 1923)

—— 'The resistances of psycho-analysis', in *The Standard Edition of the Collected Works of Sigmund Freud* 19:212–22. (Hogarth Press, London 1925)

—— *The Question of Lay Analysis: conversations with an impartial person*, in *The Standard Edition of the Collected Works of Sigmund Freud* 20:179–250. (Hogarth Press, London 1926)

—— 'Analysis terminable and interminable', in *The Standard Edition of the Collected Works of Sigmund Freud* 23:211–53. (Hogarth Press, London 1937a)

—— 'Constructions in analysis', in *The Standard Edition of the Collected Works of Sigmund Freud* 23:257–71. (Hogarth Press, London 1937b)

—— *An Outline of Psychoanalysis*, in *The Standard Edition of the Collected Works of Sigmund Freud* 23:141–207. (Hogarth Press, London 1940)

FREUD, S. AND BREUER, J., *Studies on Hysteria*, in *The Standard Edition of the Collected Works of Sigmund Freud* 2. (Hogarth Press, London 1895)

FROMM, E., *To Have or To Be?* (Harper and Row, London 1976)

GARDNER, S., *Irrationality and the Philosophy of Psychoanalysis*. (Cambridge University Press, Cambridge 1993)

GARFIELD, S. L., *The Practice of Brief Therapy*. (Pergamon, NY 1989)

GARFIELD, S. L. AND BERGIN, L. E. (EDS.), *Handbook of Psychotherapy and Behaviour Change* (3rd ed.). (Wiley, NY 1986)

GARTRELL, N., HERMAN, J., OLARTE, S., FELDSTEIN, M. AND LOCALIO, R., 'Psychiatrist–patient sexual contact: results of a national survey', *American Journal of Psychiatry* 143:1126–31, 1986

GAY, P., *Freud: a life for our time*. (J. M. Dent and Sons, London 1988)

GELLNER, E., *The Psychoanalytic Movement*. (Paladin, London 1985)

GINSBURG, H. AND OPPER, S., *Piaget's Theory of Intellectual Development: an introduction*. (Prentice-Hall, Englewood Cliffs, NJ 1969)

GLEICK, J., *Chaos: making a new science*. (Heinemann, London 1988)

GOODMAN, N., 'When Is Art?', *The Arts and Cognition* (D.

Perkins & B. Leondar, eds.). (Johns Hopkins University Press, Baltimore 1977)

GRAHAM, H., *The Human Face of Psychology*. (Open University Press, Milton Keynes, 1986)

GREENBERG, L. S., 'Advances in clinical intervention research: a decade review', *Canadian Psychology*, 22, 1:25–34, 1981

GREENBERG, L. S. AND PINSOF, W. M., *The Therapeutic Process: a research handbook*. (Guildford, NY 1986)

GROTSTEIN, J. S., 'Reflections on a century of Freud: some paths not chosen', *British Journal of Psychotherapy*, 9, 2:181–7, 1992

GRÜNBAUM, A., *The Foundations of Psychoanalysis: a philosophical critique*. (University of California Press, Berkeley 1984)

GUGGENBUHL-CRAIG, A., *Power in the Helping Professions* (9th ed.). (Spring Publications, Dallas, Texas 1989)

HALMOS, P., *The Faith of the Counsellors*. (Constable, London 1965)

HARE, R., 'Ethical therapy', *Psychiatric Ethics* (2nd ed., S. Bloch and P. Chodoff, eds.). (Oxford University Press, Oxford 1991)

HARRÉ, R., 'What is scientific about psychotherapy', *The British Psychological Society Psychotherapy Section Newsletter* 11:14–17, 1991

HATTIE, J. A., SHARPLEY, C. F. AND ROGERS, H. J., 'Comparative effectiveness of professional and paraprofessional helpers', *Psychological Bulletin* 95:534–41, 1984

HEIDEGGER, M., *Being and Time* (trans. J. Macquarrie and E. Robinson). (Basil Blackwell, Oxford 1962)

HEIDER, J., *The Tao of Leadership*. (Wildwood House, Aldershot, Hampshire 1986)

HEIMANN, P., 'On countertransference', *International Journal of Psycho-Analysis* 31:81–4, 1950

HILGARD, E. R., *Divided Consciousness: multiple controls in human thought and action*. (Wiley, NY 1986)

HILGARD, E. R., ATKINSON, R. L. AND ATKINSON, R. C., *Introduction to Psychology* (9th ed.). (Harcourt Brace Jovanovich, NY 1987)

HOLMES, J. AND LINDLEY, R., *The Values of Psychotherapy*. (Oxford University Press, Oxford 1989)

HOLMES, J., 'Response to J. Masson's "The tyranny of psycho-therapy"', *Psychotherapy and Its Discontents* (W. Dryden and C. Feltham, eds.):29–36. (Open University Press, Milton Keynes 1992)

HOLROYD, J. AND BRODSKY, A., 'Psychologists' attitudes and practices regarding erotic and non-erotic physical contact with patients', *American Psychologist* 32:843–9, 1977

HOPKINS, J., 'The unknown Freud: an exchange', *The New York Review of Books*, 41, 3:34–5, 1994

HOWARD, A., 'What, and why, are we accrediting?', *Counselling*, 3, 2:90–2, 1992

HOWARTH, I., 'Psychotherapy: who benefits?', *The Psychologist*, 2, 4:149–52, 1989

HOWE, D., *On Being a Client: understanding the process of counselling and psychotherapy.* (Sage, London 1993)

HUSSERL, E., *Phenomenological Psychology.* (Nyhoff, The Hague 1977)

IHDE, D., *Experimental Phenomenology: an introduction.* (State University of New York, Albany 1986)

JACOBSON, E., *Progressive Relaxation.* (University of Chicago Press, Chicago 1938)

JACOBY, R., *Social Amnesia: a critique of conformist psychology from Adler to Laing.* (Harvester Press, Hassocks 1975)

JAMES, W., *The Varieties of Religious Experience.* (Macmillan (1985), NY 1890)

JAMIESON, A. AND JONES, C., 'The BAC basic principles of counselling', *Counselling* 4:155–6, 1993

KARDENER, S., FULLER, M. AND MENSCH, L., 'A survey of physicians' attitudes and practices regarding erotic and non-erotic physical contact with patients', *American Journal of Psychiatry* 130:1077–81, 1973

KARDENER, S. H., 'Sex and the physician–patient relationship', *American Journal of Psychiatry* 131:1134–6, 1973

KAZDIN, A. E., 'Comparative outcome studies of psychotherapy: methodological issues and strategies', *Journal of Consulting and Clinical Psychology* 54:729–57, 1986

KIRSCHENBAUM, H. AND HENDERSON, V. L., *The Carl Rogers Reader.* (Constable, London 1990a)

—— *Carl Rogers: Dialogues*. (Constable, London 1990b)

KITZINGER, C., 'Feminism, psychology and the paradox of power', *Feminism and Psychology* 1:111–29, 1991

—— 'Thomas Szasz: the myth and the man', *The Psychologist*, 4, 2:120–2, 1992

KLEIN, M., 'The origins of transference', *International Journal of Psycho-Analysis* 33:433–8, 1952

—— *Narrative of a Child Analysis*. (Hogarth Press, London 1961)

KLINE, F., ADRIAN, A. AND SPEVAK, M., 'Patients evaluate therapists', *Archives of General Psychiatry* 31:113–16, 1974

KLINE, P., *Psychology and Freudian Theory: an introduction*. (Methuen, London 1984)

—— 'Problems of methodology in studies of psychotherapy', *Psychotherapy and Its Discontents* (W. Dryden and C. Feltham, eds.). (Open University Press, Milton Keynes 1992)

KOESTLER, A., *The Sleepwalkers: a history of man's changing vision of the universe*. (Hutchinson, London 1959)

LAING, R. D., *The Divided Self*. (Tavistock Publications, London 1960)

—— *Self and Others*. (Penguin, Harmondsworth 1961)

—— *The Politics of Experience and the Bird of Paradise*. (Penguin, Harmondsworth 1967)

—— *The Voice of Experience: experience, science and psychiatry*. (Allen Lane, London 1982)

LAING, R. D. AND ESTERSON, A., *Sanity, Madness and the Family*. (Penguin, Harmondsworth 1965)

LAPLANCHE, J. AND PONTALIS, J. B., *The Language of Psycho-Analysis* (trans. D. Nicholson-Smith). (Hogarth Press, London 1985)

LEO, J., 'Talk is as good as the pill', *Time* Magazine, 26 May 1986:88

LERNER, B., *Therapy in the Ghetto*. (Johns Hopkins University Press, Baltimore, 1972)

LLEWELYN, S., 'The sexual abuse of clients by therapists', paper delivered to the BPS Annual Conference, 1992

LOMAS, P., *The Case for a Personal Psychotherapy*. (Oxford University Press, Oxford 1981)

LUBORSKY, L. AND SINGER, B., 'Comparative studies of

psychotherapies: is it true that everyone has won and all must have prizes?', *Archives of General Psychiatry* 32:995–1008, 1975

—— 'Therapist success and its determinants', *Archives of General Psychiatry* 42:602–11, 1985

MAIR, K., 'The myth of therapist expertise', *Psychotherapy and Its Discontents* (W. Dryden and C. Feltham, eds.) (Open University Press, Milton Keynes 1992)

MALAN, D., 'On assessing the results in psychotherapy', *British Journal of Medical Psychology* 32:86–105, 1959

—— *A Study of Brief Psychotherapy.* (Tavistock, London 1963)

MALCOLM, J., *Psychoanalysis: The Impossible Profession.* (Pan, London 1982)

—— *In the Freud Archives.* (Knopf, NY 1984)

MALUCCIO, A. N., *Learning from Clients.* (Free Press, NY 1979)

MASLOW, A., *Towards a Psychology of Being.* (Van Nostrand Reinhold, NY 1968)

MASSON, J., *The Oceanic Feeling: the origins of religious sentiment in India.* (University of Toronto Press, Toronto 1980)

—— *The Assault on Truth: Freud's suppression of the seduction theory.* (Penguin, Harmondsworth 1984)

—— *The Dark Science: women, sexuality and psychiatry in the 19th century.* (Virago, London 1986)

—— *Against Therapy: emotional tyranny and the myth of psychological healing.* (Fontana, London 1988)

—— *Final Analysis: the making and unmaking of a psychoanalyst.* (HarperCollins, London 1991)

—— 'The tyranny of psychotherapy', *Psychotherapy and Its Discontents* (W. Dryden and C. Feltham, eds.). (Open University Press, Milton Keynes 1992)

—— *My Father's Guru.* (HarperCollins, London 1993a)

—— 'Issues of power in the psychotherapeutic relationship', paper delivered to the 6th Annual Conference of the Society for Existential Analysis, November 1993b

MASTERS, W. H. AND JOHNSON, V. E., *Human Sexual Response.* (Churchill, London 1966)

—— *Human Sexual Inadequacy.* (Churchill, London 1970)

MAY, R., *Psychology and the Human Dilemma.* (W. W. Norton & Co., NY 1967)

—— *Love and Will.* (W. W. Norton & Co., NY 1969)

—— *Freedom and Destiny.* (Delta, NY 1981)

—— *The Discovery of Being: writings in existential psychology.* (W. W. Norton & Co., NY 1983)

—— 'Transpersonal or transcendental?', *The Humanistic Psychologist*, 14, 2:87–90, 1986

MAY, R., ANGEL, E. AND ELLENBERGER, H., *Existence.* (Clarion, NY 1958)

MAYS, D. T. AND FRANKS, C. M. (EDS.), *Negative Outcome in Psychotherapy and What do Do about It.* (Springer, NY 1985)

MCCARTNEY, J. L., 'Overt transference', *Journal of Sex Research* 2:227–37, 1966

MCCONNAUGHY, E. A., 'The personality of the therapist in psychotherapeutic practice', *Psychotherapy*, 24, 3:303–14, 1987

MCCORD, J., 'A thirty year follow-up of treatment effects', *American Psychologist* 3:284–9, 1978

MCLEOD, J., 'The client's experience of counselling and psychotherapy: a review of the research literature', *Experiences of Counselling in Action* (D. Mearns and W. Dryden, eds.). (Sage, London 1990)

MEARNS, D. AND THORNE, B., *Person-Centred Counselling in Action.* (Sage, London 1988)

MILLER, A., *Thou Shalt Not Be Aware: society's betrayal of the child.* (Pluto Press, London 1985)

MILLER, J., *The Body in Question.* (Cape, London 1978)

MISIAK, H. AND SEXTON, V. S., *Phenomenological, Existential and Humanistic Psychologies: a historical survey.* (Grune & Stratton, NY 1973)

MURGATROYD, S., 'A framework for intervention', *Counselling Psychology Review*, 8, 3:4–7, 1993

NACHT, S., 'Reflections on the evolution of psychoanalytic knowledge', *International Journal of Psycho-Analysis* 40:32–42, 1969

OBHOLZER, K., *The Wolf-Man Sixty Years Later: conversations with Freud's controversial patient* (trans. M. Shaw). (Routledge and Kegan Paul, London 1982)

OLDFIELD, S., *The Counselling Relationship: a study of the cli-*

ent's experience. (Routledge and Kegan Paul, London 1983)

OMER, H. AND LONDON, P., 'Metamorphosis in psychotherapy: end of systems era', *Psychotherapy: theory, research and practice* 25:171–84, 1988

ORLINSKY, D. E. AND HOWARD, K. I., 'Process and outcome in psychotherapy', *Handbook of Psychotherapy and Behaviour Change* (3rd ed., S. L. Garfield and A. E. Bergin, eds.) (Wiley, NY 1986)

OWEN, I., 'The tower of Babel: searching for core clinical, theoretical and ethical issues in psychotherapy', *Counselling Psychology Quarterly*, 5, 1:67–78, 1992

—— 'Core skills for psychotherapy', *Counselling Psychology Review*, 8, 2:15–23, 1993a

—— 'The personalities of psychotherapists', *Counselling Psychology Review*, 8, 3:10–14, 1993b

PERLS, F. S., *Gestalt Therapy Verbatim.* (Real People Press, Moab, Utah 1969)

—— *The Gestalt Approach and Eye Witness to Therapy.* (Bantam Books, NY 1976)

PERSAUD, R., 'Talking your way out of trouble', *Sunday Times*, 26 September 1993, Style and Travel section:8–9

PETERS, T., *Liberation Management.* (Macmillan, London 1992)

PILGRIM, D., 'Psychotherapy and social blinkers', *The Psychologist* 2:52–5, 1991

PLASIL, E., *Therapist.* (St Martins Press, London 1985)

POPE, K. S. AND BOUHOUTSOS, J. C., *Sexual Intimacies between Therapists and Patients.* (Praeger, NY 1986)

POPE, K. S., KEITH-SPEIGEL, P. AND TABACHNICK, B., 'The human therapist and the (sometimes) inhumane training system', *American Psychologist* 41:147–58, 1986

POPE, K. S., TABACHNICK, B. AND KEITH-SPEIGEL, P., 'Ethics of practice: the beliefs and behaviors of psychologists as therapists', *American Psychologist* 42:993–1006, 1987

POPE, K. S. AND VETTER, U., 'Prior therapist–patient involvement among patients as seen by psychologists', *Psychotherapy* 28:429–38, 1991

POPE, K. S., 'Therapist–client sexual involvement: a review of the research', *Clinical Psychology Review* 10:477–90, 1990

POPPER, K., *Logic of Scientific Discovery* (revised ed.). (Hutchinson, London 1960)

REASON, P. AND ROWAN, J., *Human Enquiry: a sourcebook of new paradigm research.* (Wiley, Chichester 1981)

RICKMAN, G., *Philip K. Dick: in his own words* (revised ed.). (Fragments West/The Valentine Press, Long Beach, California 1988)

RIEFF, P., *Freud: the mind of the moralist* (3rd ed.). (University of Chicago Press, London 1979)

ROGERS, C. R., *On Becoming a Person.* (Houghton Mifflin, Boston 1961)

—— *A Way of Being.* (Houghton Mifflin, Boston 1980)

ROSEN, R. D., *Psychobabble.* (Avon Books, NY 1979)

ROSS, C. A., *Multiple Personality Disorder: diagnosis, clinical features, and treatment.* (Wiley, NY 1989)

ROWAN, J., 'Response to K. Mair's "The myth of therapist expertise"', *Psychotherapy and Its Discontents* (W. Dryden and C. Feltham, eds.). (Open University Press, Milton Keynes 1992)

RUSSELL, J., *Out of Bounds: sexual exploitation in counselling and therapy.* (Sage, London 1993)

RUSSELL, J., DEXTER, G. AND BOND, T., 'A Report on Differentiation between Advice, Guidance, Befriending, Counselling Skills and Counselling'. (British Association for Counselling and the Department of Employment 1993)

RUSTIN, M. AND RUSTIN, M., 'Relational preconditions for socialism', *Further Contributions to the Theory and Technique of Psychoanalysis* (J. Richards, ed.). (Hogarth Press, London 1960)

RUTTER, P., *Sex in the Forbidden Zone.* (Unwin Hyman, London 1990)

SACKS, O, *The Man Who Mistook His Wife for a Hat.* (Pan, London 1986)

SAINSBURY, E., NIXON, S. AND PHILLIPS, D., *Social Work in Focus: clients' and social workers' perceptions in long-term social work.* (Routledge and Kegan Paul, London 1982)

SALMON, P., 'Psychotherapy and the wider world', *The Psychologist* 2:50–1, 1991

SARTRE, J.-P., *Being and Nothingness: an essay on phenomeno-*

logical ontology (trans. H. Barnes). (Routledge (1991), London 1956)

SCHAFER, R., *A New Language for Psychoanalysis*. (Yale University Press, London 1976)

SCHIMEK, J. G., 'Fact and fantasy in the seduction theory: a historical review', *Journal of the American Psychoanalytic Association* 35:937–65, 1985

SEDGWICK, P., *PsychoPolitics*. (Pluto Press, London 1982)

SHAFFER, J. B. P., *Humanistic Psychology*. (Prentice-Hall, Englewood Cliffs, NJ 1978)

SHARPE, E., 'The psycho-analyst', *International Journal of Psycho-Analysis* 28:1–6, 1947

SHEPARD, M., *The Love Treatment: sexual intimacy between patients and psychotherapists*. (Peter Wyden, NY 1971)

SHLIEN, J. M., 'A countertheory of transference', *Client Centered Therapy and the Person Centered Approach* (R. Levant and J. Shlien, eds.). (Praeger, NY 1984)

SIEGHART, P., *Statutory Registration of Psychotherapists: report of a profession's joint working party*. (Plumbridge, Cambridge 1978)

SKINNER, B. F., *Science and Human Behavior*. (Macmillan, NY 1953)

—— *Beyond Freedom and Dignity*. (Knopf, NY 1971)

SMAIL, D., 'Towards a radical environmentalist psychology of help', *The Psychologist* 2:61–5, 1991

SMITH, D. L., *Hidden Conversations: an introduction to communicative psychoanalysis*. (Routledge, London 1991)

—— 'On the eve of a revolution: Freud's concepts of consciousness and unconsciousness in "Studies on Hysteria" and the "Project for a Scientific Psychology"', *British Journal of Psychotherapy*, 9, 2:150–6, 1992

SMITH, M. L. AND GLASS, G. V., 'Meta-analyses of psychotherapy outcome studies', *American Psychologist* 32:752–60, 1977

SMITH, M. L., GLASS, G. V. AND MILLER, T. I., *The Benefits of Psychotherapy*. (Johns Hopkins University Press, Baltimore 1980)

SPANOS, N., 'Hypnosis, demonic possession and multiple personality', *Altered States of Consciousness and Mental Health: a cross-cultural perspective* (C. A. Ward, ed.). (Sage, Newbury Park, California 1989)

SPERRY, R. W., 'Perception in the absence of neocortical commisures', *Perception and Its Disorders* (Res. Publ. ARNMD, vol. 48). (The Association for Research in Nervous and Mental Diseases, NY 1970)

SPINELLI, E., 'An analysis of *est*', Archives of the Edale Research Group, 1979

—— *The Interpreted World: an introduction to phenomenological psychology.* (Sage, London 1989)

—— 'Sex, death and the whole damn thing: the case of Stephen R', *Journal of the Society for Existential Analysis* 3:39–53, 1992

—— 'The unconscious: an idea whose time has gone?', *Journal of the Society for Existential Analysis* 4:19–47, 1993

STILES, W. B., SHAPIRO, D. A. AND ELLIOTT, R., 'Are all psychotherapies equivalent?', *American Psychologist* 41:165–80, 1986

STILES, W. B. AND SHAPIRO, D. A., 'Abuse of the drug metaphor in psychotherapy process-outcome research', *Clinical Psychology Review* 58:352–9, 1988

STONE, A., 'Sexual misconduct by psychiatrists: the ethical and clinical dilemma of confidentiality', *American Journal of Psychiatry* 140:195–7, 1983

STORR, A., 'The concept of cure', *Psychoanalysis Observed* (C. Rycroft, ed.). (Routledge and Kegan Paul, London 1966)

—— *The Art of Psychotherapy.* (Butterworth/Heinemann, London 1979)

STRACHEY, J.,'The nature of the therapeutic action of psychoanalysis', *International Journal of Psychoanalysis* 15:117–26, 1934

STRUPP, H., FOX, R. AND LESSLER, K., *Patients View Their Psychotherapy.* (Johns Hopkins University Press, Baltimore 1969)

SULLIVAN, H. S., *Conceptions of Modern Psychiatry.* (W. W. Norton & Co. (1953), NY 1940)

SZASZ, T., *The Manufacture of Madness.* (Granada, St Albans 1973)

—— *The Myth of Mental Illness: foundations for a theory of personal conduct* (revised ed.). (Harper & Row, NY 1974a)

—— *Law, Liberty and Psychiatry*. (Routledge and Kegan Paul, London 1974b)

—— *The Ethics of Psychoanalysis: the theory and method of autonomous psychotherapy* (revised ed.). (Basic Books, NY 1974c)

—— *The Myth of Psychotherapy: mental healing as religion, rhetoric, and repression*. (Doubleday, Garden City, NY 1978)

—— *The Theology of Medicine*. (Oxford University Press, Oxford 1979)

—— 'Taking Dialogue as Therapy Seriously: words are the essential tool of treatment', *Journal of the Society for Existential Analysis* 3:2–9, 1992a

—— *Our Right to Drugs: the case for a free market*. (National Book Network, Inc., NY 1992b)

SZYMANSKA, K. AND PALMER, S., 'Therapist–client sexual contact', *Counselling Psychology Review* 8, 4:22–33, 1993

TART, C. T. (ED.), *Transpersonal Psychologies*. (Routledge and Kegan Paul, London 1975)

TAYLOR, J. AND WAGNER, N. N., 'Sex between therapists and clients: a review and analysis', *Professional Psychology* 7:593–601, 1976

THORNE, B., 'Person-centred therapy', *Individual Therapy: a handbook* (W. Dryden, ed.). (Open University Press, Milton Keynes 1992)

THORNTON, E. M., *Freud and Cocaine*. (Blond & Briggs, London 1983)

TORREY, E. F., *Witchdoctors and Psychiatrists: the common roots of psychotherapy and its future*. (Aronson, NY 1986)

—— *Freudian Fraud: the Malignant Effect of Freud's Theory on American Thought and Culture*. (HarperCollins, NY 1992)

TOWNSEND, C., 'What's in a name?', *Counselling* 4:252, 1993

TROUPP, C., 'If you can't trust your therapist . . .', *Guardian*, 28 February 1991: 23

VALLE, R. S. AND KING, M. (EDS.), *Existential-Phenomenological Alternatives for Psychology*. (Oxford University Press, NY 1978)

VALLE, R. S. AND HALLING, S. (EDS.), *Existential-Phenomenological Perspectives in Psychology*. (Plenum Press, London 1989)

VALLE, R. S., 'The emergence of transpersonal psychology', *Existential-Phenomenological Perspectives in Psychology* (R. S. Valle and S. Halling, eds.). (Plenum Press, London 1989)

VINSON, J. S., 'Use of complaint procedures in cases of therapist—patient sexual contact', *Professional Psychology: Research and Practice* 18:159–64, 1987

WANN, T. W. (ED.), *Behaviorism and Phenomenology: contrasting bases for modern psychology*. (University of Chicago Press, Chicago 1964)

WELDON, F., *Affliction*. (HarperCollins, London 1994)

WHYTE, L. L., *The Unconscious before Freud*. (Julian Friedmann Publishers Ltd, London 1978)

WINNER, E., *Invented Worlds: the psychology of the arts*. (Harvard University Press, London 1982)

WINNICOTT, D. W., *The Maturational Process and the Facilitating Environment*. (Hogarth Press, London 1965)

—— *Playing and Reality*. (Tavistock, London 1971)

WITTGENSTEIN, L., *Philosophical Investigations*. (Macmillan, NY 1953)

—— 'Conversations on Freud; excerpt from 1932–3 lectures', in *Philosophical Essays on Freud* (R. Wollheim and J. Hopkins, eds.). (Cambridge University Press, Cambridge 1982)

WOLPE, J., *The Practice of Behavior Therapy*. (Pergamon Press, NY 1969)

YALOM, I., *Existential Psychotherapy*. (Basic Books, NY 1980)

INDEX

abuse, 14, 15, 17, 66, 93, 99–116, 120–2, 126–30, 134, 202, 276, 281
  see also power
acceptance, 329
accommodation, 289, 290
adaptation, 289
advice, 27
Aebi, J., 86–8, 90
analytic interpretation, 198–9, 203–16
anxiety, 295, 370
arousal, 91
art, definition of, 43–4
assertiveness training, 240
assimilation, 289, 290
attraction, 111–16
Axline, V. M., 35–6

Beck, A. T., 26, 67, 132
befriending, 28
behaviourism, 26, 89, 164, 238, 245, 255
'being', 288, 291–2, 299–314, 330, 331, 350, 359, 360–1, 366, 368–9, 372
'being for', 317–18
'being-in-the-world', 288, 340, 360, 369
'being with', 287, 315–17
beliefs, 50, 84–5, 90, 238, 250, 281, 307, 347–51
  see also irrational beliefs

Berman and Norton, 82
body, 344, 347
bracketing, 231, 297–8
Braude, Stephen, 153–4
British Association for Counselling (BAC), 22, 23, 27, 29, 33–5, 40–1, 81, 103, 110, 119, 125, 366
British Medical Association, 61

Calestro, Dr Kenneth, 50–1
Casement, Patrick, 203–16, 308
categories, definition of, 42–4
causality, linear, 163–9, 230
change, 59, 86–7, 253–4, 264, 314, 353–4
chaos theory, 166–8, 371
Chertok, Louis, 183
children, 109, 126–7, 163
choice, 295–7
clients, 16, 87, 90, 92, 319–21, 331, 372
  beliefs of, 281, 347–51
  challenge to beliefs of, 352–4
  cognitive-behavioural approach to, 238–43
  and conditional unconditionality, 264–7
  dependency of, 121, 199
  experience of, 339
  humanistic approaches to, 256–7
  past experiences of, 175–8
  and self-construct, 351–2

391